Philip B. Whyman • Alina I. Petrescu

The Economics of Brexit

Revisited

palgrave
macmillan

Philip B. Whyman
Lancashire Sch of Bus & Ent, LIEBR
University of Central Lancashire
PRESTON, UK

Alina I. Petrescu
School of Business
University of Central Lancashire
PRESTON, UK

ISBN 978-3-030-55947-2   ISBN 978-3-030-55948-9   (eBook)
https://doi.org/10.1007/978-3-030-55948-9

This Palgrave Macmillan imprint is published by the registered company Springer Nature Switzerland AG.
The registered company address is: Gewerbestrasse 11, 6330 Cham, Switzerland

Panel A

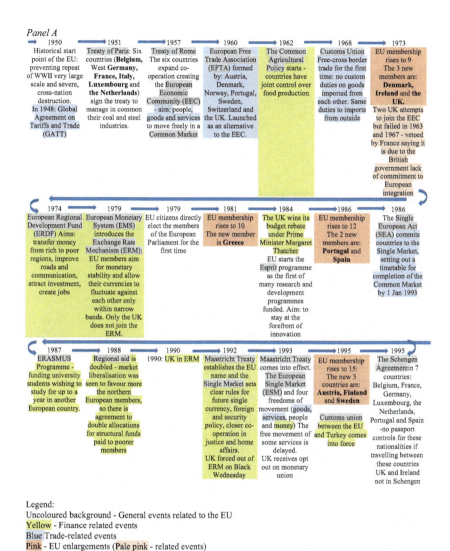

Legend:
Uncoloured background - General events related to the EU
Yellow - Finance related events
Blue Trade-related events
Pink - EU enlargements (Pale pink - related events)
Grey - Most significant event/treaty
Bold font - Names of new member states

Fig. 1 Main European Union and selected UK events related to integration, finance and trade, 1950–present

Panel B.

1997	1999	2001	2002	2004	2004	2005
Treaty of Amsterdam - plans to reform EU institutions, give the EU a stronger presence in the world, concentrate more EU resources on employment and the rights of EU citizens	European Monetary Union (EMU): Euro for commercial and financial transactions in 11 countries and in 2001 for Greece.. Not in the Euro Area: Denmark, Sweden, UK	Treaty of Nice opens the way for more EU enlargements, reforming EU voting rules; comes into effect in 2003.	Euro notes and coins in 12 countries create the Eurozone. The Euro continues to be adopted by more countries.	EU membership rises to 25: The new 10 countries are: **Check Republic, Cyprus, Estonia, Hungary, Malta, Latvia, Lithuania, Poland, Slovenia, Slovakia** UK, Ireland and Sweden are the only countries to open borders without constraints.	Treaty of the European Constitution signed by 25 countries Aim: to streamline democratic decision making and management	Voters in France and Netherlands are given a say and they reject the European Constitution. Accession negotiations begin in Croatia and Turkey

2007	2007	2009	2010	2013	2015	2016
EU has a special partnership with 78 countries in Africa and the Caribbean and Pacific region. EU is the world biggest provider of development assistance to poor countries	EU membership rises to 27: The two new countries are: **Bulgaria** and **Romania**	Lisbon Treaty - signed by EU leaders in 2007 – focus upon improving competitiveness and introducing certain elements from the earlier constitution proposals. The Credit Crunch and Eurozone crisis begin.	Iceland and Montenegro become EU candidate countries 2011 Estonia adopts the Euro - the 17th participant in the Eurozone	EU membership rises to 28: with **Croatia** The European Stability Mechanism is enacted. It includes emergency funding mechanisms and tighter fiscal supervision (2014): Latvia-18th in Eurozone,	The Eurozone has > 340 million people in 15 countries. Last to have joined the in Eurozone up to present (2020): Lithuania in 2015, as the 19th participant.	18 Feb: Voters in UK are given a say and they decide to leave the EU - Announcement of the EU Referendum 23 June Referendum takes place 24 June Result: Brexit

2017	2018	2019	2020	2021
13 Mar: Vote in the UK Parliament to trigger Article 50 29 Mar: Article 50 triggered (Start of a negotiation period of 2 years)	14 Nov: UK Government agrees draft Withdrawal Agreement with EU	Oct: UK and EU agree a revised Withdrawal Agreement and then extension of Brexit date to 31 Jan 2020 12 Dec: UK General election - a Conservative Party win	31 Jan: UK formally withdraws from the EU (on terms agreed in October 2019) Since March: Coronavirus world-wide pandemic - UK and many countries impose severe, unprecedented social and economic restrictions. EU free movement of labour impinged by many countries in lockdown. World-wide full economic consequences (e.g. on trade, jobs) yet to be ascertained. 31 December at 11 PM: End of Brexit transition period (unless an extension is jointly agreed by all parties)	From 1 January: UK can continue negotiations on further various deals with the EU and/or the World.

Legend:
Uncoloured background - General events related to the EU
Yellow - Finance related events
Blue Trade-related events
Pink - EU enlargements(Pale pink-related events)
Green - Brexit related events
Grey - Most significant event/treaty
Bold font - Names of new member states

PREFACE

The publication of our previous volume, *The Economics of Brexit: A Cost-Benefit Analysis of the UK's Economic Relationship with the EU*, followed closely upon the result of the 2016 European referendum, which had proven to be a surprise (or shock) to many commentators and a decisive turning point for the UK. The book sought to outline and evaluate the available evidence relating to how Brexit might be expected to have an economic impact upon the UK, and present this material in an accessible form, both to economic specialists and to policy makers, but just as importantly to a more general readership who are interested in the issues and points raised in the debate over Brexit and would like to disentangle the probable from the hyperbole.

Books, however, grow old, particularly those focusing upon a topical subject matter and seeking to provide the evidence base to facilitate a fast-moving popular debate. This is particularly the case when writing about Brexit, which has dominated discourse in the UK, Europe and, to a lesser but still significant extent, globally, for the past three years. During this time, new economic studies have been undertaken, new models of Brexit have been devised (and often subsequently been rejected), and evidence has begun to emerge about the economic consequences of the uncertainty that has prevailed over the final form that Brexit will adopt.

This book has, therefore, sought to build upon the evidence presented in the previous book whilst noting the changed economic environment. The UK has now withdrawn from the EU and is scheduled to emerge from a transition period to a new, independent status, by the end of 2020. This book has retained the basic structure as its predecessor, since the questions to be answered are similar, whether considering if Brexit offers a viable alternative to continued EU membership (as in the previous book), or evaluating predicted impact likely to arise as a result of Brexit and considering the optimum form that Brexit might take (in this volume).

Thus, the book contains an extended analysis of a broader range of economic studies which have had a significant effect upon the expectations of economic actors in relation to the likely future effects of Brexit, not least those of policy makers charged with designing a form of new trading relationship with the EU that maximises economic advantage and minimises associated costs. The budgetary implications of Brexit are now much clearer, as are proposals for a future independent migration system and the form of future trading relationship that Prime Minister Johnson is championing in ongoing trade negotiations with the EU, whilst the significance of the Irish border issue has been examined in relation to the choice of post-Brexit model. Other economic aspects such as final trade effects remain indeterminate at present, in relation to both the EU and new trade agreements with the rest of the world, as these will need time to develop. However, the predictions made by new studies in relation to trade, inward investment and regulation are discussed and evaluated in more detail.

One aspect only briefly discussed in the earlier book concerns the potential inherent in certain forms of Brexit, for greater economic policy flexibility and the UK's independence from significant elements of EU rules and regulations. This is one of the key considerations for policy makers, since the ability to use a wider range of economic policy instruments has the potential to support and transform the UK economy in the post-Brexit period and will help to determine whether future generations will perceive Brexit to have been an economic success or a failed experiment. Yet, this policy flexibility has a potential opportunity cost, in that there is a trade-off between close market access to the EU and greater policy independence. To put this another way, this is a choice between short-term damage limitation or medium-term potential opportunities. Consequently, this book seeks to examine this question in some detail, outlining how greater economic policy independence could be used by an imaginative government to deliver many of the objectives that have remained elusive over recent decades.

Many of the economic impacts that are likely to arise from Brexit are tied closely to the future economic, political and security relationship that remains to be forged with the UK's nearest neighbours. The current timetable is for this to be agreed by the end of the transition period, so that by

1 January 2021, policy makers will have decided how to resolve the Brexit trade-off and what form of trading environment will exist between the UK, the EU and the rest of the world. Businesses will want to have greater certainty over the new trading rules that will apply when exporting to different nations, and they will wish to understand how the regulatory regime within which they operate may evolve in the future. Even as these fundamental choices become clearer, the detail is likely to remain a work in progress beyond the end of the transition period. If a closer relationship with the EU is preferred, this will take a period of time to finesse a positive working relationship between negotiating partners who have not always shown themselves in a good light. Similarly, if a more independent relationship is pursued, then it will take time to negotiate future trade relationships with other countries, and for UK policy makers to settle upon the forms of regulation and new economic policy strategies that may reinvigorate the productive foundations of the economy. Therefore, the issues discussed in this book, and the evidence presented, will have an enduring relevance to those forging these new economic relationships as decisions of magnitude need to be based upon an understanding of the best available evidence. We, the authors, hope that this book can play a small part in helping to inform and challenge all readers who, in great part or in small, will help build this post-Brexit future.

Preston, UK   Philip B. Whyman
                                                           Alina I. Petrescu

Acknowledgements

There are a large number of people we wish to thank for their assistance, directly or indirectly, in the preparation of this book.

First, we wish to thank our respective families for their forbearance during the countless hours we have been locked in our respective studies. For your patience and goodwill, we would like to dedicate this book to you: AP—my husband, child, mum and dad; PBW—Claire, Barbara and Boyd.

Second, we thank Ruth Jenner and her colleagues at Palgrave Macmillan for their support for this project and patience during the almost inevitable overruns. I hope you are pleased with the final product and agree that it was worth the wait!

Third, we would like to thank our colleagues at the University of Central Lancashire, and research collaborators elsewhere (Mark, Brian, Tunde), since our single-minded dedication to this project has proven to be more than a tad distracting for our other work. Thanks for the comradeship.

Any remaining errors and omissions, we gladly attribute to each other!

Lancaster and Nether Edge
May 2020

Contents

ABBREVIATIONS

BBC	British Broadcasting Corporation
BCC	British Chambers of Commerce
BIS	Department for Business, Innovation and Skills
BoE	Bank of England
Brexit	Britain exiting the European Union
CAP	Common Agricultural Policy
CBI	Confederation of Business Industry
CEP	Centre for Economic Performance
CET	Common external tariff
CFP	Common Fisheries Policy
CGE	Computable general equilibrium
CIPD	Chartered Institute of Personnel and Development
CPB NL	Central PlanBureau (Bureau for Economic Policy Analysis) in Netherlands
CU	Customs Union
ECB	European Central Bank
EEA	European Economic Area
EEC	European Economic Community
EFTA	European Free Trade Association
EMS	European Monetary System
EMU	European Monetary Union
EP	European Parliament
EPA	Economic Partnership Agreement
ERM	Exchange Rate Mechanism
ESM	European Single Market
ESRC	Economic and Social Research Council
EU	European Union

FDI	Foreign direct investment
FTA	Free Trade Agreement
GATS	General Agreement on Trade in Services
GATT	General Agreement on Tariffs and Trade
GDP	Gross domestic product
GNI	Gross national income
HMG	Her Majesty's Government
HMRC	Her Majesty's Revenue and Customs
HoC	House of Commons
IMF	International Monetary Fund
IT	Information technology
LSE	London School of Economics
M&A	mergers and acquisitions
MAC	Migration Advisory Committee
MEP	Member of the European Parliament
MFN	Most Favoured Nation
NAFTA	North American Free Trade Agreement
NIESR	National Institute of Economic and Social Research
NiGEM	National Institute's Global Econometric Model (a macroeconomic simulation model)
NTBs	Non-tariff barriers
OBR	Office for Budget Responsibility
OECD	Organisation for Economic Co-operation and Development
ONS	Office of National Statistics
IoD	Institute of Directors
PAYE	Pay-as-you-earn tax
PTA	Preferential trade agreement
PwC	PricewaterhouseCoopers
R&D	Research and Development
RES	Royal Economic Society
RIAs	Regulatory Impact Assessments
SBE	Society of Business Economists
SEA	Single European Act
SIM	Single internal market
SME	Small and medium-sized enterprise(s)
SOC	Standard Occupational Classification
TFEU	Treaty on the Functioning of the European Union
TPP	Trans-Pacific Partnership
TTIP	Transatlantic Trade and Investment Partnership
TUC	Trades Union Congress
UK	United Kingdom
UN	United Nations

UNCTAD	United Nations Conference on Trade and Development
USA	United States of America
USITC	US International Trade Commission
VAR	Vector autoregressive model
VAT	Value-added tax
WDI	World Development Indicators
WERS	Workplace Employment Relations Survey
WTD	Working Time Directive
WTO	World Trade Organization
WWII	The Second World War

LIST OF FIGURES

LIST OF TABLES

INTRODUCTION[1]

The 2016 European referendum proved to be a decisive turning point for the UK as, despite the position adopted by the majority of the political and (big) business establishment, 51.9% of the electorate voted to withdraw from the European Union—a margin of more than 1.2 million people. This decision may arguably represent "the most significant moment of political choice and potential rupture since the Second World War, and in peacetime, possibly since the repeal of the Corn Laws in the nineteenth century", having shaken "to its core the world-view that the big contours of the UK's economic policy were set and resided outside the reach of democratic contest" (Kelly and Pearce, 2019: 1, 4). Orthodoxies that seemed to be set in stone and unchangeable, in the decades before the 2016 referendum result, were suddenly open for discussion and debate. Apparent permanence and inevitability were overturned by a narrow but sufficiently clear-cut democratic decision of the UK electorate. For better or worse, this decision will have a significant impact upon the lives of UK citizens, in a number of different areas, not the least of which is the economy.

As the UK rediscovers its independence, it will necessitate a structural change in its economy and a reconfiguring of economic policy to facilitate this process. Brexit will inevitably pose both challenges and opportunities for UK exporters and those engaged in trade more widely, in terms of seeking to maintain existing trading links with consumers and supply chains within other EU member states, whilst simultaneously seeking to

---

[1] If you want to read further generalist material on the debate leading up to the EU Referendum, Gill (2015) provides a good introductory reading list.

take advantage of new and more rapidly expanding markets elsewhere in the world. There will be challenges for government seeking to rebuild the UK's industrial base and increasing both the productivity and international competitiveness of UK businesses. The continued attraction of inward investment will be a key part of this approach, but so will attempts to increase R&D and technological innovation within UK companies. It will involve the repatriation of a significant element of regulation and its redesign with a greater focus on UK rather than EU needs. Similarly, it will encompass a new approach to the inward migration of labour and, to the extent that this may be more restricted in the future, a strategy would be required to ensure the re-skilling of the existing UK labour force to meet business requirements. Finally, it will require government to reject the economic orthodoxy of the past half century and ensure a sufficient level of aggregate demand to provide sufficient incentives for businesses to invest and produce, thereby increasing employment and productivity.

Therefore, the first objective of this book is to outline the main options available to policy makers, in how the UK economy might be better adapted to the challenges and opportunities presented by Brexit.

It is vital that policy makers and other economic actors (e.g. business leaders, consumers and workers) have accurate information on which to base their future strategies, whether for the management of the economy, future investment decisions in productive capacity or whether it is preferable to increase or restrain individual consumption. Similarly, for opinion formers such as journalists and other commentators, it is important that their perceptions about the economic news items of the day are based upon solid foundations. Yet there is a problem here since there is no single definitive study which satisfactorily deals with all of the relevant costs and benefits arising from Brexit (Portes, 2013: F4-5; Webb et al., 2015:4; Miller et al., 2016: 5, 12).

One significant problem for economic analysis to overcome is that there is no comparable historical precedent to Brexit against which to calibrate economic models. Although both Algeria and Greenland have previously withdrawn from the EU, the Bank of England is correct in stating that "there is no precedent of an *advanced* [my emphasis] economy withdrawing from a trade agreement as deep and complex as the European Union" (BoE, 2018:3). To the extent that Brexit is unique, this creates difficulties for economic researchers who rely upon the use of historical data and examine the lessons to be learnt from precedent to make predictions about future behaviour. As a result, economic studies have depended more heavily than usual upon a number of (sometimes questionable) assumptions and co-opting results from previous studies which were focused upon only slightly related economic questions. Consequently, their predictions are subject to considerable uncertainty (Harari and Thompson, 2013; HM Treasury, 2016: 124).

This is quite a serious problem, as policy makers and significant economic actors are desperate to base their decision making upon the firm foundation of the best available evidence, and this has often been shaky at best. Indeed, it is perhaps not surprising, therefore, that so many of the studies thus produced have been criticised as being inaccurate (Capital Economics, 2016: 3). What limited economic evidence is available from the post-referendum period has not been in line with some of the more negative predictions made by these studies. As a result, *The Times* newspaper has suggested that the reputations of economists will be judged over the accuracy of those predictions that have been forthcoming from econometric modelling teams.[2] Given the seeming inability of a large section of mainstream economics to recognise weaknesses in the global economy prior to the 2008 financial crisis, the inference is that the repute of the discipline might be under threat if its response to the analysis of Brexit is found to be less than satisfactory.

Hence, the second objective of this book is to evaluate the available evidence relating to how Brexit might have an economic impact upon the UK, in order to assess the rigour of the studies and hence the likely accuracy of their conclusions.

It is too easy, when writing a book of this type, for the prior convictions of the authors to dominate over an objective review of the evidence (Harari and Thompson, 2013). In this volume, we have sought to avoid this temptation and the fact that the authors have rather different initial degrees of enthusiasm or scepticism for the EU has perhaps helped in this respect. However, we leave it to the reader to decide how ultimately successful we have been in this respect.

The book is constituted of nine chapters.

Chapter 1 provides a detailed examination of the mainstream 'consensus' economic studies, which have formed the basis for many of the

---

[2] https://www.ft.com/content/e66852f0-3249-11e6-ad39-3fee5ffe5b5b;   http://researchbriefings.parliament.uk/ResearchBriefing/Summary/CBP-7893

comments made during and after the European referendum, but which also form the basis for much of the advice currently being presented to policy makers. To the extent that the predictions made by these studies are inaccurate, not only were the electorate presented with flawed information upon which to make their decision during the recent referendum, but policy makers and businesses are basing their current decisions upon this imprecise foundation.

The following five chapters explore key elements that should form the basis of any economic impact study. Chapter 2 examines the fiscal benefit that should accrue to the UK following Brexit, as either payments to the EU budget will be eliminated entirely, as would be the case in a free trade agreement (FTA) or reliance upon World Trade Organization (WTO) rules, or these payments would be substantially removed in the case of other forms of preferential trade association. Chapter 3 examines the potential impact upon UK trade with the EU following Brexit, whilst Chap. 4 does likewise with the inflow of foreign direct investment (FDI). These are the two areas where theorists anticipate that Brexit will incur the most significant costs. In contrast, Chapter 5 assesses the potential for significant benefit to accrue to the UK economy, once regulations are repatriated and redesigned for national rather than super-national economic requirements. Chapter 6 explores the issue of inward migration and the economic consequences of net EU migration being restricted following withdrawal.

Chapter 7 evaluates the potential economic impact that may occur due to dynamic rather than static factors. These range from the extent that the degree of openness has upon productivity, to evaluating the evidence relating EU membership to economic growth.

Chapter 8 is concerned with a range of options that the UK may wish to incorporate in any post-Brexit economic strategy. This area is, for the authors, potentially *the* most significant means of influencing the economic impact of Brexit.

Finally, Chap. 9 outlines the range of options available for the UK to consider in its negotiation of a new trade relationship with the EU but, perhaps just as (if not more) importantly in the long term, how the UK might seek to build upon existing historical and cultural ties to forge new preferential trade relationships with the rest of the world.

REFERENCES

Bank of England [BoE]. (2018). *EU Withdrawal Scenarios and Monetary and Financial Stability: A Response to the House of Commons Select Committee*, Bank of England, London. Retrieved February 18, 2020, from https://www. bankofengland.co.uk/-/media/boe/files/report/2018/eu-withdrawal-scenarios-and-monetary-and-financial-stability.pdf?la=en&hash=B5F6EDCDF90 DCC10286FC0BC599D94CAB8735DFB.

Capital Economics. (2016). *The Economics Impact of 'Brexit': A Paper Discussing the United Kingdom's Relationship with Europe and the Impact of 'Brexit' on the British economy*, Woodford Investment Management LLP, Oxford. Available via: https://woodfordfunds.com/economic-impact-brexit-report/.

Harari, D., & Thompson, G. (2013). The Economic Impact of EU Membership on the UK, *House of Commons Library Briefing Paper* SN/EP/6730. Available via: http://researchbriefings.parliament.uk/ResearchBriefing/Summary/ SN06730#fullreport.

HM Treasury. (2016). *HM Treasury Analysis: The long term economic impact of EU membership and the alternatives, Cm 9250*. London: The Stationery Office. Available via: https://www.gov.uk/government/uploads/system/uploads/ attachment_data/file/517415/treasury_analysis_economic_impact_of_eu_ membership_web.pdf.

Kelly, G., & Pearce, N. (2019). Introduction: Brexit and the Future of the British Model of Democratic Capitalism. In Kelly, G., & Pearce, N. (Eds.), Britain Beyond Brexit, *Political Quarterly*, 90(S2): 1–11.

Miller, V., Lang, A., Smith, B., Webb, D., Harari, D., Keep, M., & Bowers, P. (2016). Exiting the EU: UK Reform Proposals, Legal Impact and Alternatives to Membership, *House of Commons Library Briefing Paper* No. HC 07214. Available via: http://researchbriefings.parliament.uk/ResearchBriefing/ Summary/CBP-7214#fullreport.

Portes, J. (2013). Commentary: The Economic Implications for the UK of Leaving the European Union, *National Institute Economic Review*, No. 266, F4-9. Available via: http://www.niesr.ac.uk/sites/default/files/commentary.pdf.

Webb, D., Keep, M., & Wilton, M. (2015). In Brief: UK-EU economic relations, *House of Commons Library Briefing Paper (HC 06091)*, The Stationery Office, London. Available via: http://researchbriefings.parliament.uk/Research Briefing/Summary/SN06091.

CHAPTER 1

The Elusive Economic Consensus over Brexit

One of the most notable claims made during the 2016 referendum campaign was that there was a broad consensus amongst economists, that Brexit would prove damaging to the UK economy. This was a claim repeated by leading figures from the political, business and trade union spheres,[1] and was used by the 'Remain' campaign sought to use this apparent consensus to 'frame' the referendum debate. It appeared to be reflected in a survey of economists, undertaken by Ipsos-MORI for *The Observer* newspaper in May 2016, albeit that the 88% view that Brexit would be broadly damaging to the UK economy might have been influenced by the composition of respondents, only a minority of which being British citizens living in the UK at the time of the survey (Ipsos-MORI 2016). Nevertheless, this majority opinion is still impressive amongst a professional group notorious for disagreement.

This view was not without challenge. Economists more favourable towards Brexit described this 'consensus' as the "Great Brexit Consensus

---

[1] Exponents of this viewpoint included former Chancellor of the Exchequer Osborne, former Prime Minister Cameron, former Governor of the Bank of England Carney, the head of the IMF Lagarde, Director General of the CBI, Fairbairn (CBI via PwC, 2016). See https://mainlymacro.blogspot.co.uk/2016/05/economists-say-no-to-brexit.html; https://www.theguardian.com/politics/2016/may/28/economists-reject-brexit-boost-cameron; https://www.ft.com/content/e66852f0-3249-11e6-ad39-3fee5ffe5b5b; http://www.politico.eu/article/george-osborne-economic-case-against-brexit-not-a-conspiracy-eu-referendum-date-june-23/.

© The Author(s) 2020
P. B. Whyman, A. I. Petrescu, *The Economics of Brexit*,
https://doi.org/10.1007/978-3-030-55948-9_1

1

Deceit" and "a lot of economic nonsense" (Economists for Brexit 2016a). Most memorably, it also led the then Secretary of State for Justice, Michael Gove, to declare that "people in this country have had enough of experts from organisations … with acronyms saying that they know what is best and getting it consistently wrong".[2] In the 'rough and tumble' of political discourse, it is perhaps inevitable that Gove was characterised as denouncing experts in general,[3] rather than focusing his comments upon those organisations he described as "distant, unaccountable and elitist".

In the years following the referendum, claims of an economic consensus have been used to justify continuous campaigning for the UK government to pursue as close an economic relationship as possible with the EU.[4] Indeed, until the advent of the Johnson premiership, it was a common assumption, shared by leading political figures, that Brexit would prove harmful to the UK economy and therefore negotiations on future arrangements with the EU should be tailored to limit any such damage.

There are two questions which arise from this quite pervasive and influential narrative. The first is to ascertain whether or not an overwhelming consensus of opinion did and still does exist amongst economists, that Brexit will prove harmful to the UK economy, and, if so, how will this transmission mechanism operate and how will the impact be manifest. The second question concerns the reliability of those economic studies which have helped to form opinion. If they are rigorous and their methodology beyond reproach, then economic and political actors can feel confident in their predictions. If, however, studies are built upon rather unstable foundations—where models deviate from the untidiness of the real world and assumptions made to simplify modelling are questionable—then such economic analysis as has been conducted needs to be interpreted more cautiously, with these limitations in mind. Moreover, given the claimed

[2] https://www.youtube.com/watch?v=GGgiGtJk7MA.

[3] http://www.ft.com/cms/s/0/3be49734-29cb-11e6-83e4-abc22d5d108c.html#ixzz4ExYoJJNI; http://www.telegraph.co.uk/business/2016/06/21/in-defence-of-experts-whether-they-support-leave-or-remain/; https://www.theguardian.com/commentisfree/2016/jun/09/michael-gove-experts-academics-vote; http://www.huffingtonpost.co.uk/entry/professor-brian-cox-michael-gove-experts_uk_5777dceee4b073366f0f20b5.

[4] https://www.tuc.org.uk/news/governments-brexit-threats-hitting-jobs-says-tuc; https://www.cbi.org.uk/articles/what-comes-next-the-business-analysis-of-no-deal/; https://www.theguardian.com/politics/2019/may/16/brexit-political-mess-crushing-disaster-uk-business-cbi-chief-carolyn-fairbairn.

consensus over Brexit, *The Times* newspaper noted that "economics itself is on the line. If leaving the EU turns out to be beneficial, the profession will enter a crisis that will dwarf its inability to see the global financial crisis coming".[5]

DIFFERENT METHODOLOGIES, DIFFERENT CONCLUSIONS

The difficulty in reaching firm conclusions, in relation to the economic impact of Brexit, is a "formidably difficult exercise" (Miller et al. 2016: 12), given that many of the costs and benefits are subjective and the analysis is heavily dependent upon a range of assumptions (Thompson and Harari 2013: 5; Webb et al. 2015: 4; Miller et al. 2016: 5, 12). Indeed, Portes (2013: F5), noted that

> there is no single 'right' answer, because there is no single counterfactual. We simply do not know what the broad parameters of the relationship between the UK and the EU would be after British exit, nor do we know how the British economy would change and adapt to its new status outside the EU. This suggests that, rather than producing point estimates of the economic impact of exit, it is more sensible and informative to try to identify plausible alternative scenarios, which can then be used to model potential impacts on different assumptions about the post-exit economic environment.

Given the difficulties inherent in predicting the economic consequences of Brexit, this book has sought to present the findings of a wide range of studies, together with the data on which many of them are based, to enable general conclusions to be reached.

One central difficulty for economists concerns the lack of a historical precedent for a country the size and complexity of the UK withdrawing from the EU. Whilst Algeria (in 1962) and Greenland (in 1985) both left the EU when they gained their independence from France and Denmark, respectively, neither of these nations is sufficiently similar to the UK to provide sufficient precedence for Brexit.[6] To that extent, Brexit might be regarded as what economists term a 'black swan' event—that is, something that is known to exist, but observed so infrequently that when they do arrive, they are unexpected. Nevertheless, the lack of a close historical

---

[5] https://www.ft.com/content/e66852f0-3249-11e6-ad39-3fee5ffe5b5b.
[6] Although it might be worth noting in passing that in the five years following withdrawal from the EU in 1985, the Greenland economy grew by an average of 5.7% (Blake 2016: 5).

precedent has meant that economists have typically used one of four approaches when seeking to estimate the economic effects of Brexit (Sampson, 2017: 167–8; HMG 2018b: 21–2). These are as follows:

1. historical case studies and synthetic counterfactual analysis;
2. simulations using computable general equilibrium (CGE) trade models;
3. reduced-form evidence, combining gravity models and elasticity of income per capita to trade;
4. macroeconomic models.

Historical and Counterfactual Analysis

The first set of studies combines historical analyses of the trade gain from joining the EU, before assuming that Brexit operates in an identical but opposite fashion. Some early studies suggest that membership of the EU raised net (i.e. trade creation less trade diversion) intra-EU trade by between 16% (Badinger and Breuss 2011: 290) and 34% (Portes 2013: F5–6). However, others suggested that UK trade gains were significantly smaller than this EU average—perhaps as little as 3% (Miller and Spencer 1977; Portes 2013). Later studies examining the impact arising from the creation of the single internal market (SIM) estimated benefits *for the EU economy as a whole* ranged from 1.1–1.5% (Monti and Buchan, 1996) to between 2.6% and 3% (Harrison et al. 1994; Roeger and Sekkat 2002; Straathof et al. 2008). The EU's own Cecchini et al. (1988) report proposed a higher value of 4.5–6.5% of total EU GDP. Estimates of UK benefits arising from the formation of the SIM ranged from an initial 0.8% of UK GDP, rising to 1.49% in the medium term as a result of dynamic effects (Harrison et al. 1994: 23), to 1.8% of UK GDP (HM Treasury 2016: 1–2). Interestingly, one of these studies estimated that more integrated EU member states, such as Belgium and the Netherlands, benefitted by 6.39% and 7.73% of their national incomes, respectively. Thus, it would appear that the UK tended to gain from deeper European integration, but at a much lower level than more integrated member states (Allen et al. 1998: 468; Deutsche Bank 2013: 5).

A second variant of this approach concerns synthetic counterfactual analysis, where the historical record is contrasted with a hypothetical comparator of what might have happened if different decisions had been taken.

The method adopted is to select a baseline of similar countries who did not make the change under investigation—in this circumstance, they did not join the EU—and to compare the development paths for accession economies against this baseline. Using this method, Bayoumi and Eichengreen (1997) estimated that EU membership produced an average benefit of 3.2% of GDP for the original six participants, whilst Straathof et al. (2008) estimated that European trade integration had increased EU GDP by between 2% and 3%. Utilising data over a longer time period, Boltho and Eichengreen (2008) suggested that the formation of the EU may have boosted participant GDP by up to 5% over the period. Focusing upon the UK rather than the average EU member state, Campos et al. (2014) suggested that UK GDP was around 8.6% higher after ten years of EU membership, whilst Crafts (2016) suggested the total effect over the UK's this was closer to 10% of GDP.

There are, not surprisingly, a number of weaknesses with this approach. Isolating the effects of EU integration from other contemporaneous events is "an impossible challenge", and it would be "naïve" to expect that Brexit will have identical but opposite effects to accession to the EU (Sampson, 2017: 168). Moreover, the validity of the synthetic counterfactual methodology depends crucially upon (i) the selection of the time period selected for the analysis; (ii) the choice of baseline comparator countries; (iii) there being no 'shock' which might significantly impact upon outcomes; and (iv) the country in question should not be an outlier (Bouttell et al. 2018: 676). Unfortunately for studies of Brexit impact, all of these criteria are problematic. The UK's withdrawal from the EU is, by definition, an example of both a shock and an outlier amongst the countries constituting the analysis.

The choice of baseline comparator countries can additionally cause problems for the analysis. For example, Campos et al. (2014) utilised a previous selection of countries first adopted in a study by Böwer and Turrini (2010: 6), which comprised 10 Organisation for Economic Co-operation and Development (OECD) and 16 developing or emergent nations. The inclusion of developing or emergent nations in the baseline was justifiable for Böwer and Turrini since their study examined the impact of ten new member states joining the EU in 2004, eight of which were undergoing their own transition from command to market economies. However, it is harder to justify Campos et al. (2014) using this selection of comparator nations to investigate the impact of EU membership upon the UK. Thus, whilst it may be argued that Australia, Canada, Japan,

Norway and New Zealand may form a potential comparator group for the UK, it is much harder to justify the inclusion of Brazil, Columbia, China, Morocco, Russia, Thailand, Tunisia, Ukraine and Uruguay. This may have led the Campos et al. (2014) study to over-estimate the impact of EU membership on the UK.

Nevertheless, whilst the historical analyses have their methodological difficulties, and consequently their estimates should be treated with a degree of caution, they do point towards two conclusions: first, that EU membership has produced a net economic gain for the *average* member state and, second, that the UK's net gain was significantly more modest. These are two helpful insights to keep in mind when interpreting the economic evidence presented throughout this book.

Macroeconomic Models

Macroeconomic models tend to be data-driven. One variant of this approach is the vector autoregressive (VAR) model, which is widely used in short-run economic forecasting. Its advantage is that it allows each variable to affect all other variables in the model, whilst each variable is influenced by cumulative causation (past lags). For example, consumption impacts on GDP but is also affected by changes in GDP, whilst both impact on employment which, in turn, influences both GDP and consumption.

A second, and perhaps the most prominent type of macroeconomic models used today by central banks, economic institutions (such as the International Monetary Fund or IMF and the European Union or EU), policy makers and many academic econometricians, relates to dynamic stochastic general equilibrium (DSGE) models. The Bank of England, for example, uses a DSGE model, as does the Federal Reserve in the USA. This approach developed out of the Kyland and Prescott's (1977) "real business cycle" (new classical school) approach, which assumed continuous and instantaneous market clearing, such that the economy would shift effortlessly to full employment equilibria, whilst assumptions of rational expectations implied no role for active fiscal or monetary policy. In this view of the world, changes in aggregate demand would have no effect and the sole cause for the business cycle would be productivity or technological shocks. Not surprisingly, early variants of DSGE models are often at odds with observed stylised facts.

Later versions of DSGE models included New Keynesian theoretical insights, such that, in the short run, frictions may prevent sticky prices and wages, thereby allowing for monetary policy to influence the development of aggregate demand. However, in the long run, neo-classical assumptions prevailed, implying an economy always tending towards full employment and there being no room for active economic policy measures. Some of these unrealistic assumptions can be tempered in DSGE models, through the incorporation of financial imperfections (Rannenberg et al. 2015). However, DSGE models do still remain flawed, as the importance of aggregate demand and business cycle effects remain overlooked as explanations for changes in output and unemployment, whilst asset price bubbles are still not incorporated even after the inability of DSGE models to predict the 2008 financial crisis (Andrle et al. 2017: 27; Dullien 2017: 12–14).

An alternative form of New Keynesian macroeconomic model, which shares considerable similarity with certain types of DSGE approaches, includes the National Institute's Global Econometric Model (NiGEM).[7] This shares similar micro-foundations, such as rational expectations and a supply determined long-run equilibrium.[8] It is a global macroeconomic model and therefore tends to be widely used by those seeking to understand the linkages between countries and how a shock in one nation can impact upon others. As such, it is perhaps natural that many economic institutions, such as the IMF, OECD, National Institute of Economic and Social Research (NIESR) and HM Treasury, utilised the NiGEM simulation model for their Brexit analysis.

DSGE and New Keynesian models claim superiority over VAR and other forms of macro-econometric modelling due to micro-foundations. However, this strength is also their weakness, given that many aspects of neo-classical and New Keynesian theory are controversial. For example, neither deals very well with Keynesian insights into aggregate demand acting as the primary driving force behind economic activity, whilst demand deficiency and involuntary unemployment can persist beyond the short run if not properly corrected (King 2012: 3). Consequently, post-Keynesian alternatives such as E3ME and GINFORS have been developed, to draw behavioural characteristics from historical data (Lutz et al.

---

[7] https://nimodel.niesr.ac.uk/nigem-intro/nigemintro.php.
[8] https://mainlymacro.blogspot.com/2016/09/economics-dsge-and-reality-personal.html.

2010; Pollitt 2016). With the exception of a sole study from the University of Cambridge, however, studies adopting an econometric analysis of the economic impact of Brexit have not considered utilising these alternative models. This is a pity as their use would have helped to settle the concern that the narrow range of methods adopted by study authors, and the questionable nature of some of their attendant foundation assumptions, might be overtly biasing the results produced. The fact that many of the models produce similar results is not necessarily an indication of their veracity, but might instead reflect a herd instinct amongst economists, to follow precedent and use similar tried and trusted techniques, irrespective of whether they are in fact the best tool for the job.

CGE Simulations

Computable general equilibrium (CGE) models are built from neo-classical microeconomic foundations (Pollitt et al. 2019). They assume that economic agents (i.e. firms, households and government) optimise their behaviour so as to maximise their personal gains. This requires a further assumption that each has perfect knowledge; otherwise, such optimisation could not occur in conditions of uncertainty. It is taken for granted that the economy will automatically return to a long-term full employment market clearing equilibrium, despite the insight provided by Keynesian critique that this often does not occur and involuntary unemployment persists for long periods, partly due to hysteresis. Prices are assumed to be perfectly flexible and output determined by supply side factors. Finally, neo-classical foundations imply that there is a fixed supply of money and hence capacity constraints and crowding out can occur. The difference between DSGE and CGE models tends to be that the former focuses upon the dynamic changes exhibited in the economy over time, and is therefore better placed to understand cyclical effects arising from the business cycle or shifts in monetary and/or fiscal policy, whereas CGE modelling is primarily concerned with understanding the long-run impact of shocks or policy changes.

CGE models start from a similar starting point to input-output models (Leontief 1986), by developing a social accounting matrix to identify the linkages between different sectors in an economy. In this way, a change in one sector can be followed through as it impacts upon other sectors, through supply chain ripple effects or broader changes in aggregate demand. However, whereas input-output models focus upon the impact of demand through Keynesian multiplier analysis, CGE models focus upon identifying changes in the monetary flows between economic actors following their behavioural response to stimuli (West 1995). It is possible to include post-Keynesian insights into CGE models, such as the significance of path dependency, so that what happens in the short run is an important determinant of the long run and that government policy can influence the trajectory of growth and technological progress. The money supply can be treated as endogenous, implying that there is no crowding out or capacity constraints unless the economy is operating near full employment in which case there will begin to be constraints experienced upon further investment and output growth in the real economy. Prices can be modelled as sticky, rather than perfectly flexible, and output determined by aggregate demand and not supply side factors. However, this reconfiguration of CGE models does not typically occur.

There have been a large number of economic studies which have adopted the CGE approach to predict the economic impact of Brexit. These include the static analysis conducted by the Centre for Economic Performance-London School of Economics (CEP-LSE) team (e.g. Dhingra et al. 2017), Aichele and Felbermayr (2015), RAND (Ries et al. 2017), OECD (Kierzenkowski et al. 2016), Her Majesty's Government or HMG (2018a, 2018b), Centre for Economic Policy Research (CEPR; Vandenbussche et al. 2017), CPB NL (Rojas-Romagosa 2016), Rabobank (Erken et al. 2018) and the University of Bonn (Jafari and Britz 2017). These studies produced a range of estimates of how the introduction of trade barriers might increase UK export costs in the advent of a 'no deal' (World Trade Organization [WTO] option), which ranged between 6% and 13% (averaging 8.5%), for both goods and services. More detailed predictions as to the effect on the UK economy more generally are shown in Fig. 1.1 and Table 1.1 located at the end of this chapter.

Many of these studies include assumptions regarding the imposition of future non-tariff barriers (NTBs) drawn from existing work examining trade barriers between the EU and the USA. Thus, for example, both the CEPR, CEP-LSE and RAND studies assume that NTBs facing UK exports to the SIM will be 75% the level currently experienced by US exports to the EU, under the WTO scenario. Other studies, for example, Jafari and Britz (2017), used estimates for NTB ad-valorem cost increase equivalents drawn from previous studies (Egger et al. 2015) and assumed that the UK would incur around half of the rates currently experienced by non-EU nations. There is little justification for these assumptions, however, except for the vague belief that NTBs are unlikely to be quite as large as the USA because the UK starts from a position of perfect alignment with EU

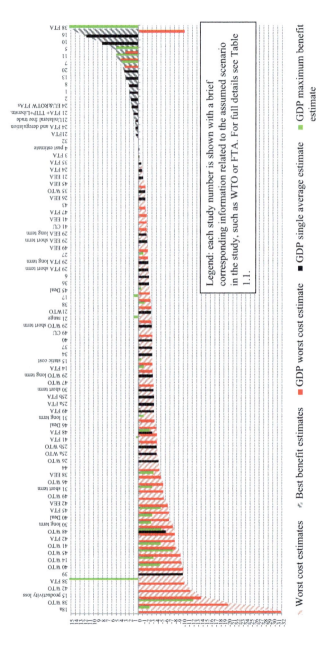

Fig. 1.1 Estimated net costs and net benefits of EU membership (% GDP), based on significant studies derived from Table 1.1. Source: Authors' review of significant studies quantifying net costs and benefits. Notes: Negative numbers show estimates of net costs; positive numbers show estimated net benefits. Please see Table 1.1 for correspondence between the number of study shown on the horizontal axis and the respective study (Table 1.1. offers more detail on estimates)

Table 1.1 Meta-analysis of the summary of net costs or net benefits, and of competences in significant cost-benefit studies (chronological order)

Study	Study number and scenario	GDP estimate %GDP min estimate	%GDP (single) estimate	%GDP max estimate	Budget	SIM	FDI	Sector	Growth & product**	BOP	Macro policy	Exch Rate	Labour migration	Reg8*	Industrial policy	Conclusions
Burkett et al, 1996	1		2		√	√		√	√	√	√	√	√	√	√	Early study, focused more on costs of EU membership than benefits
Leach [IOD], 2000	2		1.75		√	√	√					√				Net cost of EU membership (hence net benefit of Brexit) = 1.75% GDP
USITC, 2000	3 FTA		-0.02			√	√	√	√	√		√				Using a Global Trade Analysis Project (GTAP) general equilibrium trade model, the study concludes that UK withdrawal from the EU, combined with a subsequent FTA with NAFTA countries, would result in a 0.02% decline in UK GDP.
Gasiorek et al, 2002	4 past estimate		2		√	√	√	√				√		√		Using a CGE model, this study estimated the gains to the UK from EU membership to be net +2% UK GDP, between 1973 and 1985.
Milne, 2004	5	5		3	√	√	√	√				√				Net cost of EU membership 3-5% GDP
Pain & Young, 2004	6		-2.25		√	√	√	√								Simulation utilising the NIESR macroeconomic model of the UK economy. Net cost of Brexit = 2.25% GDP in the long run
Minford et al, 2005	7	3.2		3.7		√		√								Utilised the trade and macro models of the Cardiff University Macroeconomics Research Group. Findings indicate EU membership net cost: 3.2-3.7% UK GDP
Ilkovitz et al, 2007	8		2.1			√	√									European Commission study examining the benefits for the EU as a whole (no figures for the UK in isolation) arising from the SIM, 1992-2006. Estimated EU GDP 2.1% higher.
Eichengreen and Bolitho, 2008	9				√	√	√	√	√					√	√	Historical literature review approach, focusing primarily on trade (SIM) and competition. Estimated net benefit of approximately 5% EU(15) GDP.
Gaskell and Persson, 2010	10		8											√		Narrow focus on the cost of EU regulation. Estimate: costs UK economy £32.8bn p.a. (or approx. 8% of 2009 UK GDP). The benefit-cost ratio is positive, however, albeit significantly smaller than the net benefits of national regulation (1.02/1.58).
CBI, 2013	11	4		5					√							Conclusion: net benefit arising from EU membership is in the region of 4-5% of UK GDP p.a. (p.11)
Drew and Bond (Eds.) [Regents Report], 2013	12		N/A		√	√	√	√				√			√	A series of individual case studies. No summary conclusions reached.
Campos et al, 2014	13		2.8						√							Synthetical counterfactual approach estimates that the UK growth rate was 0.7% GDP p.a. higher due to EU membership
CEP-LSE studies: Ottaviano et al, 2014a and 2014b; Dhingra et al, 2015 and 2015b	14 FTA / 14 WTO	-3.1 / -9.5		-1.1 / -3.3	√	√			√							Use a standard quantitative static general equilibrium trade model with multiple sectors, countries and intermediates. Conclusion: Static losses lie between -1.1% UK GDP in the optimistic (FTA) scenario, and -3.1% UK GDP in the pessimistic (WTO) scenario; dynamic losses, although not explored in detail in the analysis, are reported as increasing potential losses from Brexit to between -3.3% UK GDP (FTA) and -9.5% UK GDP (WTO option)
BertelsmannStiftung, 2015	15 static cost / 15 productivity loss	-3 / -14		-0.6	√											Depending on the degree of trade policy isolation, UK real GDP could fall by between 0.6 and 3.0% by 2030 (static costs), whilst lower investment and innovation may lower productivity and increase losses to 14% of UK GDP (dynamic costs) in the longer term.
Congdon, 2014	16		11.5		√								√	√		Focused upon cost of EU membership – estimated at 11.5% of UK GDP (£185bn p.a.)
Mansfield, 2014	17	-2.6	0.1	1.1	√	√	√							√		Long-term impact between -2.6% and +1.1% of GDP, with, in the author's view, a best estimate of +0.1%.
Springford and Tilford, 2014	18		N/A			√	√	√								Focusing on trade effects. Conclusion: "The UK has very little to gain by quitting the EU and much to lose"
Aichele and Felbermayr, 2015	18a	-0.1 static -2.5 dynamic & migration		-2.47 static -31.8 dynamic & migration	√	√	√					√				IFO CGE model (34 sectors) for static analysis; dynamic effects drawn from conclusions reached from previous literature. Static analysis suggests virtually no loss for EEA, but -2.5% if WTO; dynamic and migration effects increase this significantly depending upon which studies estimates are drawn and assumptions as to the likely reduction in migration figures.
Bank of England, 2015	19		N/A		√	√			√		√				√	Focused on policy consequences of EU membership leading to economic openness
Business for Britain, 2015	20		3.2		√	√	√	√					√	√		Net cost of EU membership (and hence net benefit from Brexit): £12.6bn (3.2% UK GDP) or £933 per household
Ciuriak et al, 2015	21 range / 21WTO / 21EEA / 21FTA / 21FTA+TTIP+liberalisation	-2.76	-2.76 / -1.03 / 0.6 / 1.07	1.07	√	√	√									Estimated impact of Brexit, ranged from: (a) -2.76% UK GDP (WTO option) by 2030 (b) -1.03% UK GDP (EEA option) (c) FTA with EU combined with further FTAs with other leading economies, such as Australian FTA with China, Japan, India and ASIEN, would boost the UK economy by around 0.6% of UK GDP (d) A combined FTA, TTIP and liberalisation option would boost UK GDP by 1.07% of UK GDP. Depending upon the combination of options adopted, the UK could therefore face a net cost of 2.76% GDP to a small net gain of perhaps +1.07% UK GDP.
Irwin, 2015	22		N/A		√	√	√					√	√	√		Net costs (unquantified). Impact of Brexit = "severe".
McFadden and Tarrant, 2015	23		N/A		√	√	√							√		Primarily a critique of other studies, the report nevertheless concludes that Brexit is likely to prove negative for the UK, particularly due to trade effects.
Booth et al, 2015	24 WTO / 24 FTA / 24 FTA and deregulation / 24 EU&ROTW FTAs		-2.2 / -0.8 / 0.64 / 1.55		√	√		√								Utilising a GTAP computable general equilibrium model (CGE), the study generates a range of possible scenarios: the worst case (WTO) scenario reduces UK GDP by -2.2% by 2030, a FTA option has only a modest reduction in UK GDP of -0.8% whilst a FTA accompanied by significant deregulation would result in a small net gain of 0.64%, compared to the best case scenario, where the UK negotiates comprehensive FTAs with both the EU and elsewhere in the world, combined with significant deregulation, producing a net benefit to of 1.55% of UK GDP. The most feasible range, produced by the report, is assumed to lie between -0.81 to +0.64% of UK GDP.

Table 1.1   (continued)

Study	Scenario	Value		Value													Conclusions
Webb et al [HoC Library], 2015	25		N/A		√	√	√								√	√	No conclusions reached
Rojas-Romagosa [CEPB], 2016	25a FTA	-3.4 FTA			√	√	√		√						√		Utilising the CEPB CGE model for the world economy, combined with estimates for NTBs derived from gravity model results contained within the academic literature. Predictions range from a cost associated with Brexit followed by a FTA of 3.4% UK GDP, to a slightly higher 4.1% if trading according to WTO rules.
	25a WTO	-4.1 WTO															
HM Treasury (2016)	25b FTA	-3.4 FTA				√	√		√								Utilising a combination of VAR and gravity modelling, the results of which are then fed into the NiGEM macroeconomic model to determine the final results, the Treasury report predicted that Brexit would cause of a loss of UK GDP in the region of 3.8% if joining the EEA, 6.2% if negotiating a FTA with the EU, and 7.5% if trading according to WTO rules.
	25b WTO	-4.1 WTO															
IMF, 2016	26 EEA	-1.4			√	√	√		√		√						Utilising a combination of VAR, gravity and NiGEM simulation models, the IMF predicted that Brexit would lead to a loss of around -1.4% UK GDP in its limited (EEA) scenario by 2021, whereas in a more adverse (WTO) scenario, this potential loss compared to the baseline was -4.5% UK GDP.
	26 WTO	-4.5															
Punhani and Hill, 2016 – Credit Suisse Report	27	-2		-1					√								Predicts Brexit causing uncertainty and declining business investment and GDP falling by 1-2%
Miller, 2016 [HoC Library]	28		N/A		√	√	√	√							√		No conclusions reached
NIESR, 2016	29 WTO short term	-2.9			√	√	√	√				√	√				Analysis using the NiGEM general equilibrium econometric model. In the short term (2020), the net cost of Brexit was predicted to vary from -1.9% (EEA option), -2.1% (FTA) to -2.9% (WTO). In the longer term (2030), the net cost of Brexit declined slightly in the case of the EEA option to -1.8%, remained constant for the FTA option at -2.1% but increased slightly in the case of the WTO option at -3.2% of UK GDP.
	29 FTA short term	-2.1															
	29 EEA short term	-1.9															
	29 WTO long term	-3.2															
	29 FTA long term	-2.1															
	29 EEA long term	-1.8															
Kierzenkowski et al [OECD], 2016	30 short term	-3.3			√	√	√		√		√						Using CGE and NiGEM models, the OECD forecast that Brexit would result in a shortfall of -3.3% UK GDP by 2020, whereas longer term effects would range from -2.7% UK GDP (FTA option) to -7.7% (WTO option) by 2030.
	30 long term	-7.7		-2.7													
PwC, 2016	31 short term	-5.5		-3.0	√	√	√								√	√	Utilised CGE model. Short term costs (by 2020) between 3-5.5% GDP; longer term costs are lower, at 1.2-3.5% UK GDP by 2030, as uncertainty resolved. However, average GDP per capita in 2030 would be similar after 'Brexit', being around 25-28% higher than in 2015 in the two exit scenarios, compared to an estimated 29% with continued EU membership
	31 long term	-3.5		-1.2													
Capital Economics [Woodford Report], 2016	32		0.2			√	√								√	√	Slightly more plausible that the net impact of 'Brexit' will be modestly positive
TUC, 2016	33		N/A												√		Report takes growth predictions from Treasury, IFS, LSE and IMF studies. Using this data, the TUC predict that Brexit will result in average wages falling by between £28 and £48 per week by 2030
JP Morgan, 2016	34 yearly		-3														Reports views of 12 financial institutions and the HM Treasury (2016) report – predicting that GDP would be reduced by 1% GDP for every year that uncertainty persists, thus 2-3 years of negotiations would reduce GDP by up to 3% of GDP.
Felbermayr et al, 2017	35 FTA	-0.6 FTA (re: Korea)				√		√			√						Gravity model to estimate the trade effects of EU membership combined with static CGE model of international trade. Predictions are that trading under WTO rules post-Brexit would cost the UK 1.4% of GDP per capita, whereas a comprehensive FTA (such as that negotiated between the EU and South Korea) would produce a lower 0.6% drop in UK GDP per capita.
	35 WTO	-1.4 WTO															
Felbermayr et al, 2018a	36		-2.3			√		√			√						The report used a combination of CGE and gravity analysis. Its focus concerned the potential trade and broader economic impact of a dissolution of the EU. As such Brexit only featured at the margins. Nevertheless, the conclusions were that the UK GDP would likely contract by 2.3%.
Bank of England, 2018	37		-3		√	√	√	√			√						Reports views of 12 financial institutions and the HM Treasury (2016) report – predicting that GDP would be reduced by 1% GDP for every year that uncertainty persists, thus 2-3 years of negotiations would reduce GDP by up to 3% of GDP.
Dhingra et al, 2017 STATIC ANALYSIS DYNAMIC ANALYSIS	38 38 EEA 38 FTA 38 WTO	-1.3 -3.3 EEA -10.2 FTA -13.3 WTO		-2.7 -4.9 EEA - 15.3 FTA -20.0 WTO	√		√	√									Static analysis using CGE model (31 sectors, 31 global regions). Dynamic analysis is based upon Feyrer (2009a) estimates for trade openness and productivity. These give rise to significantly higher cost forecasts.
Crafts, 2016	39		-10														Conclusions drawn from the results produced by previous studies examining the trade gain from economic integration and reversing it for Brexit.
Menon et al, 2019		GDP PER CAPITA	GDP PER CAPITA	GDP PER CAPITA	√	√		√				√	√				This analysis is based upon the same CEP trade (CGE) model (31 sectors, 35 regions) as for previous studies - for further discussion, see Menon et al (2018) and Dhingra et al (2017). Please note that the forecasts made by this report relate to GDP per capita, and as such, no direct comparisons can be made with the previous studies listed in this table. For the same reason, the results are not illustrated in Fig. 1.1.
Static trade effects		-1.7 May's Deal	-2.5 Johnson's deal	-3.3 WTO													
Dynamic trade effects		-4.9 May's Deal	-6.4 Johnson's deal	-8.1 WTO													
Static trade & restrictive migration effects		-3.1 May's Deal	-3.9 Johnson's deal	-4.7 WTO													
Dynamic trade & restrictive migration		-3.5 May's Deal	-4.3 Johnson's deal	-5.1 WTO													
Menon et al, 2019 [UKCE]	40																This analysis is based upon the same CEP trade (CGE) model (31 sectors, 35 regions) as for previous studies - for further discussion, see Menon et al (2018) and Dhingra et al (2017).

Table 1.1 (continued)

Study						Checks	Description
Reis et al [RAND], 2017 TRADE ONLY	41 EEA 41 CU	-1.7 EEA -1.8 CU		-1.9 FTA -4.9 WTO		√ √	Similar approach to Dhingra et al (2016), using structural gravity (SG) model. FDI estimates are produced by reversing (symmetrically) historical effects pertaining to previous boosts to FDI from economic nitration.
TRADE & FDI	41 FTA 41 WTO	0.6 FTA EU&US		-4.1 FTA -8.2 WTO			
Erken et al, 2017	42 EEA 42 FTA 42 WTO	-6.5 EEA		-8.0 FTA -11.5 WTO		√ √ √	Used the NiGEM macroeconomic model developed by NIESR, alongside a productivity model developed by Rabobank.
Gudgin et al, 2017a	43		-1.5		√ √ ... √		The analysis uses a CBR macroeconomic model, which was developed from post-Keynesian foundations. The study utilises assumptions on how different variables will respond to the Brexit shock, leading to the prediction that Brexit will result in UK GDP falling below the pre-2016 trend rate by 1.5% in 2026.
Jafari and Britz, 2017	44		-4.6		√ √		CGE model. Variables include trade (tariffs and NTBs), FDI and migration.
HMG, 2018a No migration effects	45 Deal 45 EEA 45 WTO	-0.6 Deal -1.4 EEA -2.5 Deal		-4.9 FTA -7.7 WTO -6.7 FTA -9.3 WTO		√ √ √ √ √	Combines GETRADE static CGE model (5 sector groups, eleven modelled sectors) with dynamic elements added. NTBs are estimated using a combination of gravity models, together with direct cost estimation, evidence from stakeholders, existing literature and insights from government policy leads.
Assumes zero EEA migration							
Hantzsche et al [NIESR], 2018	46 Deal 46 WTO	-3.9 Deal & FTA		-5.5 WTO		√ √ √ √ √	The analysis uses the NiGEM model, supplemented by a number of assumptions based upon estimates drawn from the existing literature. It assumes that leaving a trade bloc has a symmetric but opposite effect to joining a similar bloc. On this basis, it forecasts that trade according to WTO rules would result in the UK GDP falling by 5.5% in the medium term, and 3.9% if a FTA was agreed.
Menon et al, 2018 Static trade effects		-1.7 deal	-3	-3.3 WTO		√ √ √ √ √	This analysis is based upon earlier work by Dhingra et al (2017), using a CEP trade model (31 sectors, 35 regions) and feeding this into a CGE model. Assumptions relating to tariffs and NTBs were also drawn from Dhingra et al (2017), where NTBs are assumed to be equivalent to a different % of US-EU barriers depending upon which Brexit option is selected. It does not model FDI.
Dynamic trade effects		-4.9 deal		-8.1 WTO			
Static trade & migration combined		-3.1 deal		-4.7 WTO			
Dynamic trade & migration combined		-4.7 deal		-9.9 WTO			
Arregui and Chen [IMF], 2018	48 FTA 48 WTO	-2.5 FTA -5 WTO	+3 FTA -6 WTO	-4 FTA -8 WTO		√ √ √ √ √	Feeding trade elasticities from previous studies (i.e. Felbermayr et al, 2018a) into a CGE model, and combining this effect with assumptions made regarding declines in inward migration, produce estimates that Brexit will lead to a 3% fall in UK GDP if a FTA is agreed, and 6% if trading under WTO rules.
Hantzsche and Young [NIESR], 2019	49 EEA 49 CU 49 FTA 49 WTO	-2 EEA -3 CU	-3.5 FTA	-5.6 WTO		√ √ √ √ √	This study uses the same approach as previously published as Hantzsche et al (2018), namely using the NiGEM model, supplemented by a number of assumptions based upon estimates drawn from the existing literature. It assumes that leaving a trade bloc has a symmetric but opposite effect to joining a similar bloc, and therefore assumes that goods trade with the EU will decline by 40% and service trade by 60%. It predicts that UK GDP would decline by around 2% if trade relations with the EU were unchanged, but the UK was subject to continued uncertainty, whereas a customs union arrangement would result in a drop of 3% over the medium term, a FTA 3.5% and trading on the basis of WTO rules 5.6%.

Notes: In blue highlight: studies used in this chapter to denote 'consensus' studies..
On green background: eighteen studies added in the second edition of this book, numbered: 18a, 25a, 25b, 35-49.

Sources: The Authors.

standards and regulations, with future deviation only occurring gradually and in part. But it could be argued that this could have been better replicated by assuming a starting point of perhaps 20–25% of the EU-US NTBs, rising to perhaps 30–50% over time. This would have generated significantly lower predicted Brexit costs in this group of studies.

Reduced-Form Evidence Using Gravity Modelling

Reduced-form analysis seeks to estimate the effect of EU membership upon trade flows, typically using what is known as a 'gravity model'. This economic approach borrows from Isaac Newton's Law of Gravitation, developed in his book *Philosophiae Naturalis Principia Mathematica* published in 1687. The familiar expression holds that the gravitational force between two masses is proportional to the product of the two masses and inversely proportional to the square of their distance. The economic 'gravity model' derives from the work on Tinbergen, in the early 1960s, although refined by Deardorff (1995) by utilising the Heckscher-Ohlin neo-classical model as the basis for the approach. It seeks to estimate differences between predicted and actual trade patterns with other nations, whilst taking account of other factors such as their relative size, wealth and spatial location relative to their trading partner(s). The geographical distance between two countries can be measured as the spatial distance (miles, kilometres) between the capitals of the countries taken into consideration, or alternatively, transportation costs could be used to proxy transaction costs.

Early gravity model analysis found, like the earlier *ex post* studies, only limited trade effects arising from European integration. However, as discussed in more detail in Chap. 3, later studies found European integration producing more significant effects, ranging from 36% to 84% (Baier et al. 2008; Felbermayr et al. 2018a; Felbermayr et al. 2018b). Gravity model predictions of changes to trade flows are combined with estimates of the elasticity of income per capita to trade (the percentage change in trade with respect to a percentage change in income) to calculate the predicted effect of EU membership on income per capita. The global estimate recorded prior to the 2008 financial crisis was around 1.4, indicating that international trade was expanding faster than the growth in global GDP (Borin et al., 2017: 5). If Brexit is assumed to result in a symmetric reversal of this effect, as the benefits derived from EU membership on income per capita are withdrawn, the analysis would predict net trade-related Brexit costs.

Various economic studies have utilised this approach. The dynamic modelling completed by the CEP-LSE team is the most prominent. However, these studies often did not construct their own gravity models but rather utilised examples drawn from the existing academic literature. Dhingra et al. (2017), for example, used gravity and elasticity of income per capita to trade estimates both drawn from previous studies (Baier et al. 2008 and Feyrer 2009a, respectively). Other studies which utilised gravity modelling included PwC (2016), the Mulabdic et al. (2017), the Baker et al. (2016), Centre d'Études Prospectives et d'Informations Internationales (CEPII; Mayer et al. 2018), Institute for Economic Research–Centre for Economic Studies (IFO-CESifo; Felbermayr et al.

2017; Felbermayr et al. 2018a; Felbermayr et al. 2018b), HMG (2018b) and the Bank of England (BoE 2018). The IMF (2016) based its analysis upon the CESifo gravity model, whilst the Kierzenkowski et al. (2016) drew upon the estimates produced by Foumier et al. (2015). The range of predictions generated by this group of studies is more diverse than those studies using CGE analysis. Predicted increases in costs for UK goods exporters ranged from 8–10% (Felbermayr et al. 2017, Felbermayr et al. 2018b; Mulabdic et al. 2017; HMG, 2018b) to 20–1% (Arregui and Chen 2018; Mayer et al. 2018). Similarly, for service exports, the range was even wider, ranging from 6–7% (Mayer et al. 2018; Mulabdic et al. 2017) to 34% (Felbermayr et al. 2018b).

The use of gravity modelling to forecast the impact of Brexit is, however, problematic. This is firstly because whilst this approach predicts the levels of trade well in a statistical sense, as long as the assumption of *ceteris paribus* remains true, Brexit involves changes in far more than a few trade barriers. It includes regulatory divergence, the formation of new preferential trade agreements (PTAs) with countries outside of the EU, and shifts in national economic policy to accommodate these changes. Thus, there are insufficient data points to allow the proper calibration of the gravity model, leading to problems of selection bias (Minford 2016: 5–6). The surprising variation in gravity model results may reinforce suspicions as to their suitability to model Brexit (Gudgin et al. 2017b: 5).

A second issue concerns the impact that improvements in technology, particularly applications facilitating remote communication, together with improvements in transportation technology and accompanying reductions in transport costs, are likely to have in reducing the relative trade cost advantage for neighbouring compared to more distant countries (Deardorff 1995: 24). Technological advances can reduce time cost elements of trade, through faster modes of travel and/or technological alternatives to physical interaction for service industries. Consequently, trade flows are likely to shift, over time, as cost advantages relating to spatial distance become less relevant and hence trade with more distant countries may become more attractive.

The changing composition of trading partners can also affect trade flows. For example, a shift towards a less egalitarian distribution of income in a particular nation may favour exporters of luxury goods but reduce demand for more basic staples, whilst a change in a nation's industrial base (and with it, supply chains) might impact upon trade flows irrespective of spatial factors (Deardorff 1995: 24–5).

A fourth issue relates to the range of studies which appear to demonstrate that shared historical and cultural ties facilitate trade, whilst cultural differences impede the flow of information and communications between individuals and companies from different countries (Fletcher and Bohn 1998; Hofstede 1980, 1994; Kogut and Singh 1988). The significance of cultural, linguistic and historical ties can be witnessed by the fact that Britain's largest single trading partner remains the USA, despite its geographical distance from the UK. Commonwealth trade also remains more significant for the UK than for other EU member states, reflecting elements of a shared history and the reflections of the UK's maritime past. Brexit may, therefore, reverse part of the trade diversion away from Commonwealth nations which occurred upon the UK's accession to the EU.

Fifth, because gravity models utilise historical data, it follows that trade barriers were much higher for most of the period under investigation than in 2020; the average EU common external tariff (CET), for example, was 17% in 1973, the date of UK accession, whereas it currently lies between 2.3% and 3% (see Chap. 3 for further discussion). Consequently, much of the data utilised in gravity models will reflect time periods when the advantages of joining regional trade associations were higher than the current time period. Hence, the advantages accruing from EU membership are likely to change over time (Gudgin et al. 2017b: 19). This is not a problem if the purpose of the gravity model is to estimate the average trade effects for a group of countries over a historical time period, but it does become a problem if the results are used to predict future effects for the UK's withdrawal from the EU, when *current* trade costs (and hence the costs of withdrawal) are lower than for the majority of the time period under investigation. Gravity models can be adjusted to take account for this effect, but this does not appear to have occurred in the economic models examining Brexit.

Sixth, gravity models depend upon the assumption that observed elasticities remain constant even when the change in commercial relationships is rather large, such as would be the case if Brexit led to the imposition of tariff barriers. This is unlikely (Minford et al. 2015: 10–11). Trade flows may follow a cyclical pathway, impacted by business cycle conditions, and thus, elasticities change with prevailing international demand. If global growth is below its long-run trend, then the elasticity of trade will also be below its long-run trend (Borin et al., 2017: 7). Hence, modelling elasticities of trade without consideration of international business cycles would appear to be a mistake. In addition, structural changes in the global economy, such as a slowing of global integration and technological advances, may lead to the creation of a "new normal", with trade income elasticity trends declining significantly since the 2008 global financial crisis (ECB 2016: 6, 9; Borin et al., 2017: 5). If this is the case, then the elasticities used in Brexit studies drawn from earlier studies will have over-estimated the impact of any reduction in UK-EU trade following Brexit.

Finally, the forecasts made by gravity modelling appear to be inconsistent with the fact that the share of UK exports to EU member states has been in decline over the past decade, since its predictions would suggest that this trade should have grown in importance over this time period (Blake 2016: 4). As a consequence, it would appear that the use of gravity modelling in Brexit studies is problematic, as it is likely to over-estimate trade-related costs (Blake 2016: 3,16; HM Treasury 2016: 129).

INFLUENTIAL 'CONSENSUS' STUDIES

The wide range of economic studies summarised in Table 1.1, seeks to capture the salient research approaches utilised by a broad range of these studies, the number of factors included in their analysis and summarising their results. A brief perusal will highlight the absence of unanimity amongst economic research teams in terms of the predicted impact deriving from Brexit. There are more studies which predict Brexit to impose net costs (rather than benefits) upon the UK economy averaging around 2–3% of UK GDP at the end of a 10–15-year time period, equivalent to shaving around 0.2% off UK growth rates for the next decade. Yet, this does not immediately equate to the economic consensus, declared by those critical of Brexit, nor the claims of dire consequences if certain forms of Brexit are adopted. The explanation is, however, quite straightforward as certain types of study, undertaken by international economic organisations (Arregui and Chen 2018; IMF 2016; Kierzenkowski et al. 2016), government departments (HM Treasury 2016; HMG, 2018b), central banks (Bank of England 2018), independent research organisations (NIESR—Baker et al. 2016; Ebell and Warren 2016; Hantzsche et al. 2018; Hantzsche and Young 2019) and academic bodies (CEP-LSE—Ottaviano et al. 2014a, Ottaviano et al. 2014b; Dhingra et al. 2015a, 2015b, Dhingra et al. 2016; Dhingra et al. 2017; Menon et al. 2018), are perceived as producing more rigorous analysis, utilising favoured methodological approaches.

The 200-page report, produced by HM Treasury in 2016, is a good example of how the 'consensus' studies influenced economic actors as it became widely used as a reference point for many of the claims made in the European referendum campaign and thereafter. Its predictions that Brexit would impose substantial and *permanent* costs upon the UK, totalling between 3.4% and 9.5% of its GDP depending upon the type of trade arrangement subsequently negotiated, were cited by former Chancellor of the Exchequer, Osborne, to claim that withdrawal from the EU would be the "most extraordinary self-inflicted wound" and that those supporting 'Brexit' were "economically illiterate".[9] This is despite the analysis being arguably "inevitably coloured" by the then government stance set firmly against the UK withdrawing from the EU (Gudgin et al. 2017a: 6).

There are, in addition, a further set of reports produced by prominent organisations, who based their conclusions not upon their own independent analysis but rather based upon the results produced by the consensus studies. For example, the Trades Union Congress (TUC 2016: 1, 3, 9) relied upon the results generated by HM Treasury, CEP-LSE, OECD and NIESR studies to substantiate their claims on employment-related Brexit impact, whilst the Institute for Fiscal Studies (IFS) based its prediction of a shortfall in UK fiscal balances upon the forecasts made by the 'consensus' studies (Emmerson and Pope 2016: 14; Emmerson et al. 2016: 18). Even the Office for Budget Responsibility (OBR) forecast for the UK economy, which intimately informs the economic policy strategy of the government, was based upon the conclusions reached by the NIESR, IMF, OECD and HM Treasury reports, rather than undertaking its own independent analysis (OBR 2016: 9, 47). As a result, a 'consensus' group of studies does emerge from this larger literature, and it is their predictions which has largely permeated into the public consciousness. For ease of comparison, this group of studies is highlighted in blue in Table 1.1.

There are, furthermore, a number of other studies which might be viewed as further extending this group of 'consensus' studies. These include work completed by the CEPR (Vandenbussche et al. 2017), the World Bank (2017), the US RAND Corporation (Ries et al. 2017), the Netherlands Bureau for Economic Policy Analysis (CPB NL; Rojas-Romagosa 2016), the French CEPII (Mayer et al. 2018), and a partnership between the German research bodies, the IFO and the CESifo

---

[9] http://www.theguardian.com/politics/2016/apr/18/george-osborne-brexit-campaigners-case-is-economically-illiterate.

(Felbermayr et al. 2017; Felbermayr et al. 2018a; Felbermayr et al. 2018b). Many of these reports had a significant influence outside of the UK. However, they were not fundamental in forming the perception within the country of their being an economic consensus that Brexit will incur significant economic costs and that more independent trading relationships will incur greater costs than a closer relationship with the EU.

Choice of Models and Their Micro-Foundations Influences Results

All of the 'consensus' studies used either CGE, DSGE or macroeconomic (NiGEM) models, with some additionally using gravitational modelling to determine expected changes in trade flow. Each of these techniques is founded upon neo-classical or New Keynesian theoretical precepts. This is perhaps not surprising because this represents the economics mainstream orthodoxy. However, it does raise a question regarding the extent to which the micro-foundations of these modelling techniques might influence their results. There has been, to date, only one study which has used a very different macroeconomic modelling approach, namely using the Centre for Business Research (CBR; University of Cambridge) macroeconomic model of the UK economy (UKMOD), which is founded upon post-Keynesian theoretical insights. Consequently, it is instructive to note that this study estimated that the medium-term economic impact of Brexit would be a mere 1.5% of UK GDP (Gudgin et al. 2017a: 38–9). This is significantly lower than the results produced by the 'consensus' studies.

Comparison between different model types is instructive and suggests two things. Firstly, the micro-foundations of macroeconomic models do appear to be significant and may bias results. Even if identical assumptions are used as the basis of the analysis, the models produce different results. Hence, it is deeply problematic for the 'consensus' studies to have used variations of the same set of modelling approaches, and it is even more troublesome that leading figures from the business and policy-making communities have uncritically internalised their findings without considering whether it might be more appropriate to draw their evidence from a broader range of sources, utilising a variety of different modelling techniques. Secondly, the Cambridge study highlights the importance of the assumptions that models depend upon, and which, in this case, made a very large difference in the results produced. The assumptions adopted by HM Treasury produced a severe downward bias compared to those adopted in the Cambridge study—that is, predicting a fall in UK GDP of

6–7% rather than 1.5%. Whereas one conclusion implies that Brexit will produce short-term costs that can easily be accommodated by the UK economy or countered by a more active economic policy, the other forecasts recession, job losses and a significantly slower rate of prosperity growth over a decade or more.

The Crucial Role of Assumptions in Economic Models

Economics models are built upon a range of assumptions required to simplify the analysis of what otherwise could be a complex and confusing array of variables and inter-relationships. To the extent that these assumptions simplify but allow the model to closely replicate observed reality, then this is helpful; to the extent that they deviate from stylised facts, the predictions made by the model become less useful as a guide to future behaviour.

The economic models seeking to predict the economic impact of Brexit used a large number of assumptions. Unfortunately, too many of these were questionable.

There were, for example, a number of simple factual inaccuracies included in many of the models. For example, many studies used figures for average 'most favoured nation' (MFN) tariff costs of 5% (Ebell and Warren 2016: 125; HM Treasury 2016: 99) and 5.3% (IMF 2016: 16), whereas average *trade-weighted* 'MFN' tariffs are estimated as being between 2.3% and 3% (Thompson and Harari 2013: 8; WTO 2015: 75; World Data Bank 2020). Similarly, fiscal savings following the UK's withdrawal from the EU were under-estimated by certain studies, using a figure of 0.3% of UK GDP (IMF 2016: 22) rather than the correct figure of 0.53%, as explained in Chap. 2 of this book.

The composition of the models was particularly problematic, since those variables most likely to deliver positive Brexit impact were generally either omitted or assumed to have little effectiveness. For example, regulation was often omitted entirely (Ottaviano et al. 2014a, Ottaviano et al. 2014b; Dhingra et al. 2015a, 2015b, Dhingra et al. 2016; HM Treasury 2016: 136; Dhingra et al. 2017; Menon et al. 2018), despite claims made by other theorists that regulatory savings might provide one of the more significant benefits arising from Brexit (Congdon 2014: 30; Business for Britain 2015: 122–3; Capital Economics 2016: 13). Where it was included, its impact was typically dismissed as having only a marginal effect, since the UK already enjoyed considerable regulatory flexibility (HMG 2018a: 6,

39–49; Kierzenkowski et al. 2016: 7, 29–31). The treatment of migration was a little better, but assumptions concerning post-Brexit reductions in flows from European Economic Area (EEA) nations were often arbitrary (HM Treasury 2016: 136; Arregui and Chen 2018: 16; BoE 2018; Hantzsche et al. 2018: F35: 15–17; Hantzsche and Young 2019: F35). The impact of exchange rates was not included in all models, despite the obvious mitigation to rising trade costs which might arise if the UK were to trade under WTO rules, whilst the potential gain from the UK being able to negotiate its own trade deals was almost universally ignored. Finally, none of the studies included a meaningful consideration of how policy changes could influence the ultimate impact of Brexit. This narrow range of variables included in the 'consensus' models leads to selection bias and has the effect of skewing the results unnecessarily towards forecasting negative results arising from Brexit, rather than providing a comprehensive analysis of the problem.

Another concerning assumption, employed by the 'consensus' studies, concerns the expectation that the effects of de-integration are symmetric but opposite to those related to greater economic integration (HM Treasury 2016: 129–30, 166; BoE 2018). In effect, leaving the EU is assumed to generate equal but opposite economic effects to joining it. However, there is little justification for this approach. When the UK joined the EU, the CET stood at 17%, whereas the trade-related average MFN EU tariff is 3% or lower. As a result, it is most unlikely that similar magnitudes of trade creation and diversion will be experienced following Brexit. It is more likely that supply chains will remain more or less intact, at least for the short run, whilst changes in exchange rates may mitigate any increase in trade costs. If trade reductions occur, they are more likely to be gradual.

As noted earlier in the chapter, most 'consensus' studies either estimated changes in UK–EU trade themselves, using gravity modelling, or they used estimates produced by previous studies. These trade estimates were then combined with estimates of the elasticity of income for trade to arrive at their predictions for the trade-related impact upon UK GDP. These elasticities are typically drawn from the existing academic literature. For example, the Bank of England uses Feyrer (2009a, 2009b), whilst the IMF (Arregui and Chen 2018: 11–13) uses estimates derived from Felbermayr et al. (2018). Yet, also noted earlier in this chapter, elasticities vary over time, either due to structural changes, such as those observed following the 2008 global financial crisis, or due to business cycle effects.

Consequently, the use of earlier literature is likely to over-estimate income elasticities, as much of their data will relate to the pre-2008 period, which will cause their calculations to over-estimate Brexit-related trade costs, whilst none of the Brexit studies allow for the possibility that elasticities may vary according to the business cycle and instead apply a constant value to their analysis.

A second issue, relating to this analysis, concerns the estimates made by the studies of any anticipated increase in trade barriers which may arise due to Brexit. The problem is that whilst the level of MFN tariffs levied by the EU against non-member states is known, it is very difficult to forecast the magnitude of any changes in NTBs. As a result, as noted earlier in this chapter, some of the studies resorted to assuming that future NTBs facing the UK are likely to be a proportion of those experienced by US exporters. These assumptions varied enormously, from 25% to 50% with favourable variants of free trade agreement (FTA) agreed between the UK and the EU, to a range between 66% to 100% if trading according to WTO rules (Ottaviano et al. 2014b: 6–7; Dhingra et al. 2017; Arregui and Chen 2018: 13–14). These assumptions are obviously arbitrary, but the choice makes a substantial difference to the predictions made by the gravity model once these assumptions are inputted. For example, the cost of NTBs used in the CEP-LSE analysis, which is drawn from the previous academic literature and not measured by the research team themselves, accounted for *ten times* the estimated tariff effect in their analysis (Ottaviano et al. 2014b: 6; Dhingra et al. 2017; Menon et al. 2018).

This part of the analysis, undertaken by 'consensus' studies, is questionable on two further grounds. The first is that estimates drawn from the existing literature are typically the result of research teams focused upon measuring the boost to trade that countries received as a result of forming PTAs with other nations. Their results are the average effect for a *basket of countries*, rather than specifically predicting any impact upon the UK, and therefore, it is unlikely that Brexit will cause an equivalent but opposite effect in terms of UK-EU trade. Since the UK sells a smaller proportion of its total exports to other EU member states, it is therefore probable that any such reduction in trade, following the UK's independence, will be smaller than would have been the case for the average drawn from the basket of countries, and hence the trade-related Brexit would be much lower than the models forecast (Blake 2016: 32; Gudgin et al. 2017b: 6–7, 10–11). Moreover, given that the UK emerges from Brexit with (at least temporarily) an identical set of regulations and standards as the remainder of the EU, it would appear inconceivable that initial trade barriers will be comparable to other nations whose regulatory systems and standards have always been quite distinct.

One further, rather troubling assumption made relating to NTBs, concerns the ability of the EU to reduce future trade barriers faster than the rest of the world. The CEP-LSE study, for example, suggested that this reduction in NTBs would occur 40% faster within the EU than for the UK if trading according to WTO rules, and 20% faster even if the UK joined the EEA or negotiated an FTA with the EU (Ottaviano et al., 2014b: 7; Dhingra et al. 2017; Menon et al. 2018). This assumption generated the largest single element of predicted Brexit cost in the CEP-LSE analysis. Similarly, whilst HM Treasury does not include forecasts for future reforms across the SIM within its analysis, it does suggest that, should these occur, costs arising from Brexit may rise by an additional 4% of UK GDP (HM Treasury 2016:8). The problem with these assumptions is that past performance does not necessarily infer future performance. Indeed, since the EU had a disproportionate success in reducing NTBs in the past, this is likely to make it more difficult to reduce barriers further in the future, as the easiest gains to achieve will already have been made and only more difficult NTBs remaining. If those 'low hanging fruit' of NTB reductions have already been picked, an alternative hypothesis might be entertained, namely that the EU is only able to reduce future barriers at the same speed, or slower, than the world at large. Indeed, the same paper that the CEP-LSE cites as the basis of their future NTB assumption, notes that price differentials between EU and OECD nations were being gradually *reduced* over time, implying that the EU's initial advantage in reducing trade barriers had actually ceased and was being gradually eroded (Méjean and Schwellnus 2009: 9–10).

A related assumption was employed, by a number of the 'consensus' studies, that no PTA could be negotiated during the Article 50 and transition period, thus leading to the UK having to trade according to WTO rules irrespective of whether it subsequently proved to be possible to negotiate an FTA or membership of a customs union or indeed the EEA (Kierzenkowski et al. 2016: 19, 21, 32; BoE 2018: 14–15, 43, 48). This assumption is slightly odd because the OECD themselves, in the same report, noted that a previous FTA between the EU and Australia was completed in three years, whilst similar agreements were completed with South Korea and Mexico in four years. Moreover, given the UK's starting point as fully aligned with the EU and that any regulatory divergence will only occur gradually post-independence, it is unlikely that it will take this long to negotiate an FTA between the two parties. The UK Johnson administration has expressed their determination to complete an FTA with the EU by the end of the transition period (11 months), which EU negotiators have described as challenging but not impossible, albeit that this may be more difficult to achieve given the emergence of the COVID-19 virus.

One particularly troublesome assumption, employed in most 'consensus' studies, relates to the claimed link whereby a fall in trade, between the UK and the EU, would result in a reduction in the UK's openness and hence produce resulting reductions in competition, slower adoption of new technology and declining rates of growth in productivity (Dhingra et al. 2015a: 4, Dhingra et al. 2015b: 16–17; Armstrong and Portes, 2016: 4; HM Treasury 2016: 13–15,131,176–7,185; IMF 2016: 9; Kierzenkowski et al. 2016: 31; BoE 2018: 25–6). The theoretical justification is drawn from previous literature (e.g. Fournier et al., 2015; Égert and Gal, 2016) and is examined in more detail in Chap. 7. Nevertheless, for the purposes of the discussion in this chapter, the fragility of the theoretical causation chain is quite straightforward. For example, there is nothing implicit in Brexit that inevitably reduces UK *global* trade. Very few 'consensus' studies even try to estimate the potential for future UK FTAs with non-EU nations. Yet, even if total UK trade does decline, the presumption that openness has a *direct* causal impact upon technology and productivity is contested. Indeed, in NIESR and IMF studies, no attempt was made to incorporate any imputed productivity effects arising from a fall in openness, because of a concern over the robustness of this supposed relationship and a desire to focus upon better understood and more significant economic relationships (Ebell and Warren 2016: 122; IMF 2016: 58). The main reason for this decision is that it is likely that openness may be acting as a proxy for other variables so that any observable effect actually derives from variables such as business confidence and expectations, rates of investment, capital accumulation and changes in productive capacity. Each of these, in turn, is influenced by the level of aggregate demand, which can be affected by changes in international trade but additionally by government policy. Similarly, whilst the size of the marketplace is one determinant of certain types of foreign direct investment (FDI), other significant factors include the rate of growth of the economy, the levels of human capital in the workforce, prevailing regulation and aspects related to government policy.

Inward migrant labour flows are included in a number of the 'consensus' study models because neo-classical growth theory would predict that a reduction in the quantity of labour inputs results in a fall in GDP (HM Treasury 2016: 66; Kierzenkowski et al. 2016: 6). Whether this is indeed the case or not, the pertinent point here is that the models were built upon this expectation and therefore would make their forecasts on this basis. Consequently, the level of assumed reduction in EU migrant labour would have a significant impact upon model results. Hence, it is troublesome that the variation between studies varied so widely. For example, whilst some assumed numbers to be reduced by 50,000 per annum (Hantzsche et al. 2018: F35: 15–17; Hantzsche and Young 2019: F35), others chose 150,000 (BoE 2018), whilst yet other studies differentiated migration reductions depending upon whether the UK negotiated an FTA with the EU or traded according to WTO rules (Arregui and Chen 2018: 16). There is no obvious rationale for these choices. For those earlier studies, the difficulty in predicting future government immigration policy post-Brexit is acknowledged, but this is not a similar excuse for later studies, when the direction of policy had been determined, if not final clarification on all details.

Even where heterogeneity of labour was acknowledged (Nickell and Salaheen 2015; Portes 2016: 17), there was an expectation that this would negatively impact on productivity (Menon et al. 2018: 9–12). There is, however, no *a priori* reason why this is the case. UK post-Brexit immigration policy proposes restricting the numbers of unskilled migrant workers but to simultaneously *increase* the inflow of skilled workers. Consequently, even if there is a fall in the total numbers of inward migrants, the expectation that there will be an increase in the proportion of more highly skilled labour. Since the latter would be expected to raise UK productivity, *ceteris paribus*, the ultimate impact on growth would depend on whether the labour supply (quantity) or productivity (quality) effect predominates.

One penultimate assumption, adopted by the 'consensus' studies, relates to the extent of uncertainty caused by (i) Brexit itself and (ii) the Brexit process. Any substantive change in public policy results in a degree of uncertainty until the implications become better understood by the economic actors affected by the decision. Thus, Brexit was always likely to cause a degree of uncertainty, more so for more independent forms of Brexit, such as reverting to trading according to WTO rules. However, the political process of the past few years will have added to this level of uncertainty as government oscillation, a failure to stick to negotiating objectives and the lack of a parliamentary majority, all combined to confuse even political insiders as to the ultimate resolution.

Uncertainty affects expectations and can therefore have a significant impact upon the economy. It is not, therefore, surprising that this variable was included in some of the 'consensus' studies (HM Treasury 2016: 132, 153; IMF 2016: 55–6; Kierzenkowski et al. 2016: 6, 12–13, 20; BOE 2018: 35). However, the difficulty in modelling uncertainty is that it is difficult to define. Some theorists seek to solve this issue by modelling uncertainty as if it is equivalent to risk, and therefore, any increase in risk premia, interest rates or bond spread can be used as proxies. This is, however, unsatisfactory because risk is based upon known probability distributions, whilst uncertainty is not. This issue is discussed in more detail in Chap. 8.

The final assumption, contained in all the 'consensus' studies, is that government would remain passive and not respond to reinforce advantages or mitigate negative consequences arising from Brexit (Ebell and Warren 2016; HM Treasury 2016; IMF 2016: 30). Whilst this undoubtedly simplifies the modelling, it also assumes away one of the greatest potential advantages likely to arise from the UK's independence from the EU (Baker et al. 2016: 117; Blake 2016: 5). It is, moreover, not credible as it would mean the Treasury negating its own core function of managing the UK economy (Blake 2016: 2).

Drivers of Brexit Impact

Whilst it is enlightening to note how significant the assumptions included in the 'consensus' studies have been in generating a set of results critical towards Brexit, the means by which the models predict this impact will be felt by the UK economy is also instructive. For those models that distinguish between different time periods, the primary short-term effects focused upon a combination of economic uncertainty and shocks to the financial system, reducing confidence and *deferring* investment (Kierzenkowski et al. 2016: 7; PwC 2016: 21,30), causing a tightening of financial conditions due to increased interest rate spreads in the financial markets (IMF 2016: 56–7). The deferral of investment, rather than its cancellation, is a crucial prediction, as it implies an initial slowing of the economy followed by a faster than average 'catching up' period which is, indeed, what the IMF (2016: 31) analysis depicts.

In the medium to long term, the more significant factors were predicted to be a reduction of trade with the EU together with a fall in FDI (IMF 2016: 58; Kierzenkowski et al. 2016: 7, 24–5, 31). Here, the CEP-LSE studies are rather interesting because the main economic impact is not anticipated to flow from direct (tariff) effects, since these only reduce UK GDP by a predicted 0.14% even in the 'pessimistic' WTO scenario, but rather a combination of current and future NTB effects. In the static 'optimistic' model, the net economic effect from Brexit would be a small economic *gain*, and the 'pessimistic model' a small loss, without the assumption (previously discussed) that the EU would reduce trade barriers more effectively than the rest of the world. Moreover, it is only when dynamic effects are introduced into the analysis—based entirely upon results drawn from previous academic studies—that sizeable Brexit-related costs are forecast (Ottaviano et al. 2014a: 4; Ottaviano et al. 2014b; Menon et al. 2018: 8).

Many of the models include a migration variable, which predicts that a reduction in migration from EEA nations would significantly reduce UK GDP (Kierzenkowski et al. 2016: 25–9; Menon et al. 2018: 9–12), which would in turn have a possible detrimental productivity effect (Menon et al. 2018: 9–12). IMF researchers suggest that a 1% increase in migrant share in the UK adult population increases productivity by between 0.4% and 0.5%, and consequently, reversing this effect would result in lower inward migration result from Brexit reducing UK GDP by between 0.6% and 1% by 2030. (Arregui and Chen 2018: 16). Unfortunately, there would appear to be a discrepancy in this calculation since the two studies in question suggest effects of 0.2% (Jaumotte et al. 2016: 17) and between 0.1% and 0.6%, respectively, for most OECD nations, albeit that a minority of countries recorded no significant measurable effect (Boubtane et al. 2015: 16). Using the two assumed reductions in migration numbers used in the IMF analysis, namely 120,000 (FTA scenario) and 150,000 (WTO scenario), respectively, this equates to 0.23% (FTA option) and 0.29% (WTO option) of the UK adult population.[10] Combining the estimates from the two IMF studies with these population assumptions produces the forecast that UK GDP would be reduced by between 0.46% and 0.58% in 20 (not 10) years. That, of course, assumes that any reduction in migration from

---

[10] https://www.ons.gov.uk/aboutus/transparencyandgovernance/freedomofinformationfoi/projectedukadultpopulationfor2018.

EEA nations led to an overall fall in net inward migration into the UK, and was not offset by any increase in migration from other countries.

One variable typically excluded from 'consensus' models concerns changes to UK regulations which could occur once the transition period ends, depending upon the eventual economic relationship agreed between the UK and the EU. Moreover, of those studies which do include regulation as a variable, both assume that it will have little positive impact for the UK economy due to the nation's already low levels of regulation (Crafts 2016: 263; HMG 2018a: 6, 39–49; Kierzenkowski et al. 2016: 7, 29–31). There is an irony in this conclusion, of course, since the CEP-LSE case for assuming that the EU would secure faster reductions in NTBs, when compared to the global average, on the basis that the EU had a track record of success in this area. Yet, HMG and the OECD use this same argument to argue that the successful track record of the UK in reducing regulatory impact will preclude significant further gains. Moreover, it also ignores research which suggests that national (UK) regulation can be a better fit for an individual economy, when compared to pan-national rules which have to be drafted to apply to distinctly different circumstances, as such national regulation may have a better benefit-to-cost ratio than EU regulation (Gaskell and Persson 2010: 10; HMG 2013: 41–2).

One final difference between how the 'consensus' studies predict Brexit transmission will occur, relates to whether or not the studies include the exchange rate within their macroeconomic modelling. Given the predicted impact upon economic uncertainty, FDI and trade, there would be an expectation that the value of sterling would fall, and this would help to at least partially offset some of these effects, by making UK exports more attractive and encouraging a degree of import substitution (Ebell and Warren 2016: 133; IMF 2016: 31; Kierzenkowski et al. 2016: 21). Perhaps due to the neo-classical micro-foundations imbuing the macroeconomic models used by the 'consensus' studies, there is an assumption that inflation rises to quite rapidly choke off much of this improvement in competitiveness (IMF 2015: 105; BoE 2018: 36–8). More astonishingly, the Bank of England assumes that interest rates would rise in order for it to meet its inflation target, with rates even rising to 5.5% in the worst-case scenario (BoE 2018: 36–8, 47–53). Given that UK interest rates have remained at or below 0.75% for the last decade and that the Bank's own forecasts for Brexit imply a significant slowdown in the economy, the act of raising interest rates to this point would be astonishing if contemplated, and an act of economic vandalism if implemented. Nevertheless, however unlikely, the inclusion of this assumption in the Bank of England's model leads to a much more adverse forecast for the economic outcome of a WTO Brexit than would otherwise be the case.

A more realistic assumption for exchange rates might be gleaned from a recent report, produced by the IMF (2015: 107,118), which suggests that a 10% devaluation might be expected to lead, *on average*, to an increase of around 1.5% of a nation's GDP over the medium term. Once again, caution has to be applied. This is a study of multiple economies and this is a finding across the whole of this sample. The effect for the UK might be greater or smaller than this average.

Dissenting Studies

The fact that the 'consensus' studies have been most influential in the Brexit debate does not detract from the fact that there are a number of studies which forecast either a net positive impact arising from withdrawal from the EU, or alternatively predict a much milder Brexit cost of the magnitude which could be easily offset through the operation of active government policy. One study, for example, predicts a net gain of 0.64% UK GDP if an FTA was negotiated with the EU, and a net cost of 2.2% if trading according to WTO rules, with an additional benefit equivalent to 1.55% of UK GDP if an ambitious programme of deregulation was enacted following independence (Booth et al. 2015: 5). Another study forecast a 1.7% UK GDP gain due to regulatory and fiscal savings, combined with supply side effects driven by a reduction in consumer prices following a drop in tariffs levied against the rest of the world (Economists for Brexit 2016b: 31). A third study predicted a net gain approximating 1.35% of UK GDP (Business for Britain 2015: 55,827).[11] It is worth noting that there has been criticism aimed at the methodology adopted by the economists for Brexit analysis in particular, and, indeed, the assumptions made relating to the adoption of zero tariffs with all nations would appear to be at odds with stated government policy, as it would automatically remove the incentive for other nations to negotiate FTAs with the UK.

---

[11] The report predicted that each UK household could gain £933 per year. Since the Office of National Statistics (ONS) calculates that there are 27 million households in the UK, this equates to a net Brexit gain of £25.2bn (1.35% UK GDP). See http://www.ons.gov.uk/peoplepopulationandcommunity/birthsdeathsandmarriages/families/bulletins/familiesandhouseholds/2015-11-05.

The CBR, of the University of Cambridge, rejected the use of gravity, CGE and DSGE models, in favour of its own macroeconomic model of the UK economy (UKMOD), developed from post-Keynesian theoretical principles. Its modelling assumptions included business investment declining by 15% in the short term, due to uncertainty, but recovering almost all of this fall by the end of the five-year focus for the report, whilst exports would decline by 10% but with four-fifths of this gap replaced by non-EU markets over a two-decade period. Imports were anticipated to fall by around 4%, before recovering due to income elasticities and UK economic growth, whilst FDI would similarly decline by one-third, before recovering two-thirds of this loss within two years. Exchange rate depreciation of 12% would increase export competitiveness and improve the trade balance, whilst net migration would decline to 190,000 per annum. Finally, fiscal spending was assumed to increase by 6% per annum to 2021, as discretionary government measures eased the Brexit transition (Gudgin et al. 2017a: 36–7). Taken as a whole, these assumptions would appear to be more realistic than many of the 'consensus' studies. Nevertheless, regulation was omitted from the list of variables, which was a slight oversight.

The Cambridge modelling results suggest that depreciation in the value of sterling is likely to almost completely offset the negative effect arising from uncertainty, resulting in a postponement (not a cancellation) of investment, and thereby facilitating a rapid recovery in UK growth from an initial slowing. In the medium term, reduction in trade causes a further slowing of the economy thereafter, but this is partially offset by the fiscal policy response undertaken by government. Hence, the net result is predicted to result in UK GDP being only 1.5% below trend by 2026, and with GDP per capita remaining unchanged (Gudgin et al. 2017a: 38–9).

The Need for More Comprehensive Analysis

This chapter has demonstrated the inadequacy of the claim that there was ever a consensus amongst economists on the predicted impact of Brexit. Whilst there are certainly areas of agreement between all economists in the various studies, for example, that barriers to trade tend to reduce trade, and that a reduction in the regulatory burden placed on (particularly small) business may provide a boost to the economy, yet there is considerable divergence in the magnitude of the predicted effects.

The fact that most of the 'consensus' studies have used rather similar models and methodologies, and consequently reached broadly similar conclusions, does in and of itself not meet the test of utilising completely independent evidence to reinforce the conclusions reached by each study (Blake 2016: 40). At their most basic, VAR, CGE and NiGEM simulation models operate by comparing predicted outcomes against a baseline projection of current trends and, as such, they must make a number of assumptions upon which the analysis is based. Yet, it is important that this simplification does not deviate too far from reality or else the predictive power of the forecasts will be significantly weakened and bias introduced into the results. Developing models on the basis of micro-foundations is an advantage only if these theoretical insights concur with observed reality and do not reflect an idealised textbook alternative reality. Moreover, the fact that Brexit is a unique event (or shock) makes its analysis more difficult.

Lord David Owen, the former Foreign Secretary, explained his concern in this way:

> You rig the [economic] model by what you put into it. If the Chancellor tells the Treasury to put in the following parameters, you get one kind of result. They have admitted they have not seen it necessary to present a model of what would be the benefits of going out of the EU. So we hear a lot about the risks of leaving, but nothing about the risks of remaining, which I believe are infinitely greater.[12]

In essence, Lord Owen is reiterating the critical effect of assumptions skewing the results of the model, but also suggesting that the comparison with the baseline projection is flawed because it is based upon the assumption that were the UK to remain a full member of the EU, its current situation would remain essentially unchanged in the future. This is unlikely for a number of reasons, whether the desire on behalf of many within the EU to pursue ever-closer integration, or because the Eurozone will require additional measures taken for its long-term sustainability which will inevitably change the nature of EU membership even for those countries which do not currently wish to participate in the single currency. As Business for Britain (2015: 712) so amusingly explain the difficulty with this status quo assumption, "one might as well produce a weather forecast for Manchester on the assumption that it is never going to rain".

---

[12] Lord Owen: 'There is no need to be afraid of leaving the EU', *The Daily Telegraph*, 28 May 2016. Available via: http://www.telegraph.co.uk/news/2016/05/28/lord-owen-there-is-no-need-to-be-afraid-of-leaving-the-eu/.

A second area where most of the 'consensus' models are flawed is in what they do, and do not, contain in their models. Portes (2013: F5) suggests that this should include examination of the impact upon trade, fiscal savings (from not having to contribute to the EU budget), investment, regulation, migration and the impact upon the financial sector. To this list should be added the effect upon the balance of payments, and through this whether growth is constrained, together with the impact of changes in the exchange rate and the effect of government policy. Other studies have sought to introduce what they term a dynamic analysis, where the association between openness, competition and productivity is hypothesised as generating a causal link whereby the former influences the development of the latter. This is not universally accepted, however (see the discussion in Chap. 7), and, indeed, openness may in fact be little more than a proxy for other factors, such as investment, capital accumulation and economies of scale—all factors which are influenced by changes in aggregate demand. Consequently, the inclusion of results linked to openness should be treated with a degree of caution.

A final flaw with the 'consensus' results is not necessarily in the construction of the models themselves, but rather in their interpretation. There have been numerous examples, during the 2016 referendum campaign and afterwards, where the predictions made by this self-selected group of economic studies are treated as though they were objective "facts" rather than economic simulations based upon a range of sometimes questionable assumptions (Blake 2016: 44–51). Rather than claim that this demonstrates how Brexit *will* impact negatively upon the UK economy, a more measured interpretation would be to explain that these models make *predictions* about what *might* happen following Brexit, based upon certain simplifying assumptions and assuming that other factors do not change (*ceteris paribus*). This approach would not inspire as many newspaper headlines, but it would at least have the virtue of responsibility.

REFERENCES

Aichele, R., & Felbermayr, G. (2015). *Costs and Benefits of a United Kingdom Exit from the European Union*. IFO Institut, Munich. Available via: https://ged-project.de/wp-content/uploads/2015/04/Costs-and-benefits-of-a-United-Kingdom-exit-from-the-European-Union.pdf.

Allen, C., Gasiorek, M., & Smith, A. (1998). The Competition Effects of the Single Market in Europe. *Economic Policy, 27*, 439–486.

Armstrong, A., & Portes, J. (2016). Commentary: The Economic Consequences of Leaving the EU. *National Institute Economic Review*, *236*, 2–6.
Andrle, M., Brůha, J., & Solmaz, S. (2017). On the Sources of Business Cycles: Implications for DSGE Models, *European Central Bank Working Paper* 2058, ECB, Frankfurt. Retrieved March 19, 2020, from https://www.ecb.europa.eu/pub/pdf/scpwps/ecb.wp2058.en.pdf?911a7a9596dac1b5db11a26e1bc8bfa6.
Arregui, N., & Chen, J. (2018). *United Kingdom—IMF Country Report* No 18/317, International Monetary Fund, Paris. Retrieved March 18, 2020, from https://www.imf.org/en/Publications/CR/Issues/2018/11/14/United-Kingdom-Selected-Issues-46354.
Badinger, H., & Breuss, F. (2011). The Quantitative Effects of European Post-War Economic Integration. In M. Jovanovic (Ed.), *International Handbook on the Economics of Integration* (pp. 285–315). Cheltenham: Edward Elgar.
Baier, S. L., Bergstrand, J. H., Egger, P., & McLaughlin, P. A. (2008). Do Economic Integration Agreements Actually Work? Issues in Understanding the Causes and Consequences of the Growth of Regionalism. *World Economy*, *31*(4), 461–497.
Baker, J., Carreras, O., Ebell, M., Hurst, I., Kirby, S., Meaning, J., Piggott, R., & Warren, J. (2016). The Short-Term Economic Impact of Leaving the EU. *National Institute Economic Review*, *236*, 108–120.
Bank of England. (2018). *EU Withdrawal Scenarios and Monetary and Financial Stability: A Response to the House of Commons Select Committee*, Bank of England, London. Retrieved March 18, 2020, from https://www.bankofengland.co.uk/-/media/boe/files/report/2018/eu-withdrawal-scenarios-and-monetary-and-financial-stability.pdf?la=en&hash=B5F6EDCDF90DCC10286FC0BC599D94CAB8735DFB.
Bayoumi, T., & Eichengreen, B. (1997). Is Regionalism Simply a Diversion? Evidence from the Evolution of the EC and EFTA. In T. Ito & A. O. Krueger (Eds.), *Regionalism vs. Multilateral Arrangements*. Chicago: University of Chicago Press.
Blake, D. (2016). *Measurement Without Theory: On the Extraordinary Abuse of Economic Models in the EU Referendum Debate*, Cass Business School, London. Available via.
Boltho, A., & Eichengreen, B. (2008). The Economic Impact of European Integration, *CEPR Discussion Paper* No. 6820. Available via: http://eml.berkeley.edu/~eichengr/econ_impact_euro_integ.pdf.
Booth, S., Howarth, C., Persson, M., Ruparel, R., & Swidlicki, P. (2015). *What if...?: The Consequences, Challenges and Opportunities Facing Britain Outside EU*, Open Europe Report 03/2015, London. Available via: http://openeurope.org.uk/intelligence/britain-and-the-eu/what-if-there-were-a-brexit/.
Borin, A., Di Nino, V., Mancini, M., & Sbracia, M. (2017). The Cyclicality of the Income Elasticity of Trade, Banca D'Italia Working Paper No 1126, Bank of

Italy, Rome. Available via: https://www.bancaditalia.it/pubblicazioni/temi-discussione/2017/2017-1126/en_tema_1126.pdf.

Boubtane, E., Dumont, J-C., & Rault, C. (2015). Immigration and Economic Growth in the OECD Countries 1986–2006, *CESifo Working Paper* No. 5392. Retrieved March 24, 2020, from https://www.cesifo.org/DocDL/cesifo1_wp5392.pdf.

Bouttell, J., Craig, P., Lewsey, J., Robinson, M., & Popham, F. (2018). Synthetic Control Methodology as a Tool for Evaluating Population-Level Health Interventions. *Journal of Epidemiol Community Health, 72*(8), 673–678.

Böwer, U., & Turrini, A. (2010). EU Accession: A Road to Fast-track Convergence? *Comparative Economic Studies, 52*(2), 181–205.

Business for Britain. (2015). *Change or Go: How Britain Would Gain Influence and Prosper Outside an Unreformed EU*, Business for Britain, London. Available via: https://forbritain.org/cogwholebook.pdf.

Campos, N. F., Coricelli, F., & Moretti, L. (2014). Economic Growth from Political Integration: Estimating the benefits from membership in the European Union using the synthetic counterfactuals method, *IZA Discussion Paper Series 8162*, Bonn. Available via: http://anon-ftp.iza.org/dp8162.pdf.

Capital Economics. (2016). *The Economics Impact of 'Brexit': A Paper Discussing the United Kingdom' Relationship with Europe and the Impact of 'Brexit' on the British Economy*, Woodford Investment Management LLP, Oxford. Available via: https://woodfordfunds.com/economic-impact-brexit-report/.

Cecchini, P., Catinat, M., & Jacquemin, A. (1988). *The European Challenge 1992: The Benefits of a Single Market, prepared for the Commission of the European Communities*. Aldershot: Gower.

Confederation of British Industry (CBI). (2013). *Our global future: The business vision for a reformed EU*. CBI, London. Available via: http://www.cbi.org.uk/media/2451423/our_global_future.pdf#page=1&zoom=auto,-119,842.

Congdon, T. (2014). *How Much Does the European Union Cost Britain?* UKIP, London. Available via: http://www.timcongdon4ukip.com/docs/EU2014.pdf.

Crafts, N. (2016). The Impact of EU Membership on UK Economic Performance. *Political Quarterly, 87*(2), 262–268.

Deardorff, A. V. (1995). Determinants of Bilateral Trade: Does Gravity Work in a Neo-classical World? *NBER Working Paper* 5377. Retrieved March 17, 2020, from https://www.nber.org/papers/w5377.pdf.

Deutsche Bank. (2013). *The Single European Market—20 Years On*, Deutsche Bank, Frankfurt. Available via: https://www.dbresearch.com/PROD/DBR_INTERNET_EN-PROD/PROD0000000000322897/The+Single+European+Market+20+years+on%3A+Achievements,+unfulfilled+expectations+%26+further+potential.pdf.

Dhingra, S., Huang, H., Ottaviano, G., Pessoa, J. P., Sampson, T., & Van Reenen, J. (2016). The Costs and Benefits of Leaving the EU: Trade Effects, *CEP Discussion Paper* No. 1478, London School of Economics Centre for Economic

Performance, London. Available via. Retrieved March 20, 2020, from http://cep.lse.ac.uk/pubs/download/dp1478.pdf.

Dhingra, S., Huang, H., Ottaviano, G., Pessoa, J. P., Sampson, T., & Van Reenen, J. (2017). The Costs and Benefits of Leaving the EU: Trade effects, *Centre for Economic Performance Discussion Paper* No. 1478. Retrieved March 18, 2020, from http://cep.lse.ac.uk/pubs/download/dp1478.pdf.

Dhingra, S., Ottaviano, G. I. P., & Sampson, T. (2015a). *Should We Stay or Should We Go? The Economic Consequences of Leaving the EU*, Centre for Economic Performance, LSE. Available via: https://ideas.repec.org/e/pot15.html.

Dhingra, S., Ottaviano, G. I. P., & Sampson, T. (2015b). *Britain's Future in Europe*, LSE, London. Available via: http://www.sdhingra.com/brexit-writeup.pdf.

Dullien, S. (2017). *How Much Progress Has the Mainstream Made? Evaluating Modern DSGE Models from a Post-Keynesian Perspective*. Retrieved March 19, 2020, from http://www.postkeynesian.net/downloads/events/Dullien_2017.pdf.

Ebell, M., & Warren, J. (2016). The Long-Term Economic Impact of Leaving the EU. *National Institute Economic Review, 236*, 121–138.

ECB. (2016). Understanding the Weakness in Global Trade: What is the New Normal?, ECB Occasional Paper Series No 178, European Central Bank, Frankfurt. Available via: https://www.ecb.europa.eu/pub/pdf/scpops/ecbop178.en.pdf. Accessed 29 October 2020.

Economists for Brexit. (2016a). *A Vote for Brexit: What Are the Policies to Follow and What Are the Economic Prospects?* Economists for Brexit, London. Available via: http://www.economistsforbrexit.co.uk/a-vote-for-brexit.

Economists for Brexit. (2016b). *The Economy After Brexit*, Economists for Brexit, London. Available via: https://static1.squarespace.com/static/570a10a460b5e93378a26ac5/t/5722f8f6a3360ce7508c2acd/1461909779956/Economists+for+Brexit+-+The+Economy+after+Brexit.pdf.

Égert, B. and Gal, P. (2016), *The Quantification of Structural Reforms in OECD Countries: A New Framework*. OECD Working Paper No 1354, OECD, Paris. Available via: https://www.oecd.org/competition/reform/The-quantification-of-structural-reforms-in-OECD-countries-a-new-framework.pdf.

Egger, P., Francois, J., Manchin, M., & Nelson, D. (2015). Non-Tariff Barriers, Integration and the Transatlantic Economy. *Economic Policy, 30*(83), 539–584.

Emmerson, C., & Pope, T. (2016). Winter Is Coming: The Outlook for the Public Finances in the 2016 Autumn Statement, *IFS Briefing Note BN188*, Institute for Fiscal Studies, London. Available via: https://www.ifs.org.uk/uploads/publications/bns/BN188.pdf.

Emmerson, C., Johnson, P., & Mitchell, I. (2016). The EU Single Market: The value of membership versus access to the UK, Institute for Fiscal Studies, London. Available via: http://www.ifs.org.uk/uploads/publications/comms/R119%20-%20The%20EU%20Single%20market%20-%20Final.pdf.

Erken, H., Hayat, R., Meijmerikx, M., Prins, C., & de Vreede, I. (2017). *The Permanent Damage of Brexit*, Rabobank, Utrecht. Retrieved March 18, 2020, from https://economics.rabobank.com/publications/2017/october/the-permanent-damage-of-brexit/.

Erken, H., Hayat, R., Meijmerikx, M., Prins, C., & de Vreede, I. (2018). *Assessing the Economic Impact of Brexit: Background report*, Rabobank, Utrecht. Retrieved March 18, 2020, from https://economics.rabobank.com/publications/2017/october/assessing-economic-impact-brexit-background-report/.

Felbermayr, G., Fuest, C., Gröschl, J., & Sthlker, D. (2017). Economic Effects of Brexit on the European Economy, EconPol Policy Report 04, IFO, Munich. Retrieved March 18, 2020, from https://www.ifo.de/DocDL/EconPol_Policy_Report_04_2017_Brexit.pdf.

Felbermayr, G., Gröschl, J., & Heuiland, I. (2018a). Undoing Europe in a New Quantitative Trade Model, IFO Working paper 250, University of Munich. Retrieved March 18, 2020, from https://www.ifo.de/DocDL/wp-2018-250-felbermayr-etal-tarde-model.pdf.

Felbermayr, G., Gröschl, J., & Steininger, M. (2018b). *Brexit Through the Lens of New Quantitative Trade Theory*, CESifo. Retrieved March 18, 2020, from https://editorialexpress.com/cgi-bin/conference/download.cgi?db_name=MWITSpring2018&paper_id=63.

Feyrer, J. (2009a). Trade and Income: Exploiting Time Series in Geography, *NBER Working Paper* 14910. Retrieved March 27, 2020, from https://www.nber.org/papers/w14910.pdf.

Feyrer, J. (2009b). Distance, Trade and Income: The 1967 to 1975 Closing of the Suez Canal as a Natural Experiment, *NBER Working Paper* 15557. Retrieved March 27, 2020, from https://www.nber.org/papers/w15557.pdf.

Fletcher, R., & Bohn, J. (1998). The Impact of Psychic Distance on the Internationalisation of the Australian Firm. *Journal of Global Marketing, 12*(2), 47–68.

Fournier, J.-M., Domps, A., Gorin, Y., Guillet, X., & Morchoisne, D. (2015). Implicit Regulatory Barriers in the EU Single Market: New Empirical Evidence from Gravity Models, *OECD Economics Department Working Paper* No. 1181, OECD Publishing. Retrieved March 17, 2020, from http://www.oecd.org/officialdocuments/publicdisplaydocumentpdf/?cote=ECO/WKP(2014)77&docLanguage=En.

Gaskell, S., & Persson, M. (2010). *Still Out of Control? Measuring Eleven Years of EU Regulation*, Second Edition, Open Europe, London. Available via: http://archive.openeurope.org.uk/Content/documents/Pdfs/stilloutofcontrol.pdf.

Gudgin, G., Coutts, K., & Gibson, N. (2017a). The Macro-economic Impact of Brexit: Using the CBR Macroeconomic Model of the UK Economy (UKMOD), *Centre for Business Research Working Paper* No. 483. Available via: http://www.cbr.cam.ac.uk/fileadmin/user_upload/centre-for-business-research/downloads/working-papers/wp483revised.pdf.

Gudgin, G., Coutts, K., Gibson, N., & Buchanan, J. (2017b). *Defying Gravity: A Critique of Estimates of the Economic Impact of Brexit*, Policy Exchange, London. Retrieved March 10, 2020, from https://policyexchange.org.uk/wp-content/uploads/2017/06/Defying-Gravity-A-critique-of-estimates-of-the-economic-impact-of-Brexit.pdf.

Hantzsche, A., Kara, A., & Young, G. (2018). *The Economic Effects of the Government's Proposed Brexit Deal*, NIESR, London. Retrieved February 17, 2020, from https://www.niesr.ac.uk/sites/default/files/publications/NIESR%20Report%20Brexit%20-%202018-11-26.pdf.

Hantzsche, A., & Young, G. (2019). The Economic Impact of Prime Minister Johnson's New Brexit Deal, *National Institute Economic Review*, 250: F34-7. Retrieved March 20, 2020, from https://www.niesr.ac.uk/publications/economic-impact-prime-minister-johnsons-new-brexit-deal.

Harrison, G., Rutherford, T., & Tarr, D. (1994). *Product Standards, Imperfect Competition, and Completion of the Market in the European Union*, World Bank Policy Research Working Paper No. 1293. Available via: https://www.gtap.agecon.purdue.edu/resources/download/3524.pdf HM Treasury, 2005.

HM Treasury. (2016). *HM Treasury Analysis: The Long Term Economic Impact of EU Membership and the Alternatives*, Cm 9250, The Stationery Office, London. Available via: https://www.gov.uk/government/uploads/system/uploads/attachment_data/file/517415/treasury_analysis_economic_impact_of_eu_membership_web.pdf.

HMG. (2018a). *EU Exit: Long-Term Economic Analysis*, Cm 9742, HMSO, London. Available via: https://assets.publishing.service.gov.uk/government/uploads/system/uploads/attachment_data/file/760484/28_November_EU_Exit_-_Long-term_economic_analysis__1_.pdf.

HMG. (2018b). *EU Exit: Long-Term Economic Analysis—Technical Reference Paper*, HMSO, London. Retrieved February 28, 2020, from https://assets.publishing.service.gov.uk/government/uploads/system/uploads/attachment_data/file/759763/28_November_EU_Exit_Long-Term_Economic_Analysis_Technical_Reference_Paper.PDF.

HMG [HM Government]. (2013). *Review of the Balance of Competences Between the United Kingdom and the European Union—The Single Market*, The Stationery Office, London. Available via: https://www.gov.uk/government/uploads/system/uploads/attachment_data/file/227069/2901084_SingleMarket_acc.pdf.

Hofstede, G. (1980). Cultural Consequences: International Differences in Work Related Values. *World Development, 1*(9), 11–17.

Hofstede, G. (1994). The Business of International Business Is Culture. *International Business Review, 3*(1), 1–13.

IMF. (2015). *Adjusting to Lower Commodity Prices*, IMF World Economic Outlook, Washington DC. Retrieved February 18, 2020, from https://www.imf.org/en/Publications/WEO/Issues/2016/12/31/World-Economic-Outlook-October-2015-Adjusting-to-Lower-Commodity-Prices-43229.

IMF. (2016). *United Kingdom: IMF Country Report*, No. 16/169, IMF, Washington DC. Available via: https://www.imf.org/external/pubs/ft/scr/2016/cr16169.pdf.

Ipsos-MORI. (2016). *Economists Views on Brexit*. Available via: https://www.ipsos-mori.com/Assets/Docs/Polls/economists-views-on-brexit-2016-charts.pdf and https://www.ipsos-mori.com/Assets/Docs/Polls/economists-views-on-brexit-2016-tables.pdf.

Jafari, Y., & Britz, W. (2017). 'Brexit—An Economy Wide Impact Assessment Looking into Trade, Immigration and Foreign Direct Investment', University of Bonn. Retrieved March 17, 2020, from https://www.gtap.agecon.purdue.edu/resources/download/8405.pdf.

Jaumotte, F., Koloskova, K., & Saxena, S. C. (2016). *Impact of Migration on Income Levels in Advanced Economies*, International Monetary Fund, Washington DC. Retrieved March 24, 2020, from https://www.imf.org/en/Publications/Spillover-Notes/Issues/2016/12/31/Impact-of-Migration-on-Income-Levels-in-Advanced-Economies-44343.

Kierzenkowski, R., Pain, N., Rusticelli, E., & Zwart, S. (2016). *The Economic Consequences of Brexit: A Taxing Decision*, OECD Economic Policy Paper No. 16, OECD, Paris. Retrieved March 18, 2010, from https://www.oecd.org/economy/The-Economic-consequences-of-Brexit-27-april-2016.pdf.

King, J. E. (2012). *The Microfoundations Delusion: Metaphor and Dogma in the History of Macroeconomics*. Cheltenham: Edward Elgar.

Kogut, B., & Singh, H. (1988). The Effect of National Culture on the Choice of Entry Mode. *Journal of International Business Studies, 19*(3), 411–432.

Kyland, F., & Prescott, E. (1977). Rules Rather than Discretion: The Inconsistency of Optimal Plans. *Journal of Political Economy, 85*(3), 473–492.

Leontief, V. (1986). *Input–output Economics* (2nd ed.). Oxford: Oxford University Press.

Lutz, C., Meyer, B., & Wolter, M. I. (2010). The Global Multisector/Multicountry 3E-Model GINFORS: A Description of the Model and a Baseline Forecast for Global Energy Demand and CO2-emissions. *International Journal of Global Environmental Issues, 10*(1-2), 25–45.

Mayer, T., Vicard, V., & Zignago, S. (2018). The Cost of Non-Europe, Revisited, *Banque de France Working Paper* 2018-06. Retrieved March 12, 2020, from http://www.cepii.fr/PDF_PUB/wp/2018/wp2018-06.pdf.

Méjean, I., & Schwellnus, C. (2009). Price Convergence in the European Union: Within Firms or Composition of Firms? *Journal of International Economics, 78*(1), 1–10.

Menon, A., Portes, J., Levell, P., & Sampson, T. (2018). *The Economic Consequences of the Brexit Deal*, UK in a Changing Europe, London. Retrieved February 14, 2020, from http://ukandeu.ac.uk/wp-content/uploads/2018/11/The-economic-consequences-of-Brexit.pdf.

Miller, M., & Spencer, J. (1977). The Static Economic Effects of the UK Joining the EEC: A General Equilibrium Approach. *Review of Economic Studies, 44*(1), 71–93.

Miller, V., Lang, A., Smith, B., Webb, D., Harari, D., Keep, M., & Bowers, P. (2016). Exiting the EU: UK Reform Proposals, Legal Impact and Alternatives to Membership, *House of Commons Library Briefing Paper* No. HC 07214. Available via: http://researchbriefings.parliament.uk/ResearchBriefing/Summary/CBP-7214#fullreport.

Minford, P. (2016). *The Treasury Report on Brexit: A Critique*, Economists for Brexit, London. Available via: http://static1.squarespace.com/static/570a10a460b5e93378a26ac5/t/5731a5a486db439545bf2eda/1462871465520/Economists+for+Brexit+-+The+Treasury+Report+on+Brexit+A+Critique.pdf.

Minford, P., Mahambare, V., & Nowell, E. (2015). *Should Britain Leave the EU? An Economic Analysis of a Troubled Relationship*. Cheltenham: IEA and Edward Elgar.

Monti, M., & Buchan, D. (1996). The Single Market and Tomorrow's Europe – A Progress Report from the European Commission. Office of the Official Publications of the European Communities, Luxembourg and Kogan Page, London. Available via: http://aei.pitt.edu/42345/1/A5494.pdf.

Mulabdic, A., Osnago, A., & Ruta, M. (2017). Deep Integration and UK-EU Trade Relations, *World Bank Policy Research Working Paper* 7947, World Bank, Washington DC. Retrieved March 18, 2020, from http://documents.worldbank.org/curated/en/853811484835908129/Deep-integration-and-UK-EU-trade-relations.

Nickell, S. J., & Salaheen, J. (2015). The Impact of Immigration on Occupational Wages: Evidence from Britain. *Bank of England Staff Working Paper* No. 574. Available via: http://www.bankofengland.co.uk/research/Documents/workingpapers/2015/swp574.pdf.

OBR [Office for Budget Responsibility]. (2016). Economic and Fiscal Outlook—November 2016, Cm 9346, The Stationery Office, London. Available via: http://cdn.budgetresponsibility.org.uk/Nov2016EFO.pdf.

Ottaviano, G., Pessoa, J. P., & Sampson, T. (2014a). The Costs and Benefits of Leaving the EU. CEP mimeo. Available via: http://cep.lse.ac.uk/pubs/download/pa016_tech.pdf.

Ottaviano, G. I. P., Pessoa, J. P., Sampson, T., & Van Reenen, J. (2014b). *Brexit or Fixit? The Trade and Welfare Effects of Leaving the European Union*, Centre for Economic Performance 016, LSE. Available via: https://ideas.repec.org/p/cep/ceppap/016.html.

Pollitt, H. (2016). *Summary of E3ME Modelling*, Cambridge Econometrics. Retrieved March 18, 2020, from https://ec.europa.eu/energy/sites/ener/files/documents/20161219_-_technical_report_on_macroeconomic_results_e3me.pdf.

Pollitt, H., Lewney, R., & Mercure, J-F. (2019). Conceptual Differences between Macro-Economic and CGE Models, Cambridge Econometrics, Cambridge. Retrieved March 10, 2020, from https://www.iioa.org/conferences/27th/papers/files/3597_20190430081_IIOApaperE3MEsession.pdf.

Portes, J. (2013). Commentary: The Economic Implications for the UK of Leaving the European Union. *National Institute Economic Review*, No. 266, F4-9. Available via: http://www.niesr.ac.uk/sites/default/files/commentary.pdf.

Portes, J. (2016). Immigration, Free Movement and the EU Referendum. *National Institute Economic Review, 236*, 14–22.

PwC [PricewaterhouseCoopers LLP]. (2016). *Leaving the EU: Implications for the UK Economy*, PricewaterhouseCoopers LLP, London. Available via: http://news.cbi.org.uk/news/leaving-eu-would-cause-a-serious-shock-to-uk-economy-new-pwc-analysis/leaving-the-eu-implications-for-the-uk-economy/.

Rannenberg, A., Schoder, C., & Strasky, J. (2015). *The Macroeconomic Effects of the Euro Area's Fiscal Consolidation, Central Bank of Ireland Technical Research Paper* 03/RT/2015. Retrieved March 19, 2020, from https://www.central-bank.ie/docs/default-source/publications/research-technical-papers/research-technical-paper-03rt15.pdf.

Ries, C., Hafner, M., Smith, T., Burwell, F., Egel, D., Han, E., Stepanek, M., & Shatz, H. (2017). After Brexit: Alternative Forms of Brexit and Their Implications for the United Kingdom, Europe and the United States, RAND, Santa Monica, Calif., and Cambridge, UK. Retrieved March 18, 2020, from https://www.rand.org/pubs/research_reports/RR2200.html.

Roeger, W., & Sekkat, K. (2002). 'Macroeconomic Effects of the Single Market Program After 10 Years', background paper of the European Commission, Brussels, II- A- 1/W D(2002).

Rojas-Romagosa, H. (2016). *Trade effects of Brexit for the Netherlands*, CPB Netherlands Bureau for Economic Analysis, The Hague. Retrieved March 18, 2020, from https://www.cpb.nl/sites/default/files/omnidownload/CPB-Backgroud-Document-June-2016-Trade-effects-of-brexit-for-the-netherlands.pdf.

Sampson, T. (2017). Brexit: The Economics of International Disintegration. *Journal of Economic Perspectives, 31*(4), 163–184.

Straathof, B., Linders, G. J., Lejour, A., & Mohlmann, J. (2008). *The Internal Market and the Dutch Economy: Implications for Trade and Economic Growth*, Document No 168, CPG Netherlands Bureau for Economic Policy Analysis, The Hague. Retrieved March 17, 2020, from https://www.cpb.nl/sites/default/files/publicaties/download/internal-market-and-dutch-economy-implications-trade-and-economic-growth.pdf.

Thompson, G., & Harari, D. (2013). The Economic Impact of EU Membership on the UK, *House of Commons Library Briefing Paper* SN/EP/6730. Available via: http://researchbriefings.parliament.uk/ResearchBriefing/Summary/SN06730#fullreport.

TUC. (2016). *Better Off In—Working People and the Case for Remaining in the EU*, TUC, London. Available via: https://www.tuc.org.uk/sites/default/files/BetteroffIN.pdf.

Vandenbussche, H., Connell, W., & Simons, W. (2017). *Global Value Chains, Trade Shocks and Jobs: An Application to Brexit*. London: CEPR.

Webb, D., Keep, M., & Wilton, M. (2015). In Brief: UK-EU Economic Relations, *House of Commons Library Briefing Paper (HC 06091)*, The Stationery Office, London. Available via: http://researchbriefings.parliament.uk/ResearchBriefing/Summary/SN06091.

West, G. R. (1995). Comparison of Input–Output, Input–Output + Econometric and Computable General Equilibrium Impact Models at the Regional Level. *Economic Systems Research, 7*(2), 209–227.

World Data Bank. (2020). Tariff Rate Series. World Development Indicators. Available online via: https://data.worldbank.org/indicator/TM.TAX.MRCH.SM.AR.ZS.

WTO [World Trade Organization]. (2015). *World Tariff Profiles 2015*, WTO, Geneva. Available via: https://www.wto.org/english/res_e/booksp_e/tariff_profiles15_e.pdf.

CHAPTER 2

The Fiscal Impact of Brexit

One of the main areas where even detractors of Brexit concede that the UK will benefit from withdrawal from the EU concerns the saving of the annual contributions paid to that organisation.[1] However, the calculation of net budgetary contributions to the EU is not quite as straightforward as it might appear, however, for a number of different reasons, including

1. The composition of the EU budgetary process is itself slightly opaque, due to the way in which budget payments are set, the resources over which the EU lays claim and the fact that contributions depend to a large extent upon the relative national income of member states. Thus, should the UK achieve a higher (lower) growth rate relative to other member states, it will incur higher (lower) retrospective demands for contributions to the EU budget than were initially anticipated.

2. Net payments to the EU must take into account the UK rebate, and how this may change (or cease to exist) over time, and also the range of payments received from the EU. It is easy to justify payments made directly to the UK government and also farmers, since this is part of EU agricultural subsidies (the Common Agricultural Policy [CAP]) administered by the UK government. However, it is more contentious to justify the inclusion of funding achieved by private

---

[1] Additional savings may arise from a reduction in UK representation in the various EU institutions.

© The Author(s) 2020
P. B. Whyman, A. I. Petrescu, *The Economics of Brexit*,
https://doi.org/10.1007/978-3-030-55948-9_2

sector organisations (including UK universities) in research and/or training programmes, secured through competitive bidding.

3. The timing of calculating the payments is different when comparing Treasury and EU Commission estimates of net payments, with the result that they often present quite different estimates. Hence, there will be some discrepancy between different studies, depending upon which data sources they have chosen (Browne et al. 2016: 40). To take one example, the Institute for Fiscal Studies typically use figures from the EU Commission, whereas this chapter draws its data from HM Treasury.

4. The level of fiscal savings will partially depend upon whether the UK's future arrangement with the EU involves an element of fiscal contribution to secure participation in EU programmes.

For something as apparently clear-cut as UK budgetary contributions to the EU, therefore, estimating the likely fiscal benefit arising from Brexit is a little more complicated than might be expected.

COMPOSITION AND SIZE OF THE EU BUDGET

The EU budget has increased, over time, from 0.5% of community gross national income (GNI) in 1973 to its present 1% level (Browne et al. 2016: 6). It is set for a 5–7-year Multiannual Financial Framework in order to provide a stable funding platform. For 2014–2020, the budget was set at €960 billion, which implies an average of €137.14 billion per year. This settlement represents a cash increase over the previous financial period, but a real terms (after inflation) decrease (from 1.12% EU GNI), which represents the first such real terms reduction in the EU budget (HM Treasury 2014: 5; Keep 2015: 3).[2]

In practice, however, it is a little more complicated for two reasons. Firstly, the EU budget fails to include additional elements which are essentially off balance sheet (HMG 2014: 26). These include €36.8 billion worth of allocations to an Emergency Aid Reserve, a European Globalisation Fund, a Solidarity Fund, a Flexibility Instrument and the European Development Fund (EDF). If included in the core EU budget, this would represent an increase of 0.04% of total EU GNI. Secondly, the

[2] http://www.consilium.europa.eu/uedocs/cms_data/docs/pressdata/en/ecofin/139831.pdf

appropriation commitments are increased by what is described as a 'margin' of around 0.28% of EU GNI, presumably in order to provide a degree of flexibility to EU expenditures intended to cover a relatively long time period. Hence, the total appropriations (payments made into the EU budget) necessary to cover this total sum (i.e. core budget + margin) represents 1.23% of EU GNI up until 2020 (see Table 2.1).

Having established the magnitude of EU budgetary expenditures, the contributions can be established for each member state. This primarily derives from what the EU has established as its 'own resources', namely (HM Treasury 2014: 9–10)

(i) GNI-based contributions (currently representing approximately 74% of total EU revenue) vary according to the relative affluence of member states. It is calculated that the UK's share of this revenue category was 14.5% in 2014;

(ii) VAT contributions (13% of EU revenue), based upon a slightly complicated set of assumptions and capped to limit excessive variations. The pertinent point is that the UK's share of contributions to the EU budget under this category was 16% in 2014;

(iii) Customs duties (12% of EU revenue) levied on goods imported from non-member states. It is estimated that the UK contributed 16.1% of the revenue under this category;

(iv) Sugar levies (less than 1% of EU revenue) are charged on the production of sugar;

(v) A small proportion (approximately 1%) of EU revenue lies outside of the 'own resources' and includes contributions from non-EU member states to participate in certain programmes, taxes paid on EU staff salaries, interest on late payments and fines levied upon companies breaching competition law.

Customs duties and sugar levies comprised the initial basis for EU funding, reflecting its early focus upon agricultural production and its establishment of a customs union (described as a 'common market' in UK discourse), later augmented by value-added tax (VAT) contributions and, more latterly, the rising importance of revenues calculated according to the relative affluence of member states. The volatility in calculating net payments to the EU budget is largely due to the inherent nature of the 'own resources' system (HM Treasury 2014: 13–14). Moreover, the complexity inherent within the 'own resources' approach therefore partly

Table 2.1 Multiannual Financial Framework EU 28 for 2014–2020, adjusted for 2017 (€m, 2017 prices)

Commitment appropriations	2014	2015	2016	2017	2018	2019	2020	Total 2014–2019
1. Smart and inclusive growth	**52,756**	**77,986**	**69,304**	**73,512**	**76,420**	**79,924**	**83,661**	**513,563**
1.a. Competitiveness for growth and jobs	16,560	17,666	18,467	19,925	21,239	23,082	25,191	142,130
1b. Economic, social and territorial cohesion	36,196	60,320	50,837	53,587	55,181	56,842	58,470	371,433
2. Sustainable growth: Natural resources	**49,857**	**64,692**	**64,262**	**60,191**	**60,267**	**60,344**	**60,421**	**420,034**
Of which market related expenditure and direct payments	43,779	44,190	43,951	44,146	44,163	44,241	44,264	308,734
3. Security and citizenship	1737	2456	2546	2578	2656	2801	2951	17,725
4. Global Europe	8335	8749	9143	9432	9825	10,268	10,510	66,262
5. Administration	8721	9076	9483	9918	10,346	10,786	11,254	69,584
Of which administrative expenditure of the institution	7056	7351	7679	8007	8360	8700	9071	56,224
6. Compensation	**29**	**0**	**0**	**0**	**0**	**0**	**0**	**29**
Total commitment appropriations	**121,435**	**162,959**	**154,738**	**155,631**	**159,514**	**164,123**	**168,797**	**1,087,197**
As a percentage of GNI	0.90%	1.17%	1.05%	1.04%	1.04%	1.04%	1.03%	1.04%
Total payment appropriations	**135,762**	**140,719**	**144,685**	**142,906**	**149,713**	**154,286**	**157,358**	**1,025,429**
As a percentage of GNI	1.01%	1.02%	0.98%	0.95%	0.97%	0.97%	0.96%	0.98%
Margin available	0.22%	0.21%	0.25%	0.28%	0.26%	0.26%	0.27%	0.25%
Own resources ceiling as a percentage of GNI	1.23%	1.23%	1.23%	1.23%	1.23%	1.23%	1.23%	1.23%

Source: Europa EU (2016)

reflects the historical development of the EU and the difficulty in securing a more streamlined approach, when this would inherently involve individual nations who benefit from any changes and others who are required to make larger contributions as a result. The evolution and significance of each source of EU revenue is illustrated in Fig. 2.1.

In terms of EU expenditure, the initial dominance of the CAP, which can be noted in Fig. 2.2, has been reduced somewhat due to the dramatic expansion of cohesion and structural funds to promote regional development across all member states. Thus, in the current budgetary framework, 47% of total spending commitments relate to regional policy, 39% for CAP and sustainable development, with the balance incorporating administration (6%), external policy (6%) and issues relating to migration, public

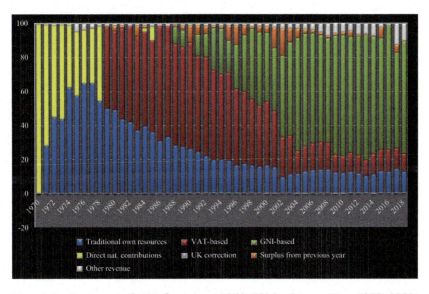

Fig. 2.1 Structure of EU financing, 1958–2018. *Sources:* For 1970–2008: European Commission (2009). Financial Report EU budget 2008. Publication and accompanying dataset. Last accessed 15 August 2016. For 2009–2014: European Commission (2015). Financial Report EU budget 2014. Publication and accompanying dataset. Last accessed 15 August 2016. For 2015–2016: European Commission (2016). Definitive Adoption (EU, Euratom) 2016/150 of the European Union's general budget for the financial year 2016. Last accessed 15 Aug 2016. For 2017–2018: European Commission (2020)

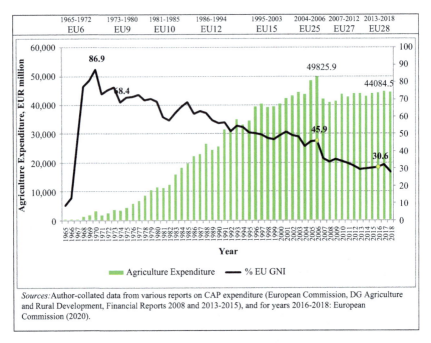

Fig. 2.2 Agriculture expenditure as part of the EU GNI, 1965–2015 (€m). *Sources: Author-collated data from various reports on CAP expenditure (European Commission, DG Agriculture and Rural Development, Financial Reports 2008 and 2013–2015)*

health, consumer protection, culture and youth policy (2%) (Keep 2015: 6–7).

Financial Management and Fraud

One issue which typically arises, when considering the EU budget, concerns accusations of financial mismanagement and/or fraud. This criticism derives from the annual reports produced by the European Court of Auditors (ECA), which assess the financial management of the EU's finances. In its opinion, the latest set of accounts to be assessed, in 2012, was found to be legal and regular, but that 4.8% of EU expenditure was subject to 'material error'. In essence, this means that spending did not conform to the rules established to guide EU expenditure. Data collected through monitoring sampling, undertaken across different categories of EU expenditure, indicate that errors were not confined to specific sectors, with agricultural support estimated to have a material error of perhaps 3.8% of total expenditure, rural development 7.9%, regional policy, energy and transport 6.8%, employment and social affairs 3.2%, external relations 3.3% and research 3.9%.

The auditors argued that this did not necessarily equate to fraud, and nor is almost 5% of the total EU budget necessarily wasted—the complexity inherent in administering a series of programmes across a large number of nations, each at different levels of development, and with different practices concerning the distribution and monitoring of public expenditure. That is why the ECA themselves have set an error ceiling of 2% as acceptable for EU spending programmes—a rate that would be difficult to justify in public spending programmes within a single nation (HMG 2014: 30). Nevertheless, the failure to meet even this generous target creates cause for concern about deficiencies in eligibility assessment and compliance monitoring which require corrective action. Consequently, for the nineteenth consecutive year, the ECA provided only partial assurance as to the accuracy of the EU's accounts (HM Treasury 2014: 21–24).

UK CONTRIBUTIONS TO THE EU BUDGET

The UK has been an almost continuous net contributor to the EU's budget, the one exception being in 1975 (see Table 2.2).

The UK is currently the second largest net contributor to the EU, after Germany, but only the sixth largest when these payments are averaged per capita (per person), as illustrated in Fig. 2.3.

The UK Rebate

One early acknowledgement of distributional concerns raised by the 'own resource' system resulted in the adjustment of the UK's net contributions paid into the EU budget by means of a correction or abatement—normally described as a 'rebate'. Given that the UK had a relatively efficient and small agricultural sector and that CAP expenditures were a majority of EU spending at the time of its accession to the EU, the UK received relatively small expenditures from the EU budget. At the same time, as a trading nation, the UK's share of customs duties and VAT receipts were disproportionately large, thereby requiring a disproportionately high

Table 2.2 UK net contributions to the EU/EC budget (£m), 1973–2020

Year	Gross contribution	Negotiated refunds	Rebate	Total contribution (after rebate and refunds)	Public sector receipts	Net contribution (Gross contribution—rebate and refunds—public sector receipts)	GDP, chained volume measures, seasonally adjusted (£m)	Net contribution as % GDP
1973	181			181	79	102	781,583	0.013
1974	181			181	150	31	762,257	0.004
1975	342			342	398	−56	750,912	−0.007
1976	463			463	296	167	772,852	0.022
1977	737			737	368	369	791,889	0.047
1978	1348			1348	526	822	825,111	0.100
1979	1606			1606	659	947	855,933	0.111
1980	1767	98		1669	963	706	838,462	0.084
1981	2174	693		1481	1084	397	831,931	0.048
1982	2863	1019		1844	1238	606	848,700	0.071
1983	2976	807		2169	1522	647	884,520	0.073
1984	3204	528		2676	2020	656	904,639	0.073
1985	3940	61	166	3713	1905	1808	942,519	0.192
1986	4493		1701	2792	2220	572	972,239	0.059
1987	5202		1153	4049	2328	1721	1,024,346	0.168
1988	5138		1594	3544	2182	1362	1,083,629	0.126
1989	5585		1154	4431	2116	2315	1,111,618	0.208
1990	6355		1697	4658	2183	2475	1,175,573	0.211
1991	5807		2497	3309	2765	544	1,162,605	0.047
1992	6738		1881	4857	2827	2030	1,167,268	0.174
1993	7985		2539	5446	3291	2155	1,196,331	0.180
1994	7189		1726	5463	3253	2211	1,242,342	0.178
1995	8889		1207	7682	3665	4017	1,273,790	0.315
1996	9133		2412	6721	4373	2348	1,305,527	0.180

Year	Gross contribution	Negotiated refunds	Rebate	Total contribution (after rebate and refunds)	Public sector receipts	Net contribution (Gross contribution—rebate and refunds—public sector receipts)	GDP, chained volume measures, seasonally adjusted (£m)	Net contribution as % GDP
1997	7991		1733	6258	4661	1597	1,355,853	0.118
1998	10,090		1378	8712	4115	4597	1,405,272	0.327
1999	10,287		3171	7117	3479	3638	1,453,448	0.250
2000	10,517		2085	8433	4241	4192	1,503,408	0.279
2001	9379		4560	4819	3430	1389	1,548,124	0.090
2002	9439		3099	6340	3201	3139	1,584,110	0.198
2003	10,966		3559	7407	3728	3679	1,636,169	0.225
2004	10,895		3593	7302	4294	3008	1,675,011	0.180
2005	12,567		3656	8911	5329	3582	1,728,273	0.207
2006	12,426		3569	8857	4948	3909	1,776,462	0.220
2007	12,456		3523	8933	4332	4601	1,819,641	0.253
2008	12,653		4862	7791	4497	3294	1,814,526	0.182
2009	14,129		5392	8737	4401	4336	1,737,448	0.250
2010	15,197		3047	12,150	4768	7382	1,771,321	0.417
2011	15,357		3143	12,214	4132	8082	1,798,603	0.449
2012	15,746		3110	12,636	4169	8467	1,825,204	0.464
2013	18,135		3674	14,461	3996	10,465	1,864,255	0.561
2014	18,777		4416	14,361	4583	9778	1,912,866	0.511
2015	19,717		4913	14,804	4315	10,489	1,957,920	0.535
2016	18,896		5026	13,870	4584	9286	1,995,478	0.465
2017	17,058		4302	12,756	4144	8612	2,033,234	0.424
2018	19,970		4451	15,591	4492	11,027	2,061,408	0.535
2019[a]	20,197		4662	15,535	4993	10,541		0.535

(continued)

Table 2.2   (continued)

Year	Gross contribution	Negotiated refunds	Rebate	Total contribution (after rebate and refunds)	Public sector receipts	Net contribution (Gross contribution—rebate and refunds—public sector receipts)	GDP, chained volume measures, seasonally adjusted (£m)	Net contribution as % GDP
2020[a]	20,433		4319	**16,114**	5147	**10,967**		
2021[a]	21,145		4251	**16,894**	5938	**10,956**		
2022[a]	21,430		4567	**16,863**	5905	**10,957**		

Note [a]figures for 2019–22 are OBR forecasts, drawn from HM Treasury (2019: 17)

Sources: HM Treasury (2015); ONS, UK National Accounts (2016, 2019); HM Treasury (2019); ONS, UK Balance of Payments—The Pink Book (2019)

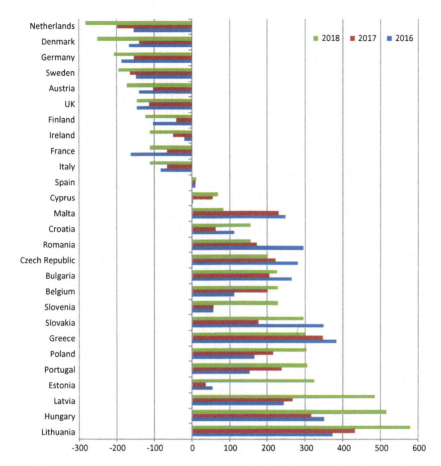

Fig. 2.3 EU net contribution per capita, by member state (in €), 2016–2018—ranked from largest to smallest total net contribution in 2018. *Notes:* Negative figures denote a member state being a net contributor of funds to the EU budget; positive figures denote being a net recipient of funds from the EU budget. Not showing Luxembourg as the figures are high for the graph scale. *Source:* Authors' calculations based on data from the European Commission (2020) and OECD 2020 population data series

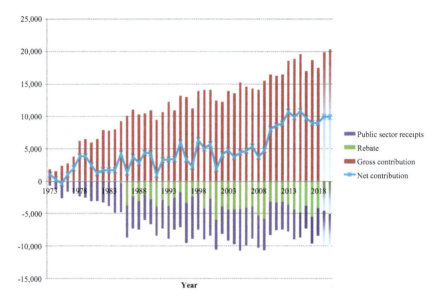

Fig. 2.4 UK contributions to and receipts from the EU budget real terms (£m at 2015 prices), 1973–2020. *Note:* Figures for 2019–2020 are forecasts rounded to the nearest £100 million. *Sources:* HM Treasury (2016); ONS, UK National Accounts *(2016)*

contribution to the EU budget. In 1984, the UK was the third poorest EU member state, in terms of GNI per capita, and yet making the second largest net contribution to the EU budget (HMG 2014: 15). Unsurprisingly, this led to political tensions and the rebate was negotiated to provide an ex post facto adjustment to reduce net contributions to a more equitable position.

The initial 1985 rebate lowered UK contributions by two-thirds and calculated by subtracting the UK's percentage share of expenditure from the UK's percentage share of VAT contributions, then multiplying this by 0.66 and finally multiplying this sum by the total amount of EU expenditure.[3] This rebate is valuable to the UK (see Fig. 2.4), amounting to £4.9 billion in 2014 and signifying that the UK's net contribution

[3] http://register.consilium.europa.eu/doc/srv?l=EN&f=ST%205602%202014%20INIT

would have been just under 50% larger had the rebate not been applied (see Table 2.4).

It should be noted that the UK is not the only member state to benefit from a budgetary correction mechanism. For example, Austria, Denmark, Germany, the Netherlands and Sweden are all net contributors to the EU budget and who receive one or more forms of contribution adjustments, to prevent what might otherwise be termed an 'excessive' budgetary burden (HMG 2014: 27; Business for Britain 2015: 369–370). Thus, the UK is certainly not unique in the EU for having what are regarded as disproportionate and inequitable funding burdens ameliorated (EU Commission 2014). Despite this fact, the UK abatement has been subject to periodic criticism from the Commission and other member states (Business for Britain 2015: 182; Capital Economics 2016: 28), and indeed, before the UK's withdrawal, there were proposals being discussed which would have gradually removed the UK rebate in its entirety.[4]

As a fiscal matter, any decision to remove or reform the rebate would require unanimity in the Council of Ministers, and hence, whilst the UK remained a member of the EU, it could have vetoed the proposals, although previous UK governments have accepted reductions in the rebate to secure concessions on other areas of fiscal spending—a fact which had a significant impact upon UK fiscal contributions to the EU (Business for Britain 2015: 182; Keep 2015: 15; Webb et al. 2015: 9–12; Begg 2016: 44). See Table 2.3.

Table 2.3 Percentage of UK rebate lost due to 2005 changes

Year	Actual size of UK rebate in nominal prices (€m)	Value of UK rebate had 2005 changes not been made in nominal prices (€m)	Lost value of the UK rebate
2008	6114	6416	4.7%
2009	6057	7407	18.2%
2010	3553	5670	37.3%
2011	3623	5978	39.4%
2012	3835	6726	43.0%
2013	4073 (Est)	7480 (Est)	45.5%

Source: Business for Britain (2014: 4)

[4] https://www.independent.co.uk/news/uk/politics/brexit-eu-budget-rebate-gunther-oetinger-second-referendum-remain-a8580616.html;   https://www.ft.com/content/5ce33318-4e1e-11e8-a7a9-37318e776bab

Gross Versus Net Contributions

One controversy, which arose during the 2016 referendum campaign, concerns whether it is more appropriate to refer to *gross* or *net* contributions to the EU budget. This is an interesting question to consider because the answer partly depends upon what the presentation of the figures is seeking to demonstrate. In regular conversation, for example, if an individual is asked about their income, they will most likely reply giving their gross income, rather than what they actually receive into their bank accounts after tax and other deductions. Nor will it be very likely that they will think to add back into the calculation of their income what they might receive in tax credits or social security benefits, and even less the net benefit they might personally receive through the provision of those public services which their tax payments help to fund, less any additional fees or charges involved in utilising these public services. The more complex net income calculation may provide the more accurate answer, but it is unlikely to be the one give, even if the individual concerned was an economics professor!

Nevertheless, economists aim to be a little more precise. Hence, if the intention is to highlight the total liability to the UK should anticipated payments not occur and the rebate is assumed to have been abolished, then the gross figure is appropriate. It might also be justified when considering whether any divergence between the efficiency of nationally, as opposed to supra-nationally, determined forms of expenditure may affect the economic impact experienced by the UK economy (Congdon, 2014: 19–22). However, if the intention is to emphasise the magnitude of UK fiscal expenditure over which the UK has only indirect control, then gross payments less the rebate might be an appropriate figure. By contrast, if the intention is to estimate the magnitude of public finances that could be repatriated following withdrawal—that is, over which the UK government has 'taken back control'—then the *net* contribution is more appropriate.

Official estimates of net UK contributions to the EU are given in what is known as *The Pink Book* (ONS 2019, Table 9.9). In 2015, the last year before the referendum debate, the net contribution was given as £10.5 billion (equivalent to £202 million per week), whereas for 2018, the most recent year for which data is available, this figure is £11 billion. This figure relates to total contributions transferred to the EU by the UK government after the rebate has been deducted and after taking account of the receipts received back *by the public sector* from the EU for participation in various programmes, such as the CAP or regional development funding.

There is, however, an alternative estimate produced, by the EU, which includes into its calculations an additional amount received by the UK *private sector* due to their participation in EU programmes. These most notably include research funding won by UK universities, through a competitive process, from the Horizon 2020 research programme, and the Erasmus student mobility scheme. The Treasury estimates that in 2013, these payments to private organisations totalled in the region of £1.4 billion (HM Treasury 2015: 14), whereas the EU estimated this private benefit to be in the region of £2.2 billion in 2017 (HMT 2019: 15). If this is subtracted from the net public sector receipts, it gives a final net financial impact upon the UK economy from the EU budget of around £8.3–8.8 billion per year.

The range of different estimates of UK contributions to the EU budget, therefore, range from around £19.2 billion gross payments to between £11 billion net contributions for the UK government and public sector, and around £8.8 billion for both public and private sectors (ONS 2019, Table 9.9). Each of these figures can be used for certain circumstances. For example, the £11 billion net contribution estimate would be preferable when seeking to estimate the impact of withdrawal from the EU upon expected fiscal savings to government following Brexit, because it outlines the magnitude of expected additional fiscal resources that would be available for an independent UK government once Brexit is completed. The EU figure might arguably be useful when seeking to calculate the net economic impact upon the UK economy as a whole. However, this does assume that the UK government would replicate EU spending decisions following withdrawal, otherwise private sector organisations which would no longer receive the £2.5bn difference between the figures. This highlights the important difference between money secured *indirectly* through competitive bidding to various EU run programmes, by private sector organisations such as universities or public limited companies (PLCs), compared with direct transfers to public sector bodies. There is a significant degree of volatility in research funding, for example, and while participation in EU programmes has been an undoubted benefit for many universities over the past few decades, there is no assurance that this would continue into the future, irrespective of government guarantees and the fallout from Brexit.[5] Hence, the £11bn (0.53% UK GDP) figure is perceived to be the most reliable for economic studies, and, indeed, most economic studies therefore use this figure (e.g. HM Treasury 2014; Ottaviano et al. 2014: 2; Dhingra et al. 2014: 3; Capital Economics 2016: 3).

Misuse of Statistics

It is difficult to avoid mention, at this point, of the controversy relating to the *Vote Leave* campaign bus slogan:

"We send the EU £350 million a week—let's fund the NHS instead".

This has been denounced by many as being factually inaccurate[6] and complaints on this issue were made to the Independent Press Standards Organisation and latterly to the High Court,[7] albeit that neither were upheld. Criticism centres around three elements of this statement:

1. The suggestion that £350 million per week would be better spent upon the National Health Service was criticised as a general 'aspiration'[8] because it was not subsequently enacted by the government following the referendum. This reflects an important difference between General Election campaigns, where political parties make, and are expected to fulfil, manifesto promises should they gain control of the levers of power, and referendums where participants may

---

[5] https://royalsociety.org/-/media/news/2019/brexit-uk-science-impact.pdf; https://www.theguardian.com/education/2017/dec/03/eu-university-funding-grants-decline-brexit-horizon-2020; https://www.ukro.ac.uk/Documents/factsheet_brexit.pdf?pubdate=20191030

[6] https://www.theguardian.com/commentisfree/2017/sep/18/boris-johnson-350-million-claim-bogus-foreign-secretary; https://www.independent.co.uk/news/uk/politics/brexit-latest-news-vote-leave-director-dominic-cummings-leave-eu-error-nhs-350-million-lie-bus-a7822386.html

[7] https://www.pressgazette.co.uk/ipso-rule-boris-johnsons-350m-to-eu-figure-made-in-telegraph-column-not-significantly-inaccurate/; https://www.ipso.co.uk/rulings-and-resolution-statements/ruling/?id=18520-17; https://www.judiciary.uk/wp-content/uploads/2019/07/2019ewhc-1709-admin-johnson-v-westminster-mags-final.pdf

[8] http://www.independent.co.uk/news/uk/politics/brexit-350-million-a-week-extra-for-the-nhs-only-an-aspiration-says-vote-leave-campaigner-chris-a7105246.html

win the argument but (as in this case) not find themselves in office and therefore unable to enact their preferred outcomes.

2. The use of the word 'send'[9] would seem to imply that the full (gross) contribution was transferred to the EU, whereas this does not occur until the UK's rebate is deducted. Whilst a case can certainly be made that the UK rebate may not have survived in the long term even had the UK remained a member of the EU,[10] this does not justify it being omitted from the figure stated as being 'sent' to the EU. The gross fiscal cost after rebate deductions in 2016 was approximately £275 million per week (Emmerson and Pope 2016: 1).

3. If, however, the intention of this slogan was to estimate the magnitude of public finances that could be repatriated following withdrawal—that is, over which the UK government has 'taken back control'—then the *net* contribution figure (£212 million) should have been used. The UK Statistics Authority argued that this was a "clear misuse of official statistics"[11] which was potentially capable of misleading voters,[12] whilst a Treasury Select Committee found the lack of qualification sitting alongside the Vote Leave slogan as "deeply problematic".[13]

It would be remiss and unbalanced, however, to imply that these were the only occasions when the UK Statistics Authority and the Treasury Select Committee criticised the use of statistics in the referendum campaign. Indeed, the latter report extends the following criticisms over the misuse of statistics during the referendum campaign:

1. Claims made by *Stronger in Europe* that withdrawal would increase consumer prices were criticised due to their use of out-of-date

---

[9] http://www.theguardian.com/politics/reality-check/2016/may/23/does-the-eu-really-cost-the-uk-350m-a-week

[10] https://standpointmag.co.uk/issues/july-august-2019/the-350-million-wasnt-a-lie-heres-why/

[11] https://www.statisticsauthority.gov.uk/wp-content/uploads/2017/09/Letter-from-Sir-David-Norgrove-to-Foreign-Secretary.pdf; https://www.statisticsauthority.gov.uk/news/uk-statistics-authority-statement-on-the-use-of-official-statistics-on-contributions-to-the-european-union/

[12] https://fullfact.org/europe/350-million-week-boris-johnson-statistics-authority-misuse/

[13] https://publications.parliament.uk/pa/cm201617/cmselect/cmtreasy/122/12204.htm, paragraph 36.

sources and unrealistic assumptions over tariff levels set by a newly independent UK.[14]

2. Claims made by the Prime Minister and Chancellor relating to the economic models discussed in the previous chapter misrepresented key aspects of the economic studies.[15]

3. Claims made by *Britain Stronger in Europe*, the former Deputy Prime Minister (Clegg), former Chief Secretary to the Treasury (Alexander) and repeated in the government leaflet distributed during the referendum campaign, that 3 million jobs are dependent upon UK trade with the EU, were criticised as "misleading",[16] a "wild overstatement" (Capital Economics 2016: 18) and "totally implausible, and certainly not based on evidence" (Portes 2013: F8–9). The reason is quite simple—that even the worst-case predictions of Brexit impact upon trade would accept that most of this trade would continue and therefore the impact upon employment (if any) would be far smaller than this headline figure. PwC (2016: 3), for example, suggested that any such employment effects would be perhaps a tenth of the more publicised claims, whilst any increase in trade with the rest of the world could mitigate or offset any such effect.

Consequently, it would be fair to conclude that many of the participants, individuals and campaigning groups on both sides of the argument, were less than stringent in their use of official statistics during and after the referendum campaign. This highlights the importance of, where possible, examining the data yourself and making an educated judgement about the veracity of competing claims. Indeed, this is hopefully one of the contributions that this book can make to the ongoing debate of the UK's future relationship with the EU.

THE UNCERTAINTY OF FUTURE BUDGETARY DEVELOPMENTS

When producing their estimates of the economic impact of Brexit, those studies which incorporate a fiscal element tend to project potential budgetary savings arising from Brexit on the basis that future developments do not impact upon this level of budgetary savings. This simplifies the

---

[14] Ibid., paragraphs 44–45.
[15] Ibid., paragraph 74.
[16] Ibid., paragraphs 50–51.

analysis but at the cost of underestimating these likely effects. These might include the following:

(a) Future growth of the EU budget and consequent increase in UK fiscal contributions
(b) The financial settlement with the EU
(c) The cost incurred in preparation for UK exit from the EU
(d) Which model of trade relationship the UK negotiates with the EU following Brexit
(e) The macroeconomic impact arising from Brexit and consequences for the national budget

For the first factor, it can be noted that the historical development of UK budgetary contributions has been variable, but following a steadily increasing trend (see Fig. 2.5). There are many causes to this phenomenon, including (i) the natural growth in a budget fixed at a certain percentage of EU GDP; (ii) UK growth rates being faster than the EU average during the recent Eurozone crisis, and therefore the UK has to pay an increasing share of EU expenditure; (iii) the EU budget as a whole being expanded over time, from 0.5% of EU GDP in the 1970s to a little over

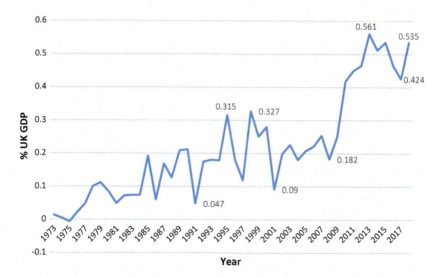

Fig. 2.5 UK net contributions to the EU budget (% of UK GDP), 1973–2015. *Sources:* HM Treasury *(2019); ONS, UK National Accounts (2019)*

1% of GDP today; and (iv) the UK rebate being eroded through negotiating exemptions as a means to leverage additional change within the organisation. However, there is a reasonable expectation that the EU budget will continue to increase during the next budgetary period. This may arise out of the need to provide further support to the single currency (MacDougall 1977: 20; HMG 2014: 37–8), to expand current programmes or to enable the EU to provide a sufficient fiscal stimulus in current and future economic crises (Begg 2016: 41).

The 2021–2027 EU budget remains subject to debate, yet it is worth noting that the EU Commission has proposed an increase to 1.114% of EU GDP and the European Parliament has proposed 1.3%.[17] Either of these options would have resulted in significant increases in UK fiscal contributions to the EU budget. If the UK currently contributes £11bn to an EU budget set at 1% of EU GDP, the expectation would be that UK payments might have risen by between 11% and 30%, ceteris paribus, if either of these proposals were accepted. Hence, economic studies projecting Brexit impact for the next decade should take into account the potentially higher fiscal savings the UK will make in the future compared to the baseline of continued EU membership.

The second factor relates to the financial settlement negotiated as part of the draft Withdrawal Agreement between the UK government and the EU. This 'divorce bill' is intended to wind up the UK's membership of the EU by calculating the assets and liabilities arising from past and future policy commitments made whilst a member of the organisation. There are three main components of the financial settlement, namely

1. Continued EU membership contributions during the transition period, negotiated as part of the withdrawal agreement, and intended to last until the end of 2020;
2. The UK's outstanding commitments or Reste à Liquider (RAL),[18] which arise out of decisions taken during the period of the UK's membership of the EU, but where spending is ongoing past the end of 2020; and
3. Remaining net liabilities (after assets have been offset)—the largest element of this relates to the estimated £8.6bn pension liability.

---

[17] https://www.euractiv.com/section/economy-jobs/linksdossier/eu-faces-tough-post-brexit-test-with-2021-2027-budget/

[18] https://op.europa.eu/en/publication-detail/-/publication/b3ea5d9a-e4c2-11e9-9c4e-01aa75ed71a1/language-en

It is difficult to provide a precise estimate of the final cost of the financial settlement because certain elements depend upon the movement in exchange rates (as the payment is calculated in Euros) and changes in future EU budgets can also have an effect as part of the UK's contribution to the EU budget reflects the UK's share of total EU GDP and is thereby determined retrospectively; if the UK outperforms the rest of the EU, then its share of contributions to the EU budget rises, and vice versa (HOCCPA 2018: 9–10). This figure will not be known until 2022. Nevertheless, the best estimate made by the Office for Budget Responsibility (OBR) is that the total cost is likely to be around £32.9bn and comprised £8.9bn from participation in the EU budget during the transition period until the end of 2020, £19.2bn due to RAL and £4.8bn relating to remaining net liabilities.[19] Compared to earlier estimates, the latter category appears to have increased significantly (HM Treasury 2019: 67). Seventy-five per cent of these payments are expected to have been made by the end of 2023, but others, primarily pension liabilities, will potentially extend many years into the future, whilst the EU's use of a rather unfavourable actuarial discount rate for pension liabilities mitigates against the option of early payment (HOCCPA 2018: 12; HM Treasury 2019: 68).[20] All of this assumes that the transition period will terminate at the end of 2020 as currently envisioned. If it is further extended, perhaps because of difficulties for negotiations caused by responding to the COVID-19 virus,[21] then further costs would be incurred.

One additional element not included in the financial settlement calculations refers to the UK's commitment to contribute a further £3bn to the EDF in the post-Brexit period. The rationale for not including this sum is that the UK remains committed to spending 0.7% of its GDP upon overseas aid and if it did not spend this money through the EDF, it would be mandated to do so via another mechanism. Thus, the Treasury did not include this sum in its estimates of the cost of withdrawal from the EU as it did not represent additional expenditure over and above that which would have occurred in any case (HOCCPA 2018: 11).

A related factor concerns the cost for the UK government arising from preparations for withdrawal from the EU. The best available estimate

---

[19] https://commonslibrary.parliament.uk/research-briefings/cbp-8039/
[20] https://commonslibrary.parliament.uk/brexit/the-eu/withdrawal-agreement-bill-the-financial-settlement/
[21] https://www.dailymail.co.uk/news/article-7720395/Boris-Johnson-vows-NOT-extend-Brexit-transition-period-past-December-2020.html; https://www.brookings.edu/blog/order-from-chaos/2020/03/26/brexit-is-not-immune-to-coronavirus/

produced thus far, by the National Audit Office, suggests that government departments have spent around £4.4 billion, between June 2016 and 31 January 2020 (NAO, 2020). Approximately £301 million of this sum derived from existing budgets, consequently around £4.1bn represented funding provided specifically to facilitate Brexit. This is unlikely to represent the end of this expenditure as there will be a requirement for information provision to assist exporters to comply with new trading rules, such as the operation of a rule of origin scheme (for all Brexit scenarios excepting a customs union), whilst it is probable that further investment will be required to strengthen goods and passenger infrastructure given the need for more customs checks for EU imports and the anticipated rise in trade with the rest of the world. There will be further areas of expenditure related to agriculture and fisheries support, research and student mobility schemes, and so forth. Thus, Brexit is likely to have more significant impact upon the future scope of public expenditure than is simply covered by measuring the benefit arising from no longer transferring a significant net fiscal transfer to the EU.

The future trade relationship that the UK negotiates with the EU will have a fourth impact upon the future development of UK public finances, especially if this includes an element of financial contribution towards EU programmes. Around half of the preferential trade options, available to the UK (discussed in more detail in Chap. 9), would involve varying degrees of fiscal transfers to the EU (see Table 2.4). The closest forms of trade relationship would be likely to carry the most significant fiscal costs, as members of the European Economic Area (EEA) are expected to make a

Table 2.4 Estimated fiscal impact from different future trading relationships with the EU

	Gross		Net		UK net	
	£m	% GDP	£m	% GDP	£bn	% GDP
Norway—EEA	620	0.76%	310	0.38	4.4	0.22
Turkey—customs union	n/a	n/a	n/a	n/a	3[a]	0.14[a]
Swiss—bilateral	420	0.13	410	0.13	2.1	0.09
South Korea—FTA	0	0	0	0	0	0
Greenland—WTO	0	0	0	0	0	0
Hong Kong—unilateral free trade	0	0	0	0	0	0

[a] Authors' estimate

significant contribution towards EU programmes, whereas the more independent and less intimate the relationship, the less of a fiscal burden may be required, if, indeed, any contribution is necessitated at all. Thus, should the UK participate in the EEA on the same terms as Norway, the overall net savings to the UK from Brexit might be as low as £5.6 billion, whereas if the UK negotiated a Free Trade Agreement (FTA) on a similar basis to the deal offered to Canada, there would be no fiscal cost involved, and therefore the final budgetary saving for the UK would remain at around £11 billion.

This calculation is complicated because the studies, discussed in Chap. 1, suggest that the closest trading relationships to full EU membership carry greater economic benefits (or lower costs). The significance of the economic impact of Brexit is that it would only require a 0.9% permanent reduction in the level of output in order to eliminate Brexit's £11 billion net budgetary saving or a 0.9% net boost to the economy in order to double Brexit's net fiscal benefit (Capital Economics 2016: 29; Emmerson and Pope 2016: 2). The range of economic studies, produced over the past two decades, have predicted effects ranging from large economic benefits to equally large economic costs, with the majority of the studies suggesting a more moderate impact of between plus or minus 2–3% of UK GDP (see Table 1.1). Thus, the net fiscal position is likely to depend upon whether this predicted economic impact occurs as expected and, if so, whether the effect is larger than the level of net fiscal savings.

One claim, made by the Liberal Democrats during the 2019 General Election campaign, suggested that cancelling Brexit and remaining in the EU would result in the UK economy being 1.9% larger by 2024/2025 and hence generate a 'remain bonus' equivalent to £14 billion per annum or £50 billion accumulated over a five-year period.[22] The problem with this estimate, of course, is that it is based upon the predictions made by the same group of economic studies discussed in Chap. 1 of this book, and it is therefore tainted with the flawed assumptions that underpinned these studies. Consequently, it is likely that the claim is over-stated, with both the magnitude and even the existence of a 'remain bonus' remaining uncertain.

[22] https://www.libdems.org.uk/the-remain-bonus;   https://www.bbc.co.uk/news/election-2019-50486538;   https://www.channel4.com/news/factcheck/factcheck-libdem-manifesto-and-the-remain-bonus;   https://www.ifs.org.uk/election/2019/article/liberal-democrat-manifesto-an-initial-reaction-from-ifs

The consideration of future budgetary exposure to the EU might appear a little odd since the UK has withdrawn from the EU and there is no immediate prospect of the submission of an application to re-join. However, the significance is two-fold. Firstly, it relates to how economic studies incorporate fiscal impact into their calculations of Brexit. Rather than simply projecting forward estimates of fiscal savings of either 0.3% or 0.53% of UK GDP as a gain from Brexit, based upon the payments into the current EU budget cycle, these calculations should reflect the probability that future UK contributions would rise, in line with larger EU budgets, and hence ongoing Brexit *ongoing* savings would be significantly higher than the values used in economic studies; perhaps 11–30% higher, if the Commission or European Parliament succeed in getting their budget proposals ratified. In addition, *non-recurring* financial settlement costs should be built into these models, implying that there would likely be little fiscal gains from Brexit for the first two years followed by benefits of perhaps 0.6% of UK GDP thereafter. The choice of Brexit option is likely to have an impact on this amount, although the current UK proposal of an FTA with the EU would involve no budgetary contributions (unlike EEA and customs union alternatives), whilst considerations regarding potential future participation in certain EU programmes would, if adopted, slightly lower future fiscal gains.

The final point that the future performance of the UK economy is likely to have a greater impact upon future fiscal developments is, of course, quite accurate. This is, after all, what all economic analysis is seeking to predict. If Brexit proves to be a success, then fiscal gains will increase commensurately; if, however, the economy weakens significantly as a result, then the impact upon fiscal policy will likely outweigh the initial savings made through no longer contributing to the EU budget. Unfortunately, the problems inherent in forecasting economic and fiscal impacts, which were discussed in the previous chapter, make it difficult to reach a firm conclusion.

References

Begg, I. (2016). The EU Budget and UK Contribution. *National Institute Economic Review, 236*, 39–47.

Browne, J., Johnson, P., & Phillips, D. (2016). *The Budget of the European Union: A Guide, IFS Briefing Note BN181*. London: Institute for Fiscal Studies.

Business for Britain. (2014). The UK's EU Rebate: How Much Did Tony Blair Give Away?. Briefing note.

Business for Britain. (2015). *Change or Go: How Britain Would Gain Influence and Prosper Outside an Unreformed EU*, Business for Britain, London. Available via: https://forbritain.org/cogwholebook.pdf.

Capital Economics. (2016). *The Economics Impact of 'Brexit': A Paper Discussing the United Kingdom' Relationship with Europe and the Impact of 'Brexit' on the British Economy*, Woodford Investment Management LLP, Oxford. Available via: https://woodfordfunds.com/economic-impact-brexit-report/.

Congdon, T. (2014). How much does the European Union cost Britain?, UKIP, London. Available via: http://www.timcongdon4ukip.com/docs/EU2014.pdf.

Dhingra, S., Ottaviano, G., & Sampson, T. (2014). Should We Stay or Should We Go? The Economic Consequences of Leaving the EU, Centre for Economic Performance Election Analysis Discussion Paper, London. Available via: http://cep.lse.ac.uk/pubs/download/EA022.pdf

Emmerson, C., & Pope, T. (2016). Winter is Coming: The Outlook for the Public Finances in the 2016 Autumn Statement. *IFS Briefing Note BN188*, Institute for Fiscal Studies, London. Available via: https://www.ifs.org.uk/uploads/publications/bns/BN188.pdf.

EU Commission. (2014). *Commission Working Document on calculation, financing, payment and entry in the budget of the correction of budgetary imbalances in favour of the United Kingdom ("the UK correction") in accordance with Articles 4 and 5 of Council Decision 2014/xxx/EU, Euratom on the system of own resources of the European Union*, COM(2014) 271, European Commission, Brussels. Available via: https://eur-lex.europa.eu/legal-content/EN/TXT/PDF/?uri=CELEX:52014DC0271&from=EN.

Europa EU. (2016). *Budget Figures and Documents*. Available via: http://ec.europa.eu/budget/mff/figures/index_en.cfm.

European Commission (2009). Financial Report EU budget 2008. Publication and accompanying dataset. Last accessed 15 August 2016.

European Commission (2015). Financial Report EU budget 2014. Publication and accompanying dataset. Last accessed 15 August 2016.

European Commission (2016). Definitive Adoption (EU, Euratom) 2016/150 of the European Union's general budget for the financial year 2016. Last accessed 15 Aug 2016.

European Commission. (2020). *EU Expenditure and Revenue 2014–2020*. DG Budget Data. Available online via: https://ec.europa.eu/budget/graphs/revenue_expediture.html.

HM Treasury. (2014). *European Union Finances 2014: Statement on the 2014 EU Budget and Measures to Counter Fraud and Financial Mismanagement*, Cm 8974, The Stationery Office, London. Available via: https://www.gov.uk/government/uploads/system/uploads/attachment_data/file/388882/EU_finances_2014_final.pdf.

HM Treasury. (2015). European Union Finances, 2015: Statement on the 2015 EU Budget and Measures to Counter Fraud and Financial Mismanagement, Cm 9167, The Stationery Office, London, UK. Available via https://www. gov.uk/government/uploads/system/uploads/attachment_data/ file/483344/EU_finances_2015_final_web_09122015.pdf.

HM Treasury. (2016). *HM Treasury Analysis: The Long Term Economic Impact of EU Membership and the Alternatives*, Cm 9250, The Stationery Office, London. Available via: https://www.gov.uk/government/uploads/system/uploads/ attachment_data/file/517415/treasury_analysis_economic_impact_of_eu_ membership_web.pdf.

HM Treasury. (2019). European Union Finances, 2018: Statement on the 2018 EU Budget and Measures to Counter Fraud and Financial Mismanagement, CP 114, June The Stationery Office, London. UK.

HMG [HM Government]. (2014). *Review of the Balance of Competences Between the United Kingdom and the European Union – EU Budget*, The Stationery Office, London. Available via: https://www.gov.uk/government/uploads/ system/uploads/attachment_data/file/332762/2902399_BoC_EU_ Budget_acc.pdf.

HOCCPA [House of Commons Committee of Public Accounts]. (2018). *Existing the EU: The Financial Settlement*, HC 973, House of Commons, London. Available via: https://publications.parliament.uk/pa/cm201719/cmselect/ cmpubacc/973/973.pdf.

Keep, M. (2015). 'EU Budget 2014–2020', *House of Commons Library Briefing Paper (HC 06455)*, The Stationery Office, London. Available via: http:// researchbriefings.files.parliament.uk/documents/SN06455/SN06455.pdf.

MacDougall, D. (1977). *The Role of Public Finance in the European Communities*, Office for the Official Publications of the European Communities, Luxembourg.

NAO [National Audit Office] (2020). Existing the European Union: The Cost of EU Exit Preparations, HC 102, National Audit Office, London. https://www. nao.org.uk/wp-content/uploads/2020/03/The-cost-of-EU-Exit- preparations.pdf

ONS [Office for National Statistics]. (2019). *Pink Book – Geographical Breakdown of the Current Account*, The Stationery Office, London, UK. Available via: https://www.ons.gov.uk/economy/nationalaccounts/balanceofpayments/ bulletins/unitedkingdombalanceofpaymentsthepinkbook/2019.

ONS [Office of National Statistics] UK National Accounts. (2016). *Gross Domestic Product, Chained Volume Measures: Seasonally Adjusted*. Available via: https:// www.ons.gov.uk/economy/grossdomesticproductgdp/timeseries/abmi/bb.

Ottaviano, G. I. P., Pessoa, J. P., Sampson, T., & Van Reenen, J. (2014). *Brexit of Fixit? The Trade and Welfare Effects of Leaving the European Union*, Centre for Economic Performance 016, LSE. Available via: https://ideas.repec.org/p/ cep/ceppap/016.html.

Portes, J. (2013). Commentary: The economic implications for the UK of leaving the European Union, *National Institute Economic Review*, No. 266, F4-9. Available via: http://www.niesr.ac.uk/sites/default/files/commentary.pdf.

PwC [PricewaterhouseCoopers LLP]. (2016). *Leaving the EU: Implications for the UK economy*, PricewaterhouseCoopers LLP, London. Available via: http://news.cbi.org.uk/news/leaving-eu-would-cause-a-serious-shock-to-uk-economy-new-pwc-analysis/leaving-the-eu-implications-for-the-uk-economy/.

Webb, D., Keep, M., & Wilton, M. (2015). In Brief: UK-EU economic relations, *House of Commons Library Briefing Paper (HC 06091)*, The Stationery Office, London. Available via: http://researchbriefings.parliament.uk/ResearchBriefing/Summary/SN06091.

CHAPTER 3

Brexit and Trade

The impact of Brexit upon international trade has been the primary concern expressed by those critical towards Brexit. This is not surprising because the early EU initiatives were focused upon the promotion of trade integration amongst member states through lowering barriers to trade, with the anticipated result that trade would increase, thereby promoting faster economic growth. Hence, reversing this logic would infer that withdrawal from the EU might reduce trade and hence lower UK GDP. This chapter, therefore, seeks to examine this issue.

THE ECONOMIC THEORY OF TRADE

Long-established theories of international trade tend to explain the flow of goods and services between countries in terms of comparative advantage derived from differences in the opportunity costs of production. This could arise because of differences in productivity, which is often termed 'Ricardian' comparative advantage, or due to differences in factor abundance and/or intensity, known as 'Heckscher-Ohlin' comparative advantage. The hypothesis is that countries will possess a relative advantage in one industry, from which it will export, and be less competitive in another, from which it will import. To the extent that these competitive advantages exist and are relatively evenly distributed between nations, the potential benefits from specialisation and trade between these nations are self-evident (Portes 2013: F9).

© The Author(s) 2020 71
P. B. Whyman, A. I. Petrescu, *The Economics of Brexit*,
https://doi.org/10.1007/978-3-030-55948-9_3

The theory of international trade is, however, complicated by three factors. The first is that when considering the costs and benefits arising from trade agreements, standard economic trade theory predicts that specialisation in areas of relative advantage, when combined with the lowering of trade barriers, should benefit the free trade agreement *as a whole*. It does not, however, unambiguously follow that *all* participating nations benefit equally. Indeed, it is quite conceivable that some may lose from the process. The distribution of gains and losses, within and between individual participant nations, means that interpretation of trade flows in the absence of considering these additional impacts becomes problematic. For example, if, by joining a free trade agreement, a nation benefitted from lower prices paid by consumers, but simultaneously experienced a growing trade deficit and consequently lower future employment and growth potential, would that nation be said to have benefitted from the trade arrangement? Focus upon microeconomic gains for consumers might suggest this is the case, but if the productive potential of the nation shrank as a result, the macroeconomic consequences would be negative.

Secondly, simplified discussions of Ricardian theory start from the premise that two nations possess very different factor endowments and specialise in diverse product ranges—that is, textiles and wine, or cheese and cars. Yet, a cursory inspection of trade flows demonstrates that a large proportion of international trade occurs between countries with relatively similar profiles. It might have once been the case that the UK exported manufactured goods (perhaps textiles) and imported non-manufactured items (perhaps food and wine), yet the majority of current UK trade takes place with other developed nations sharing broadly similar factor endowments and industrial structures. The UK both imports cars from, and exports cars to, Germany. To account for this apparent paradox, new trade theories have sought to explain these trading patterns by emphasising differences in consumer tastes and economies of scale within different industries, as determining specialisation of production and trade between nations (Bernard et al., 2007: 106–8).

The third factor concerns the distribution of industries in which competitive advantage occurs, reinforced by the terms of trade pertaining to each industry. If one economy has a greater number of industries which possess competitive advantages over another economy, and/or the terms of trade are such to maintain or reinforce this beneficial position, then it is likely that the former economy will generate a trade surplus and the latter a trade deficit. The consumers in the deficit nation may have an initial benefit of lower prices for their imported goods, but the nation will have to sell assets or borrow to meet its trade obligations. Unless this situation is ultimately resolved and brought back into balance, the deficit nation may suffer growth constraints, and those same consumers, even if all of them remain in employment, are likely to have slower growing incomes than in the surplus nation (McCombie and Thirwall 1994).

In a simplified economic model of the world, where the relative exchange values of currencies are primarily determined by international trade and foreign direct investment (FDI), the exchange rate might resolve differences in competitive advantage over time. However, the vast majority of foreign exchange trading today is related to financial speculation rather than financing international trade in goods and services. Indeed, one estimate is that the global value of all traded goods and services equates to a mere four days' worth of global foreign exchange trading (Singh 2000: 16). Hence, this equilibrating mechanism may not act in a smooth and timely fashion. Moreover, the principle of cumulative causation would suggest that those firms or countries which have an initial competitive advantage have the potential to retain and bolster this over time (Myrdal 1957: 12–13). The gains from trade are therefore not evenly distributed. Consequently, whilst the economic textbook theory of growth would indicate that it should be to everyone's advantage to encourage specialisation and free trade, the reality is not always so clear cut.

Theoretical Effects of Trade Integration

There are a number of reasons to expect that trade integration may result in increased trade flows, greater specialisation and hence efficiency. Adam Smith noted that the size of the market limited the degree of specialisation of labour, and therefore, an expansion of the marketplace, through the creation of a customs union or a single market, should encourage a greater division of labour and specialisation (Baldwin 1989: 260). Endogenous growth theory allows for economic growth to be positively influenced through increased competition arising from an expanded market, together with increasing returns to scale and scope due to increased specialisation of inputs, technology spillovers and the integration of more integrated supply chains (Baldwin 1989: 7–8, 36; Baldwin and Venables 1995). Moreover, trade policy might also have growth effects (Baldwin and Seghezza, 1996).

Yet, neo-classical growth theory suggests that trade integration can have only a minor (and short-term) impact upon economic development. The more competitive the economy, the smaller the impact of trade integration upon competition and prices (Allen et al. 1998: 447). The so-called Washington consensus that trade liberalisation will improve performance has been criticised for its supply side assumptions (Gnos and Rochon, 2005: 188) and for its record of generating poor macroeconomic outcomes—that is, low growth, repeated economic crises, a failure to produce full employment, secure current account balance and distributional inequalities (Arestis, 2005: 252; Davidson 2005: 209). Thus, when viewed in a broader context, the evidence that trade openness has predictable, robust and systematic impact upon economic growth rates is quite weak (Rodrik 2006: 975).

There have been a number of studies which have found a positive relationship between international trade and national income (Edwards 1998; Feyrer 2009; Frankel and Romer 1999; Rodriguez and Rodrik 2000). The inference is that increasing trade boosts national income. However, it is equally plausible that the direction of causality could run the other way—that is, richer countries tend to engage in more trade. In order to seek to identify causality, economic models have shifted from cross-sectional to time series data, and gravity models have gained in prominence, as will be seen later in this chapter.

Consideration of partial forms of trade liberalisation, through preferential trade agreements (PTAs), provides an additional form of complication because these agreements reduce one element of economic distortion from free trade, by reducing tariffs between participants, whilst simultaneously worsening another, by increasing the geographical tariff variance (Adams et al. 2003: 11). PTAs can enhance economic welfare for participating nations by enabling them to shift production from higher- to lower-cost members of the trade agreement ('trade creation'), but this is offset (in part or in full) if trade is shifted from lower-cost (more efficient) non-participants to higher-cost PTA members ('trade diversion'). This can be most clearly demonstrated in the case of customs unions like the EU, with a common external tariff (CET) facing non-participating nations; if this is lower than previous national tariff regimes, it should contribute towards trade creation, but if this tariff wall is higher, then it creates trade diversion (Viner 1950). The economic impact of trade integration will therefore depend upon the balance of these two effects (Europe Economics 2013: 11). Moreover, this also implies that PTAs are likely to have differential effects upon the various participants, with some gaining disproportionate benefits and others smaller benefits or even net economic costs (Panagariya 2000). The realisation of economies of scale has similarly ambiguous effects, as cost reduction gains achieved by firms located within participating nations could be offset by a trade suppression effect outside the PTA (Corden 1972).

The evidence concerning the net effect of PTAs is indeterminate. Certain studies find greater trade creating than diverting effects (Wonnacott and Lutz, 1989; DeRose 2007), whereas others, when controlling for factors such as size and relative income levels, found only weak evidence that distance and trade volumes point towards the significance of developing regional PTAs based upon a 'natural trading partner' hypothesis (Bhagwati and Panagariya 1999). Similarly, studies examining the trade performance of prominent PTAs, such as MERCOSUR and North American Free Trade Agreement (NAFTA), found significant trade diversion, which meant that net trade effects tended to be small, short-lived or insignificant (Gilbert et al. 2001; Krueger 1999; Soloaga and Winters 2001). One reason for finding few significant effects derived from regional PTAs might be that technological advances that have produced quite dramatic cost reductions in transport and communications (Carnoy et al. 1993; Rustin 2001: 18). Thus, there is no longer a particularly noticeable advantage to be gained from forming regional PTAs to realise lower transportation costs. Another potential reason might be that other factors such as shared culture and language, economic policy and institutional variables also have an effect in determining trade flows (Adams et al. 2003: 34–5).

The introduction of PTAs would, therefore, appear to represent a second best solution *for the global economy as a whole* when compared to multilateral trade liberalisation, of the type advanced by the World Trade Organization (WTO) (Adams et al. 2003: 22). However, this is made more difficult to achieve because the differential effects experienced by individual nations are likely to make some prefer a variety of PTA options under which they gain greater advantage.

TRENDS IN TRADE DEVELOPMENT

International trade has, over a long time period, grown faster than total global output. Since the mid-1800s, global population has increased by 6-fold, output 60-fold, but the value of international trade 140-fold (Maddison 2008; WTO 2013: 46). Between 1950 and the turn of the century, the value of exports rose from 5.5% of global GDP to 17.2% (WTO 2013: 47). Similarly, the 5.6% average growth in world trade, between 1985 and 2011, was almost twice as fast as the average 3.1% GDP growth rate during the same period (WTO 2013: 56). This rapid expansion in trade has been facilitated by reduced tariff and transport costs, together with a general catching-up effect arising from renewed trade activity in formerly more restricted economies in China and the former Soviet Union. Moreover, technological advances have in effect 'shrunk' the size of the globe as far as trade is concerned or, as Feyrer (2009: 31) explains the process, "technology changes the nature of distance over time".

UK Trade Development

The UK is the tenth largest goods exporter in the world (2.5% global market share) and is second only to the USA in the export of commercial services (6.5% of global service exports) (WTO, 2019: 100, 102). This represents a decline from the UK's former status as eighth largest goods exporter in the world in 1980 (WTO 2013: 60–3). Following global trends, trade has represented a rising share of UK national income (see Fig. 3.1). Interestingly, however, trade was comparatively more significant for the UK than for many other advanced economies prior to its accession to the EU than subsequently.

UK trade with the EU has grown during the period of its membership, with part of this increase due to the expansion resulting from an increase in the number of member states. Correcting for the 'Rotterdam effect',[1] trade with the EU peaked at around 60% of total UK trade in the early 1990s, before declining to 49% in 2018 (ONS 2019: 96–9, The Pink Book, Table 9.1). In terms of UK exports, the EU single internal market (SIM) purchases 45.3%, whereas the EU supplies 52.6% of UK imports (ONS 2019: 96–9, *The Pink Book*, Table 9.1). Excluding the effect of EU expansion, trade with the original EU(8) member states rose from around

---

[1] Rotterdam's position as a major shipping hub complicates data because UK exports destined for India may first be shipped to Rotterdam and is recorded as trade with the Netherlands rather than the ultimate destination, whilst oil imports from the Middle East may be similarly shipped via Rotterdam and be recorded as an EU import. The degree of distortion is uncertain; however, the ONS adopts what it terms as a "realistic assumption" that half of all UK trade with the Netherlands masks non-EU origination (for imports) or destination (for exports) (Webb et al. 2015: 7–8).

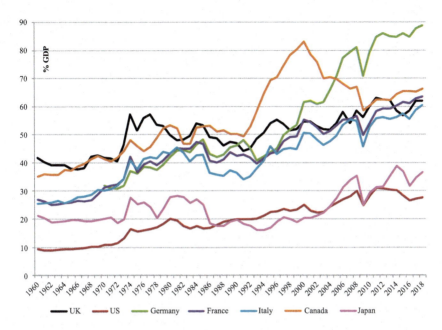

Fig. 3.1 Total trade relative to GDP in selected countries, 1960–2019. Source: World Bank (2020)

28% in 1973 to a peak of almost 50% around the turn of the century, before falling back again to around 40% in 2018 if using OECD (2020) figures or 38.1% if relying upon ONS measurements[2] (see Fig. 3.2).

Deficit

The UK runs a significant trade deficit with the rest of the EU, which peaked at 4.55% of UK GDP in 2015 (IMF 2016), before declining slightly to 3.1% in 2018 (ONS 2019: 5). It runs a trade deficit with the majority of EU member states except for Ireland, Cyprus, Greece, Malta and Estonia; in all cases except Ireland, this surplus is marginal (see Fig. 3.3). For a number of member states, this trade surplus with the UK exceeds 1% of their national incomes—that is, the Netherlands, Poland,

[2] https://researchbriefings.parliament.uk/ResearchBriefing/Summary/CBP-7851#fullreport.

Fig. 3.2 The share of UK trade with the EU(8), measured as % of total UK trade, 1973–2018. Source: OECD (2020). Notes: EU(8) economies comprise the eight EU member states of 1973 apart from the UK, namely Belgium, the Netherlands, Luxembourg, France, Italy, Germany, Ireland and Denmark. Data from 2018 is the most recently available

Czech Republic, Belgium, Hungary, Latvia, Lithuania and Slovakia (Irwin 2015: 11). Whilst for the EU(28) as a whole, the EU's trade surplus with the UK is equivalent to around 0.6% of their GDP per annum (Irwin 2015: 11). Nevertheless, it remains the case that most of the UK's trade deficit with the EU arises from the original EU(6) member states. Thus, the UK's trading weakness is not a recent product of newer member states undercutting UK goods through a lower cost base, but rather an entrenched feature associated with the UK's membership of the EU. Long-term participation in economic integration has resulted in a widening of the UK's trade deficit over time.

Largely because of this trade deficit with the EU, the UK's total trade deficit for 2018 was 1.8% of GDP (ONS 2019: 6). Taking into consideration investment incomes and transfer payments, alongside trade in goods and services, the UK's current account deficit stood at 4.3% of UK GDP in 2018, which was a small decline from its previous record level of 5.2% UK GDP in 2016 (ONS 2019: 3). This is the largest current account deficit amongst G7 economies (ONS 2019: 4).

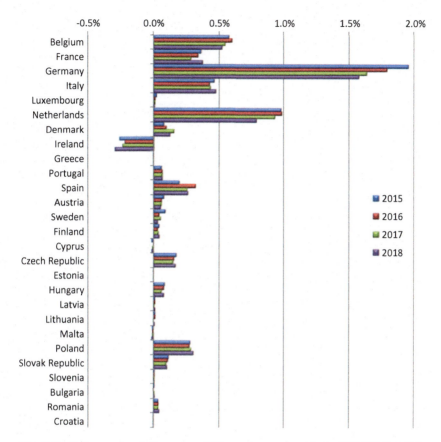

Fig. 3.3 Balance of trade for various EU member states with the UK, 2015–2018, expressed as % of UK GDP. Source: IMF (2020). Note: A positive balance of trade for the EU member state signifies a trade deficit for the UK

In contrast to its trade deficit with the EU, the UK runs a trade surplus equivalent to 1.3% of UK GDP with the rest of the world. It runs a significant trade surplus with NAFTA economies (i.e. the USA, Canada and Mexico) and a smaller but still significant surplus with Australasia and Oceania (see Fig. 3.4). Of the 67 nations with which the UK has a trade surplus, the 10 largest are the USA, Ireland, Switzerland, Australia, South

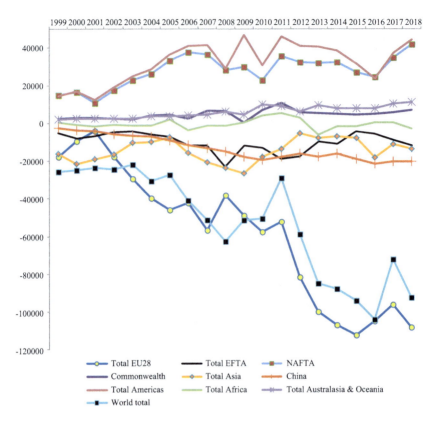

Fig. 3.4 UK current account balance with trade blocs and selected countries, 1999–2018, in £m. Note: The Commonwealth includes here the following countries: India, Canada, South Africa and Australia. Source: ONS (2019)

Korea, the UAE, Singapore, Guernsey, Saudi Arabia and Gibraltar.[3] Those countries with whom the UK currently runs its largest trade deficits are all EU or European Economic Area (EEA) member states, with the exception of China (the largest single deficit) and India (tenth largest).

Trade deficits are a sign that the economy is living beyond its means—purchasing more than it is selling. If an individual did the same, they

---

[3] https://assets.publishing.service.gov.uk/government/uploads/system/uploads/attachment_data/file/836787/190924_UK_trade_in_numbers_full_web_version_final.pdf.

would either be forced to use savings to cover the gap between income and expenditure or become indebted. For countries, it is a similar effect, albeit that there are more channels available to finance the trade deficit. The UK has generally relied upon net inflows of FDI to perform this function. Greenfield FDI creates additional capacity and is generally viewed as having positive impact upon the host economy, whereas the purchasing of formerly UK-owned businesses has a more mixed effect. Similarly, portfolio investment, although temporarily enhancing inward flows of capital, more often worsens the balance of payments position and hence makes it more difficult to finance the trade deficit (World Data Bank 2016).

Trade deficits, if uncorrected, can have a direct impact upon the growth potential of the real economy. They have an immediate effect of reducing aggregate demand and thereby weakening economic performance. The latest figures for the UK's global trade deficit are approximately equivalent to 2.4% of its GDP.[4] Hence, the UK has 2.4% less national product than it would otherwise have done had trade balance been achieved. If combined with a low-income elasticity for UK exports, however, this effect can be quite pronounced and of longer duration, weakening the growth potential of the country. This constrained growth theory will be discussed in more detail in Chap. 7.

The EU—A Declining Market for UK Trade

A second trend, which can be distinguished from trade data, concerns the fact that the EU is a declining market for UK exporters and importers. This trend can be observed in Fig. 3.2. Moreover, Oxford Economics suggested that, even in the absence of Brexit, the EU would be likely to purchase a declining share of UK exports in the future—forecast to decline to 37% of UK exports by 2035 and 30% by 2050 (Slater 2016). Part of this reason could be due to continued after-effects of the Eurozone crisis (Springford and Tilford 2014: 7), and the damaging policy response implemented by the leading EU nations (Baimbridge et al. 2012). Alternatively, it could reflect the rising share of trade currently being undertaken with emerging and developing nations and because they are forecast to provide the majority of global growth in the medium term (CBI 2013: 9).

[4] https://www.ons.gov.uk/economy/nationalaccounts/balanceofpayments/bulletins/uktrade/august2019#the-total-trade-deficit-widened-in-the-12-months-to-august-2019.

Despite this relative decline, EU member states are likely to remain amongst the UK's largest export markets in the medium term (see Fig. 3.5), as the realisation of new trade links with areas of faster growing markets is not an instantaneous process (Springford and Tilford 2014: 3; HMG 2018: 21). Trade with the BRIC (Brazil, Russia, China and India) economies may prove to be of considerable value for UK exports in the medium term, but these markets have not been successfully penetrated to date, and consequently, the potential to expand trade in NAFTA and Australasia might be of more immediate significance in the short run.

EUROPEAN TRADE INTEGRATION

A fundamental objective of the 1957 Treaty of Rome concerned the promotion of European economic integration. This was pursued initially through the creation of a customs union in 1968 and more latterly through

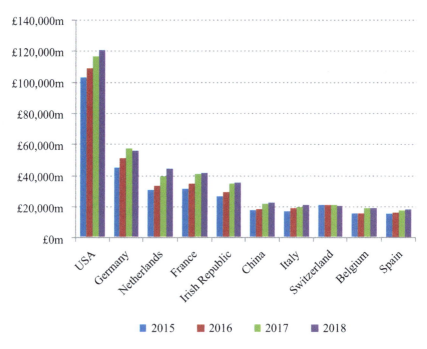

Fig. 3.5 The UK's top ten export markets in the world in 2018 (£m). Source: ONS (2019)

the creation of the SIM in 1993 (Europe Economics 2013:9; HMG 2013: 16, 22, 25–6). Whereas the former focused upon removing tariff barriers to trade in goods between EU member states and erecting a CET against the rest of the world, the latter sought to create a more integrated market, whilst strengthening competition policy and extending EU competence to areas of research and development, social and environmental policy.

A fundamental aspect of this approach was outlined in Article 7A, which necessitated the abolition of restrictions upon the free movement of people and capital (inputs), in addition to goods and services (outputs), known more popularly as the 'four freedoms' (EC 1996: 15; Europe Economics 2013) (see Fig. 3.6). These principles were more recently formalised in Article 3 of the Treaty on the EU and Articles 28–66 of the Treaty on the Functioning of the EU (TFEU) (Bank of England 2015:

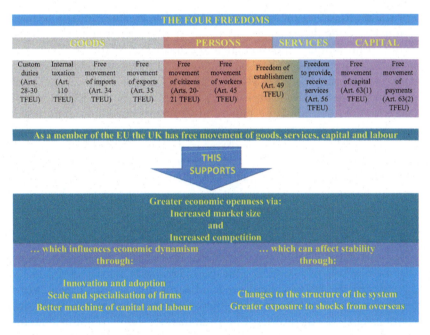

Fig. 3.6 The four freedoms according to the Treaty of Rome—overview and theoretical means of achieving dynamic effects. Notes: TFEU stands for Treaty on the Functioning of the European Union (2007); Art(s). stands for Article(s). Source: Authors' compilation of EU information based on material developed by the Bank of England (2015: 11)

17). The freedom of movement of economically active EU nationals was included in the Treaty of Rome, but this principle was extended through the creation of European citizenship via the Maastricht Treaty. Article 45 of the TFEU includes the right to move and reside freely within the territory of the EU member states without discrimination (HMG 2013: 24). Articles 63–66 of the TFEU further provide for the free movement of capital between EU member states and also between EU member states and outside nations, subject to certain restrictions intended to protect national tax systems, outlaw transactions related to criminal or terrorist activity, and where temporary capital controls might be required to protect the single currency (HMG 2013: 26; Bank of England 2015: 20).

Empirical Studies—Initial Impact of EU Membership

For the six founding members of the EU, trade creation appears to have dominated trade diversion (Eicher et al., 2012; Allen et al. 1998; Magee 2008). One estimate indicated that the formation of the EU customs union may have raised intra-EU trade by 20%, whilst trade diversion amounted to only around 3.8% (Badinger and Breuss 2011: 290). This is perhaps not particularly surprising, as the CET set by the EU(6) was in line with rates previously pertaining in Germany and France, and lower than that of Italy, albeit higher than prior rates in the three Benelux nations. Therefore, the creation of free trade between the EU(6) member states would be likely to create additional trade, whilst the common tariff they employed was not sufficiently higher than previous rates to cause trade to be diverted to less efficient producers within this trade barrier.

The success of the establishment of the initial EU customs union, for its six founder member nations, led many commentators to anticipate that UK accession to the EU would result in 'dynamic gains', arising from the more intensive competition and potential for realising economies of scale that membership of a larger European market would deliver (HMG 1970: 26). Indeed, the 1970 White Paper *Britain and the European Communities* predicted that a combination of these dynamic factors, together with membership of a fast-growing European market, should result in a significant improvement to the UK's balance of payments (HMG 1970: 37).

Unfortunately, the UK's accession to the EU did not deliver such positive results. For example, when the UK joined the EU, the CET stood at an average of 17% (Badinger 2005: 50), which meant an increase in the UK's external tariff barrier. The result was a dramatic reorientation of UK trade towards other EU member states, shifting from around 20% to 40% within less than two decades from accession (Gasiorek et al. 2002: 425–6). Contemporaneous studies indicated significant trade diversion and consequently only negligible net trade benefits derived from the early years of EU membership. HM Treasury's own calculations would suggest that whilst the initial benefit derived from EU membership for most EU nations was an increase in inter-EU trade of around 38%, this was only 7% for the UK and, moreover, accession diverted trade from non-member states by 4% (Portes 2013: F5-6). Thus, the net benefit was only a mere 3% increase in trade. Given the Treasury's estimate that a 1% increase in trade share of GDP leads to an increase in growth of around 0.2%, then this would suggest that the trade effects arising from the UK's accession to the EU were likely to have been in the region of only 0.6% of UK GDP. Furthermore, if the loss of previous tariff revenue is included in the calculation, then accession to the EU may have had a negative impact on the UK economy (Miller and Spencer 1977: 82–5, 90).

UK accession produced a net 0.05% boost to EU(6) GDP per annum, due to the expansion of exports sold within the UK market (Miller and Spencer 1977: 90). The resultant increase in UK import penetration combined with a contraction in UK exports to the global market, due to the imposition of the CET (CEPG 1979: 31–2). Hence, the UK's comparative trade balance deteriorated (Winters 1985: 352). This had been predicted in advance of membership and should, therefore, not have come as too much of a surprise to the government of the time (HMG 1970: 42; Wall, 2012: 350). Moreover, the combination of the CET, alongside the incorporation of the Common Agricultural Policy (CAP), resulted in a 20% increase in food prices in the UK, which in turn caused a 0.67% averse shift in the terms of trade (Miller and Spencer 1977:77; CEPG 1979; Fetherston et al., 1979: 399).

The macroeconomic impact upon the UK economy was partially obscured by the 1974 global recession. However, the impact may be inferred by the fact that the loss of output in the UK was more pronounced than in other developed nations (CEPG 1979: 32). One estimate suggests that by 1977, net UK exports were around £2bn lower than would have been expected on the basis of trends prior to EU membership (Fetherston et al., 1979: 405). Moreover, this negative trade impact has never been corrected, and the UK has suffered an almost continuous trade deficit with the EU from the point of accession to the present period.[5] This has imposed a depressing effect on the UK economy (CEPG 1979: 28; Fetherston et al., 1979: 400). High net fiscal transfers to the EU were calculated to have depressed UK production by an additional 1–2% compared to a steady-state position, with unemployment 100,000–200,000 higher, inflation 2–3% higher and national income 2–3.5% lower than necessary (CEPG 1979: 28–9). Taking into account the deterioration in the UK balance of payments and the constraint imposed upon economic growth, together with the drain imposed by fiscal transfers to the EU budget and the cost of the CAP, one estimate has suggested that UK national income was fully 15% lower in 1977/1978 than it would have been had the UK not joined the EU (Fetherston et al., 1979: 405–6). Even should part of this analysis be flawed, it would seem reasonable to conclude that the initial shock, resulting from the UK joining the EU, had a negative impact upon the UK economy.

Empirical Studies—Medium-Term Impact of EU Membership

There have been a number of studies which have sought to estimate the impact of EU membership and the introduction of the SIM for its member states. These typically comprise a combination of static and dynamic gains. The former are more immediate and derive primarily from the removal of barriers to trade, whereas the latter are more medium or long term and may arise from the impact of competition, the realisation of economies of scale and restructuring of markets. Static effects are likely to be smaller than dynamic effects, but are more certain to calculate, as the latter depend upon longer-term theoretical estimations which may or may not come to pass.

Prior to the establishment of the SIM, the European Commission produced the Cecchini Report, which predicted economic benefits pertaining to the creation of the SIM to be in the region of 4¼% to 6½% of EU GDP (Cecchini et al. 1988). This report suggested that benefits derived from further reductions in trade barriers were likely to be minor, perhaps between 0.2% and 0.3% of EU GDP, which is interesting given the prominence provided to the potential of this type of dynamic gains included in the CEP-LSE analysis discussed in Chap. 1. Medium-term dynamic effects by contrast, such as enhancing competition and realising economies of

---

[5] This topic is explored in more detail in Chap. 7.

scale, were expected to provide the majority of forecast benefits (Emerson et al., 1988; HMG 2013: 63). A subsequent study, undertaken by Baldwin (1989: 249), suggested that these forecasts were likely to be too conservative, and by adding potential productivity gains, Baldwin claimed that economic effects were likely to be between 40% and 250% higher (HMG 2013: 65). Unfortunately, subsequent *ex post facto* (after the event) analyses found these predictions to be over-optimistic.

The European Commission commissioned further studies into the impact of the SIM. For example, Monti and Buchan (1996) estimated its introduction to have increased EU output by between 1.1% and 1.5% by 1994. A second study, completed on the tenth anniversary of the foundation of the SIM, concluded that real GDP would have been an average of between 0.8% and 2.1% lower across participant nations had this measure not been implemented. Another suggested further modest gains of 0.5% by 2022 (Roeger and Sekkat 2002). A more recent study calculated that the introduction of the SIM may have raised EU GDP by around 2.18% between 1992 and 2006, thereby reducing the aggregate price-cost mark-up by 9% and boosted total factor productivity by 0.5% (Ilzkovitz et al., 2007). These predictions were subsequently slightly reduced, when extending the period under examination to 2008, with the revised economic boost being calculated to be approximately 2.13% (HMG 2013: 68–70). Most of these effects were from static analysis, with the dynamic effects proving to be much weaker than anticipated. Harrison et al. (1994) produced a slightly higher estimated gain for the EU of approximately 2.6% of EU GDP, whilst Straathof et al. (2008) produced a slightly higher estimate of 3%.

If accurate, these effects should have resulted in demonstrable improvements in the growth record of EU member states when compared to reference nations such as the USA, yet this was not the case (Badinger and Breuss 2011: 296, 308). This either suggests that the study's conclusions were over-optimistic or else that other factors (perhaps the depressing effect of the single currency and supportive economic framework) predominated any such trade effect upon economic growth.

Assessing trade impact over a longer time period, 1956–1973, and utilising a counterfactual analysis, Bayoumi and Eichengreen (1997) estimated that the annualised impact of the formation of the EU customs union for the six founder members was around 3.2% over the period. Viewing the impact of trade integration over a longer, 50-year period since 1958, Boltho and Eichengreen (2008) estimated that the whole period of European integration, from the Treaty of Rome to the date of their study, had boosted EU GDP by perhaps 5%, although SIM effects were relatively small. Conducting a similar exercise over a similar times-cale, however, Straathof et al. (2008) estimated that European trade inte-gration had increased EU GDP by only between 2% and 3%.

Other studies have found that European integration has succeeded in reducing trade barriers to a level lower than for other equivalent trading blocs (De Sousa et al. 2012), whilst competitive pressures have increased (Europe Economics 2013) and average mark-up over costs in manufactur-ing have been reduced by around 32% by the end of the 1990s (Badinger 2007). However, not all findings in the various studies were unambigu-ously positive. For example, the establishment of the SIM was noted to have encouraged a spate of cross-border mergers and acquisitions, as the EU's global share of such deals rose from just under 10% in 1985 to 28.8% two years later (EC 1996). Yet, whilst stimulating the development of pan-national supply chains, this development was also found to reduce the domestic share of home markets by an average of 5.4% in the 15 sectors examined in the study, inferring depressed opportunities for domestic firms in their home markets (Allen et al. 1998: 453).

Gravity models can be used to estimate differences between predicted and actual trade patterns with other nations, whilst taking account of other factors such as their relative size, wealth and spatial location relative to their trading partner(s). As noted in Chap. 1, the importance of prox-imity can be over-estimated, as cultural, linguistic and historical ties are also significant factors, whilst technological advance and the falling cost of transportation, together with the growing significance of service sector exports, are also likely to detract from more simplistic versions of gravity modelling analysis.

Early gravity model analysis found, like the earlier *ex post* studies, only limited trade effects arising from European integration. Yet, this was later criticised as underestimating the true effects (Baier et al. 2008: 464, 493). The argument is a little technical as it relates to the inclusion of the GDP of trade partners skewing the results because these variables are too closely related (correlated), thereby creating what is known as a multicollinearity effect. If the GDP of all trading partners is omitted from the analysis, it does show a much higher rate of trade creation (Europe Economics 2013: 55–6). However, the fact that this 'solution' omits key predictive variables from the model, namely the affluence of each of the trading nations, would appear equally problematic for an analysis seeking to investigate factors which influence the development of trade, given that the wealth and growth of individual economies are certainly two such key factors. Nevertheless, later studies, using this revised approach, have suggested a much more significant effect, with one suggesting that that EU membership has enhanced goods trade by around 84%[6] since 1956 (Baier et al. 2008), whilst another estimated goods trade expanding by 36%, with a significantly larger 82% trade creation in services (Felbermayr et al. 2018a; Felbermayr et al. 2018b).

Turning from the impact of European integration on the whole of the EU and focusing upon the specific impact upon the UK economy, the evidence would suggest that European integration has produced considerably less benefit for the UK than for the majority of EU member states. For example, the Treasury estimated that the creation of the SIM increased inter-EU trade by 9% for the UK, resulting in the Treasury ready-reckoner predicting a benefit to UK GDP of around 1.8% of GDP (HM Treasury, 2005: 1–2). These conclusions are supported by evidence that the UK gained less than the EU average from the establishment of the SIM, as smaller economies recorded the largest gains, due to their proportionally greater exposure to trade as a share of their economy (Allen et al. 1998: 468; Deutsche Bank 2013: 5). Harrison et al. (1994: 23) produced similar findings, suggesting that the UK's benefit from the SIM was a lowly 0.8% of UK GDP, rising to 1.49% in the medium term as a result of dynamic effects, whereas comparable benefits to Belgium and the Netherlands were in excess of 6.39% and 7.73% of their national incomes, respectively.

Adopting a broader approach, which moves beyond a narrow focus upon trade integration to incorporate regulatory effects associated with the SIM and misallocation of resources resulting from the impact of the CAP, a study by Minford et al. (2005) estimated that UK GDP was between 2% and 3% *lower* than it might otherwise have been because of EU membership. There is some supportive evidence for this conclusion that can be drawn from work examining the trade diversion caused by the high tariff walls protecting agriculture within the EU. Indeed, Sapir

[6] It perhaps should be noted that this same study estimated that the expansion in trade ascribed to other FTAs enacted in more recent times was in the region of 64.5%, whilst the EEA produced a lesser but still creditable 52.5% boost to trade. Placed in this relative context, the study suggests that EU membership produced a slightly larger expansion in trade than FTA alternatives, but interestingly, that FTAs would appear to boost trade more than the closest form of economic integration with the EU outside full membership, namely joining the EEA.

(1992) found that this negative impact was larger than more positive trade creation effects created by the formation of the EU's customs union.

The SIM has not, therefore, produced the unambiguous positive economic benefits that its advocates predicted. Intra-EU trade effects have certainly occurred, although these were far lower for the UK than for the EU as a whole. Given the Treasury's ready-reckoner calculation, this would suggest that the UK has received a boost to GDP, over the period since the SIM was established, of perhaps 1.8% of GDP. This is a welcome boost, but hardly of the magnitude that would be disastrous for the UK economy were the UK to exit the SIM when it withdraws from the EU. In addition, it should be noted that the risks associated with trade diversion increase when the rest of the world is growing faster than the nations within the SIM, which has been the case over the past few decades (Europe Economies 2013: 71). Trade effects do not seem to have resulted in a reduction in unit costs in the UK, whilst the period since the creation of the SIM has coincided with a 0.4% fall in annual R&D expenditure (Europe Economics 2013: 62–6).

THE PREDICTED TRADE-RELATED IMPACT FROM BREXIT

The impact on trade, arising from Brexit, will depend upon the form of trade agreement that the UK is able to negotiate both with the EU and with other nations across the globe. Thus, the net effect will derive from a combination of protecting existing supply chains with firms located within other EU member states and expanding global trade networks. This will also determine whether Brexit leads to a retraction in UK trade and openness or allows a reorientation towards greater global trade patterns. The final chapter in this book discusses a number of the most prominent Brexit options in more detail. However, for the purposes of this chapter, it is useful to outline the likely effect of the UK failing to reach a PTA with the EU, within the negotiating timescale, and consequently having to revert to trading according to WTO rules. The possibility of this 'no deal' scenario has given rise to claims that the UK economy would 'fall off a cliff edge'—an opinion still widely held amongst sections of the business community and political establishment, even though the evidence for this proposition does not look as robust when subjected to more detailed examination (Whyman 2018).

Tariffs Under the 'WTO Option'

The WTO is the successor to the previous General Agreement on Tariffs and Trade, and it seeks to apply the principle of non-discrimination to international trade, such that one member does not treat another member less advantageously, with the exceptions of regional free trade agreements (FTAs) and customs unions such as the EU. Outside of these derogations, each nation should apply the same level of tariffs applied to its 'most favoured nation' (MFN) to all trading partners. This would preclude any punitive tariffs being imposed by a disgruntled EU, should withdrawal negotiations with the UK not proceed as it anticipates.

There has been a global trend towards falling tariff barriers over the past three decades (see Fig. 3.7) as multilateral trade liberalisation has succeeded in reducing average (mean) tariff rates significantly, with particularly large falls amongst developing and intermediate nations. For almost the entirety of this period, EU average tariffs have been below 5%, and for

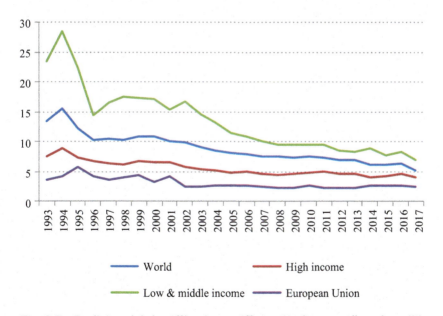

Fig. 3.7 Declining global tariff barriers: tariff rate, simple mean, all products (%), 1993–2017. Source: World Data Bank (2020)

the past decade and a half, approximating 3%. This is considerably lower than the CET value of 17% when the UK first joined the EU.

Headline tariff figures can be a little misleading because this does not take into account the relative importance, in terms of the value of goods sold. Accordingly, calculating tariff rates to take account of those sectors in which most trade value occurs, the 2017 EU *trade-weighted* average MFN tariff is estimated to lie between 2.25% and 3% for non-agricultural products (UNCTAD 2020; World Data Bank 2020; WTO 2019), with a higher 14.2% (simple average) for agricultural products (WTO 2019). Average overall rates are illustrated in Fig. 3.8 and are disaggregated by selected sectors in Fig. 3.9. As a result, the current average trade-weighted set of EU MFN tariffs facing UK exporters, if trading under WTO rules, is not substantial and it is significantly lower than the average rate of 17% in 1968 (Badinger 2005: 50). Hence, the cost for the UK of trading with the EU on the basis of WTO rules is substantially lower than it would have been five decades previously.

One reason for average trade-weighted tariffs on non-agricultural goods being so low is that in 2018, around 27.5% of these products were traded duty free (i.e. without tariffs applied), whilst a further 35.6%

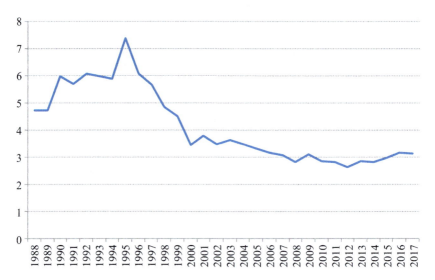

Fig. 3.8 EU tariff rate, most favoured nation, weighted, 1988–2017, (%). Source: World Data Bank (2020)

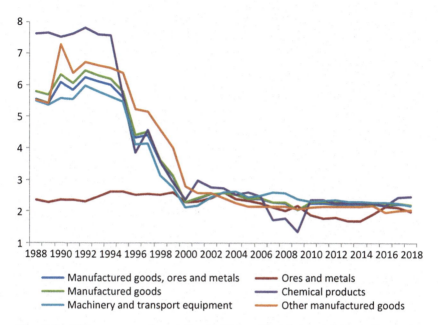

Fig. 3.9 EU average trade-weighted MFN tariffs (%) for trade with developed nations, 1988–2018. Source: UNCTAD (2020)

received a tariff below 5% and, indeed, 91.1% of all non-agricultural goods received tariffs below 10% (WTO 2019b). For agricultural produce, the level of tariffs levied was significantly higher, although, even here, fully 31.0% of all products were traded tariff free. These figures are comparable with tariffs the EU encounters when exporting to other nations, for example, to the USA and Switzerland, where trade-weighted tariffs applied to non-agricultural products were only 1.3% for the USA and 1.0% for Switzerland, and for agricultural products these were 2.1% for the USA to 2.7% for Switzerland (WTO 2019b).

To place this average level of tariffs into context, there has only been one year in which the Euro has not experienced more than a 5% fluctuation in its value from its average rate, since its establishment in 1999, yet this has seemingly had little noticeable impact upon the ability of UK companies to trade in the SIM (Business for Britain 2015: 54; Capital Economics 2016: 15). Moreover, it is the generally accepted conclusion, amongst economists, that tariff rates of 5% or below have relatively little impact upon trade (WTO 2015: 179). Thus, it is likely that, overall, the impact upon UK–EU trade is not likely to be particularly significant (Portes 2013: F5-6). This helps to explain why, for those studies which separate out tariff effects from other contributory factors, there is only a relatively minor negative effect upon trade flows and the economy as a whole.

Low average tariff levels do, however, obscure significant variance between sectors (Thompson and Harari 2013: 8; Booth et al. 2015: 27). This is illustrated in Fig. 3.10.[7] The highest tariffs (above 15%) are imposed upon dairy produce, sugars and confectionery, cereals, beverages and tobacco, and animal products. Fish, fruit, vegetables and plants receive lower but still significant tariff rates ranging between 10% and 15%. Agrifood exports will be hardest hit if no PTA is agreed with the EU, although it is estimated that this accounts for only around 5% of total UK exports to the SIM (Lawless and Morgenroth 2019: 197). Outside of the food and drink sector, other industries likely to incur a reasonably high tariff rate include clothing (11.5%), which represents around 1.4% of UK exports; textiles (6.6%), representing about 1.63% of UK exports; footwear (4.2%), representing around 0.27% of UK exports; and chemicals (4.5%), which represents around 12% of UK exports (Lawless and Morgenroth 2019: 197). The fact that tariff costs are concentrated upon a relatively small group of industries does make it easier for policy makers, should they so choose, to develop policy measures aimed at providing support for certain sectors compliant with WTO rules.

Low levels of MFN tariffs for finished products are not, however, the only concern for UK industry. The growth of global supply chains means that around half of trade in non-fuel products is in intermediate rather than finished goods. Indeed, if financial services are included in the calculation, the intermediate's share of exports increases (CBI 2013: 61), and hence, the imposition of tariffs upon these intermediate products, as well as the final exported product, can amplify the impact of any tariff regime. Fortunately, for most industries, the average MFN tariffs payable upon intermediate inputs are relatively low. WTO (2015: 179,184) data

[7] When countries join the WTO, they make certain commitments as to the maximum tariff they will charge for each commodity line. These are then described as final bound tariffs. If the country charges tariffs above this level, they can be taken to WTO dispute settlement. Tariffs can be set below this level as long as this is non-discriminatory, unless via a PTA (such as an FTA or customs union). For the UK, the MFN tariff rates will be the most relevant figure to consider.

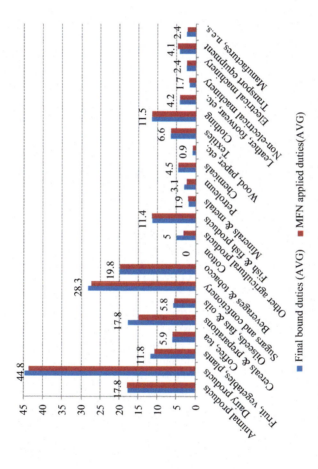

Fig. 3.10 Average EU final bound duties and MFN applied tariffs. Source: Authors' interpretation based on data from WTO (2019b)

suggests that average MFN duties paid upon intermediate inputs lie at or below 2% for the majority of export sectors—that is, petroleum, mining, office equipment, media, metals and metal products, medical equipment, chemicals and electrical machinery. Most other manufacturing, plastics and transport equipment received tariff rates of around 3%, with wood products and vehicles levied at a little over 4%, with textiles around 5%, and with only agriculture and food products receiving significant tariffs of around 7% and 9%, respectively.

One point that is worth noting, however, is that the UK has a current trade deficit with the EU in the majority of these markets, and therefore, were the UK to impose equivalent tariffs upon those goods imported from the EU, it would have a greater impact upon the sales of EU produce. This should reduce import penetration, given the higher prices for EU imports, and may result in a shift in focus to satisfying the demands of the domestic market for some of these producers. Higher tariff rates would have a negative impact upon consumers, who would pay higher prices for produce as a result of the imposition of tariffs, and it may impose upward pressure upon inflation.

Tariff barriers are not the only form of protectionism, and as they have declined, non-tariff barriers (NTBs) have become more prominent (De Sousa et al. 2012). NTBs can include the following (Deardorff and Stern 1985: 13–14; Europe Economics 2013: 12; UNCTAD, 2013: 14–15; Miller et al. 2016: 18–20; UNCTAD 2019):

i. Physical barriers and quantity controls—including exchange or customs controls, together with the imposition of quotas or voluntary export restraints on the importation of certain goods

ii. Technical barriers—including sanitary and phytosanitary measures, production and environmental standards, health and safety regulation, labelling, trademarks and advertising regulations

iii. Fiscal barriers—including differing rates of excise duties and VAT, alongside state aid (subsidies) for specific domestic industries

iv. Government trade policy measures—including public procurement restrictions, competition policy and the granting of exclusive franchises

v. Legal barriers—including licensing restrictions, poor protection of intellectual property rights and restrictions on foreign ownership, together with the prohibition of, or restrictions placed upon, access to raw materials

vi. Domestic content rules—typically requiring the local sourcing of a minimum percentage of a goods content or employment of a given proportion of the skilled workforce drawn from the domestic labour market

vii. Anti-dumping measures—preventing goods being exported at a price below production costs

Unlike tariffs, the direct measurement of NTBs is highly challenging, leading to reliance upon indirect estimates (Anderson and Van Wincoop 2004: 696). This increases the imprecision of macroeconomic modelling of trade impact upon the national economy, which necessarily seek to include NTBs as a key determinant (Fugazza and Maur 2008: 476; Kee et al. 2009: 172). Moreover, not all NTBs act in the same way and have quite distinct economic effects. Requirements to provide product information and labelling impact upon consumer demand directly, whilst conditions pertaining to certain forms of technology or product attributes will impact upon the supply side of the economy. Certain NTBs have a larger fixed cost effect, which may discourage market entry. Furthermore, whilst tariffs do not apply to trade in services, NTBs can have a direct impact, whether through technical rules or standards applied to service delivery, the non-recognition of qualifications or restrictions placed upon work visas to facilitate service delivery.

Due to the heterogeneous nature of NTBs, economic studies seeking to estimate their effect tend to adopt one of two approaches. The first is to try to estimate impact directly, by measuring the change to the frequency of trade following the introduction of an NTB (Henn and McDonald 2014). However, since direct measurement is not always possible, many studies use an indirect approach, estimating the effects of NTBs from observed market anomalies, such as deviations between domestic and world prices (Andriamananjara et al. 2004; Bradford 2003), or by identifying residuals from gravity models of trade (Deardorff and Stern, 1997). Clearly, differences between domestic and world prices might be due to factors other than NTBs, and similarly, not all gravity model residuals are necessarily evidence of NTB effects. Nevertheless, studies seek to calculate a tariff-equivalent cost effect imposed by the NTB under investigation.

The estimates produced by these studies vary considerably. One prominent study calculates that NTBs have, on average, only around 87% the impact of an equivalent tariff (Kee et al. 2009: 191). Another found that reducing tariffs by 10% would boost trade by 2%, whereas reducing NTBs by a similar magnitude would result in an improvement of trade flows of a slightly lower 1.7% (Hoekman and Nicita 2011: 2075). Other studies have found similar effects (Bouët et al. 2008; Bratt 2017). Differentiating between different types of NTBs, however, appears to produce noticeably different results. Thus, technical controls (i.e. standards, health and safety regulations, capital controls) and public procurement measures would appear to have a larger effect upon the goods targeted than direct import controls, whilst state aid and subsidies have the smallest impact upon trade (Kinzius et al. 2018: 18-19). Depending upon the type of NTB introduced, these studies found a trade reducing effect of between 4% and 12% (Kinzius et al. 2018: 26). Finally, one study which differentiated between NTB effects for specific groups of countries found that, in 2008, NTBs for the EU(10) raised trade costs by approximately 4.9% (Fugazza and Maur 2008: 483). This was less than the EU tariffs imposed at the time.

One difficulty in estimating NTBs concerns their variability. In certain sectors (e.g. mining, petroleum, manufacturing and paper), NTBs are virtually non-existent; in another (e.g. textiles, food, beverages and tobacco), NTBs apply to the majority of items traded. Hence, tariff-equivalent costs can be as high as 125% for sugar and 100.3% for dairy goods, even though the mean tariff-equivalent NTB barrier may be closer to 7.7% (Anderson and Van Wincoop 2004: 693, 703).

It is difficult to reach firm conclusions as to the likely NTBs that an independent UK will face should it prove to be impossible to negotiate a PTA with the EU and the UK reverts to trading according to WTO rules. Results drawn from a decade or more ago would suggest that NTBs are likely to have an effect upon trade somewhat less than the prevailing tariff rate. Since the EU average trade-weighted tariff lies between 2.3% and 3%, that would imply a total combined tariff and non-tariff cost for UK exporters seeking to sell into the EU SIM of perhaps 4.3–5%. This estimate is lower than that produced by Fugazza and Maur (2008) which, when added to EU tariff rates, would produce a combined tariff and non-tariff rate of between 7% and 8%, whilst the insights produced by Kinzius et al. (2018) would suggest that if certain types of NTBs were preferred over others, this combined NTB-related increase in costs for UK exporters could be higher.

The Bank of England (2018: 16) calculated its own estimates relating to EU NTBs which, if accurate, suggests that these have grown in more recent years and are approximately three times the level of trade-weighted tariffs. Interestingly, later in the same report, difficulties in quantifying the likely impact of NTBs are acknowledged, and it is conceded that NTBs may indeed impose costs either similar to, or double, tariff effects (Bank of England 2018: 17). This is a wide range of predicted effects to be advanced by a single report. However, this would suggest that NTBs might impose additional costs upon UK exports within the SIM, under a WTO option, of between 2.25% and 9%, giving rise to total trade costs of between 4.5% and 12%. It is perhaps worth noting that even the more inflated of these estimates are still lower than the competitive gain enjoyed by UK exporters following the exchange rate depreciation.

Economic Models—Trade Predictions

The reason for dedicating so much of this chapter to outlining evidence relating to the past impact of different phases of European integration upon international trade is because many of the economic studies seeking to forecast the impact of Brexit hypothesise that it involves a winding-back of this process. Thus, if the advent of the EU customs union increased intra-EU trade in the UK by 7%, or 3% after trade diversion effects are included, and the SIM by a further 9%, then were Brexit to culminate in the UK withdrawing from the SIM and customs union in their entirety, then this may reverse the previous process and result in a decrease in intra-EU trade of around 12%.

This simplistic conclusion is, of course, dependent upon the assumption of a symmetric relationship—that is, that exiting the EU is an exact mirror image of entry—which is unlikely (Portes 2013: F5-6). Yet, it is the simplest starting point when seeking to predict possible trade impact. Using the Treasury's ready-reckoner, that a 1% change in trade leads to an approximate 0.2% change in GDP, then an assumption of a simple reversal of former European integration effects would be expected to result in a 2.4% drop in UK GDP over time. This conclusion is, of course, rather simplistic. It ignores the potential for trade expansion for an independent UK, free to negotiate its own trade deals with the rest of the world. It also ignores the fact that trade barriers were much higher (17%) when the UK joined the EU than now prevail (2.3–3%), and therefore, the benefit of accession would be much larger than the cost of leaving.

Other economics studies have adopted a variety of approaches to estimate trade effects arising from a variety of different Brexit scenarios. These have variously included 'soft' versions of Brexit, primarily EEA or customs union options, to 'harder' forms of Brexit, such as FTAs and trading according to WTO rules. In the former, greater access to the SIM would be gained through acceptance of the freedom of movement of labour and/or acceptance of the continuing dominance of EU rules on goods standards, competition and industrial policy. For FTA or WTO options, neither of these would apply, but the trade-off would be less integration to the SIM. *Ceteris paribus*, there would be an expectation that a closer economic relationship with the EU would result in smaller reductions in UK-EU trade, but smaller potential future trade gains from the reorientation of trade focus to the rest of the world, whereas a less integrated (more independent) economic relationship would result in smaller future trade with the EU but larger trade with non-EU nations. The net trade effect arising from Brexit would therefore depend upon which effect proved to be larger—the loss of trade arising through less integration with the EU, set against potential future trade gains achieved through PTAs with non-EU countries and the refocusing of UK exports upon more rapidly growing areas of the world economy.

A number of the most prominent examples of these studies were outlined in Chap. 1, along with a critique of their methodological underpinnings. Not all of these studies disaggregate their predicted effects so that trade effects can be distinguished from general economic impact. One feature of the earlier examples of Brexit studies is the lack of consideration of potential future trade with the rest of the world. In effect, they only really considered the debit side of the trade ledger. Accordingly, the results produced emphasised the loss of trade associated with Brexit. In addition, many of these studies subsequently sought to associate this finding with a reduction in the openness of the UK economy, and thereby make a link to dynamic losses arising from poorer productivity growth.

The CEP-LSE set of studies is a good example of this process, where initial estimate of negative trade effects amount to barely 1.07% of UK GDP even assuming the imposition of tariffs and NTBs with future trade occurring under WTO rules (Ottaviano et al. 2014b: 8; Dhingra et al., 2014: 5; Dhingra et al. 2015: 17; Dhingra et al. 2016: 5). This static impact was further inflated due to rather unlikely assumptions of future reductions in NTBs in the EU, from which an independent UK would no longer benefit—the effect being to triple the initial static trade impact. Moreover, dynamic assumptions related to productivity had the effect of further tripling the predicted trade-related impact of Brexit (Ottaviano et al. 2014a: 4). Gasiorek et al. (2002: 438–442) produce a similar set of results, predicting relatively modest initial (static) trade effects arising from Brexit, but larger (although still relatively moderate) dynamic effects, particularly focused upon manufacturing value-added. Other studies suggested that Brexit trade effects might result in relatively modest losses to UK GDP, of perhaps 0.5% or 1.2% GDP if an FTA was negotiated with the EU, compared to between 1.77% and 2% if trade occurs under WTO rules (CEPR 2013; PwC 2016: 9), or alternatively 1.2%.

A different method, adopted by economics research teams, involves the use of gravity models to predict changes in future trade flows due to alterations in trade costs between nations. Trade patterns are hypothesised to be significantly affected by the wealth of a nation and its geographical setting in relation to countries with which it wishes to trade. Increased trade costs, due to tariffs or NTBs, with EU member states who are both relatively wealthy and located geographically close to the UK, can thereby have profound effects upon trade flows.

The HM Treasury (2016: 129) study, for example, predicted an almost instantaneous decline in UK trade with the EU of perhaps 45–50%. This seems to be most unlikely, even if trading under WTO rules, with trade-weighted tariffs averaging around 2.3–3%, and NTBs not likely to be more than twice this magnitude. A later follow-up study, used gravity modelling techniques to estimate the likely NTBs that UK exporters would experience when selling into the EU SIM, suggested that NTBs would impose more than three times the cost upon exporters as tariffs levied by the EU under the WTO option, and increase export costs by 8% even under an FTA (HMG 2018: 36). Once again, this seems rather high—the normal expectation is for NTBs to be approximately twice the magnitude of tariff barriers. Nevertheless, directly as a result of these NTB estimates, it was predicted that trading according to WTO rules would reduce UK GDP by 7.7% due to trade costs alone or 4.9% if an FTA was negotiated with the EU (HMG, 2018: 7). The second Treasury report is consistent, therefore, in predicting significantly higher trade-related Brexit costs to other comparable studies.

A second set of studies, whilst continuing to reply upon gravity modelling, 'borrowed' results from a paper by Baier et al. (2008: 485–6), whose focus was upon the possible boost to trade arising from different forms of trade agreement between different nations across the globe. Their findings suggested that EU membership produced the largest trade effect, followed by other types of agreement—that is, European Free Trade Association, EEA and a hybrid average formed of other unspecified PTAs. The results were acknowledged to be larger than previous studies, but this was explained, not altogether successfully, by reference to improvements in gravity modelling techniques. Nevertheless, these results were interpreted by later studies as predicting that withdrawal from the EU and reliance upon an FTA would result in trade losses of around 45%, whereas trading according to WTO rules would be likely to result in a decline in trade of between half and two-thirds (Sampson, 2017: 172; Hantzsche et al., 2018: 13–14).

Other studies produced quite different predicted trade effects. The OECD (2016: 19–20) suggested that UK exports would fall by only around 8.4% following Brexit if the UK relied upon WTO MFN trade rules, and 6.4% if it negotiated an FTA with the EU. Its forecast for a 5% negative effect upon UK GDP arises partly because the OECD assumed that no FTA could be negotiated within the Brexit timescale, but primarily due to assumptions of an almost halving of inward FDI flows and dynamic (productivity) effect, rather than trade effects *per se*. Studies undertaken by the Institute for Economic Research (IFO) suggest that reductions in UK exports to the EU may be only 3.9% if a comprehensive FTA (similar to the agreement between the EU and South Korea) was introduced and 12.1% if trade occurred under WTO rules (Felbermayr et al., 2017, Felbermayr et al. 2018a, Felbermayr et al. 2018b). A study undertaken by the IMF (2016: 58) concurred that an initial drop in FDI inward flows would have a negative effect upon the UK economy, but this study concluded that such effects would be temporary and easily reversible, whilst dynamic (productivity) effects were considered to be of only marginal importance. Trade effects, by contrast, were considered to produce the bulk of longer-term impact.

Studies by Business for Britain (2015: 53, 770–2, 793–9) and Minford et al. (2005, 2015: 9, 16–20) suggested much lower Brexit-related trade costs—the former predicting losses of around £4.8bn for agricultural and goods export sectors, derived from average EU tariffs of 4.3%, whereas the latter predicted an increase in trade if the UK pursued unilateral zero tariffs.

Adopting a slightly different approach, an ESRI study used a disaggregated analysis to identify potential trade effects in each sub-sector of the UK economy. Their findings were that UK exports to the EU could decline by 22% if trade occurred under WTO rules (Lawless and Morgenroth 2016: 17). This would imply a 10% reduction in total UK exports. However, sterling's exchange rate depreciation since 2016 would fully negate the impact of tariff costs for 90% of exported products (Lawless and Morgenroth 2016: 14–16; Gudgin et al., 2017: 8).

The Loss of Future Trade Benefits from EU Membership

One regular feature of studies examining the trade impact of Brexit concerns the EU's ability to realise additional future trade benefits, through either a further reduction in trade barriers more rapidly than that achieved by the world as a whole or the negotiation of PTAs with other nations on terms that are more favourable than those the UK as an independent nation could achieve. The inference is that not only would the UK suffer the consequences of lower current trade benefits as a result of Brexit, but that it would miss out on these future predicted benefits.

It is difficult to assess the viability of these hypothetical scenarios. It is worthy of note that, to date, the SIM has been established for a quarter of a century and has not been very successful in securing completely unfettered trade in services. This, however, can be taken as evidence of the probability of it achieving significant future success in this area to be rather slight or that, should it occur, there would be significant gains that could be realised and this would benefit the UK given its competitive advantage in financial and business services (Monteagudo et al. 2012; Portes 2013: F6). Moreover, as noted earlier in this chapter, the EU Commission's own Cecchini Report appeared to downplay the potential for future dynamic gains through NTB removal.

A number of studies have, nevertheless, included in their calculations potential future benefits that could arise from the EU's negotiation of two major new FTAs, namely the Transatlantic Trade and Investment Partnership (TTIP) with the USA and the Economic Partnership Agreement (EPA) with Japan. Noting historical precedence, these trade deals are predicted to lower consumer prices within the EU, through reducing or removing trade barriers on a range of goods and thereby increasing competitive pressures (Dhingra et al., 2014: 6; Dhingra et al. 2015: 18). The Commission's own analysis predicts that the TTIP would result in a significant increase in trade volumes between the EU and the USA, with a permanent boost to the EU economy of 0.5% of GDP and a similar 0.4% benefit to the USA (CEPR 2013; EC, 2013: 2, 6–7). This analysis has, however, been undermined by the vetoing of the TTIP by the US Trump administration. Consequently, whilst Brexit would mean that the UK does not benefit from any of these potential benefits, they are unlikely to prove to be as significant as presented in many of these studies, because of difficulties inherent in actually securing future intra-EU reductions in barriers and because the TTIP in particular seems moribund for the foreseeable future.

Focusing upon potential lost opportunities is, of course, only one side of the balance sheet, as independence from the EU would mean that the UK could negotiate its own FTAs or EPAs with other countries. This subject is dealt with in more detail in Chap. 9. However, it is reasonable to assume that the current close links between the UK and both the USA and Japan might facilitate future trade deals that should benefit all signatories. Certainly, the comments made by the previous US President appear to have been superseded by a more favourable attitude, announced by his predecessor and leading members of Congress, towards a US–UK FTA.[8]

There are, furthermore, a number of other uncertainties relating to the future development of the EU, which may impact upon the UK in the future. For example, the turbulence within the Eurozone continues as it struggles with the after-effects of the financial crisis[9] having only barely recovered to the level of economic activity recorded at the start of 2008 (HMG 2013: 52–3).

CONCLUSIONS

The evidence presented in this chapter would appear to indicate that economic integration and the negotiation of PTAs generally produce favourable results in terms of expanding trade and related economic welfare. The UK's membership of the EU has been associated with economic benefits, although these were less than those experienced by many other member states, due to factors such as trade diversion given the UK's more global (rather than regional) historical trade patterns. Given that one anticipated

[8] https://www.theguardian.com/politics/2016/apr/22/barack-obama-brexit-uk-back-of-queue-for-trade-talks; http://www.wsj.com/articles/a-new-american-deal-for-europe-1466974978?mod=wsj_review_&_outlook&cb=logged0.1996315843048233; http://www.politico.com/story/2016/06/brexit-us-britain-trade-deal-224776; http://www.telegraph.co.uk/news/2017/01/27/congress-pushes-donald-trump-form-bilateral-trade-deal-uk/
[9] https://www.theguardian.com/business/2016/sep/27/deutsche-bank-how-did-a-beast-of-the-banking-world-get-into-this-mess

effect of Brexit is likely to be a reduction in UK-EU trade, it is likely that this will result in a net cost for the UK. However, it is most unlikely that Brexit will result in a mirror image to the integration caused by the UK's accession to the EU in 1973. EU tariff barriers were set at an average rate of 17% at that point, compared to a trade-weighted MFN average of between 2.25% and 3% in 2020. Moreover, there is some evidence to suggest that trade linkages are highly persistent once they are established (McCallum, 1995; Anderson and Van Wincoop 2004), which would suggest that UK trade patterns with the EU might be fairly robust irrespective of any impact from Brexit. However, confusingly, there also appears to be evidence that suggests that once trade becomes interrupted for any reason, it may take a long time to recover (Beestermöller and Rauch, 2014), which might infer a fragility in trade relationships.

The future of trade with the EU depends upon the type of relationship agreed following the withdrawal process. Yet, only a few of those same studies contain a serious and rigorous attempt to assess the growth potential for future non-EU trade, preferring to reply on backward-looking gravity models to emphasise the significance of local trading partners. This is a pity, since 55% of UK exports already flow outside the EU, and this share was likely to increase whether or not the Brexit had occurred. To the extent that non-EU trade expands, it has the potential to compensate, in full or in part, for any loss of trade with the EU.

The significance of the CEP-LSE analysis is through its suggestion that the UK may experience only minor static costs if it proves possible to negotiate an FTA with the EU—a level of costs which have already been more than compensated for by the depreciation of sterling. Reliance upon WTO rules is predicted to have a more substantial cost, even though trade-weighted average MFN tariffs would be only between 2.3% and 3% (WTO 2015: 75; World Data Bank 2020). With the majority of those studies reviewed in this chapter suggesting that NTBs are likely to have at most a similar impact upon trade costs, this is likely to produce combined additional costs for UK exporters in the region of 4.3–6%. This would be unwelcome, but hardly the 'cliff-edge' scenario that some commentators have claimed.

Taking all of this into account, it would seem reasonable to conclude that UK withdrawal from the EU is likely to result in a short-term reduction in trade with EU member states, whilst trade expansion in the rest of the world is indeterminate given the reluctance of the current set of studies to assess this potential. Longer-term dynamic effects will depend upon the interplay of competitive and industrial policy effects that are not fully explored in the studies examined in this chapter. Consequently, given the low levels of MFN tariffs, even when combining with NTB estimated effects, it is quite possible that Capital Economics (2016: 2) are accurate in their summation that even should the UK fail to secure an FTA with the EU, and revert to trading under WTO rules, this would be "an inconvenience rather than a major barrier to trade". If, however, an FTA can be agreed between the two parties, any negative trade effects should be more modest.

References

Adams, R., Dee, P., Gali, J., & McGuire, G. (2003). The Trade and Investment Effects of Preferential Trading Arrangements: Old and New Evidence, *Productivity Commission Staff Working Paper*, Canberra. Retrieved December 11, 2019, from https://www.pc.gov.au/research/supporting/preferential-trade-agreements/tiepta.pdf.

Allen, C., Gasiorek, M., & Smith, A. (1998). The Competition Effects of the Single Market in Europe. *Economic Policy, 27*, 439–486.

Anderson, J. E., & Van Wincoop, E. (2004). Trade Costs. *Journal of Economic Literature, 42*(3), 170–192.

Andriamananjara, S., Dean, J. M., Feinberg, R., Ferrantino, M. J., Ludema, R., & Tsigas, M. (2004). *The Effects of Non-Tariff Measures on Prices, Trade, and Welfare: CGE Implementation of Policy-Based Price Comparisons*, United States International Trade Commission (USITC), Washington DC. Retrieved March 3, 2020, from https://www.usitc.gov/publications/332/ec200404a.pdf.

Arestis, P. (2005). Washington Consensus and Financial Liberalisation. *Journal of Post Keynesian Economics, 27*(2), 251–270.

Badinger, H. (2005). Growth Effects of Economic Integration: Evidence from the EU member states. *Review of World Economics / Weltwirtschaftliches Archiv, 141*(1), 50–78.

Badinger, H. (2007). Has the EU's Single Market Programme Fostered Competition? Testing for a Decrease in Mark-up Ratios in EU Industries. *Oxford Bulletin of Economics and Statistics, 69*(4), 497–519.

Badinger, H., & Breuss, F. (2011). The Quantitative Effects of European Post-War Economic Integration. In M. Jovanovic (Ed.), *International Handbook on the Economics of Integration* (pp. 285–315). Cheltenham: Edward Elgar.

Baier, S. L., Bergstrand, J. H., Egger, P., & McLaughlin, P. A. (2008). Do Economic Integration Agreements Actually Work? Issues in Understanding the Causes and Consequences of the Growth of Regionalism. *World Economy, 31*(4), 461–497.

Baimbridge, M., Burkitt, B., & Whyman, P. B. (2012). The Eurozone as a Flawed Currency Area. *Political Quarterly, 83*(1), 96–107.

Baldwin, R. E. (1989). *On The Growth Effects of 1992*, NBER Working Paper No. 3119, NBER, Cambridge MA. Available via: http://www.nber.org/papers/w3119.pdf.

Baldwin, R. E., & Venables, A. J. (1995). Regional Economic Integration. In G. Grossman & K. Rogoff (Eds.), *Handbook of International Economics* (Vol. III, pp. 1597–1644). Amsterdam: Elsevier.

Baldwin, R. E., & Seghezza, E. (1996). Testing for trade-induced investment-led growth (NBER Working Paper No. 5416). Available via: http://www.nber.org/papers/w5416.

Bank of England. (2015). *EU Membership and the Bank of England*, Bank of England, London. Available via: http://www.bankofengland.co.uk/publications/Documents/speeches/2015/euboe211015.pdf.

Bank of England. (2018). *EU Withdrawal Scenarios and Monetary and Financial Stability: A Response to the House of Commons Select Committee*, Bank of England, London. Retrieved February 18, 2020, from https://www.bankofengland.co.uk/-/media/boe/files/report/2018/eu-withdrawal-scenarios-and-monetary-and-financial-stability.pdf?la=en&hash=B5F6EDCDF90DCC10286FC0BC599D94CAB8735DFB.

Bayoumi, T., & Eichengreen, B. (1997). Is Regionalism Simply a Diversion? Evidence from the Evolution of the EC and EFTA. In T. Ito & A. O. Krueger (Eds.), *Regionalism vs. Multilateral Arrangements*. Chicago: University of Chicago.

Beestermöller, M., & Rauch, F. (2014). A Dissection of Trading Capital: Cultural Persistence of Trade in the Aftermath of the Fall of the Iron Curtain. FREIT [Forum for Research on Empirical International Trade] Working Papers, No. 697. Available via: http://www.freit.org/WorkingPapers/Papers/TradePatterns/FREIT697.pdf

Bernard, A. B., Jensen, J. B., Redding, S. J., & Schott, P. K. (2007). Firms in International Trade. *Journal of Economic Perspectives, 21*(3), 105–130.

Bhagwati, J., & Panagariya, A. (1999). Preferential Trading Areas and Multilateralism—Strangers, friends or foes? In J. Bhagwati, P. Krishna, & A. Panagariya (Eds.), *Trading Blocs: Alternative Approaches to Analyzing Preferential Trade Agreements* (pp. 33–100). Cambridge, MA; London: MIT Press.

Boltho, A., & Eichengreen, B. (2008). The Economic Impact of European Integration, CEPR Discussion Paper No. 6820. Available via: http://eml.berkeley.edu/~eichengr/econ_impact_euro_integ.pdf.

Booth, S., Howarth, C., Persson, M., Ruparel, R., & Swidlicki, P. (2015). *What If...?: The Consequences, Challenges and Opportunities Facing Britain Outside EU*, Open Europe Report 03/2015, London. Available via: http://openeurope.org.uk/intelligence/britain-and-the-eu/what-if-there-were-a-brexit/.

Bouët, A., Decreux, Y., Fontagn, E. L., Jean, S., & Laborde, D. (2008). Assessing Applied Protection Across the World. *Review of International Economics, 16*(5), 850–863.

Bradford, S. (2003). Paying the Price: Final Goods Protection in OECD Countries. *The Review of Economics and Statistics, 85*(1), 24–37.

Bratt, M. (2017). Estimating the Bilateral Impact of Non-Tariff Measures on Trade. *Review of International Economics, 25*(1), 1–25.

Business for Britain. (2015). *Change or Go: How Britain Would Gain Influence and Prosper Outside an Unreformed EU*, Business for Britain, London. Available via: https://forbritain.org/cogwholebook.pdf.

Capital Economics. (2016). *The Economics Impact of 'Brexit': A Paper Discussing the United Kingdom' Relationship with Europe and the Impact of 'Brexit' on the British Economy*, Woodford Investment Management LLP, Oxford. Available via: https://woodfordfunds.com/economic-impact-brexit-report/.

Carnoy, M., Castells, M., Cohen, S. S., & Cardosa, F.-H. (1993). *The New Global Economy in the Information Age*. University Park, PA: Pennsylvania State University Press.

CBI [Confederation of British Industry]. (2013). *Our Global Future: The Business Vision for a Reformed EU*, CBI, London. Available via: http://www.cbi.org.uk/media/2451423/our_global_future.pdf#page=1&zoom=auto,-119,842.

Cecchini, P., Catinat, M., & Jacquemin, A. (1988). *The European Challenge 1992: The Benefits of a Single Market, Prepared for the Commission of the European Communities*. Aldershot: Gower.

CEPG [Cambridge Economic Policy Group]. (1979). *Cambridge Economic Policy Review* No. 5, Gower Press, London. Available via: http://cpes.org.uk/om/cambridge-economic-policy-review-volume-5.

CEPR. (2013). *Trade and Investment Balance of Competence Review*, Department for Business Innovation and Skills, London. Available via: https://www.gov.uk/government/uploads/system/uploads/attachment_data/file/271784/bis-14-512-trade-and-investment-balance-of-competence-review-project-report.pdf.

Corden, M. (1972). Economies of Scale and Customs Union Theory. *Journal of Political Economy, 80*(3), 465–475.

Davidson, P. (2005). A Post Keynesian View of the Washington Consensus and How to Improve It. *Journal of Post Keynesian Economics, 27*(2), 207–230.

De Sousa, J., Mayer, T., & Zignago, S. (2012). Market Access in Global and Regional Trade. *Regional Science and Urban Economics, 42*(6): 1037-1052. Available via: http://econ.sciences-po.fr/sites/default/files/file/tmayer/MA_revisionRSUE_jul2012.pdf.

Deardorff, A. V., & Stern, R. M. (1985). *Methods of Measurement of Nontariff Barriers*, United Nations Conference on Trade and Development, UNCTAD/ST/MD/28, United Nations, Geneva. Retrieved March 3, 2020, from https://unctad.org/en/Docs/c1em27d2_en.pdf.

Deardorff, A. V., & Stern, R. M. (1997). Measurement of Non-Tariff Barriers. OECD Economics Department Working Paper No. 179.

DeRose, D. A. (2007). The Trade Effect of Preferential Arrangements: New Evidence from the Australian Productivity Commission, *Peterson Institute for International Economics Working Paper* 07-1, Washington DC. Retrieved December 12, 2019, from https://www.piie.com/sites/default/files/publications/wp/wp07-1.pdf.

Deutsche Bank. (2013). *The Single European Market—20 Years On*, Deutsche Bank, Frankfurt. Available via: https://www.dbresearch.com/PROD/DBR_INTERNET_EN-PROD/PROD0000000000322897/The+Single+Europea n+Market+20+years+on%3A+Achievements,+unfulfilled+expectations+%26+fu rther+potential.pdf.

Dhingra, S., Huang, H., Ottaviano, G., Pessoa, J.P., Sampson, T., & Van Reenen, J. (2016). The Costs and Benefits of Leaving the EU: Trade Effects, *CEP Discussion Paper* No. 1478, London School of Economics Centre for Economic Performance, London. Retrieved March 20, 2020, from http://cep.lse.ac.uk/pubs/download/dp1478.pdf.

Dhingra, S., Ottaviano, G., & Sampson, T. (2014). Should We Stay or Should We Go? The Economic Consequences of Leaving the EU, Centre for Economic Performance Election Analysis Discussion Paper, London. Available via: http://cep.lse.ac.uk/pubs/download/EA022.pdf.

Dhingra, S., Ottaviano, G., & Sampson, T. (2015). *Britain's Future in Europe*, LSE, London. Available via: http://www.sdhingra.com/brexitwriteup.pdf.

EC [European Commission]. (1996). Economic Evaluation of the Internal Market, *European Economy Reports and Studies*, No. 4, Office for Official Publications of the European Communities, Luxembourg. Available via: http://ec.europa.eu/archives/economy_finance/publications/archives/pdf/publication7875_en.pdf.

Edwards, S. (1998). Openness, Productivity and Growth: What Do We Really Know? *Economic Journal, 108*(447), 383–398.

Eicher, T., Henn, C., & Papageorgiou, C. (2012). Trade Creation and Diversion Revisited: Accounting for Model Uncertainty and Unobserved Bilateral Heterogeneity. *Journal of Applied Econometrics 27*(2), 296–321.

Emerson, M., Aujean, M., Catinat, M., Goybet, P., & Jacquemin, A. (1988). *The Economics of 1992*. Oxford: Oxford University Press. Available via: http://ec.europa.eu/economy_finance/publications/publication7412_en.pdf.

Europe Economics. (2013). *Optimal Integration in the Single Market: A Synoptic Review*, Department of Business Innovation and Skills, London. Available via: https://www.gov.uk/government/uploads/system/uploads/attachment_data/file/224579/bis-13-1058-europe-economics-optimal-integration-in-the-single-market-a-synoptic-review.pdf.

Felbermayr, G., Fuest, C., Gröschl, J., & Sthlker, D. (2017). Economic Effects of Brexit on the European Economy, EconPol Policy Report 04, IFO, Munich. Available via: https://www.ifo.de/DocDL/EconPol_Policy_ Report_04_2017_Brexit.pdf. Accessed 18 March 2020.

Felbermayr, G., Gröschl, J., & Heuiland, I. (2018a). Undoing Europe in a New Quantitative Trade Model, IFO Working paper 250, University of Munich. Retrieved March 18, 2020, from https://www.ifo.de/DocDL/wp-2018-250-felbermayr-etal-tarde-model.pdf.

Felbermayr, G., Gröschl, J., & Steininger, M. (2018b). *Brexit Through the Lens of New Quantitative Trade Theory*, CESifo. Available via: https:// editorialexpress.com/cgi-bin/conference/download.cgi?db_name= MWITSpring2018&paper_id=63 Fetherston et al., 1979.

Fetherston, M., Moore, B., & Rhodes, J. (1979). EEC Membership and UK Trade in Manufactures. *Cambridge Journal of Economics, 3*(4), 399–407.

Feyrer, J. (2009). Distance, Trade and Income: The 1967 to 1975 Closing of the Suez Canal as a Natural Experiment, *NBER Working Paper* 15557. Retrieved March 27, 2020, from https://www.nber.org/papers/w15557.pdf.

Frankel, J. A., & Romer, D. (1999). Does Trade Cause Growth? *American Economic Review, 89*(3), 379–399.

Fugazza, M., & Maur, J.-C. (2008). Non-Tariff Barriers in CGE Models: How Useful for Policy? *Journal of Policy Modelling, 30*(3), 475–490.

Gasiorek, M., Smith, A., & Venables, A. J. (2002). The Accession of the UK to the EC: A Welfare Analysis. *Journal of Common Market Studies, 40*(3), 425–447.

Gilbert, J., Scollay, R., & Bora, B. (2001). Assessing Regional Trading Arrangements in the Asia-Pacific. Policy Issues in International Trade and Commodities Study Series No. 15, UNCTAD, United Nations, Geneva. Retrieved December 13, 2019, from https://unctad.org/en/Docs/ itcdtab16_en.pdf.

Gnos, C., & Rochon, L.-P. (2005). What is Next for the Washington Consensus? *Journal of Post Keynesian Economics, 27*(2), 187–193.

Hantzsche, A., Kara, A., & Young, G. (2018). The Economic Effects of the Government's Proposed Brexit Deal, National Institute of Economic and Social research (NIESR), London. Available via: https://www.niesr.ac.uk/ sites/default/files/publications/NIESR%20Report%20Brexit%20-%20 2018-11-26.pdf. Accessed 17 December 2019.

Harrison, G., Rutherford, T., & Tarr, D. (1994). *Product Standards, Imperfect Competition, and Completion of the Market in the European Union*, World Bank Policy Research Working Paper No. 1293. Available via: https://www.gtap. agecon.purdue.edu/resources/download/3524.pdf HM Treasury, 2005.

Henn, C., & McDonald, B. (2014). Crisis Protectionism: The Observed Trade Impact. *IMF Economic Review, 62*(1), 77–118.

HM Treasury. (2005). EU Membership and Trade. Available via: https:// www.gov.uk/government/uploads/system/uploads/attachment_data/ file/220968/foi_eumembership_trade.pdf.

HM Treasury. (2016). *HM Treasury Analysis: The Long Term Economic Impact of EU Membership and the Alternatives*, Cm 9250, The Stationery Office, London. Available via: https://www.gov.uk/government/uploads/system/uploads/ attachment_data/file/517415/treasury_analysis_economic_impact_of_eu_ membership_web.pdf HM Treasury, 2005.

HMG [HM Government]. (1970). *White Paper, Britain and the European Communities: An Economic Assessment, Cmnd 4289*. London: HMSO.

HMG [HM Government]. (2013). *Review of the Balance of competences between the United Kingdom and the European Union—The Single Market*, The Stationery Office, London. Available via: https://www.gov.uk/government/ uploads/system/uploads/attachment_data/file/227069/2901084_ SingleMarket_acc.pdf.

HMG [HM Government]. (2018). *EU Exit: Long-Term Economic Analysis*, Cm 9742, HMSO, London. Available via: https://assets.publishing.service.gov.uk/ government/uploads/system/uploads/attachment_data/file/760484/28_ November_EU_Exit_-_Long-term_economic_analysis__1_.pdf.

Hoekman, B., & Nicita, A. (2011). Trade Policy, Trade Costs, and Developing Country Trade. *World Development, 39*(12), 2069–2079.

Ilzkovitz, F., Dierx, A., Kovacs, V., & Sousa, N. (2007). Steps Towards a Deeper Economic Integration: The Internal Market in the 21st Century - A Contribution to the Single Market Review, European Economy – Economic Papers No. 271. Brussels: European Commission. Available via: http://ec. europa.eu/economy_finance/publications/publication784_en.pdf.

IMF [International Monetary Fund]. (2016). *United Kingdom: IMF Country Report*, No. 16/169, IMF, Washington DC. Available via: https://www.imf. org/external/pubs/ft/scr/2016/cr16169.pdf.

IMF [International Monetary Fund]. (2020). Direction of Trade Statistics. For UK GDP: OECD statistics (2020). https://stats.oecd.org/Index. aspx?DatasetCode=SNA_TABLE1.

Irwin, G. (2015). *Brexit: The Impact on the UK and the EU*, Global Counsel, London. Available via: http://www.global-counsel.co.uk/system/files/publi- cations/Global_Counsel_Impact_of_Brexit_June_2015.pdf.

Kee, H. L., Nicita, A., & Olarreaga, M. (2009). Estimating Trade Restrictiveness Indices. *Economic Journal, 119*(534), 172–199.

Kinzius, L., Sandkamp, A-N., & Yalcin, E. (2018). Trade Protection and the Role of Non-Tariff Barriers, *CESifo Working Paper* 7419, Center for Economic Studies and Ifo Institute (CESifo), Munich. Retrieved March 3, 2020, from https://www.econstor.eu/bitstream/10419/198779/1/cesifo1_ wp7419.pdf.

Krueger, A. (1999). Trade Creation and Trade Diversion Under NAFTA, NBER Working Paper No. 7429, National Bureau of Economic Research, Cambridge, MA. Retrieved December 13, 2019, from https://www.nber.org/papers/w7429.pdf.

Lawless, M., & Morgenroth, E. L. W. (2016). The Product and Sector Level Impact of a Hard Brexit Across the EU, *ESRI Working Paper* No 550. Retrieved March 18, 2020, from https://www.esri.ie/publications/the-product-and-sector-level-impact-of-a-hard-brexit-across-the-eu.

Lawless, M., & Morgenroth, L. W. (2019). The Product and Sector Level Impact of a Hard Brexit Across the EU. *Contemporary Social Science, 14*(2), 189–207. https://doi.org/10.1080/21582041.2018.1558276.

Maddison, A. (2008). The West and the Rest in the World Economy: 1000–2030. *World Economy, 9*(4), 75–100.

Magee, C. S. (2008). New Measures of Trade Creation and Trade Diversion. *Journal of International Economics, 75*(2), 349–362.

McCallum, J. (1995). National Borders Matter: Canada-US Regional Trade Patterns. *American Economic Review, 85*(3), 615–662.

McCombie, J., & Thirwall, A. P. (1994). *Economic Growth and the Balance of Payment Constraint.* London: Macmillan.

Miller, M., & Spencer, J. (1977). The Static Economic Effects of the UK Joining the EEC: A General Equilibrium Approach. *Review of Economic Studies, 44*(1), 71–93.

Miller, V., Lang, A., Smith, B., Webb, D., Harari, D., Keep, M., & Bowers, P. (2016). Exiting the EU: UK Reform Proposals, Legal Impact and Alternatives to Membership, *House of Commons Library Briefing Paper* No. HC 07214. Available via: http://researchbriefings.parliament.uk/ResearchBriefing/Summary/CBP-7214#fullreport.

Minford, P., Mahambare, V., & Nowell, E. (2005). *Should Britain Leave the EU? An Economic Analysis of a Troubled Relationship.* Cheltenham: IEA and Edward Elgar.

Minford, P., Mahambare, V., & Nowell, E. (2015). *Should Britain Leave the EU? An Economic Analysis of a Troubled Relationship.* Cheltenham: IEA and Edward Elgar.

Monteagudo, J., Rutkowski, A., & Lorenzani, D. (2012). *The Economic Impact of the Services Directive—A First Assessment Following Implementation,* European Commission, European Economy—DG Economic and Financial Affairs, Economic Paper No. 456. Available via: http://ec.europa.eu/economy_finance/publications/economic_paper/2012/pdf/ecp_456_en.pdf.

Monti, M., & Buchan, D. (1996). *The Single Market and Tomorrow's Europe—A Progress Report from the European Commission,* Office of the Official Publications of the European Communities, Luxembourg and Kogan Page, London. Available via: http://aei.pitt.edu/42345/1/A5494.pdf.

Myrdal, G. (1957). *Economic Theory and Underdeveloped Regions.* London: Duckworth.

OECD. (2016). The Economic Consequences of Brexit: A taxing decision, OECD Economic Policy Paper, No. 16. Available via: http://www.oecd.org/eco/The-Economic-consequences-of-Brexit-27-april-2016.pdf.

OECD [Organisation for Economic Co-operation and Development]. (2020). *Trade statistics: G20 International Trade G20 (MEI).* Last updated 5 November 2019. Available via: http://stats.oecd.org/#.

ONS [Office for National Statistics]. (2019). UK Balance of Payments, The Pink Book 2019, HMSO, London. Retrieved February 28, 2020, from https://www.ons.gov.uk/economy/nationalaccounts/balanceofpayments/bulletins/unitedkingdombalanceofpaymentsthepinkbook/2019.

Ottaviano, G., Pessoa, J. P., & Sampson, T. (2014a). The Costs and Benefits of Leaving the EU, CEP mimeo. Available via: http://cep.lse.ac.uk/pubs/download/pa016_tech.pdf.

Ottaviano, G. I. P., Pessoa, J. P., Sampson, T., & Van Reenen, J. (2014b). *Brexit of Fixit? The Trade and Welfare Effects of Leaving the European Union,* Centre for Economic Performance 016, LSE. Available via: https://ideas.repec.org/p/cep/ceppap/016.html.

Panagariya, A. (2000). Preferential Trade Liberalization: The Traditional Theory and New Developments. *Journal of Economic Literature, 38*(2), 287–331.

Portes, J. (2013). Commentary: The Economic Implications for the UK of Leaving the European Union, *National Institute Economic Review,* No. 266, F4-9. Available via: http://www.niesr.ac.uk/sites/default/files/commentary.pdf.

PwC [PricewaterhouseCoopers LLP]. (2016). *Leaving the EU: Implications for the UK Economy,* PricewaterhouseCoopers LLP, London. Available via: http://news.cbi.org.uk/news/leaving-eu-would-cause-a-serious-shock-to-uk-economy-new-pwc-analysis/leaving-the-eu-implications-for-the-uk-economy/.

Rodriguez, F., & Rodrik, D. (2000). Trade Policy and Economic Growth: A Sceptic's Guide to the Cross-national Evidence. *NBER Macroeconomics Annual, 15,* 261–325.

Rodrik, D. (2006). Goodbye Washington Consensus, Hello Washington Confusion? *Journal of Economic Literature, 44*(4), 973–987.

Roeger, W., & Sekkat, K. (2002). Macroeconomic Effects of the Single Market Program After 10 Years, Background Paper of the European Commission, Brussels, II- A- 1/W D(2002).

Rustin, M. (2001). The Third Sociological Way. In P. Arestis & M. Sawyer (Eds.), *The Economics of the Third Way: Experiences from Around the World* (pp. 11–25). Cheltenham: Edward Elgar.

Sampson, T. (2017). Brexit: The Economics of International Disintegration. *Journal of Economic Perspectives, 31*(4), 163–184.

Sapir, A. (1992). Regional Integration in Europe. *Economic Journal, 102*(514), 1491–1506.

Singh, K. (2000). *Taming Global Financial Flows: Challenges and Alternatives in the Era of Financial Globalisation.* London: Zed Books.

Slater, A. (2016). Will Brexit Speed a Seismic Shift in UK Trade Patterns? *Oxford Economics Research Briefing.* Global 7 Sept 2016.

Soloaga, I., & Winters, L. A. (2001). Regionalism in the Nineties: What Effect on Trade? *North American Journal of Economics and Finance, 12*(1), 1–29.

Springford, J., & Tilford, S. (2014). *The Great British Trade-Off: The Impact of Leaving the EU on the UK's Trade and Investment*, Centre for European Reform, London. Available via: http://www.cer.org.uk/publications/archive/policy-brief/2014/great-british-trade-impact-leaving-eu-uks-trade-and-investmen Straathof et al. (2008.

Straathof, S., Linders, G.-J., Lejour, A., & Mohlmann, J. (2008). The Internal Market and the Dutch Economy: Implications for Trade and Economic Growth. CPG Netherlands Document No. 168. Available via: http://www.cpb.nl/sites/default/files/publicaties/download/internal-market-and-dutch-economy-implications-tradeand-economic-growth.pdf.

Thompson, G., & Harari, D. (2013). The Economic Impact of EU Membership on the UK, *House of Commons Library Briefing Paper* SN/EP/6730. Available via: http://researchbriefings.parliament.uk/ResearchBriefing/Summary/SN06730#fullreport.

UNCTAD [United Nations Conference on Trade and Development]. (2013). *Non-Tariff Measures to Trade.* Geneva: United Nations. Available via: http://unctad.org/en/PublicationsLibrary/ditctab20121_en.pdf.

UNCTAD. (2019). *International Classification of Non-Tariff Measures*, United Nations, Geneva. Retrieved March 3, 2020, from https://unctad.org/en/PublicationsLibrary/ditctab2019d5_en.pdf.

UNCTAD [United Nations Conference on Trade and Development]. (2020). *Most Favoured Nation (MFN) Tariff Rates, Weighted Average—EU28 (European Union), 1988-2014.* Available via: http://unctadstat.unctad.org/wds/TableViewer/tableView.aspx.

Viner, J. (1950). *The Customs Union Issue.* Oxford: Oxford University Press. 2014 edition.

Wall, S. (2012). *The Official History of Britain and the European Community* - Vol. 2. London: Routledge.

Webb, D., Keep, M., & Wilton, M. (2015). In Brief: UK-EU Economic Relations, *House of Commons Library Briefing Paper (HC 06091)*, The Stationery Office, London. Available via: http://researchbriefings.parliament.uk/ResearchBriefing/Summary/SN06091.

Whyman, P. B. (2018). Brexit: A Cliff Edge or a Small Bump in the Road? *Political Quarterly, 89*(2), 298–305.

Winters, L. A. (1985). Separability and the Modelling of International Economic Integration—UK Exports to Five Industrial Countries. *European Economic Review, 27*(3), 335–353.

Wonnacott, P., & Lutz, M. (1989). Is There a Case for Free Trade Areas? In J.J. Schott (Ed.), *Free Trade Areas and U.S. Trade Policy*. Washington, DC: Institute for International Economics.

World Bank. (2020). *Trade as Percent of GDP Report*. Available via: http://databank.worldbank.org/data/reports.aspx?source=2&series=NE.TRD.GNFS.ZS&country=GBR.

World Data Bank. (2016). Tariff Rate Series. World Development Indicators.

World Data Bank. (2020). Tariff Rate Series. World Development Indicators. Available online via: https://data.worldbank.org/indicator/TM.TAX.MRCH.SM.AR.ZS.

WTO [World Trade Organization]. (2013). *World Trade Report 2013: Factors Shaping the Future of World Trade*, World Trade Organisation, Geneva. Available via: https://www.wto.org/english/res_e/booksp_e/world_trade_report13_e.pdf.

WTO [World Trade Organization]. (2015). *World Tariff Profiles 2015*, WTO, Geneva. Available via: https://www.wto.org/english/res_e/booksp_e/tariff_profiles15_e.pdf.

WTO [World Trade Organization]. (2019). *Trade Policy Review: European Union*. Released: 10 December 2019. Retrieved March 31, 2020, from https://www.wto.org/english/tratop_e/tpr_e/s395_e.pdf.

CHAPTER 4

Foreign Direct Investment (FDI) After Brexit

The inflow of foreign direct investment (FDI) is typically associated with a variety of economic benefits, ranging from increased productivity to enhanced innovation and technological development. The UK has been relatively successful in attracting inward flows of FDI, and consequently it has been one of the areas where it is suggested that Brexit may have a negative impact. Thus, it is important to assess the veracity of predictions made by the various studies which have examined this question, to test whether these provide a firm evidence base for UK policy makers with the responsibility to manage the transition towards independence from the EU.

Definition—What Is FDI?

FDI[1] may be defined as the acquisition by firms, governments or individuals, in one (source) country, of assets in another (host) nation, for the purpose of controlling the production, distribution and/or other productive activities. It is the aspect of *control* of the productive process which distinguishes FDI from the more passive international portfolio investment—that is, where firms, governments or individuals purchase securities, including shares and bonds, in another country. Whereas portfolio investment is typically undertaken to spread risk by diversifying holdings in multiple securities, and where investors do not typically seek to influence the management of the organisation, FDI involves the concentration

---

[1] For a good overview of the theory and evidence pertaining to FDI, see Moosa (2002).

© The Author(s) 2020
P. B. Whyman, A. I. Petrescu, *The Economics of Brexit*,
https://doi.org/10.1007/978-3-030-55948-9_4

of investment specifically in order to control production. It is not usually a short-term investment, but rather seeks to acquire a long-term controlling interest (IMF 2013). The IMF (2013) defines this as exceeding 10% of equity ownership, whereas for the OECD (2008: 17), it relates to where the direct investor owning at least 10% of the voting power of the direct investment organisation.

The international business literature argues that firms consider FDI once they have developed competitive advantage(s) that they feel can be more effectively exploited through strategic location of production abroad. Hence, rather than export goods and services from a home base, they may choose to locate production overseas but maintain direct control to minimise transaction costs, whilst retaining control over organisation knowledge, technology and other elements of the production process (Morgan 1997). Assuming rational action, firms must be responding to, firstly, incentives to locate production abroad, rather than export from their existing home base, and, secondly, a separate set of incentives to internalise the production process. The latter may centre upon the perceived risk inherent within the principal-agent problem. This occurs when the owner (or principal) has to rely upon an agent to fulfil objectives established by the principal, and differences in self-interest may result in sub-optimal solutions. Resolution of the principle-agent problem may require costly solutions, such as incentivising the agent or introducing intensive monitoring of their activities. Risks may include the theft of technological knowledge or diffusion of technological knowledge, thus eroding competitive advantage. Similarly, low-quality franchise operations may result in loss of reputation and goodwill.

FDI can take a number of forms:

a) Greenfield investment—where a foreign-based company establishes a new enterprise, as a subsidiary
b) Mergers and acquisitions (M&A)—when an existing firm is taken over by a foreign owner
c) Acquisition of share capital in an existing subsidiary, joint venture or through purchasing a sizeable stake in an existing firm sufficient to ensure a lasting management involvement
d) Acquisition of loan capital, such as corporate bonds, which provides a similar involvement in the management of the enterprise as (c)
e) Lending to an existing subsidiary
f) Unremitted profit being re-invested in the host economy rather than being remitted to the home parent company.

THEORETICAL IMPACT—WHY IS FDI IMPORTANT?

FDI is associated with the import of capital, thereby increasing the supply of funding for productive investment. This is assumed to reduce interest rates and the cost of capital (Ries et al. 2017: 111). FDI is associated with the introduction of new technology (Barrell and Pain 1997; Driffield and Taylor 2006; Pain and Wakelin 1998) and innovative forms of work organisation (Bloom et al. 2012a). It may also encourage greater competition (Bank of England 2015: 38). Technological and productivity spillovers may produce beneficial externalities for domestic producers (Borensztein et al. 1998; Aitken and Harrison 1999; Driffield and Munday 2000; Bloom et al. 2012b). Furthermore, inward investment may generate an expansion in employment opportunities (Dunning 1993) and additionally provide an important source of government revenues (UNCTAD 2015: 184). Foreign-owned Trans-National Corporations (TNCs) would appear to have higher levels of productivity than domestic owned firms (Haskel et al. 2002; Griffith et al. 2004; Helpman et al. 2004; Keller and Yeaple 2009), such that the Treasury assumption is that a 1% increase in FDI stock is associated with a 0.04% increase in the level of technology, with subsequent productivity effects (HM Treasury 2016: 182). Thus, FDI is often viewed as a means of improving aggregate productivity and allocative efficiency, whilst facilitating the rising skill level of the workforce through the provision of high-skill employment opportunities (Dunning 1988; De Mello 1999; Harris and Robinson 2002).

This benign view of FDI may, however, reflect selection effects—that is, that more efficient firms tend to seek to capitalise on their existing advantages through exporting to reach a larger market, rather than the process of exporting subsequently bestows these advantages. As a result, policy measures aimed at attracting inward FDI may have only a weak impact upon aggregate productivity and technological capacity within the economy (Rodrik 2004: 30). Indeed, very few economic studies are able to substantiate significant beneficial effects and/or the direction of any causality (Görg and Greenaway 2004; Driffield et al. 2013: 25). Thus, whilst some studies indicate that completion from FDI causes rising investment and capital deepening in the domestic manufacturing sector (De Mello 1999; Driffield and Hughes 2003), others suggest that domestic firms react by reducing output and investment, at least in the short term (Buffie 1993; Aitken and Harrison 1999), with FDI replacing rather than supplementing domestic capital formation (Hejazi and Pauly 2003). FDI may cause 'reverse spillovers', by securing access to technology otherwise unavailable to the home company (Driffield and Love 2003), or by attracting skilled labour away from existing producers (Driffield and Taylor 2000; Driffield et al. 2013: 15–16). Deadweight costs may arise from a reduction in competition arising from the takeover of an existing producer, whether inadvertently or as a strategic intent to displace local producers in order to increase potential monopoly profits (Hymer 1960; Cowling and Sugden 1987). Indeed, the preface to the most recent UNCTAD (2016) report on this topic may hint at this problem when it noted that substantial recorded increases in FDI flows in recent years have not led to an equivalent increase in productive capacity.

The traditional Heckscher-Ohlin-Samuelson approach treats FDI and trade as substitutes, given that the international mobility of factors of production may substitute for international trade, as production occurs locally in the host economy rather than in the home economy and being exported to the other nation (Dunning 1988; Liu et al. 2001). However, it can also complement trade if TNCs are established to facilitate export activity (Gray 1998; Grossman and Helpman 1994: 39; USITC 2000: 4–19). WTO (2013: 84) analysis indicates a modest positive association between the foreign content of exports and the level of gross manufacturing exports, although this does not, by itself, prove causality, as FDI may have been attracted by a pre-existing superior export track record.

There is, sadly, a lack of robust evidence on the relationship between FDI and economic growth in the host economy. Whilst a number of studies have found a positive relationship *in the long run*, with a 1% rise in the FDI to GDP ratio resulting in an increase in output of between 0.26% and 0.42% (Li and Liu 2005; Busse and Groizard 2008), others found little or no evidence of FDI having a direct positive effect upon growth rates. Indeed, under certain conditions, FDI flows can negatively impact upon growth potential (Carkovic and Levine 2005; Durham 2004). Meta studies have produced conflicting results, with some finding that the link between FDI and economic growth is at best mixed, with some finding either no of limited positive effects (Görg and Strobl 2001; Görg and Greenaway 2004), whereas others identified a modest but significant effect (Bruno and Campos 2013; Iamsiraroj and Ulubaşoğlu 2015). After reviewing this limited evidence, the Bank of England (2018: 25) adopted an elasticity of 0.04 in its analysis. If accurate, this would suggest that FDI has a much smaller effect upon productivity and growth rates than trade and other variables such as innovation and capital accumulation.

Notwithstanding these reservations, the attraction of inward flows of FDI has become an important policy objective for national and regional policy makers (Young et al. 1994; Wren and Taylor 1999). Under the correct conditions, FDI may have the potential to improve the competitive position of both home and host economies, and it can enhance local economic development. However, this is not automatic and it depends upon the policy framework within which FDI operates (OECD 2008: 14; Bailey et al. 2016: 886).

DETERMINANTS OF FDI

The ability to attract inward flows of FDI depends upon many different factors, including:

1. The size and growth of the host market—current and future demand conditions signal inward investors (Pain and Lansbury 1997; Ethier 1998; Driffield and Munday 2000).
2. Access to resources or strategic assets, such as technology or production methods protected by legal patent, to which the TNC wishes to gain access (Dunning 1988).
3. The degree of openness (Pain and Lansbury 1997; Driffield et al. 2013: 27).
4. Economic stability (HMG 2013: 40).
5. The strength of commercial law, contract enforcement (including intellectual property) and the predictability of the business climate (UNCTAD 2015: 177).
6. Distance and transportation costs (Egger and Pfaffermayr 2004).
7. Infrastructure (Fredriksson et al. 2003).
8. Corporate tax rates (Hines 1996).
9. The cost of factors of production (UNCTAD 2015: 177). This can be affected by access to low-cost capital, whilst relative unit costs may be influenced by government policy, as the maintenance of a buoyant level of aggregate demand is associated with lower unit costs (Arestis and Mariscal 1997, 2000).
10. Labour skill levels and labour market flexibility (Haaland and Wooton 2007; HM Treasury 2003).
11. The quality of institutions (Wren and Jones 2012).
12. Exchange rates (Froot and Stein 1991).

13. Agglomeration (clustering) (Driffield et al. 2013: 36; Driffield and Munday 2000).
14. English language ability (HMG 2013: 40).

The relative significance of the various factors is difficult to establish and may change over time. These individual factors can be grouped together to highlight three main motivations underlying FDI, namely (UNCTAD 2015: 177):

a) *Resource-seeking investments*—that is, gaining access to raw materials or different types of technology. These firms tend to be relatively capital intensive and can be sensitive to policy or cost changes which may impact upon their long-term returns.
b) *Market-seeking investments*—primarily concerned with market *demand* (finding new markets for their products) and less concerned with inputs to their productive processes. The fact that the UK is the fifth largest economy in the world is of particular significance for inward investors; however, there will be a proportion of TNCs who operate within the UK as an "export platform" to the SIM (HMG 2013: 40) and who may consider the relocation of certain activities elsewhere within the EU following Brexit.
c) *Efficiency-seeking investments*—focus upon the cost and efficiency of their inputs (i.e. capital, labour and raw materials) and the costs inherent in maintaining their supply chains. They are sensitive to the differential costs of factors of production and the impact of economic policy decisions upon their business model, including taxation but also regulations impacting upon trading costs. In the latest available Global Competitiveness Index, produced by the World Economic Forum, the UK ranks ninth out of 144 nations.[2] The depreciation of sterling over the past few years will have further enhanced the competitive position of the UK for this group of international investors.

The significance of the different motivations may help to explain why, for example, TNCs state concern over the cost of labour within different nations, yet the majority of FDI stock is invested in high wage and relatively high tax developed economies (Weiss 1998: 186).

[2] http://reports.weforum.org/global-competitiveness-report-2014-2015/rankings/

FDI AND THE UK ECONOMY

Magnitude of FDI

The UK has been consistently effective in attracting inward flows of investment. According to the latest figures, the UK attracted a record number of foreign investment projects in 2018 (see Fig. 4.1). There was a very small dip in the *number* of FDI projects in 2016, the year of the European referendum, but rose thereafter. The *value* of FDI investment, by contrast, peaked in 2016. It is unlikely that this is due to a Brexit effect, however, otherwise decline would have continued rather than recovered in 2018. Indeed, the 2016 figure does appear to be an aberration in post-2008 flows, caused by a very large increase in mergers and acquisitions. The depreciation of sterling will have reduced the cost for such takeovers of existing UK firms, whilst the uncertainty following the

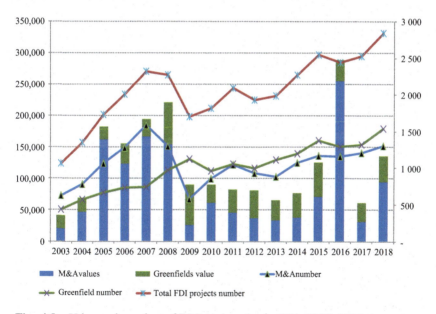

Fig. 4.1 Value and number of FDI projects in the UK, 2003–2018, at current prices (US$m). Note: Merger and acquisition (M&A) and greenfield values are shown on the left vertical axis; the numbers of M&A, greenfield and total FDI projects are shown on the right vertical axis. Source: UNCTAD (2020)

referendum result may have encouraged longer-term inward investors to take advantage of this temporarily favourable set of circumstances to bring forward purchases.

The UK has remained fairly consistently the largest recipient of inward FDI within the EU (UKTI 2015). This was the case prior to the UK joining the EU and remained so throughout the period of membership (see Fig. 4.2), with brief exceptions in the early 1980s recession and the period surrounding the introduction of the EU single currency in 1999. It is possible that one reason for this has been the success of the UK in attracting the European headquarters of firms based outside the EU (HMG 2013: 39), although government Ministers prefer to emphasise the supportive economic environment created for business activities within the UK (UKTI 2015).

Placing these achievements into a broader global context, UK attractiveness for inward FDI flows compares rather well with many larger economies and economic groupings (see Fig. 4.3). In 2018, the UK was ranked as the sixth largest recipient of inward FDI flows in the world—behind the USA, China, Hong Kong, Singapore and the Netherlands—receiving inward investment of around $64 billion (£49 billion) (UNCTAD 2019: 4). This represents a significant boost to the national economy and can facilitate a significant segment of the UK's trade deficit. In 2017, UNCTAD figures indicate that the UK was the fourth largest recipient of inward FDI, valued at $101 billion (£77.6 billion) (UNCTAD 2015: 71). It is unwise to place too much emphasis upon FDI figures or country rankings for any one individual year, as a small number of very large investments, disinvestments or trans-national intracompany loans can result in substantial volatility (UNCTAD 2015: 73, 190–7). Consequently, when viewed over the past two decades, the UK has been consistently one of the largest recipients of inward FDI amongst advanced economies and has received the largest share amongst EU economies (Driffield et al. 2013: 9–10; Bank of England 2015: 4). Indeed, over the past decade, it has ranked fourth in the world, behind the USA, China and India, hosting around 19% of new FDI projects located in Europe, compared to France with 14.7% and Germany with 12.7% (EY 2019: 11).

The UK's ability to attract inward FDI is impressive. However, when compared with world trends in FDI flows, its performance has largely reflected global trends; the two exceptions are in the immediate aftermath of the 2008 financial crisis when it performed more badly than global trends and for the two decades after 1970 when it outperformed global

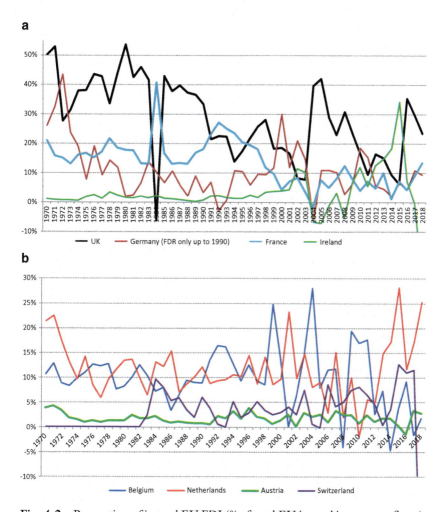

Fig. 4.2 Proportion of inward EU FDI (% of total EU inward investment flows), 1970–2018. Panel A: UK, Ireland and the two largest EU economies (Germany and France). Panel B: Belgium, Netherlands, Austria, Switzerland. Panel C: Scandinavian countries: Denmark, Finland, Sweden, Norway and Iceland. Panel D: Southern European countries: Italy, Spain, Portugal and Greece. Notes: A country's share of EU FDI is calculated as a percentage out of the total EU inward FDI for the respective year. Shares of inward FDI are shown for all countries, however: the UK, Denmark and Ireland joined the EU in 1973, Greece in 1981, Portugal and Spain in 1986, while Austria, Finland and Sweden joined in 1995. Three non-EU member states are also shown, for comparative purposes, namely Iceland, Switzerland and Norway. Source: UNCTAD (2020)

c

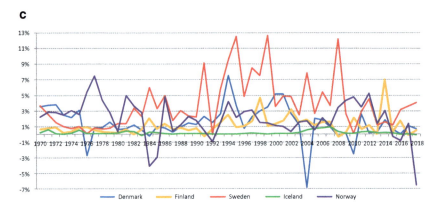

d

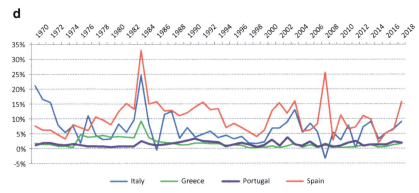

Fig. 4.2   (continued)

trends (see Fig. 4.4).[3] Thus, whilst the UK is particularly attractive as a host for FDI investment within Europe, it is largely performing in accordance with, rather than superseding, world trends. The period in the immediate aftermath of the 2008 global financial crisis witnessed a significant shift in FDI flows towards other parts of the world economy less exposed to the consequences of financial sector excess (UNCTAD 2015: 30). However,

---

[3] To interpret this figure, please note that global FDI is represented by a different scale to UK inward investment on the plural y-axes, in order to capture trends in global FDI and much smaller relative investment flows in one individual economy.

a

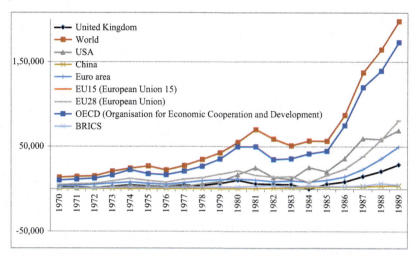

b

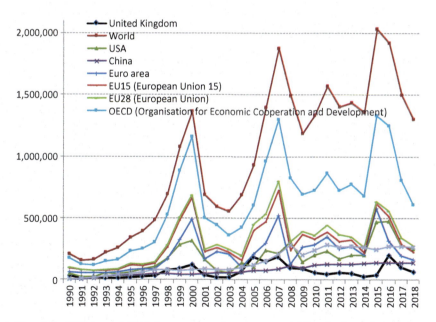

Fig. 4.3 UK inward FDI flows, comparison across world and selected countries (US$ million), Panel A. Over the period 1970–1990, Panel B. Over the period 1990–2018. Notes: Measured in million US Dollars at 2014 prices and 2014 exchange rates. Panel A and Panel B have a different scale on the vertical axis, in order to allow for an easier comparison. Source: UNCTAD (2016b) and UNCTAD (2020)

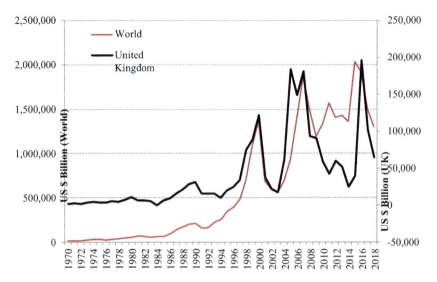

Fig. 4.4 Comparison of the flows of inward FDI into the UK and the World, 1990–2018. Source: UNCTAD (2020)

subsequent UK inward FDI flows have reverted back towards broadly following global trends.

Discussion of inward FDI should not, however, detract from the fact that the UK is a net outward investor, with a larger external than internal stock of FDI. In 2015, for example, UNCTAD (2016a: 200) records that the UK held around £1025.4 billion of outward FDI stock whereas inward investor stock in the UK accounted for £971.6 billion—a 5.5% surplus of outward over inward investment stock. Indeed, the UK remains the third largest source of outward FDI behind the USA and Germany. Outward investment may benefit the UK if it leads to the strengthening of UK firms, through facilitating technology transfer and/or economies of scale resulting from enhanced market opportunities, and it should lead to future benefits for the balance of payments as profits made overseas are partially repatriated to the home company. These advantages are longer term, however, with short-run effects being largely negative, stemming from a loss of investment and reduction in demand in the home economy arising from the outflow of this investment capital. It should additionally be noted that these values of FDI stock are significantly less significant than recorded levels of portfolio investment, which are between 10 and 15 times larger (HMG 2013: 39).

Origin of FDI

The EU is the source for approximately 40% of the stock of inward FDI for the UK (see Fig. 4.5). This proportion of inward investment has varied over the past two decades, ranging from around one third to a figure almost half of the total (Driffield et al. 2013: 9–10, 56–7; Bank of England 2015: 91; Irwin 2015: 12). The single largest source of UK inward investment, throughout this period, derives from the USA, albeit the share has declined since the 1990s, when the USA would have represented around half of the total (Bank of England 2015: 91).

Composition of FDI

Whilst the popular conception of FDI may revolve around the construction of a Japanese car plant on a 'greenfield' site, somewhere in the North East or the Midlands, the reality is that the vast majority of inward FDI into the UK involves mergers and acquisitions—that is, the takeover of an existing British company (Driffield et al. 2013:11). This is illustrated in Fig. 4.6. Relatively liberal UK laws concerning corporate ownership and the takeover of domestic companies have facilitated these purchases (Milne 2004: 21–2).

The overwhelming majority of FDI occurs in the service sector, rather than in manufacturing, and this share has been increasing in recent years (see Fig. 4.7). Thus, in 2018, approximately three quarters of inward FDI *stock* was located in the service sector, whilst manufacturing accounted for around 18% and the primary sector, which comprises mainly of mining and energy extraction industries, the remaining 8%. This is a greater proportion than for global FDI flows more generally (UNCTAD 2015: 12).

The composition of FDI matters for two main reasons. The first relates to whether or not inward investment has a significant impact upon the UK economy. It is easy to conceive that 'greenfield' investment is likely to have a net positive effect upon employment and output, because this is adding an element of production of goods or services that did not previously exist, unless, of course, it displaces existing production carried out by UK firms who may have to reduce output as a result of the new competition.

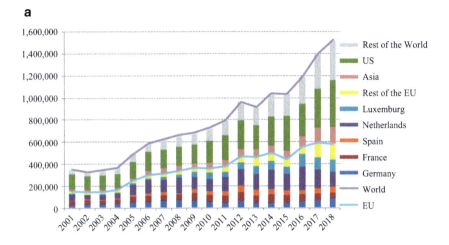

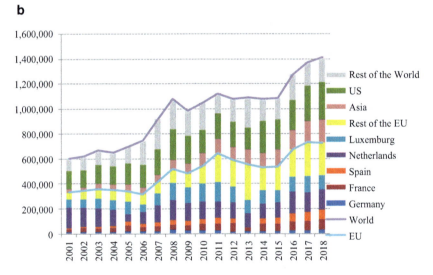

Fig. 4.5 The stock of inward and outward UK FDI, by selected geographical areas and country, 2001–2018 (in £ million). Source: ONS (2020c)

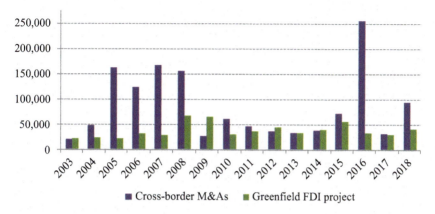

Fig. 4.6 The value of cross border mergers and acquisitions compared to green-field FDI projects in the UK, 2003–2018 (US$m). Source: UNCTAD (2020)

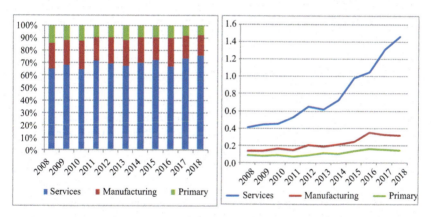

Fig. 4.7 Net inward FDI stock in the UK by sector, 2008–2018 (% and £bn). Source: Authors' compilation of data, based on ONS (2020a) and ONS (2010:79)

Yet, even here, the expectation would be that there should be efficiency gains as a result of the FDI (Hofmann 2013).

The situation is less clear cut with inward acquisition FDI involving foreign takeover of an existing UK-owned firm. Whilst this creates a positive balance of payments effect, there is no certainty that realised capital will be recirculated to benefit UK productive industry. For the business itself, the transfer of ownership may bring in new techniques, technology and/or expand operations, thereby generating additional output and employment opportunities, or it may not. Indeed, it is perfectly possible that the new owners may wish to run down UK operations of their new acquisition, in order to reduce competition for their existing operations, which is particularly serious for a host economy as the targets for FDI acquisition tend to be of higher than average quality and which were characterised by high levels of existing research and development (R&D) (Bertrand et al. 2008). Consequently, the net effect of inward FDI needs to be assessed on a case by case basis, rather than be assumed to be inevitably positive.

The second reason why the composition of FDI is important, when seeking to ascertain its potential impact upon the UK economy, relates to the diverse ability of businesses, working in different sectors, to deliver the increased dynamism that may be found in theory textbooks. For example, it may prove easier for manufacturing than in many areas of the service sector, for FDI to introduce newer forms of technology, innovation and deliver skills spillovers to the UK economy, with consequent impact upon productivity and an improvement in the balance of payments.

FDI and the UK Economy

The UK is disproportionately reliant upon the continuing flow of inward FDI (see Fig. 4.8). In part, this is a consequence of the small size and scope of its manufacturing sector. Proposals to rebalance the UK economy would, if realised, facilitate an expansion of UK manufacturing and, as a result, would reduce the over-dependence upon FDI. Brexit could facilitate this process (see Chap. 8). In the short term, however, until these effects are realised, the magnitude of FDI flows and persistence of spillover effects will remain particularly important for the UK economy.

The approximately 45,000 foreign affiliates operating within the UK economy represent less than 2% of the total number of firms, yet they account for around 13% of the UK employment and a little over a third of total output (Driffield et al. 2013: 5, 12). In the manufacturing sector, foreign-owned firms are even more pronounced, accounting for around 42% of manufacturing investment and 38% of manufacturing output (Driffield et al. 2013: 64–5). Thus, despite the difficulty experienced by economic studies in measuring the impact of possible positive spillovers upon national economies, there is limited evidence to suggest that this

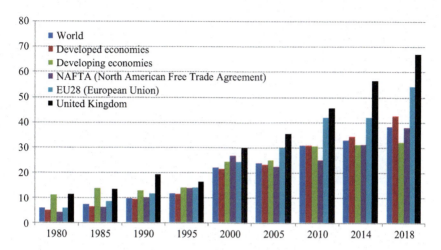

Fig. 4.8 FDI stocks as percentage of gross domestic product for the UK and selected global regions, 1980–2018. Source: UNCTAD (2020)

may provide a modest benefit to the UK (Haskel et al. 2002; Aghion et al. 2009).

One area in which FDI is particularly important for the UK economy concerns R&D expenditure, where foreign-owned firms have undertaken around half of the UK's total R&D spend for more than half a decade (see Fig. 4.9). The dominance of foreign-owned firms is even more pronounced in the motor vehicle industry, where they accounted for approximately 80% of all R&D expenditure between 2001 and 2010; the equivalent share of R&D expenditures exceeded 40% of the UK total in the consumer electronics, machinery and equipment, optical and precision instruments, computer programming, food products, beverages and tobacco, and finally the chemical sector (Driffield et al. 2013: 64).

This is important for three reasons. Firstly, R&D investment provides a boost to current aggregate demand whilst providing a simultaneous potential enlargement to future productive capacity. Secondly, R&D investment is a primary means for delivering innovation and/or technological change. Both of which will have a potential impact upon economic growth. Thirdly, this disproportionate reliance upon foreign-owned firms to deliver crucial innovation and technological advance demonstrates both the significance that FDI plays in driving the efficiency of the UK economy, but also the relative weakness of domestic firms and the consequent

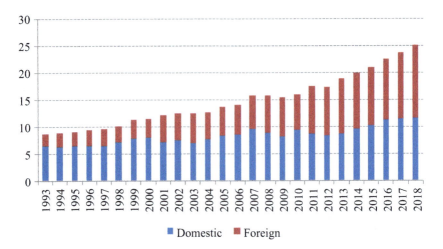

Domestic   Foreign

Fig. 4.9   Expenditure in R&D performed in UK business by foreign and domestic firms in current prices (£bn), 1993–2018. Source: The authors, based on ONS (2020b)

fragility of the UK economy due to its continued reliance upon firms with fewer natural anchors to the UK economy. Furthermore, over-reliance upon foreign-owned businesses to drive innovation and technological advance increases the UK's vulnerability to changes in the decision-making calculations made by overseas investors and the boards of foreign TNCs (Hughes 2013).

Paradoxically, therefore, Brexit can provide both a threat and an opportunity to UK prosperity. If it results in the UK being a less attractive destination for foreign-owned firms, this may result in a medium-term decline in R&D and reduce future growth potential. However, Brexit may facilitate a more active public policy focused upon the reinvigoration of the UK manufacturing industry which, if successful, would raise the share of R&D undertaken by domestic firms and boost future growth potential. It is the balance of these two forces which may, in part, determine the net impact of Brexit upon the UK economy in the medium and longer term.

The Potential Impact of Brexit upon FDI

There is relatively scant direct evidence pertaining to possible effects of Brexit on FDI flows (Ries et al. 2017: 70) or, indeed, more generally seeking to measure the impact of EU membership upon FDI, and even fewer studies which disaggregate predicted effects for individual member states (Ebell and Warren 2016: 125). The evidence which does exist appears to indicate that EU membership as a whole, and the creation of the single internal market (SIM) in particular, has coincided with an increase in inward FDI over and above the levels that might have been expected given the increase in international investment flows over time (Baldwin et al. 1996; Barrell and Pain 1998; Deutsche Bank 2013: 10; Ries et al. 2017: 70). Gravity modelling has produced estimates ranging from indeterminate effects (Brenton et al. 1999) to boosts to FDI of between 17% (Straathof et al. 2008: 70) and an upper boundary of 38% (Bruno et al. 2016: 9; Ries et al. 2017: 71).

Studies which have sought to compare EU integration with other forms of preferential trade agreement (PTA) have produced mixed results. One study suggests that membership of a customs union can encourage inward FDI flows to increase by around a fifth, whereas participation in a free trade agreement (FTA) can do so by one third (Lederman et al., 2005), whereas others found EU membership to boost inward investment by around 28%, whilst an FTA with the EU would produce a rise in FDI inflows of around 16% (Ries et al. 2017: 88). Bruno et al. (2016: 9) find no statistical difference between a country being a member of the European Free Trade Association or EFTA (European Economic Area or EEA option) and being completely independent from the EU (WTO option). The National Institute of Economic and Social Research (NIESR) analysis suggests that declines in FDI flows would be larger if trading according to WTO rules (23.7%) compared to FTAs (17.1%) and 9.7% (EEA) (Ebell and Warren 2016: 127). Other studies suggest that trading according to WTO rules might reduce inward FDI flows into the UK by around 20–27% (Dhingra et al. 2017; Hantzsche et al., 2018: 15). Nevertheless, it is fair to conclude that most studies assume that Brexit will result in a significant decline in inward FDI flows (Barrell and Pain 1998; Pain and Young 2004; Fairbairn and Newton-Smith 2016: 18; PwC 2016: 31–2). A few of the prominent gravity estimates are included in Table 4.1.

Table 4.1   Summary of key gravity model estimates, FDI and Brexit

	Gravity Results (%)	Brexit impact (%)		
		Optimistic (EEA)	Central (bilateral, FTA)	Pessimistic (WTO)
HM Treasury 2016		-10	-15/-20	-18/-26
Fournier et al. 2015	17–22 (OECD wide)			
OECD 2016		-10	-30	-45
Straathof et al. 2008	17			
Bruno et al. 2016	14/33/38 (av. 28)	-12	-25	-28
Ebell and Warren 2016 [NIESR]		-9.7	-17.1	-23.7
Ries et al. 2017	12/28		-12	-28
Bank of England, 2018: 25, 51	20		-20	-20

Limitations of Economic Estimates

The evidence on potential changes in FDI flows to the UK should be treated with caution for a number of reasons.

Firstly, certain rather prominent studies utilising gravity modelling to estimate FDI effects have not worked very well, and their analysis was thereby forced to employ a rather dubious assumption that inward investment will change in direct proportion to any trade effects arising from Brexit (HM Treasury 2016: 130–1, 174–5, 185). Moreover, this was not the only study to bundle trade and FDI effects (Emmerson et al., 2016: 32–4; PwC 2016: 55). This is despite it being well known that FDI can act a substitute for international trade, rather than necessarily being a complement, as firms take the decision that it might make financial sense to establish productive facilities abroad rather than continue to export goods made in the home nation (Gray 1998). Other studies have relied upon these estimates drawn from the existing literature, such as those studies previously mentioned seeking to calculate effects deriving from EU membership for all EU member states, and then applying (in reverse) this *average* figure to their analysis of the UK after Brexit. For example, the OECD (2016: 31) relied, in its Brexit study, upon gravity estimates from the previous study undertaken by Fournier et al. (2015: 10). Other studies have introduced an assumed causation chain into their analysis, linking FDI flows, openness and productivity (Bank of England, 2018: 25–6; Hantzsche et al., 2018: 15–17). This is questionable, as was discussed in Chap. 1 and in more detail in Chap. 7. Finally, other Brexit studies have excluded the factor altogether (Dhingra et al. 2016: 9).

It is, however, easy to over-emphasise the consequences which arise from these predictions (Capital Economics 2016: 27). Firstly because, as this chapter has indicated, there are many inter-related determinants of FDI. Withdrawal from a preferential trade agreement is unlikely to be symmetric with initial participation, as agglomeration effects, sunk costs, reluctance to disturb existing supply chains and continuing (if lower) profit streams all mitigate against sudden and dramatic change (Ries et al. 2017: 87). Rather than a sudden relocation of existing foreign-owned production out of the UK, on the day following Brexit, it is more likely that, if the UK did become less attractive for a proportion of international investors, they would respond by slowing the rate of new investment into the UK rather than relocating all existing facilities (Pain and Young 2004: 393). This still has real effects, but these will be experienced more over time and it would not, therefore, represent a sudden shock. Hence, research studies may over-estimate FDI effects unless they adjust for inertia and/or sunk cost effects.

A second reason why the small group of studies that do exist have produced such widely differing estimates of the probable impact of Brexit upon FDI relates to whether their data included all inward investment into the EU, from anywhere in the world, or was more narrowly focused upon intra-EU investment flows. For example, Straathof et al. (2008: 55) estimated that intra-EU FDI flows may reduce by up to 25%, but global flows would fall by between 11% and 13%. Similarly, Bruno et al. (2016) produced a range of estimates ranging from 13% to 32%, depending upon statistical methods adopted. Hence, it would be reasonable to conclude that those studies which focus more narrowly upon FDI originating in the EU are likely to give a misleading impression of any potential decline in inward investment into the UK following Brexit, since these are the investors most likely to experience concern about a weakening of integration between the EU and the UK, whereas international investors from the rest of the world appear to take a relatively more benign view of the future prospects for the UK as an independent nation.

Thirdly, all of the economic studies have been undertaken according to the simplifying maxim, *ceteris paribus* (all relevant factors remaining constant), and therefore they do not take into consideration any policy changes which may mitigate any negative effects. Similarly, they assume away any impact upon the perceptions of international investors which may derive from those changes which are likely to arise as a result of Brexit. These factors may include the creation of a more attractive regulatory framework for international investors, or the more active management of the exchange rate to enhance the competitive position of those firms exporting from the UK, or, indeed, alternative trade relationships which may be formed over time with the rest of the world. It would be wrong to criticise such studies for failing to include all possible future permutations in their calculations, or else models would get very complex and a simple narrative would be lost, nevertheless, this fact should lead to a degree of caution in the interpretation of the meaning of the results. The fact that a study might conclude that Brexit may lead to a fall in FDI *if nothing else changes* is not the same as a firm prediction that FDI flows *will* inevitably fall; rather it is a warning that national policy makers have to take these factors into account when they formulate policy responses to ensure that this predicted eventually does not occur.

Fourthly, the various studies tend to develop panel data by aggregating evidence drawn over a number of years. However, this obscures whether there may be differential FDI effects over time. For example, it might be a reasonable assumption to anticipate that a nation may experience greater benefits during the initial period following a reduction in trade barriers but, unless other factors change, this initial boost to FDI flows is likely to gradually diminish over time (Campos et al. 2014: 16; Bank of England 2015: 23).

Fifthly, it is difficult to isolate the impact of one variable out of so many, over a 40-year time period, and it has proven even more difficult to establish the means by which any theoretical benefit might be translated to the UK real economy (Rodrik 2008; Miller 2016: 27). For example, Ramasamy and Yeung (2010) suggest that, rather than EU membership being a decisive factor, it is rather the degree of openness of a nation which determines inward FDI flows. Yet, very few studies have sought to disentangle these two possible variables.

Finally, it is worth noting that advocates for greater regional economic integration argued that inward flows of FDI into the UK would be damaged by reluctance to join the single currency (e.g. Begg et al. 2003: 5, 28). Yet, the opposite occurred with large increases in FDI inward flows despite (or perhaps because of) the UK adopting an increasingly firm position against joining the Euro. This suggests that it may be uncertainty which is likely to pose more of a problem than distancing from European integration *per se* (Driffield et al. 2013: 44). If so, this is more easily ameliorated through government policy measures. Moreover, once the UK government has established a clear new relationship with the EU post-Brexit, previous advantages may reassert themselves and inward flows of FDI may not be deterred.

It would seem incontrovertible that many of the studies which have sought to predict future investment flows possess flaws of data and/or design, and therefore the evidential base is not particularly strong. Nevertheless, a reasonable conclusion would be to assume that a combination of economic uncertainty and a narrowing of short-term trade opportunities are likely to have a negative impact upon inward FDI flows into the UK (Portes 2013: F7), albeit that the magnitude and duration of any potential fall in FDI are more questionable. This would at least partially depend upon those factors assumed away in most economic studies—that is, the impact of related policy interventions upon stabilising the expectations of international investors and boosting UK growth prospects, alongside the nature of the trade relationships the UK is able to negotiate with the EU and the rest of the world (Mansfield 2014: 43; Capital Economics 2016: 3, 27).

ATTITUDE SURVEYS—INTERNATIONAL INVESTORS

Predictions made by econometric modelling are one source of evidence, but another derives from surveying actual or potential international investors to gauge their perceptions and interpret their future investment intentions resulting from changed circumstances. For a number of years, Ernst and Young (EY 2013, 2015) have produced 'attractiveness' surveys which purport to indicate the perceived attractiveness of the UK as a destination for international investment. The advantage of these surveys is that they seek to gather intelligence upon perceptions, motivations and intentions of those influencing the timing and location of FDI. The disadvantage of the survey is that it focuses upon the *number* of FDI projects but not their *value*.

The latest survey drew data from a "representative panel of 446 international decision makers" (EY 2019: 44). It found that the UK remained the leading destination for FDI in Europe, but the volume of projects had declined by 13% since 2017. Interestingly, this is the same percentage fall as experienced by Germany, which demonstrates the significance of factors other than Brexit contributing to this poor performance. Indeed, the largest single element of this decline for the UK concerned a 48% fall in the number of FDI projects originating from China (EY 2019: 28), perhaps as a result of that country's slowing economy and/or the impact of the trade tensions with the USA. Nevertheless, when questioned about perceived risks in the European market, Brexit was identified by participants are their greatest concern (EY 2019: 14).

Drilling down a little deeper into the EY data indicates that the vast majority of international investors—70% overall and 86% of those who already have an established presence in the UK—have not altered their FDI plans as a result of Brexit, with as many companies *increasing* investment as reducing it as a direct consequence of Brexit (see Fig. 4.10). Nevertheless, that still leaves approximately 15% of investors having frozen potential investments in the UK until Brexit has been resolved; this represents only 6% of those already established in the UK but a troublesome 20% of those considering investing in the UK for the first time (EY 2019: 16). Hence, the evidence would suggest that there is only a small risk of disinvestment, and indeed this number appears to be receding from previous surveys (EY 2019: 35), but the attraction of future investment from those not already established within the UK might prove more difficult until uncertainty has reduced. At the same time, however, there has been a significant increase in outward FDI from the UK to elsewhere within the EU, as certain industries have decided to restructure their activities in advance of UK withdrawal from the EU (EY 2019: 31).

EY (2019: 33–5) evidence would therefore suggest that the UK remains an attractive destination for inward FDI, but its attractiveness would remain weaker than previously unless or until the uncertainty surrounding the Brexit process has been resolved. The UK's formal withdrawal from the EU, completed on 31 January 2020, will have contributed to this process, but the end result of the negotiations on the future economic relationship between the two entities is likely to have an additional effect. Similarly, it could encourage government to focus upon other (non-Brexit) factors determining investment location to assuage international investor concerns (see Figs 4.11 and 4.12). These may include initiatives to boost access to skills, incentives to promote investment and R&D, measures taken to promote domestic economic growth, considerations of regulatory alignment and reducing the regulatory burden on business,

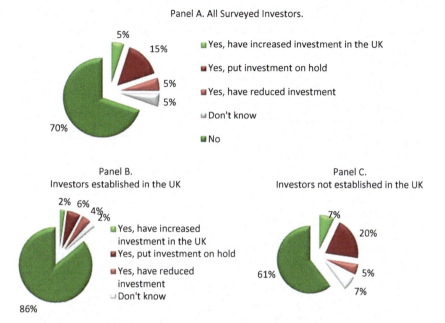

Fig. 4.10   The impact of Brexit on investment plans, EY survey results (%). Note: Authors' interpretation of data. Showing the answers given investor respondents in the year 2019 to the survey question: "Have you changed your UK investment plans (as a result of Brexit)?" Panel A: Answers from all investors (N=446 investors). Panel B: Investors established in the UK (N=284). Panel C: Investors not established in the UK (N=162). *Source*: EY (2019: 16)

public investment in infrastructure and building stronger business networks. Depending upon the form of Brexit actually delivered by the UK government, some of these issues could be more easily resolved through a closer economic relationship with the EU, whereas others could be more straightforwardly realised through a more independent form of Brexit.

A second source of survey data can be drawn from the work of IPSOS MORI in 2013, whose respondents encompassed CEOs, chairmen, CIOs, board members, directors and partners of 101 companies based in the UK. This survey did not seek to discover the perceptions and investment plans of *potential* inward investors, but rather the attitudes of those already embedded within the UK economy. The results suggest that Brexit is likely to have little impact on most inward investors, although up to 10%

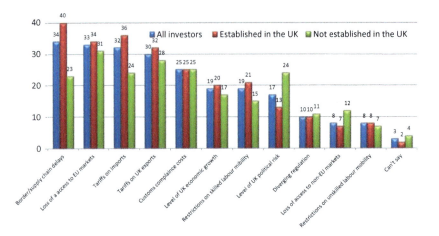

Fig. 4.11 Investors' key factors of concerned about the UK post-Brexit, survey results (%). Note: Authors' interpretation of data, showing the answers given investor respondents in the year 2019 to the survey question: "What are the key factors that you are concerned about with the UK after it leaves the European Union?" Two answers were possible. Answers collected from all investors (N=446 investors); investors established in the UK (N=284); and investors not established in the UK (N=162). *Source*: EY (2019: 40)

may seriously consider relocating at least some of their operations out of the UK, whilst a further 27% leave this option open (Punhani and Hill 2016: 10) (see Fig. 4.13).

UNCTAD survey data has the advantage of a much larger sample size than the Ernst and Young (EY 2013, 2015) or IPSOS MORI surveys, and its results indicate that the national market remains the most important determinant of FDI for both the manufacturing and service sectors (UNCTAD 2009: 18). Similarly, even during a period when potential investors were fully aware of the possible withdrawal of the UK from the EU, international investors still viewed the UK as the fourth most promising host economy for FDI (UNCTAD 2019: 26).

Using a slightly different approach, a YouGov survey carried out for the CBI found that 42% of the 415 CBI members surveyed felt that Brexit would have a slight or significant detrimental impact upon the ability of UK firms to attract inward international investment from within the EU and 32% from outside the EU. For inward FDI as a whole, 75% of

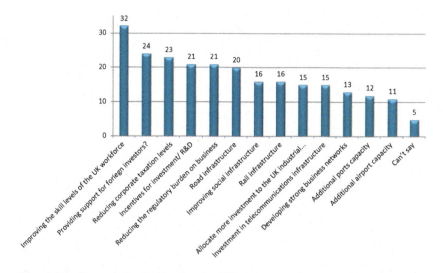

Fig. 4.12 Investors' priorities for the UK government to consider post-Brexit, survey results (%). Note: Authors' interpretation of data, showing the answers given investor respondents in the year 2019 to the survey question: "Which of the following areas should be domestic priorities for the UK Government to improve the UK's attractiveness in future?" Two answers were possible. Answers collected from all investors (N=446 investors). *Source*: EY (2019: 41)

respondents believed that this would decline, with just over half of these predicting it would do so by a significant amount.[4] This particular study is interesting for the insight that it provides into business (and particularly big business) opinion in the UK, but it is not as useful as the Ernst and Young (EY 2013, 2015) or UNCTAD surveys, given that the latter were questioning international investors—that is, the people who are likely to be undertaking the FDI themselves—rather than businesspeople within the UK, many of who have no connection with inward investment and therefore could claim no particular insight into likely future developments.

Overall, these surveys of international investor perceptions and intentions suggest that the uncertainty surrounding Brexit has damaged the attractiveness of the UK as a preferred location for production, for a number of potential investors, with a small minority (6–10%) considering

---

[4] http://news.cbi.org.uk/news/8-out-of-10-firms-say-uk-must-stay-in-eu/yougov-cbi-eu-business-poll/

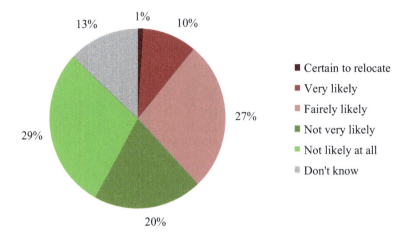

Fig. 4.13 Perception of Brexit impact on Single Market access and relocation decisions *In Answer to the Survey* Question: "In a scenario where the UK left the Single Market, how likely is it that your firm would relocate at least some of its headcount from the UK to a location within the Single Market?" Source: Based on Punhani and Hill (2016: 11)

relocating some of their existing facilities away from the UK. Nevertheless, the UK still remains amongst the most attractive locations for FDI in the world, and the top destination for inward investment within the EU, which suggests that medium-term effects are likely to be muted as long as Brexit-related uncertainty can be addressed in the short term.

POLICY RESPONSE

The appropriate policy response to managing inward flows of FDI, following Brexit, depends upon the assessment of the impact upon the UK economy. In the short term, the balance of payments gain derived from the inflow of overseas capital is certainly an advantage, particularly if trade flows to the EU are likely to be affected by whatever relationship the UK negotiates with the EU. However, in the medium and longer term, the reliance of the UK upon the continued attraction of inward flows of FDI is problematic, both because this highlights the weakness and imbalances which persist in the UK economy, but also because the spillovers which economic theory would suggest arise from inward investment are difficult to substantiate in practice. Consequently, UK policy makers may wish to consider a two-pronged approach, namely to:

1. Seek to reassure international investors in the short term, since the economy is currently over-reliant upon their contribution to certain sectors of the economy and mitigating a very large balance of trade deficit through inward flows of capital.
2. Utilise a package of measures, including an industrial strategy, to seek to rebalance the UK economy in the medium term, through facilitating the expansion of the manufacturing sector, and thereby reducing the current over-reliance upon FDI to drive R&D and raise productivity through perhaps elusive technological spillovers.

Short-term options to enhance the attractiveness of the UK as an FDI location, certainly relative to the rest of the EU, could include lowering the cost for inward investors, through reducing regulatory costs and/or taxation (Irwin 2015: 13). This approach need not be a 'race to the bottom', with the UK seeking to undercut EU standards, since cost cutting can equally be achieved through a deregulation and liberalisation agenda, or through the realisation of economies of scale through underpinning production by aggregate demand management and thereby reducing unit costs. Either approach should prove attractive to efficiency-seeking inward investors.

For market-seeking investors, however, the main determinants are the wealth and growth rate of the national economy, together with access to other international markets. Given that most FDI flowing into the UK is in services, and this sector tends to be more focused upon the national market rather than international exporting possibilities, then a macroeconomic strategy aimed at ensuring continued good levels of economic growth in the UK economy should reassure a large proportion of inward investors. The Bank of England's 2016 stimulus package and the Chancellor of the Exchequer's more recent infrastructure investment plans will assist in this regard. For a significant minority, however, the resolution of the withdrawal negotiations with the EU, and the particular model for future trade relationships selected, will have a significant bearing upon whether these investors are reassured or will gradually disinvest from the UK economy.

Case Study: Brexit and the Car Industry

One sector which is regularly discussed in the context of Brexit is the UK car manufacturing industry. Figures from its trade body, the Society of Motor Manufacturers and Traders (SMMT), highlight its importance for the UK economy, in terms of turnover (£82bn), direct (186,000) and indirect (856,000) employment, R&D investment and export earnings (12% of the total), albeit that the net trade balance in cars is a deficit of approximately £2 billion.[5] In terms of FDI inflows, the car industry represents a significant share of inward manufacturing investment, although, as the data presented earlier in this chapter indicates, manufacturing FDI represents only a small share of total investment flowing into the UK. Nevertheless, with the number of new cars sold declining for the past two years[6], and a number of manufacturing plants having closed, the UK car industry represents an important segment of the UK economy which merits particular attention.

The SMMT has been particularly vociferous in its stance that a 'no deal' Brexit would risk "permanent devastation" which may result in "destroying" the car industry, due to a combination of Brexit uncertainty delaying investment, contingency spending increasing costs, concerns over access to future skilled workers, the disruption of just-in-time supply chain logistics and the threat of tariffs on exports to the EU.[7] The SMMT claims that this would add £3.2bn a year to car manufacturing costs—equivalent to approximately 90% of the industry's R&D budget—and output could decline from 1.3 million cars in 2019 to around 1 million by 2025.[8] The heads of BMW and PSA (Citroen-Peugeot) have stated their consideration of closing UK manufacturing plants if components cannot be easily

---

[5] https://www.smmt.co.uk/industry-topics/uk-automotive/; https://commonslibrary.parliament.uk/insights/whats-driving-the-uk-car-industry-crisis/

[6] https://www.smmt.co.uk/2019/06/uk-new-car-market-falls-again-in-may/

[7] https://www.smmt.co.uk/2019/02/brexit-represents-a-clear-and-present-danger-to-uk-car-industry/;https://www.theguardian.com/politics/2018/jun/26/brexit-uncertainty-putting-860000-jobs-at-risk-warns-car-industry; https://www.independent.co.uk/news/business/news/brexit-no-deal-latest-risks-destroy-uk-car-industry-effect-house-of-commons-vote-a8728661.html;   http://fortune.com/2019/01/31/brexit-uk-auto-industry-damage/;

[8] https://www.theguardian.com/business/2019/nov/26/no-deal-brexit-would-cost-uk-car-industry-40bn-by-2024?CMP=Share_iOSApp_Other

imported from elsewhere in Europe following Brexit.[9] This is despite Tavares, Chairperson of PSA, having earlier claimed that trading according to WTO rules would in fact be a "nice opportunity" for Vauxhall, as it would encourage strengthening of supply chains and sourcing of inputs from within the UK.[10] There are, however, two problems with this simplistic narrative. The first is that the SMMT analysis rests upon the assumption that rule of origin requirements would require the UK car industry to demonstrate that 55% or 60% of a finished vehicle, to be exported into the EU single market, would contain UK content by value.[11] Current figures for the UK car industry are around 44%, albeit this figure fails to account for the fact that almost half the value of these UK components use parts sourced from elsewhere in the world. This would appear to be a time-consuming problem for the UK car industry to resolve. Yet, in both the EU-Canadian (CETA) and EU-South Korea (EU-SK) FTAs, the foreign (non-originating) content level for cars is set at 45%, which is very close to the current content for the UK industry.[12] In addition, what is known as 'cumulation of origin' rules mean that products or components originating in *any* of the parties to the agreement count towards this total (EU-SK: Section A: Rules of Origin, Article 3; CETA: Council of the EU 2016: 5, 90, Chapter 87).[13] In other words, 55% of the value of a South Korean car must come from *either* South Korea *or* the EU, and for a Canadian car exported to the EU must be from *either* Canada *or* the EU (Cooper et al. 2011: 8; EU Commission 2017: 15). If a UK-EU free trade agreement imposed similar rule of origin requirements upon the UK car industry, then this would be met quite easily with no changes to supply chains required.

[9] https://www.ft.com/content/1982d8ee-7907-11e8-bc55-50daf11b720d; https://www.bbc.co.uk/news/business-50564819; https://www.theguardian.com/business/2019/jun/27/vauxhall-astra-to-be-built-in-uk-if-ministers-avoid-no-deal-brexit.

[10] https://www.telegraph.co.uk/business/2017/03/06/psa-seals-19bn-takeover-vauxhall-opel/.

[11] https://www.smmt.co.uk/wp-content/uploads/sites/2/SMMT-Brexit-issue-paper-RULE-OF-ORIGIN-Dec-17-Update-With-New-Figures.pdf; https://www.instituteforgovernment.org.uk/printpdf/5789.

[12] https://eeas.europa.eu/sites/eeas/files/tradoc_145203.pdf.

[13] https://www.international.gc.ca/trade-commerce/trade-agreements-accords-commerciaux/agr-acc/ceta-aecg/text-texte/P1.aspx?lang=eng; https://publications.parliament.uk/pa/ld201919/ldselect/ldeucom/6/604.htm.

The second and more substantive issue raised by the SMMT thesis concerns the difficulty in isolating the impact arising from the Brexit process from the impact of other factors affecting the global car market. The question, therefore, is whether Brexit which is the main or even significant contributory cause of the UK car industry's current difficulties. The current trade dispute between the USA and China, for example, has had secondary impacts upon car manufacture in Europe, Canada and Mexico. Coinciding with a reduction in tax allowances on the purchasing of new cars in China, this shift in global demand was cited in the decisions of plant closures in the UK by Honda and Jaguar Land Rover.[14] Similarly, the trade agreement between the EU and Japan, which entered into force in February 2019, will gradually reduce barriers to Japanese companies exporting cars directly from Japan rather than locating plants in the UK or other EU member states. This will encourage further reconfiguration of Japanese car plant location.[15] Finally, and perhaps most significantly, European car manufacturing is likely to be most impacted by a shift in demand away from diesel cars, partly as a direct result of the 2015 emissions scandal, but mostly driven by more fundamental environmental concerns, as transport is responsible for approximately 27% of EU(28) greenhouse gas emissions.[16] Policy targets are to impose tighter environmental regulations in the short term and require zero emission vehicles in the medium term (HMG 2018).[17]

The European car industry is more exposed by this shift in global demand, in large part because of an earlier collaboration between certain car manufacturers and the European Commission, which actively encouraged a switch from petrol to diesel in the belief that this could lower emissions. The results were dramatic. Between 1990 and 2014, the share of

[14] https://www.bbc.co.uk/news/business-47391800;   https://www.bbc.co.uk/news/uk-england-wiltshire-48255590?intlink_from_url=https://www.bbc.co.uk/news/business/global_car_industry&link_location=live-reporting-story;   https://www.bloomberg.com/news/articles/2019-06-05/ford-set-to-close-u-k-engine-factory-as-part-of-restructuring.

[15] https://facta.co.jp/article/201907002.html, translated from the original Japanese by Oishi Kuranosuke.

[16] https://www.eea.europa.eu/data-and-maps/indicators/transport-emissions-of-greenhouse-gases/transport-emissions-of-greenhouse-gases-11;   https://ec.europa.eu/clima/policies/transport_en.

[17] https://ec.europa.eu/commission/presscorner/detail/en/IP_18_3708; http://www.europarl.europa.eu/RegData/etudes/BRIE/2019/637895/EPRS_BRI(2019)637895_EN.pdf.

the UK new car market accounted by diesel vehicles rose from 6% to 50%. This market penetration is quite low compared to the EU as a whole, where diesel car market penetration reached 60%. In the absence of Commission and national government inducements, it is estimated that the market penetration of diesel cars in Europe may have likely stabilised at around 15% market share (Cames and Helmers 2013: 3). This contrasts sharply with diesel car market share in the USA and China, which has barely exceeded 1%, whilst Japanese focus on developing petrol-electric hybrids allowed their car manufacturers to gain early mover advantage in that particular market and their share of diesel cars declined to around 1.4% (Cames and Helmers 2013).

Demand for alternatively powered vehicles (i.e. hybrid, electric and gas) currently remains constrained, in the UK and across many parts of the EU, by current battery limitations and under-developed recharging infrastructure.[18] Nevertheless, as infrastructure improves, consumer demand and policy requirements will drive substantial increased sales in zero emission vehicles. This will, in turn, require reconfiguration of manufacturing plant and the introduction of new lines of investment.

Global shifts in demand and the necessity to move away from diesel engine manufacture have impacted significantly upon the global car industry, irrespective of Brexit. The only indirect link may be that any uncertainty surrounding the future trading policy of the UK may delay or defer investment in UK plant, thereby slowing the UK industry's response to these global changes in demand and eventually undermining the attractiveness of the product for consumers. Falling demand has led to decisions to close more marginal plant to reduce excess capacity and facilitating focus upon the development of new innovative products.[19] Plant closures and job losses have occurred in Russia, Mexico, the USA and Europe (including France and Germany).[20] Indeed, in November 2019, Daimler Mercedes-Benz (10,000), Volkswagen (7000 job losses), Audi (9500) and BMW (6000) announced planned reductions in their global workforces in

---

[18] https://www.acea.be/uploads/statistic_documents/Economic_and_Market_Report_full-year_2018.pdf.

[19] https://www.bbc.co.uk/news/uk-wales-48533790; https://www.bbc.co.uk/news/business-47291627.

[20] https://www.bbc.co.uk/news/business-48340619?intlink_from_url=https://www.bbc.co.uk/news/business/global_car_industry&link_location=live-reporting-story; https://www.bloomberg.com/news/articles/2019-06-05/ford-set-to-close-u-k-engine-factory-as-part-of-restructuring.

order to reduce its cost base and enable increased investment into electric car manufacture.[21] These announcements are clearly not Brexit-related. This is not to dismiss the existence of *any* potential Brexit effect. Cost implications may arise from delays at customs checks, whilst the imposition of 8–10% tariffs in the event of trading according to WTO rules, and possible difficulties accessing sufficient skilled workers, may provide the UK car industry with further challenges. However, the UK's independence may make a contribution towards helping to resolve some of these problems for the UK car industry through, for example, policy intervention targeted upon skills development, the maintenance of a competitive exchange rate, more generous R&D credits or the use of industrial policy measures to create a domestic car manufacturing supply chain.[22] The localising of supply chains would additionally deliver additional benefits to the UK economy and reduce environmental transportation costs.

Conclusion

There is a clear and consistent consensus amongst economists, business-people and policy makers that FDI provides positive benefits for the UK economy, whether through technological and productivity spillovers in the microeconomy, or compensating for the very large trade deficit in terms of UK balance of payments. Indeed, the UK is probably more reliant upon the continuation of FDI flows, at least in the short term, than most similarly sized economies. Thus, a number of those studies, produced during the recent European referendum, sought to measure the likely impact of Brexit upon FDI flows. The conclusions appeared clear cut—that is, that withdrawal from the EU would result in a substantial drop in FDI, with consequent negative impact upon productivity and growth.

The problem with this consensus, as has been demonstrated in this chapter, is that it is based on only a small number of academic studies and opinion surveys, each of which has methodological weaknesses. Moreover, the range of forecasted impacts is quite wide and is due to different

---

[21] https://www.reuters.com/article/us-daimler-jobs/daimler-to-ax-at-least-10000-jobs-in-latest-car-industry-cuts-idUSKBN1Y312E; https://www.theguardian.com/business/2019/nov/29/daimler-to-axe-at-least-10000-jobs-worldwide

[22] https://www.theguardian.com/business/2016/nov/06/european-commission-examine-terms-uk-deal-nissan.

assumptions and data selection involved in the design of the individual studies. Surveys appear to suggest that there has thus far been a decline in inward investment following Brexit, and it is reasonable to presume that uncertainty surrounding the resolution of Brexit has dampened investment, whether inward flows or domestic forms of investment. However, it is difficult to ascribe causation because this has occurred amidst a more general global decline in FDI flows. Indeed, UNCTAD data shows that UK FDI flows have held up comparatively well when compared to the EU as a whole.

This is, however, not the end of the Brexit process. Withdrawal has not yet occurred and econometric studies, using gravity models, have forecast a much larger potential future decline in FDI, albeit with individual predictions being very heavily dependent upon data selection and the resolution of future trading arrangements. Surveys of investor perceptions indicate weakening of the attractiveness of the UK as a destination for FDI, but as yet only a very small minority of companies are considering disinvestment and those pausing investment until Brexit has been resolved remains perhaps only 6% of those already established in the UK, albeit that a larger proportion of new potential investors are preferring to delay entry into the UK market in the short term.

The data, therefore, would appear to point towards a weakening in inward flows of FDI into the UK, of a not too dissimilar nature to more general global declines in FDI flows. What is difficult to distinguish, at present, is the degree to which Brexit is having an impact and, if so, whether this is primarily related to the uncertainty it creates or a more fundamental change in investor perceptions resulting from the UK's scheduled withdrawal from the EU. This will become clear over the next year. Yet, the imprecision over Brexit impact predictions makes it more difficult for policy makers to develop a policy framework capable of stabilising investment over the medium term.

What all of the different methods agree upon, however, is that, without any corrective action being undertaken, there is likely to be a drop in inward investment, at least in the short run. Moreover, surveys indicate the areas where policy makers can focus their attention—that is, skills, infrastructure investment, promoting growth rates in the UK economy. These can be pursued irrespective of the final form of Brexit resolution, but the options available to governments might vary according to the type of Brexit solution is delivered. This topic will be developed further in Chap. 8.

REFERENCES

Aghion, P., Blundell, R., Griffith, R., Howitt, P., & Prantl, S. (2009). The Effects of Entry on Incumbent Innovation and Productivity. *Review of Economics and Statistics, 91*(1), 20–32.

Aitken, B. J., & Harrison, A. E. (1999). Do Domestic Firms Benefit from Direct Foreign Investment? Evidence from Venezuela. *American Economic Review, 89*(3), 605–618. an+Market+20+years+on%3A+Achievements,+unfulfilled+ex pectations+%26+further+potential.pdf.

Arestis, P., & Mariscal, I. (1997). Conflict, Effort and Capital Stock in UK Wage Determination. *Empirica, 24*(3), 179–193.

Arestis, P., & Mariscal, I. (2000). Capital Stock, Unemployment and Wages in the UK and Germany. *Scottish Journal of Political Economy, 47*(5), 487–503.

Bailey, D., Lenihan, H., & De Ruyter, A. (2016). A Cautionary Tale of Two "Tigers": Industrial policy "lessons" from Ireland and Hungary? *Local Economy, 31*(8), 873–891.

Baldwin, R. E., Forslid, R., & Haaland, J. I. (1996). Investment Creation and Diversion in Europe. *World Economy, 19*, 635–659.

Bank of England. (2015). *EU Membership and the Bank of England*. London: Bank of England. Available via: http://www.bankofengland.co.uk/publications/Documents/speeches/2015/euboe211015.pdf.

Bank of England. (2018). *EU Withdrawal Scenarios and Monetary and Financial Stability: A Response to the House of Commons Select Committee*. London: Bank of England. Available via: https://www.bankofengland.co.uk/-/media/boe/files/report/2018/euwithdrawal-scenarios-and-monetary-and-financial-stability.pdf?la=en&hash=B5F6EDCDF90DCC10286FC0BC599D94CAB8735DFB. Accessed on 18 February 2020.

Barrell, R., & Pain, N. (1997). Foreign Direct Investment, Technological Change and Economic Growth within Europe. *Economic Journal, 107*(445), 1770–1786.

Barrell, R., & Pain, N. (1998). Real Exchange Rates, Agglomerations, and Irreversibilities: Macroeconomic Policy and FDI in EMU. *Oxford Review of Economic Policy, 14*(3), 152–167.

Begg, D., Blanchard, O., Coyle, D., Eichengreen, B., Frankel, J., Giavazzi, F., Portes, R., Seabright, P., Venables, A., Winters, L. A., & Wyplotz, C. (2003). *The Consequences of Saying No: An Independent Report into the Economic Consequences of the UK Saying No to the Euro*. London: Britain in Europe. Available via: http://faculty.london.edu/rportes/research/BeggCommissionReport.pdf.

Bertrand, O., Nilsson-Hakkala, K., Norbäck, P-J., & Persson, L. (2008). Should R&D Champions Be Protected from Foreign Takeovers? *IFN Working Paper* No. 772, Research Institute of Industrial Economics, Stockholm. Retrieved December 11, 2019, from https://papers.ssrn.com/sol3/papers.cfm?abstract_id=1308433.

Bloom, N., Genakos, C., Sadun, R., & Van, R. J. (2012a). Management Practices Across Firms and Countries. *Academy of Management Perspectives, 26*(1), 12–33.

Bloom, N., Sadun, R., & Van Reenen, J. (2012b). Americans Do IT Better: US Multinationals and the Productivity Miracle. *American Economic Review, 102*(1), 167–201.

Borensztein, E., DeGregorio, J., & Lee, J.-W. (1998). How Does Foreign Direct Investment Affect Economic Growth? *Journal of International Economics, 45*, 115–135.

Brenton, P., Di Mauro, F., & Lücke, M. (1999). Economic Integration and FDI: An Empirical Analysis of Foreign Investment in the EU and in Central and Eastern Europe. *Empirica, 26*(2), 95–121.

Bruno, R. L., & Campos, N. F. (2013). Re-examining the Conditional Effect of Foreign Direct Investment, *Institute of Labor Economics Discussion Paper* No. 7458, Bonn. Retrieved December 13, 2019, from http://ftp.iza.org/dp7458.pdf.

Bruno, R., Campos, N., & Estrin, S. (2016). *Gravitating Towards Europe: An Econometric Analysis of the FDI Effects of EU Membership*, Mimeo. London School of Economics. Available via: http://cep.lse.ac.uk/pubs/download/brexit03_technical_paper.pdf.

Buffie, E. (1993). Direct Foreign Investment. *Crowding Out, and Underemployment on the Dualistic Economy, Oxford Economic Papers, 45*, 639–667.

Busse, M., & Groizard, J. L. (2008). Foreign Direct Investment, Regulations and Growth. *World Economy, 31*(7), 861–886.

Cames, M., & Helmers, E. (2013). Critical Evaluation of the European Diesel Car Boom: Global Comparison, Environmental Effects and Various National Strategies. *Environmental Science Europe, 25*(15), 1–22.

Campos, N. F., Coricelli, F., & Moretti, L. (2014). *Economic Growth from Political Integration: Estimating the Benefits from Membership in the European Union Using the Synthetic Counterfactuals Method* (IZA Discussion Paper Series 8162). Bonn. Available via: http://anon-ftp.iza.org/dp8162.pdf.

Capital Economics. (2016). *The Economics Impact of 'Brexit': A Paper Discussing the United Kingdom' Relationship with Europe and the Impact of 'Brexit' on the British Economy*. Oxford: Woodford Investment Management LLP. Available via: https://woodfordfunds.com/economic-impact-brexit-report/.

Carkovic, M. V., & Levine, R. (2005). Does Foreign Direct Investment Accelerate Economic Growth? In T. H. Moran, E. M. Graham, & M. Blomstrom (Eds.), *Does Foreign Direct Investment Promote Development?* (pp. 195–219). Washington DC: Institute for International Economics Center for Global Development.

Cooper, W. H., Jurenas, R., Platzer, M. D., & Manyin, M. E. (2011). *The EU-South Korea Free Trade Agreement and Its Implications for the United States, R41534*. Washington DC: Congressional Research Services.

Council of the EU. (2016). *Comprehensive Economic and Trade Agreement Between Canada, on the One Part, and the European Union and Its Member States, of the Other Part—Protocol on Rules of Origin and Origin Procedures*, 10973/16, Brussels. Available via: http://data.consilium.europa.eu/doc/document/ST-10973-2016-ADD-6/en/pdf.

Cowling, K., & Sugden, R. (1987). *Transnational Monopoly Capitalism*. London: Wheatsheaf Books.

De Mello, L. R. (1999). Foreign Direct Investment-led Growth: Evidence from Time Series and Panel Data. *Oxford Economic Papers, 51*, 133–151.

Deutsche Bank. (2013). *The Single European Market—20 Years On*. Frankfurt: Deutsche Bank. Available via. https://www.dbresearch.com/PROD/DBR_INTERNET_EN-PROD/PROD0000000000322897/The+Single+Europe.

Dhingra, S., Huang, H., Ottaviano, G., Pessoa, J. P., Sampson, T., & Van Reenan, J. (2017). Trade After Brexit. *Economic Policy, 32*(92), 651–705.

Dhingra, S., Ottaviano, G., Sampson, T., & Van Reenen, J. (2016). *The Consequences of Brexit for UK Trade and Living Standards*, Centre for Economic Performance (CEP) and London School of Economics and Political Science (LSE). Available via: http://cep.lse.ac.uk/pubs/download/brexit02.pdf.

Driffield, N. L., & Hughes, D. R. (2003). Foreign and Domestic Investment: Complements or Substitutes? *Regional Studies, 37*(3), 277–288.

Driffield, N. L., & Love, J. H. (2003). FDI, Technology Sourcing and Reverse Spillovers. *The Manchester School, 71*(6), 659–672.

Driffield, N., Love, J., Lancheros, S., & Temouri, Y. (2013). *How Attractive Is the UK for Future Manufacturing Foreign Direct Investment?* London: Foresight Government Office for Science.

Driffield, N. L., & Munday, M. C. (2000). Industrial Performance, Agglomeration, and Foreign Manufacturing Investment in the UK. *Journal of International Business Studies, 31*(1), 21–37.

Driffield, N. L., & Taylor, K. (2000). FDI and the Labour Market: A Review of the Evidence and Policy Implications. *Oxford Review of Economic Policy, 16*(3), 90–103.

Driffield, N. L., & Taylor, K. (2006). Domestic Wage Determination: Regional Spillovers and Inward Investment. *Spatial Economic Analysis, 1*(2), 187–205.

Dunning, J. H. (1988). The Eclectic Paradigm of International Production. *Journal of International Business Studies, 19*(1), 1–29.

Dunning, J. H. (1993). *Multinational Enterprises and the Global Economy*. Harrow: Addison-Wesley.

Durham, J. B. (2004). Absorptive Capacity and the Effects of Foreign Direct Investment and Equity Foreign Portfolio Investment on Economic Growth. *European Economic Review, 48*(2), 285–306.

Ebell, M., & Warren, J. (2016). The Long-term Economic Impact of Leaving the EU. *National Institute Economic Review, 236*, 121–138.

Egger, P., & Pfaffermayr, M. (2004). Distance, Trade and FDI: A Hausman-Taylor SUR Approach. *Journal of Applied Econometrics, 19*, 227–246.

Emmerson, C., Johnson, P., Mitchell, I., & Phillips, D. (2016). *Brexit and the UK's Public Finances* (IFS Report 116). Institute for Fiscal Studies, London. Available via: http://www.ifs.org.uk/uploads/publications/comms/r116.pdf.

Ernst and Young (EY). (2013). *EY's Attractiveness Survey—UK 2013*. London: Ernst and Young. Retrieved from: http://www.ey.com/Publication/vwLUAssets/.

Ernst and Young (EY). (2015). *EY's Attractiveness Survey—UK 2015*. London: Ernst and Young. Retrieved from: http://www.ey.com/Publication/vwLUAssets/.

Ernst-and-Youngs-attractiveness-survey-UK-2013-No-room-forcomplacency/$FILE/EY_UK_Attractiveness_2013.pdf.

Ethier, W. J. (1998). The New Regionalism. *Economic Journal, 108*(449), 1149–1161.

EU Commission. (2017). *Guide to the Comprehensive Economic and Trade Agreement (CETA), Publications Office of the European Union*, Luxembourg. Available via: https://trade.ec.europa.eu/doclib/docs/2017/september/tradoc_156062.pdf.

EY. (2019). Attractiveness Survey. 2019 Report. June. UK.

Fairbairn, C., & Newton-Smith, R. (2016). *Brexit—The Business View*, Lecture at London Business School, Monday 21st March. Available via: http://news.cbi.org.uk/business-issues/uk-and-the-european-union/eu-business-facts/brexit-the-business-view-pdf/.

Fournier, J.-M., Domps, A., Gorin, Y., Guillet, X., & Morchoisne, D. (2015). *Implicit Regulatory Barriers in the EU Single Market: New Empirical Evidence from Gravity Models* (OECD Economics Department Working Papers No. 1181). Available via: https://doi.org/10.1787/5js7xj0xckf6-en.

Fredriksson, P. G., List, J. A., & Millimet, D. L. (2003). Bureaucratic Corruption Environmental Policy and Inbound US FDI: Theory and Evidence. *Journal of Public Economics, 87*, 1407–1430.

Froot, K., & Stein, J. (1991). Exchange Rates and Foreign Direct Investment: An Imperfect Capital Markets Approach. *Quarterly Journal of Economics, 196*, 1191–1218.

Görg, H., & Greenaway, D. (2004). Much Ado About Nothing? Do Domestic Firms Really Benefit from Foreign Direct Investment? *World Bank Research Observer, 19*(2), 171–197.

Görg, H., & Strobl, E. (2001). Multinational Companies and Productivity Spillovers: A Metaanalysis. *Economic Journal, 111*(475), 723–739.

Gray, H. P. (1998). International Trade and Foreign Direct Investment: The Interface. In J. H. Dunning (Ed.), *Globalization Trade and Foreign Direct Investment* (pp. 19–27). Oxford: Elsevier.

Griffith, R., Redding, S., & Simpson, H. (2004). Foreign Ownership and Productivity: New Evidence from the Service Sector and the R&D Lab. *Oxford Review of Economic Policy, 20*(3), 440–456.

Grossman, G. M., & Helpman, E. (1994). Endogenous Innovation in the Theory of Growth. *Journal of Economic Perspectives, 8*(1), 23–44. Available via: https://www.researchgate.net/profile/Elhanan_Helpman/publication/4722290_Endogenous_Innovation_in_the_Theory_of_Growth/links/56adf60e08ae19a38515eda3.pdf.

Haaland, J. I., & Wooton, I. (2007). Domestic Labour Markets and Foreign Direct Investment. *Review of International Economics, 15*(3), 462–480.

Hantzsche, A., Kara, A., & Young, G. (2018). *The Economic Effects of the Government's Proposed Brexit Deal.* London: NIESR. Available via: https://www.niesr.ac.uk/sites/default/files/publications/NIESR%20Report%20Brexit%20-%202018-11-26.pdf. Accessed 17 February 2020.

Harris, R., & Robinson, C. (2002). The Effect of Foreign Acquisitions on Total Factor Productivity: Plant-level Evidence from UK Manufacturing, 1987–1992. *Review of Economics and Statistics, 84*(3), 562–568.

Haskel, J. E., Pereira, S. C., & Slaughter, M. J. (2002). *Does Inward Foreign Direct Investment Boost the Productivity of Domestic Firms?* (NBER Working Paper No. 8724). Available via: http://www.nber.org/papers/w8724.pdf.

Hejazi, W., & Pauly, P. (2003). Motivations for FDI and Domestic Capital Formation. *Journal of International Business Studies, 34*, 282–289.

Helpman, E., Melitz, M. J., & Yeaple, S. R. (2004). Export Versus FDI with Heterogeneous Firms. *American Economic Review, 94*, 300–316.

Hines, J. R. (1996). Altered States: Taxes and the Location of Foreign Direct Investment in America. *American Economic Review, 86*(5), 1076–1094.

HM Government (HMG). (2013). *Review of the Balance of Competences Between the United Kingdom and the European Union—The Single Market.* London: The Stationery Office. Available via: https://www.gov.uk/government/uploads/system/uploads/attachment_data/file/227069/2901084_SingleMarket_acc.pdf.

HM Treasury. (2003). *The Green Book: Appraisal and Evaluation in Central Government.* London: The Stationery Office. Available via: https://www.gov.uk/government/uploads/system/uploads/attachment_data/file/220541/green_book_complete.pdf.

HM Treasury. (2016). *HM Treasury Analysis: The Long Term Economic Impact of EU Membership and the Alternatives.* London: Cm 9250, The Stationery Office. Available via: https://www.gov.uk/government/uploads/system/uploads/attachment_data/file/517415/treasury_analysis_economic_impact_of_eu_membership_web.pdf.

HMG [Her Majesty's Government]. (2018). *The Road to Zero: Next Steps Towards Cleaner Road Transport and Delivering Our Industrial Strategy*, Department for Transport, London. Retrieved December 16, 2019, from https://assets. publishing.service.gov.uk/government/uploads/system/uploads/attachment_data/file/739460/road-to-zero.pdf.

Hofmann, P. (2013). *The Impact of International Trade and FDI on Economic Growth and Technological Change*. Berlin: Springer.

Foresight-Department of Business, Innovation and Science. Available via: https://www.gov.uk/government/uploads/system/uploads/attachment_data/file/277171/ep7-foreign-direct-investment-trends-manufacturing.pdf.

Hughes, A. (2013). Short-Termism, Impatient Capital and Finance for Manufacturing Innovation in the UK. In Hughes, A. (Ed.), *The Future of UK Manufacturing: Scenario Analysis, Financial Markets and Industrial Policy*, UK-RIC, Cambridge and London. Retrieved January 8, 2019, from http://www.uk-irc.org/wp-content/uploads/2015/02/Future_of_Manufacturing_ebook.pdf.

Hymer, S. (1960). *The International Operations of National Firms; A Study of Direct Foreign Investment*. Cambridge: MIT Press.

Iamsiraroj, S., & Ulubaşoğlu, M. A. (2015). Foreign Direct Investment and Economic Growth: A Real Relationship or Wishful Thinking? *Economic Modelling, 51*(C), 200–213.

IMF. (2013). *Balance of Payments Manual* (6th ed.). Washington DC: IMF. Available via: https://www.imf.org/external/np/sta/bop/BOPman.pdf.

Irwin, G. (2015). *Brexit: The Impact on the UK and the EU*. London: Global Counsel. Available via: http://www.global-counsel.co.uk/system/files/publications/ Global_Counsel_Impact_of_Brexit_June_2015.pdf.

Keller, W., & Yeaple, S. (2009). Multinational Enterprises, International Trade, and Productivity Growth: Firm-level Evidence from the United States. *The Review of Economics and Statistics, 91*(4), 821–831.

Lederman, D., Maloney, W., & Serven, L. (2005). *Lessons from NAFTA for Latin America and Caribbean Countries: A summary of Research Findings*. Washington, DC: World Bank.

Li, X., & Liu, X. (2005). Foreign Direct Investment and Economic Growth: An Increasingly Endogenous Relationship. *World Development, 33*(3), 393–407.

Liu, X., Wang, C., & Wei, Y. (2001). Causal Links Between Foreign Direct Investment and Trade in China. *China Economic Review, 12*, 190–202.

Mansfield, I. (2014). *A Blueprint for Britain: Openness Not Isolation*. London: Institute for Economic Affairs. Available via: http://www.iea.org.uk/sites/default/files/publications/files/Brexit%20Entry%20170_final_bio_web.pdf.

Miller, V. (ed.). (2016). *Exiting the EU: Impact in Key UK Policy Areas* (House of Commons Library Briefing Paper No. HC 07213). Available via: http://researchbriefings.parliament.uk/ResearchBriefing/Summary/CBP-7213#fullreport.

Milne, I. (2004). *A Cost Too Far? An Analysis of the Net Economic Costs and Benefits for the UK of EU Membership*, Civitas. London. Available via: http://www.civitas.org.uk/pdf/cs37.pdf.

Moosa, I. A. (2002). *Foreign Direct Investment: Theory, Evidence and Practice*. Basingstoke: Palgrave.

Morgan, K. (1997). The Learning Region: Institutions Innovation and Regional Renewal. *Regional Studies, 31,* 491–503.

OECD. (2008). *OECD Benchmark Definition of Foreign Direct Investment* (4th ed.). Paris: OECD. Available via: https://www.oecd.org/daf/inv/investment-statisticsandanalysis/40193734.pdf.

OECD. (2016). *The Economic Consequences of Brexit: A Taxing Decision* (OECD Economic Policy Paper No. 16). Available via: http://www.oecd.org/eco/The-Economic-consequences-of-Brexit-27-April-2016.pdf.

ONS [Office of National Statistics]. (2010). *Business Monitor MA4—Foreign Direct Investment involving UK Companies.* Available via: https://www.google.co.uk/url?sa=t&rct=j&q=&esrc=s&source=web&cd=1&cad=rja&uact=8&ved=0ahUKEwj6ioqixOrRAhWbOsAKHUblDj8QFggjMAA&url=http%3A%2F%2Fwww.ons.gov.uk%2Fons%2Frel%2Ffdi%2Fforeign-direct-investment%2F2010-ma4%2Fbusiness-monitor-ma4-2010.pdf%3Fformat%3Dcontrast&usg=AFQjCNE9OZT7jOSmlOQ5i6p088I80bn9Vw.

ONS [Office of National Statistics]. (2020a). *Foreign Direct Investment Involving UK Companies.* Inward tables. Dataset. Available via: https://www.ons.gov.uk/economy/nationalaccounts/balanceofpayments/bulletins/foreigndirectinvestmentinvolvingukcompaniesassetandliability/2018.

ONS [Office of National Statistics]. (2020b). *Business Enterprise Research and Development,* ONS, London. Available via: https://www.ons.gov.uk/economy/governmentpublicsectorandtaxes/researchanddevelopmentexpenditure/bulletins/businessenterpriseresearchanddevelopment/2018#uk-funding-of-business-rd-continues-to-grow.

ONS [Office of National Statistics]. (2020c). Foreign Direct Investment for UK companies (Directional). Released 6 February 2020. Available online via: https://www.ons.gov.uk/economy/nationalaccounts/balanceofpayments/bulletins/foreigndirectinvestmentinvolvingukcompanies/2018.

Pain, N., & Lansbury, M. (1997). Regional Economic Integration and Foreign Direct Investment: The Case of German Investment in Europe. *National Institute Economic Review, 160,* 87–99.

Pain, N., & Wakelin, K. (1998). Export Performance and the Role of Foreign Direct Investment. *Manchester School, 66*(S), 62–88.

Pain, N., & Young, G. (2004). The Macroeconomic Impact of UK Withdrawal from the EU. *Economic Modelling, 21,* 387–408. Available via: http://www.niesr.ac.uk/sites/default/files/publications/1-s2.0-S0264999302000688-main.pdf.

Portes, J. (2013). Commentary: The Economic Implications for the UK of Leaving the European Union. *National Institute Economic Review*, No. 266, F4–9. Available via: http://www.niesr.ac.uk/sites/default/files/commentary.pdf.

PricewaterhouseCoopers LLP (PwC). (2016). *Leaving the EU: Implications for the UK Economy.* London: PricewaterhouseCoopers LLP. Available via: http://news.cbi.org.uk/news/leaving-eu-would-cause-a-serious-shock-to-ukeconomy-new-pwc-analysis/leaving-the-eu-implications-for-the-uk-economy/.

Punhani, S., & Hill, N. (Credit Suisse Report). (2016). *Brexit: Breaking Up Is Never Easy, or Chea.* Zurich: Credit Suisse. Available via: https://doc.research-and-analytics.csfb.com/docView?language=ENG&format=PDF&document_id=806936650&source_id=emrna&serialid=lPu6YfMSDd9toXKa9EPxf5HiN BEoWX2fYou5bZ6jJhA%3D.

Ramasamy, B., & Yeung, M. (2010). The Determinants of Foreign Direct Investment in Services. *The World Economy, 33*(4), 573–596.

Ries, C. P., Hafner, M., Smith, T. D., Burwell, F. G., Egel, D., Han, E., Stepanek, M., & Shatz, H. J. (2017), *After Brexit: Alternate Forms of Brexit and Their Implications for the United Kingdom, the European Union and the United States*, Rand, Santa Monica, California and Cambridge, UK. Retrieved December 11, 2019, from https://www.rand.org/pubs/research_reports/RR2200.html.

Rodrik, D. (2004). *Industrial Policy for the Twenty-first Century.* Available via: https://myweb.rollins.edu/tlairson/pek/rodrikindpolicy.pdf.

Rodrik, D. (2008). Industrial Policy: Don't Ask Why, Ask How. *Middle East Development Journal*, Demo Issue, 1–29. Available via: https://www.sss.ias.edu/files/pdfs/Rodrik/Research/Industrial-Policy-Dont-Ask-Why-Ask-How.pdf.

Straathof, S., Linders, G.-J., Lejour, A., & Mohlmann, J. (2008). *The Internal Market and the Dutch Economy: Implications for Trade and Economic Growth* (CPG Netherlands Document No. 168). Available via: http://www.cpb.nl/sites/default/files/publicaties/download/internal-market-and-dutch-economy-implications-trade-and-economic-growth.pdf.

UNCTAD [United Nations Conference on Trade and Development]. (2009). *World Investment Prospects Survey 2009–2011.* Geneva: United Nations. Available via: http://unctad.org/en/Docs/diaeia20098_en.pdf.

UNCTAD [United Nations Conference on Trade and Development]. (2015). *World Investment Report 2015.* Geneva: United Nations. Available via: http://unctad.org/en/PublicationsLibrary/wir2015_en.pdf.

UNCTAD [United Nations Conference on Trade and Development]. (2016a). *World Investment Report 2016.* Geneva: United Nations. Available via. http://unctad.org/en/PublicationsLibrary/wir2016_en.pdf.

UNCTAD [United Nations Conference on Trade and Development]. (2016b). *Foreign Direct Investment: Inward Flows, Annual.* Available via: www.unctad. org/fdistatistics.

UNCTAD. (2019). *World Investment Report 2019*, UNCTAD, New York. Retrieved March 6, 2019, from https://unctad.org/en/PublicationsLibrary/ wir2019_en.pdf.

UNCTAD [United Nations Conference on Trade and Development]. (2020). *Foreign Direct Investment: Inward Flows, Annual..* Available via: www.unctad. org/fdistatistics.

United Kingdom Trade and Investment (UKTI). (2015, June 17). UK Wins a Record Number of Investment Projects and Maintains Position as Top Investment Destination in Europe. *UKTI Press Release.* Available via: https:// www.gov.uk/government/news/uk-wins-a-record-number-of-investment-projectsand-maintains-position-as-top-investment-destination-in-europe.

United States International Trade Commission (USITC). (2000). *The Impact on the US Economy of Including the United Kingdom in a Free Trade Agreement with the United States, Canada and Mexico* (Investigation No. 332–409). Washington DC: USITC.

Weiss, L. (1998). *The Myth of the Powerless State: Governing the Economy in a Global Era.* Cambridge: Polity Press.

World Trade Organisation (WTO). (2013). *World Trade Report 2013: Factors Shaping the Future of World Trade.* Geneva: World Trade Organisation. Available via: https://www.wto.org/english/res_e/booksp_e/world_trade_ report13_e.pdf.

Wren, C., & Jones, J. (2012). FDI Location Across British Regions and Agglomerative Forces: A Markov Analysis. *Spatial Economic Analysis, 7*(2), 265–286.

Wren, C., & Taylor, J. (1999). Industrial Restructuring and Regional Policy. *Oxford Economic Papers, 51,* 487–516.

Young, S., Hood, N., & Peters, E. (1994). Multinational Enterprises and Regional Economic Development. *Regional Studies, 28*(7), 657–677.

CHAPTER 5

Regulation

One of the areas where EU membership has been criticised as impacting negatively upon the UK economy concerns EU imposed rules and directives. Hence, the expectation is that Brexit would allow the UK to design its own regulations, which may diverge from those governing the EU single market. At the time this book was completed, the EU's negotiating stance is focused upon nullifying this advantage, by insisting upon what it terms to be a 'level playing field'; acceptance would ensure continued regulatory harmonisation, with the UK having to follow EU-determined rules and regulations, even after it has ceased to be an EU member.

REGULATION—BENEFIT OR BURDEN?

Regulation is introduced to solve a problem in the economy, either to curb behaviour or activity which is deemed to have negative consequences upon individuals or society in general or to resolve an incident of market failure. It may prevent collusion, enhance competition, restrict damaging environmental consequences, limit the exposure of the real economy to excessive behaviour in the financial sector, provide a minimum standard of working environment for employees and/or protect consumers against sharp business practices and unsafe products.

Regulatory harmonisation, within the SIM, is intended to encourage intra-EU trade by reducing transaction costs and facilitating the creation of cross-border supply chains (HMG 2013: 41-2; McFadden and Tarrant

© The Author(s) 2020
P. B. Whyman, A. I. Petrescu, *The Economics of Brexit*,
https://doi.org/10.1007/978-3-030-55948-9_5

2015: 41, 60). However, if effective, regulation also imposes costs upon those required to comply, particularly when regulations apply to businesses focused upon domestic (not international) trading and where rules are regarded as unnecessary or badly designed (NAO 2001: 1). Indeed, there would appear to be sufficient evidence to conclude that EU regulation is the source of the majority of the cumulative regulatory burden imposed upon UK businesses (HoC 2009: Ev76; Ambler et al. 2010: 2). As a result, 60% of the members of the Institute of Directors advocated EU regulatory reform,[1] whilst a majority of CBI (2013: 7, 11, 18) members considered that Brexit would result in a reduction in the regulatory burden on their business.

WHAT PROPORTION OF UK LAWS DERIVE FROM THE EU?

It should be a straightforward matter to calculate the proportion of UK law derived from the EU. Unfortunately, there is little conclusive data on the issue. Hence, the range of estimates ranges from 84%, which derives from a written parliamentary answer given by an undersecretary in the Ministry of Justice to the German Bundestag in April 2005 (Gaskell and Persson 2010: 37-8), to the 9% figure claimed by the then Minister of State for Europe, MacShane.[2] Using a slightly different approach, researchers from the House of Commons Library arrived at an average figure of 14.1%, for regulations and laws introduced in the UK between 1997 and 2009 (Miller 2010: 16-17).

One reason for such a discrepancy in these figures relates to the time period over which the estimate is calculated which, as illustrated in Fig. 5.1, varies significantly and hence can significantly skew the estimates produced. A second reason, however, relates to the divergent definitions of what constitutes EU law. If only those laws established through EU directives are included, then the proportion of UK laws determined by the EU is correspondingly small. If, however, all 'soft law' regulations and rules that complement these legal regulations are also included, then the proportion is much greater. Christiensen (2010: 12) calculates that, from the

---

[1] 'IoD calls on all parties to accept need for EU reform', 28 September 2015, http://www.iod.com/influencing/press-office/press-releases/iod-calls-on-all-parties-to-accept-need-for-eu-reform.

[2] http://www.publications.parliament.uk/pa/cm200405/cmhansrd/vo050322/text/50322w46.htm

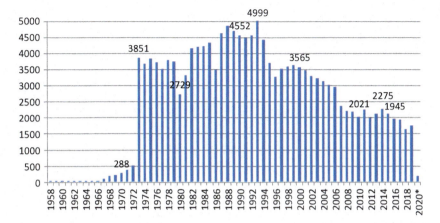

Fig. 5.1 EU legislation adopted by the UK, 1958–2020. Note: Includes all EU legislation, inclusive of regulations, decisions, directives and treaties. *For the year 2020, the data only includes the period 1 January–22 February and amounts to 180 pieces of legislation. Source: Authors' calculations based on information available on the website for All UK Legislation available via https://www.legislation.gov.uk/eu-origin

mid-1990s, soft law has exceeded the combined total number of new directives and EU regulations. In the year 2000 alone, Christiensen estimates that there were more than 2500 examples of new soft laws introduced by the EU, compared to around 800 regulations and around 100 directives. Similarly, Miller (2010: 12-13) estimates that the number of EU (soft and hard) laws peaked at over 14,000 instruments in the early 1980s, with a second, lower peak recorded in the mid-1990s. Accordingly, the House of Commons Library concludes that it is quite plausible to justify any estimate which lies between 15% and 50%, depending upon the methodology utilised (Miller 2010: 24).

CAN BREXIT DELIVER A REGULATORY BENEFIT?

In seeking to assess whether Brexit can have any significant impact upon the regulatory burden faced by UK businesses, the starting point is to assess whether the UK currently suffers from any obvious competitive disadvantage. Superficially, the answer would seem to be in the negative, as Fig. 5.2 indicates that the UK is considered to be one of the most lightly

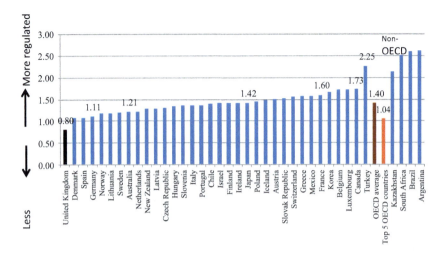

Fig. 5.2 Product market regulation index for selected countries, 2018. Source: Compiled by the authors from data available at OECD Statistics (2018). Note: Due to significant changes in methodology, the OECD product market regulation figures from 2018 are not comparable to earlier calculations made by the OECD

regulated of the OECD nations (Irwin 2015: 14; Crafts 2016: 263; Kierzenkowski et al., 2016: 7, 29-31; Springford 2016: 1; HMG 2018: 6, 39-49). However, the fact that EU regulation has not prevented the UK from maintaining a relatively liberal approach up until this point does not preclude the possibility that it has prevented an even more advantageous position for the UK, and nor does it rule out the possibility that Brexit may facilitate the realisation of this more advantageous regulatory regime. National regulation can be a better fit for an individual economy, when compared to pan-national rules which have to be drafted to apply to distinctly different circumstances.

Most UK Businesses Do Not Export into the SIM

One reason why the burden of EU regulation is considered to be excessive arises from the fact that all UK firms and organisations are subject to the rules and regulations established to form the basis of the SIM (in addition to social and environmental standards), irrespective of the fact that only a small minority of UK firms actually engage in international trade with other EU member nations. Calculating the proportion of firms that export is not altogether straightforward, however, because there are different ways of counting. There were, for example, 5.4 million private sector businesses recorded in 2015, yet only 2.45 million of these were registered for VAT and/or PAYE (BIS 2015: 1, 5; ONS, 2015). Thus, if the percentage calculation uses the figure for total number of firms in the UK, it will produce a result less than half the figure if the calculation uses only those firms registered for VAT.

The figures used by HMRC (2015: 1) suggest that, in 2014, there were approximately 143,000 businesses which exported goods to other EU member states, employing a total of 9.8 million people, with 210,000 businesses importing goods from other EU member states, employing 12.3 million. Unfortunately, there are no equivalent figures for services and therefore the estimate produced, of only 5% of UK businesses exporting goods to the EU, is too restrictive (BIS 2016: 7). If, as has been suggested, services account for around one quarter of trade with the EU by value, then a more accurate figure might be 6.25%.[3] Another complication is that the figures make it difficult to distinguish whether some firms both import and export, or whether these are distinctive activities. This matters, when calculating the number of firms that trade with the EU, because if they are distinct, the number will be around 350,000, whereas if firms both import and export, numbers could be only 210,000. Finally, using a slightly different selection of data, the ONS have produced their own estimates, which are actually quite close to the HMRC figures. They assess that around 5.2% of UK firms export and 7.4% import goods, with the equivalent figures for services being 7% and 4.9% respectively.[4] Using the earlier estimate that services account for around one quarter of trade with the EU, this would imply that around 5.7% of UK businesses export goods and services, and 6.8% import from the EU.

It is possible, of course, that SMEs might not trade with EU nations directly, but their activity may be part of a process which does so indirectly, if they participate in the supply chains of larger enterprises, who themselves do trade with the EU. One estimate is that this would affect around

---

[3] http://www.publications.parliament.uk/pa/cm201212/cmhansrd/cm120327/text/120327w0005.htm#1203281002290

[4] http://webarchive.nationalarchives.gov.uk/20160105160709/; http://www.ons.gov.uk/ons/rel/abs/annual-business-survey/exporters-and-importers-in-great-britain%2D%2D2014/sty-exporters-and-importers.html.

15% of SMEs (BIS 2016: 2). If this figure was added to the ONS estimate for direct exporters, it would indicate that a little over 20% of UK firms were involved, either directly or indirectly, in trading with EU member states.

The composition of these firms is also interesting. Given that operating beyond national borders incurs sunk costs, whether in terms of establishing a new client base, translation, search and regulatory costs (Anderson and van Wincoop 2004), it is perhaps not surprising that it is overwhelmingly the larger and most productive firms that engage in international trade (Driver 2014: 14). Indeed, one estimate suggests that 59.1% of firms exporting to the EU in 2014 have 250 or more employees (Harris and Li 2007; HMRC 2015: 7). This is not just a UK phenomenon. Indeed, the UK has a less concentrated trading profile than many leading developed nations. For example, barely 4% of US firms export, including only around 18% of US manufacturing firms and, of these, only around 15% of the value of their output is actually exported (Bernard et al. 2007: 105, 108-9). Moreover, the share of total export value accounted for by the largest exporters is actually significantly lower in the UK than in most leading developed nations, with the top 1% of exporters accounting for 80.9% of US exports, 59% in Germany, 48% in Belgium, 44% in France and 42% in the UK. When expanding the group to the top 10% of exporters, the difference narrows, as these firms account for 96.3% of US exports, 90% in Germany, 84% in both France and Belgium, together with 80% in the UK (WTO 2013: 87).

Yet, despite only a minority of UK businesses exporting to EU member states, all firms have to abide by the full set of EU regulations. This places an onerous burden upon small and medium-sized enterprises (SMEs), which represent over 99% of all private sector businesses in the UK, employing 15.6 million people, representing 60% of all private sector employment, and with a combined annual turnover of £1.8 trillion, representing 47% of all private sector turnover (BIS 2015: 1). Indeed, the EU has itself recognised the significance of this issue and proposed consultation about lightening the burden of regulations upon the smallest, micro businesses (HMG 2016: 20-1). Given that, within the SIM, it has been argued that exempting domestically orientated firms from some EU regulations would be "unworkable", as it would provide them with an unfair competitive advantage (Springford 2016: 2), the withdrawal from the SIM would enable such deregulation to take place. Hence, it is suggested that Brexit could deliver a regulatory gain for the vast majority of SMEs and those larger companies who do not trade with the EU in having to bear the cost of SIM regulations (Business for Britain 2015: 122-3; Capital Economics 2016: 13).

The Estimated Costs and Benefits of EU Regulations

There have been a number of calculations made concerning the cost of EU regulations. Congdon (2014: 5, 26-35), for example, estimated that it costs between 5.25% and 7% of UK GDP. He further disaggregated this regulatory burden into measures pertaining to climate change and renewable energy regulations of between 1.75% and 2.25% of UK GDP, social and employment regulation costing between 2.5% and 2.75% of UK GDP, financial regulation between 0.5% and 0.75% of UK GDP and the balance of regulatory costs of between 0.75% and 1.25% of UK GDP (Congdon 2014: 30). This analysis focuses rather narrowly upon the costs of regulation, rather than considering the associated benefits. Hence, whilst the effect of EU regulation such as the Temporary Agency Workers Directive imposes costs upon businesses who fall within its sphere of influence, through payment of higher wages, this has a positive macroeconomic effect in boosting demand which is likely to offset some of this cost to the economy, and yet is not included in Congdon's calculations (McFadden and Tarrant 2015: 41).

A second approach has involved use of the Regulatory Impact Assessments (RIAs), introduced by the UK government in 1998, to attempt to measure the potential costs and benefits associated with individual national and EU-originated regulations, together with the opportunity cost (or calculated risks) of not intervening (NAO 2001).[5] There are a number of weaknesses with the RIA approach, not the least of which being that only around 60% of regulations, and more particularly only 52% of EU regulations, identified costs for businesses, whilst the corresponding figures for benefits were less than in 40% of cases (Ambler et al. 2010: 13, 22). RIAs also do not tend to assess wider economic impacts, which may derive from a more regulated business reducing its output as a result of health and safety measures in the case of asbestos manufacture or energy-intensive industries in the case of environmental regulation

---

[5] A database of these RIAs are available via: http://www.legislation.gov.uk/ukia. If you would like to read more about the origin, design and application of RIAs, then you may wish to consider Dunlop and Radaelli (2016).

(Thompson and Harari 2013: 20). Moreover, in order to estimate future economic impacts, the RIA system uses a discount rate (the Social Time Preference Rate) of 3.5% per annum (HM Treasury 2003). This is a practice which Ambler et al. (2010: 18) regard as "wholly unrealistic", because the discount rate is an inadequate means of estimating future impacts amidst uncertainty about regulatory impact. This is a reasonable criticism, yet there is a need to estimate the impact of regulations over time and therefore future projections have to be discounted to take account of opportunity costs.

Whatever the weaknesses with the approach, RIA data has been utilised by research teams working with the British Chambers of Commerce (BCC) and the 'think tank' *Open Europe* to estimate the cumulative costs and benefits of EU regulations. The BCC 'Burdens Barometer' estimated the cumulative cost of the major regulations, introduced in the UK between 1998 and 2010, to total £88.3bn, with 68.8% of this, representing £60.8bn, originating from the EU.[6] By contrast, *Open Europe* calculated the cumulative cost of regulation, introduced since 1998, to have cost the UK economy £176 billion over this 11-year period, with 71% of this total, amounting to £124 billion, having its origin in the EU (Gaskell and Persson 2010: 7). Part of the reason for this discrepancy in results concerned the number of cases analysed; the *Open Europe* study examined 1950 RIAs, whereas the BCC study analysed only the largest 144 RIAs.

A detailed examination of the RIAs indicates that there are a few regulations which have a disproportionate impact upon the overall cost burden for the UK economy. For example, *Open Europe* estimates that the most significant 100 EU regulations cost the UK economy £33.3 billion per annum.[7] Hence, the costliest 5% of EU regulations impose 26.9% of the estimated burden upon UK businesses, whilst the five costliest EU regulations were estimated to cost approximately £19 billion per year and representing more than 15% of the total cost imposed by EU-derived regulations. These were:

i. The UK Renewable Energy Strategy—promotion of renewable energy, including biofuels, with a recurring cost of £4.7bn per annum

---

[6] http://www.thamesvalleychamber.co.uk/uploads/Policy/BurdensBarometer2010.pdf.
[7] http://openeurope.org.uk/intelligence/britain-and-the-eu/top-100-eu-rules-cost-britain-33-3bn/

ii. The Capital Requirements Regulation and Directive (CRD IV)—strengthening the regulation of the banking sector, with an estimated recurring cost of £4.6bn per annum

iii. The Working Time Directive—limiting working hours and requiring annual leave of 5.6 weeks per year, with a recurring cost of £4.2bn per annum

iv. The EU Climate and Energy Package—establishing targets to meet greenhouse gas reduction, embodying the EU emissions trading system, with a recurring cost of £3.4bn per annum

v. The Temporary Agency Workers Directive—guaranteeing equal pay and conditions for those working through employment agencies with employees working in businesses doing equivalent work, with a recurring cost of £2.1bn per annum

When considering regulations by type, the *Open Europe* report indicates that EU employment legislation is the largest regulatory category, costing the UK economy £38.9 billion between 1998 and 2009, and accounting for 22% of total regulatory costs, followed by EU environmental regulation (18%), and with EU health and safety regulation and EU financial regulation both accounting for 5% of total regulatory costs for the UK economy (Gaskell and Persson 2010: 8).

The conclusion that EU regulations would appear particularly burdensome for the business community is tempered by two caveats. The first is that it is possible that a proportion of these costs derive from national government's 'gold plating' EU regulations as they translate Directives into national law, through adding additional requirements, and thereby increasing burdens upon firms, consumers and employees over and above the original intent of the EU regulation (HMG 2013). National governments have some discretion over how to translate Directives into UK law, although this is not the case with EU Regulations or Decisions, where they are imposed without the requirement for national legislation (Thompson and Harari 2013: 20). Gaskell and Persson (2010: 13-14) remain sceptical that this is a significant problem, even though their database does not allow for the type of cross-national comparative analysis which would be necessary to resolve the question. However, as can be noted from the work of Christiensen (2010: 12), the number of Directives represent only a very small proportion of the total volume of the totality of EU rules and regulations, and therefore it is likely that national government 'gold plating' is not likely to be more than of marginal significance.

The more important qualification is that this analysis, thus far, has focused upon the costs but not the benefits of regulation. Yet, the purpose of regulation is to achieve a positive net benefit for the economy as a whole, even if this does place a disproportionate burden upon the business community. Hence, when seeking to determine the relative merits of individual policy interventions, it is preferable to use the Hicks-Kaldor criteria that it should be considered to be successful if the net gains exceed net costs, such that, in principle, those who gained from the measure could fully compensate the losers (Layard and Glaister 1994: 6).

The BCC analysis rejects the inclusion of forecast benefits, preferring to focus more narrowly upon the burden of regulation for businesses. Indeed, it criticises the inclusion of benefits for other stakeholders in the analysis as being "deeply flawed" and "lack credibility" (Ambler et al. 2010: 2, 17). The *Open Europe* analysis, by contrast, does include an estimation of potential benefits although they are equally critical about the veracity of certain reported benefits.[8] Nevertheless, they note that these same 100 EU regulations were estimated to produce benefits of around £58.6 billion per year, thus *exceeding* their associated costs, and producing a benefit-to-cost ratio of 1.76. For the full range of 1950 regulations, the benefit-to-cost ratio was a more modest 1.02, thus suggesting that, on balance, EU regulations probably do little net harm to the UK economy, but neither are they a particular benefit (Gaskell and Persson 2010: 10).

Are National Regulations More Beneficial to the UK Economy?

The real significance of the *Open Europe* analysis relates to its comparison of the efficiency of national vis-à-vis EU regulation. Whereas EU regulation appears to deliver a slight benefit in the form of the 1.02 benefit-to-cost ratio, national (UK) regulations were found to deliver a benefit-to-cost ratio of 2.35. In other words, whereas EU regulations have produced on average £1.02 worth of benefits for every £1 of costs imposed, UK regulations have delivered benefits of £2.35 (Gaskell and Persson 2010: 10).

A similar estimate, produced by the Department for Business Innovation and Skills (BIS), calculated that the benefit-to-cost ratio for UK regulation introduced in the year 2008–2009 was 1.85, although this figure would increase to a value of around 4 if the disproportionate impact of one rather

---

[8] http://openeurope.org.uk/intelligence/britain-and-the-eu/top-100-eu-rules-cost-britain-33-3bn/

large piece of (pensions) legislation was removed from the calculation. Breaking the figures down further, BIS estimated that primary legislation produced a net benefit-to-cost ratio of 2.82 and secondary legislation 5.57.[9] Given that BIS figures are based upon only those regulations introduced within one year, and that they only partially include recurring impacts derived from measures introduced in previous years (Gaskell and Persson 2010: 36), some discrepancy in the results is inevitable. Nevertheless, the BIS results do seem to reinforce the conclusions, reached by *Open Europe*, that national regulations are, on average, more effective in that they deliver greater net benefits than supra-national regulations. Moreover, these conclusions have been repeated in a major UK government report (HMG 2013: 41-2).

One plausible reason for this difference relates to the fact that EU regulations, by definition, have to apply across all member states and therefore must be a one-size-fits-all solution to a perceived problem. Yet, this may be expected to be less capable of accounting for differences in individual circumstances pertaining within individual nations. Consequently, supernational regulations are more likely to create friction and be less effective in achieving the desired outcome than a national alternative designed with individual circumstances in mind. Alternatively, it might be the result of EU regulations being concentrated in those areas where few net benefits may be delivered relative to other areas where national regulations predominate, such as environmental and employment legislation (Thompson and Harari 2013: 21; McFadden and Tarrant 2015: 41). This is plausible, albeit that it may still be the case that solutions may be better designed at national rather than supra-national level.

The evidence indicating a potential superiority of national over supranational regulation is not as extensive nor tested by as many different studies as is desirable if the conclusions reached are to form the basis of policy actions. Nevertheless, notwithstanding a suitable degree of caution regarding these results, there does seem to be sufficient *prima facie* evidence to raise the possibility that a shift from EU to national regulation, following Brexit, might in and of itself deliver an economic benefit to the UK economy, even if numbers of regulations and areas covered were maintained at the current level.

---

[9] http://www.publications.parliament.uk/pa/cm200809/cmhansrd/cm091021/wmstext/91021m0001.htm; https://www.theyworkforyou.com/wms/?id=2009-10-21c.55WS.1

REGULATION AFTER BREXIT

Outside of the EU, the UK has the *potential* to use its greater flexibility to devise and operate its own tailor-made regulatory framework. There are undoubted advantages in doing so. The degree of regulatory divergence from current (EU-determined) rules and standards could be modest or more substantive.

'Singapore on Thames'

One option, for the UK, is to pursue what has been described, usually by its detractors, as 'Singapore on Thames'. The proposal is that the UK could emulate the economic success enjoyed by Singapore, through a combination of lower taxation, regulation liberalisation and the attraction of increased rates of inward investment (Congdon 2014: 31).[10] This approach has a number of obvious attractions and, given the statements made by certain leading figures within the EU, the potential for a deregulatory approach to deliver competitive advantage for the UK is being taken seriously.[11]

Nevertheless, it is improbable that the UK would adopt this approach. Firstly, because a sustainable majority of public opinion would be difficult to create to support this approach (CITYPERC 2017: 3; Elliott and Kanagasooriam 2017). It is unlikely, for example, that a coalition of voters could be sustained to support a platform committed to weaken measures aimed at tackling climate change and reducing the number of days of holiday that employees are guaranteed under the Working Time Directive. Secondly, the strategy of lowering corporate tax rates tends to work for a limited number of smaller countries, when the loss of revenue is exceeded by attracting inward investment by TNCs,[12] whereas the UK is simply too large to pursue "arbitrage" or niche strategies.[13] Singapore is a city-state of

---

[10] https://www.independent.co.uk/news/business/news/sir-martin-sorrell-brexit-singapore-steroids-tax-low-regulation-a9200381.html; https://www.adamsmith.org/blog/the-singapore-on-thames-question-do-you-sincerely-want-to-be-rich

[11] https://www.euractiv.com/section/uk-europe/opinion/why-brussels-shouldnt-be-scared-of-singapore-on-thames/; https://www.ft.com/content/30a1b750-1d36-11ea-97df-cc63de1d73f4

[12] https://www.euractiv.com/section/uk-europe/opinion/why-brussels-shouldnt-be-scared-of-singapore-on-thames/

[13] https://www.euractiv.com/section/uk-europe/opinion/why-brussels-shouldnt-be-scared-of-singapore-on-thames/

5.8 million people and closely integrated into the ASEAN trading bloc, whereas the UK has a population of 66.4 million[14] and is in the process of disengaging from the European trade bloc. Moreover, UK evidence on reducing corporation tax as a means of attracting greater inward FDI flows is disappointing at best (CITYPERC 2017: 29). Finally, and most problematically for advocates of the Singapore model, concerns the fact that its prosperity has not been built upon a laissez-faire version of liberalisation but rather to a combination of active government, strategically attracting inward investment and imposing tight regulations upon the labour market (Huff 1994, 1995; Müller 1997). Economic planning was used to steer markets (Nolan 1990: 59; SEPC 1991: 14), whilst the state maintains substantial shareholdings in major domestic industries.[15]

Modest but Significant Potential Regulatory Gain

Perhaps noting the weaknesses inherent in the 'Singapore on Thames' concept, the current government has committed to maintain or raise (not lower) standards in employment, the food industry and the environment (Conservative Party 2019: 5). Even so, evidence reviewed in this chapter would seem to indicate that some advantages should still be forthcoming from the development of rules to best fit the needs of the national economy, rather than adapting EU requirements which have been devised for application across a large and diverse set of member states. The magnitude of this effect is, however, difficult to determine.

As Table 1.1 from Chap. 1 indicates, only a minority of economic studies have included regulation within their analyses. Of these, estimates vary from very positive estimates of 6% improvement in UK GDP (Congdon 2014: 5, 31), resulting from large-scale liberalisation, to modest gains of 2% (Economists for Brexit 2016: 29) and 0.7-1.3% (Booth et al., 2015: 5), down to negligible effects of 0.3% (Oxford Economics 2016; PwC 2016: 9) and 0.1% of UK GDP (HMG 2018) from those studies which assume there to be little room for future regulatory gain. Other studies, although not quantifying anticipated effects, nevertheless suggest that any

---

[14] https://www.ons.gov.uk/peoplepopulationandcommunity/populationandmigration/populationestimates/articles/overviewoftheukpopulation/august2019

[15] https://www.ft.com/content/a70274ea-2ab9-11e9-88a4-c32129756dd8; https://www.prospectmagazine.co.uk/world/the-singapore-on-thames-delusion-brexit-red-tape-economy

future regulatory divergence from EU norms will be a net cost to UK exporters, although this fails to acknowledge the benefit which might be expected for the large majority of UK businesses which do not export into the SIM (CEP 2018; Hantzsche et al. 2018). The potential benefit which could derive from shifting from EU to national forms of regulation was not costed. However, as an illustrative example, then using as a starting point the *Open Europe* estimate that the 100 most costly EU regulations impose an annual recurring burden of around £33.3bn upon the UK economy, then their replacement with similar but better targeted national forms of regulation could deliver superior benefit-to-cost ratios, which might deliver regulatory gains of 3.7% UK GDP. In reality, it is unlikely that all existing EU regulations could be so easily redesigned by national government, as environmental legislation, in particular, deals with international spillovers and is therefore more likely better determined at global (rather than European) level. Nevertheless, even assuming that only perhaps less than a third of the total number of EU regulations could be effectively redesigned with national priorities and market characteristics in mind, this would represent a net recurring benefit to the UK economy of over 1% GDP, even if no significant liberalisation was to occur.

The magnitude of regulatory gains from Brexit will, additionally, depend upon the form of trade relationship that the UK negotiates with the EU to take effect at the end of the transition period. If, for example, the UK decides to remain a full participant in the SIM, through European Economic Area (EEA) membership, then former EU rules will continue to apply and there will be minimal (if any) regulatory gains. Indeed, an Open Europe assessment is that participation in the EEA would still leave the UK with around 94% of former regulatory costs, but without the ability to participate in the determination of the rules.[16] By contrast, the negotiation of a simple form of free trade agreement (FTA) with the EU, or alternatively where trade is governed by WTO rules, would allow regulatory divergence to occur. In these circumstances, it is probable that only those firms which choose to trade with EU member states will abide by the full set of EU regulations, which will represent an economic gain for around four-fifths of UK firms.

Regulatory divergence from EU norms has the additional advantage, for an independent UK which does not remain part of a customs union

[16] http://www.theguardian.com/politics/2015/mar/16/eu-exit-norway-option-costs-thinktank

with the EU, in that it can facilitate trade agreements with other nations. Whilst much of this discussion has focused upon the potential for lowering food standards, as a consequence of seeking an FTA with the USA,[17] the UK's ability to tailor its regulations to the characteristics of its own economy and/or to align more closely with other international standards could prove economically beneficial. Furthermore, as shall be discussed in Chap. 8, it enables the UK to utilise more active forms of economic policy.

Regulatory Divergence or Level Playing Field

A shift away from regulatory convergence with EU rules has two main consequences. Firstly, it means that those firms who export into the SIM will have to comply with both national and EU standards (CEP 2018: 5). Most of these firms will also export to other countries outside of the EU, and will already be familiar with the requirement for those selling into a given market to follow its rules and regulations. Thus, regulatory divergence between the UK and EU would not greatly complicate matters, in that this would simply be another set of standards for large exporters to follow. For those firms which focused exports entirely within the SIM, the need to comply with more than one set of product and social regulations will be more of a challenge.

The second consequence is that there is likely to be a trade-off between policy flexibility and the degree of access granted by the EU into the SIM. If, for example, the UK joined the EEA—the so-called Norway option—the UK would have to continue to comply with existing and future EU-determined regulations, with little or no effective influence over their composition (a 'rule taker') as the price for facilitating relatively frictionless trade. In contrast, other forms of Brexit, such as a simple FTA or trading according to WTO rules, would facilitate regulatory divergence and greater economic policy flexibility, but at the cost of less preferential access into the EU market.

It is noticeable that regulatory divergence has been incorporated into many of the econometric models, seeking to analyse the impact of Brexit, as a form of non-tariff barrier and hence is treated as a wholly negative

---

[17] https://www.bbc.co.uk/news/business-47036119; https://www.cnbc.com/2019/06/13/chlorinated-chicken-poultry-threat-to-us-uk-trade-deal-post-brexit.html; https://www.cnbc.com/2017/01/27/american-beef-industry-sees-brexit-as-big-stakes-opportunity.html

phenomenon (CEP 2018: 6; Hantzsche et al. 2018: 18). This is not surprising, because these studies typically focus (often to the near exclusion of the domestic market and the rest of the world), upon the UK's future relationship with the EU, then any degree of regulatory divergence which does occur would indeed create an element of friction in trade relations between the two parties and would therefore be considered to have negative effects. If, however, these same studies included evidence outlined a little earlier in this chapter, concerning how national regulation has the potential to deliver economic gains, then this conclusion might be tempered somewhat and the net consequence might be more positive.

One interesting feature of the period immediately following the 2019 UK General Election is that key European leaders, together with the EU negotiating team, appear to be seeking to set out the choice architecture that will underpin future trade negotiations between the UK and the EU. For example, German Chancellor Merkel has expressed her concern that the UK will become "an economic competitor on our doorstep",[18] whilst French President Macron has claimed that regulatory divergence would lead to "unfair competition" and social "dumping".[19] Moreover, in a joint statement, the 27 EU leaders said the future relationship with Britain would have to be based on a "balance of rights and obligations and ensure a level playing field".[20]

These expressed opinions reflect earlier European Council guidelines, adopted in April 2017 (paragraph 20), which outlined the priority for EU negotiators of ensuring "a level playing field", particularly in the areas of competition, state aid, taxation, alongside social and environmental regulation.[21] This would seem to show that the EU negotiating strategy is to advance the argument that a comprehensive trade and economic relationship, between the UK and the EU, needs to be based upon a commonality of regulations. In essence, this would bring a Free Trade Agreement option closer to that of the EEA option. The UK government negotiating stance is to reject close alignment in favour of equivalence (i.e. similar but

---

[18] https://www.euractiv.com/section/uk-europe/opinion/why-brussels-shouldnt-be-scared-of-singapore-on-thames/;https://www.ft.com/content/30a1b750-1d36-11ea-97df-cc63de1d73f4

[19] https://www.connexionfrance.com/French-news/Brexit/President-Macron-welcomes-time-of-clarity-after-UK-election-result

[20] https://uk.reuters.com/article/uk-britain-election-eu/eu-says-talks-on-future-uk-relationship-will-be-complex-and-tough-idUKKBN1YH0QY

[21] https://ec.europa.eu/commission/sites/beta-political/files/level_playing_field.pdf

not identical) in key standards and technical areas, but divergence in others. This divergence of negotiating objectives is likely to dominate the second phase of the Brexit process, as the UK seeks to negotiate a new trading relationship with the EU and thereafter forge new preferential trade agreements with other countries.

CONCLUSION

The apparent nervousness demonstrated by leading figures in the EU, that the UK could utilise greater regulatory flexibility to generate competitive advantages, means that the question of regulation will feature prominently in the second phase of Brexit. The EU negotiating position is quite unambiguous; preferential access to the single market is available at the price of continued compliance to EU rules and regulations, whether in the field of product standards, social and environmental protection, restrictions imposed upon the setting of tax rates and being bound by EU rules relating to competition, procurement and state aid. Varying UK regulations from the EU status quo would be viewed as constituting unfair competition with its own producers. The advantage of this approach would be to secure a trading relationship with the EU by being bound closely to its internal development; close to being a full member, but without the influence in the determination of these regulations that this would deliver.

The alternative approach is for the UK to embrace regulatory differentiation and redesign rules to meet the particular issues pertaining in the national economy. This is expected to deliver regulatory benefits but would additionally enable UK policy makers to take advantage of the use of public procurement and state aid to enhance the capability of industrial policy and thereby promote economic transformation.[22] The consequence would be that trade with the EU single market would not be as frictionless. If a simple FTA could be agreed, free movement of goods (and those services included) would limit this downside, yet nevertheless, this would still necessitate rule of origin statements and accompanying transaction costs.

---

[22] https://www.theguardian.com/business/2019/dec/01/johnson-spots-an-opportunity-over-state-aid-and-it-may-work;   https://www.newstatesman.com/spotlight/2019/11/announcing-key-labour-leaver-policy-johnson-steps-opposition-s-toes

REFERENCES

Ambler, T., Chittenden, F., & Miccini, A. (2010). *Is Regulation Really Good for Us?* London: British Chambers of Commerce. Available via: http://www.britishchambers.org.uk/assets/downloads/policy_reports_2010/is_regulation_really_good_good_for_us.pdf.

Anderson, J. E., & van Wincoop, E. (2004). Trade Costs. *Journal of Economic Literature, 42*(3), 691–751.

Bernard, A. B., Jensen, J. B., Redding, S. J., & Schott, P. K. (2007). Firms in International Trade. *Journal of Economic Perspectives, 21*(3), 105–130.

Booth, S., Howarth, C., Persson, M., Ruparel, R., & Swidlicki, P. (2015). What if...?: The Consequences, challenges and opportunities facing Britain outside EU. Open Europe Report 03/2015, London. http://openeurope.org.uk/intelligence/britain-and-the-eu/what-if-there-were-a-brexit/.

Business for Britain. (2015). *Change or Go: How Britain Would Gain Influence and Prosper Outside an Unreformed EU.* London: Business for Britain. Available via: https://forbritain.org/cogwholebook.pdf.

Capital Economics. (2016). *The Economics Impact of 'Brexit': A Paper Discussing the United Kingdom' Relationship with Europe and the Impact of 'Brexit' on the British Economy.* Oxford: Woodford Investment Management LLP. Available via: https://woodfordfunds.com/economic-impact-brexit-report/.

CEP [Centre for Economic Performance]. (2018). *The Economic Consequences of the Brexit Deal,* UK in a Changing Europe, London. Retrieved December 17, 2019, from http://ukandeu.ac.uk/wp-content/uploads/2018/11/The-economic-consequences-of-Brexit.pdf.

Christiensen, J. G. (2010). EU Legislation and National Regulation: Uncertain Steps Towards a European Public Policy. *Public Administration, 88*(1), 3–17.

CITYPERC [City Political Economy Research Centre]. (2017). A Singapore on the Thames? Post-Brexit Deregulation in the UK, City Political Economy Research Centre, University of London. Retrieved December 18, 2019, from https://www.city.ac.uk/__data/assets/pdf_file/0005/356558/CPRMay2017.pdf.

Confederation of British Industry (CBI). (2013). *Our Global Future: The Business Vision for a Reformed EU.* London: CBI. Available via: http://www.cbi.org.uk/media/2451423/our_global_future.pdf#page=1&zoom=auto,-119,842.

Congdon, T. (2014). *How Much Does the European Union Cost Britain?* London: UKIP. Available via: http://www.timcongdon4ukip.com/docs/EU2014.pdf.

Conservative Party. (2019), *Get Brexit Done: Unleash Britain's Potential,* 2019 General Election Manifesto, The Conservative and Unionist Party, London. Retrieved December 18, 2019, from https://assets-global.website-files.com/5da42e2cae7ebd3f8bde353c/5dda924905da587992a064ba_Conservative%202019%20Manifesto.pdf.

Crafts, N. (2016). The Impact of EU Membership on UK Economic Performance. *Political Quarterly, 87*(2), 262–268.

Department for Business Innovation and Skills (BIS). (2015). *Business Population Estimates for the UK and Regions 2015*. London: BIS. Available via: https://www.gov.uk/government/uploads/system/uploads/attachment_data/file/467443/bpe_2015_statistical_release.pdf#page=3.

Department for Business Innovation and Skills (BIS). (2016). *BIS Estimate of the Proportion of UK SMEs in the Supply Chain of Exporters*. London: BIS. Available via: https://www.gov.uk/government/uploads/system/uploads/attachment_data/file/524847/bis-16-230-smes-supply-chains-exporters.pdf#page=7.

Driver, R. (2014). *Analysing the Case for EU Membership: How Does the Economic Evidence Stack Up?* London: The City UK. Available via: https://www.thecityuk.com/research/analysing-the-case-for-eu-membership-does-theeconomic-evidence-stack-up/.

Dunlop, C. A., & Radaelli, C. M. (Eds.). (2016). *Handbook of Regulatory Impact Assessment*. Cheltenham: Edward Elgar.

Economists for Brexit. (2016). *The Economy After Brexit*. London: Economists for Brexit. Available via: https://static1.squarespace.com/static/570a10a460b5e93378a26ac5/t/5722f8f6a3360ce7508c2acd/1461909779956/Economists+for+Brexit+-+The+Economy+after+Brexit.pdf.

Elliott, M., & Kanagasooriam, J. (2017). *Public Opinion in the Post-Brexit Era: Economic Attitudes in Modern Britain*, Legatum Institute, London. Retrieved December 18, 2019, from https://lif.blob.core.windows.net/lif/docs/default-source/default-library/1710-public-opinion-in-the-post-brexit-era-final.pdf?sfvrsn=0.

Gaskell, S., & Persson, M. (2010). *Still Out of Control? Measuring Eleven Years of EU Regulation* (2nd ed.). London: Open Europe. Available via: http://archive.openeurope.org.uk/Content/documents/Pdfs/stilloutofcontrol.pdf.

Hantzsche, A., Kara, A., & Young, G. (2018). *The Economic Effects of the Government's Proposed Brexit Deal*, National Institute of Economic and Social Research (NIESR), London. Retrieved December 17, 2019, from https://www.niesr.ac.uk/sites/default/files/publications/NIESR%20Report%20Brexit%20-%202018-11-26.pdf.

Harris, R., & Li, Q. C. (2007). *Firm Level Empirical Study of the Contribution of Exporting to UK Productivity Growth (Cm 7101)*. London: The Stationary.

HMRC [HM Revenue and Customs]. (2015). *UK Trade in Goods Statistics by Business Characteristics*. London: HMRC. Available via: https://www.gov.uk/government/uploads/system/uploads/attachment_data/file/476593/IDBR_OTS_2014.pdf.

HM Treasury. (2003). *The Green Book: Appraisal and Evaluation in Central Government*. London: The Stationery Office. Available via: https://www.gov.

uk/government/uploads/system/uploads/attachment_data/file/220541/green_book_complete.pdf.

HMG. (2013). *International Education: Global Growth and Prosperity*. London: The Stationery Office. Available via: https://www.gov.uk/government/uploads/system/uploads/attachment_data/file/340600/bis-13-1081-international-education-global-growth-and-prosperity-revised.pdf.

HMG (HM Government). (2016). *The Best of Both Worlds: The United Kingdom's Special Status in a Reformed European Union*, The Stationery Office, London. Available via: https://www.gov.uk/government/uploads/system/uploads/attachment_data/file/502291/54284_EU_Series_No1_Web_Accessible.pdf.

HMG [Her Majesty's Government]. (2018). *EU Exit: Long Term Economic Analysis*, Cm 9742, HMSO, London. Retrieved December 11, 2019, from https://assets.publishing.service.gov.uk/government/uploads/system/uploads/attachment_data/file/760484/28_November_EU_Exit_-_Long-term_economic_analysis__1_.pdf.

House of Commons Regulatory Reform Committee (HoC). (2009). *Themes and Trends in Regulatory Reform: Ninth Report of Session 2008–09*, Vol. II, HC 329-II, London: The Stationery Office. Available via: http://www.publications.parliament.uk/pa/cm200809/cmselect/cmdereg/329/329ii.pdf.

Huff, W. G. (1994). *The Economic Growth of Singapore*. Cambridge: Cambridge University Press.

Huff, W. G. (1995). What Is the Singapore Model of Economic Development? *Cambridge Journal of Economics, 19*(6), 735–759.

Irwin, G. (2015). *Brexit: The impact on the UK and the EU*. London: Global Counsel. Available via: http://www.global-counsel.co.uk/system/files/publications/Global_Counsel_Impact_of_Brexit_June_2015.pdf.

Kierzenkowski, R., Pain, N., Rusticelli, E., & Zwart, S. (2016). The Economic Consequences of Brexit: A Taxing Decision, OECD Economic Policy Paper No. 16, OECD, Paris. Available via: https://www.oecd.org/economy/The-Economic-consequences-of-Brexit-27-april-2016.pdf. Accessed 18 March 2020.

Layard, R., & Glaister, S. (1994). Introduction. In R. Layard & S. Glaister (Eds.), *Cost-benefit Analysis*. Cambridge: Cambridge University Press.

McFadden, P., & Tarrant, A. (2015). *What Would 'Out' Look Like? Testing Eurosceptic Alternatives to EU Membership*. London: Policy Network. Available via: http://www.policy-network.net/publications/4995/Whatwould-out-look-like.

Miller, V. (2010). *How much legislation comes from Europe?* (House of Commons Library Research Paper No. HC10/62). Available via: http://researchbriefings.parliament.uk/ResearchBriefing/Summary/RP10-62.

Müller, A. (1997). The Government in the Economic History of Singapore. *South African Journal of Economic History, 12*(1-2), 54–76.

NAO. (2001). *Better Regulation: Making Good Use of Regulatory Impact Assessments* (HC 329). London: The Stationery Office. Available via: https://www.nao.org.uk/wp-content/uploads/2001/11/0102329.pdf.

Nolan, P. (1990). Assessing Economic Growth in the Asian NICs. *Journal of Contemporary Asia, 20*(1), 41–63.

OECD [Organisation for Economic Co-operation and Development]. (2018). *OECD Product Market Regulation 2018.* June. Available via: http://stats.oecd.org/Index.aspx?DataSetCode=SNA_TABLE1#.

Office for National Statistics (ONS). (2015). *Statistical Bulletin: UK Business: Activity, Size and Location—Business Enterprises Analysed by Legal Form, Industry, Region and Employment Size Band.* London: The Stationery Office. Available via: https://www.ons.gov.uk/businessindustryandtrade/business/activitysizeandlocation/bulletins/ukbusinessactivitysizeandlocation/2015-10-06.

Oxford Economics. (2016). *Assessing the Economic Implications of Brexit.* London: Oxford Economics.

PricewaterhouseCoopers LLP (PwC). (2016). *Leaving the EU: Implications for the UK Economy.* London: PricewaterhouseCoopers LLP. Available via: http://news.cbi.org.uk/news/leaving-eu-would-cause-a-serious-shock-to-ukeconomy-new-pwc-analysis/leaving-the-eu-implications-for-the-uk-economy/.

SEPC [Singapore, Economic Planning Committee]. (1991). *Strategic Economic Plan.* Singapore: Singapore National Printers.

Springford, J. (2016). *Brexit and EU Regulation: A Bonfire of the Vanities.* London: Centre for European Reform. Available via: https://www.cer.org.uk/sites/default/files/pb_js_regulation_3feb16.pdf.

Thompson, G., & Harari, D. (2013). *The Economic Impact of EU Membership on the UK* (House of Commons Library Briefing Paper SN/EP/6730). Available via: http://researchbriefings.parliament.uk/ResearchBriefing/Summary/SN06730#fullreport.

World Trade Organisation (WTO). (2013). *World Trade Report 2013: Factors Shaping the Future of World Trade.* Geneva: World Trade Organisation. Available via: https://www.wto.org/english/res_e/booksp_e/world_trade_report13_e.pdf.

CHAPTER 6

Migration

One of the key areas of concern for the UK with regard to opting to leave the EU has been the negative consequences of free movement of labour—part of the European Single Market four freedoms (Curtice 2017). There have been, however, warnings from business-representing groups such as CBI, FSB, BCC and IoD (CIPD 2019; Open Letter to Home Secretary 2020) that skill shortages would be exacerbated and that the economy would suffer post-Brexit, in case the government devised a too restrictive immigration system.

Migration can have a positive or negative impact for the UK as a whole and also for particular indigenous groups, depending on the economic aspect analysed. Therefore, understanding the evidence in relation to migration is important since it is a significant input into the decision regarding which form of Brexit to favour and how to design a post-Brexit migration policy in order to retain as many of the benefits as possible and reduce negative effects.

Briefly put, migrants are people who move voluntarily from a country to another country. Economic migrants are in search of better economic conditions such as a higher wage or higher living standards, and this chapter focuses on this reason for migration.

Measuring migration has been problematic in terms of tracking people or deciding whether a migrant to be included in the statistics. For example, in the UK the Office for National Statistics migration figures include economic migrants as well as overseas university students, albeit students

© The Author(s) 2020
P. B. Whyman, A. I. Petrescu, *The Economics of Brexit*,
https://doi.org/10.1007/978-3-030-55948-9_6

could be staying in the UK for relatively short periods of study and, for various reasons, may not choose to work—thus their contribution to the UK economic system may be more volatile and even harder to evaluate. Indeed, migration data collected in the UK is less useful than otherwise desired (Migration Advisory Committee 2012: 46) and this can explain why studies (e.g. on the net cost or benefit of migration to the UK) produce differing results.

INSIGHTS INTO UNDERSTANDING MIGRATION, ITS MOTIVATIONS AND IMPACT

What Is Migration, How Is It Analysed and Why This Matters

Economics is the quintessentially concerned with efficient use of limited resources. Its well-known famous tools for understanding concepts are **supply and demand meeting in the market to determine prices and quantities/qualities of goods and services produced.** In its simplest form, this theoretical model[1] can be applied to the market for labour: that is where the demand for labour (firms wanting workers to fill vacancies) and the supply of labour (people in a job or looking for a job) meet to determine the price of labour, that is, the equilibrium wage (Fig. 6.1)

So, typically the *wage* is first and foremost the focus of labour market analysis, for migration studies too. The labour market will be theoretically continually adjusting, that is the wage will fluctuate. Thus, it is assumed that it will tend to reach **labour market equilibrium,** that is, the point where all firms have filled their vacancies and all workers have found a job.

Neo-classical Theory to Understand the Labour Market and Migration

A number of simplifying assumptions are made in *mainstream neo-classical* theory, such as that labour is **homogenous** (meaning all workers are the same—same education, ability, age, skills, experience), information is freely and perfectly available (about jobs and about skills for example), the labour market is perfectly mobile (transition costs are null, moving

---

[1] A model is a way to try to understand and predict the world, usually based on formulating assumptions, for example, an assumption could be that people have all the information they need to make decisions.

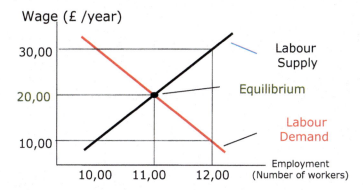

Fig. 6.1 The basic theoretical model of a labour market: Demand and supply meet and the wage as the key. *Source*: The Authors. Numbers are fictitious and only serve as examples. In this labour market, when labour supply and demand meet, the equilibrium wage is £20,000 per year and at that wage 11,000 workers are hired

from one area to another is not linked to cultural ties or barriers to movement).

Albeit simplistic and evidently unrealistic, *neo-classical migration* models remain useful for certain base-line forecasting or in analyses carried out by authors motivated in obtaining certain fast, crude predictions. In so far as they relate to a certain valid element of how labour markets could be constructed and expected to change—since they follow fundamental economic market laws of tending to equilibrium and unbounded rationality— these neo-classical models can be traced to **very many studies** that then imply a strong correlation between decreases in labour supply (if EU migration drops) and consequences to output (UK production or GDP would fall)—see for example HM Treasury, 2016: 66; Kierzenkowski et al., 2016:6.

Extensions of Neo-classical Theories Make Predictions More Real

A more realistic approach is offered in economic models of migration that assume workers to be *heterogeneous*, that is, different by ability, skill, education and so on. These models may also relax the perfect-information assumption, or the free movement of labour assumption, in favour of a realisation that culture, family ties or language poses barriers to labour mobility.

Since workers *are* different, varied and **multiple equilibrium wage levels** can exist at the same time, and the analysis becomes more difficult to predict, requiring more in-depth studies too. **Different equilibrium wages are a key aspect of interest in labour market theory regarding migration.** Theoretical developments of the labour market also include an expectation that markets are **segmented by skill level or region**, say the London plumbers' labour market or the Scottish labour market for engineers. At the same time, various levels of wages that 'clear' a market (all who need work, find work and there are no vacancies) and multi-equilibria are in place.

The Importance of Migration—Creating Efficiency and a Wage Leveller?

Wage inequalities, such as regional wage variations within a country or across various regions (e.g. the more prosperous Western Europe vs. the poorer Eastern European countries), are predicted to encourage migration from low-wage to high-wage areas. The theoretical expectation is that by allowing full labour market mobility (e.g. via the EU freedom of movement in labour markets), the outcome would **be the most efficient allocation of limited labour resources**: if workers would be allowed to move across areas (countries/labour markets) to best meet their job needs, then this would mean that firms would be most efficient in their hiring decisions and workers most efficient in finding the best job/wage for them.

In this sense, migration is theoretically the **key instrument for allowing labour markets to reach equilibrium** via an efficient allocation of labour market resources. For example, workers previously underpaid in a region could move to make best use of their human capital (knowledge and skills) in search of a better wage. Similarly, firms able and wishing to pay a higher wage would benefit from filling in their vacancies from an improved pool of talented job candidates.

Significantly, migration would theoretically **lead to wage convergence**, that is, the lowering of wage discrepancies. This is because of two effects. Firstly, with regard to the low-wage region, out-migration (here due to workers moving away from a low-wage area) would lead to a decrease in labour supply, while labour demand would not have changed, thus firms looking for workers in that area would then need to *increase* the wage to attract further workers into jobs. Secondly, since migration leads to a labour supply increase in the relatively high wage economy, the theoretical expectation would be that firms in that area would have more workers than jobs to fill, thus they could (theoretically) lower the wage. Ultimately, across both regions, this could lead to wages tending to equalise. For example, migration between a lower-wage (w_O) region (e.g. net outward migration countries) and a higher-wage (w_I) region (e.g. net inward migration countries) would lead to wages being equated across the regions at wage w^* (see Fig. 6.2).

Migration is also theoretically expected to **create efficiency and add value to an economy**. The shaded area ABC (Fig. 6.2. Panel A) shows the increase in the total value of output after migration has occurred, and this total value would not have been produced if labour were not allowed to move freely. Of note, though, is the expense incurred by the area losing migrants, denoted by the shaded trapezoid in Fig. 6.2 Panel B—the Northern Labour Market would lose this output since its labour supply has shrunk. Yet, if North and South are two regions part of an economic union (such as a nation or the EU), then the theoretical prediction is that migration would lead **to wage equalisation** and an overall **increase in output** (the shaded area ABC) that would not otherwise be produced

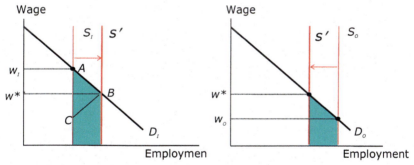

(a) The net inward migration labour markets   (b) The net outward migration labour markets

Fig. 6.2 Wage convergence in two labour markets linked by migration. (a) The net inward migration labour markets. (b) The net outward migration labour markets. Source: The Authors. Note: The supply curves (S) are vertical lines here, because migration is assumed to take place in a short period of time, that is, when there is not enough time for the supply of labour to increase via more births or graduates/trained employees entering the labour market unless migrants were allowed to move freely and if they were perfect substitutes (a migrant would be able to replace a native worker, having the exact abilities, knowledge, education, interest to work, preference for wage levels, etc.). Indeed, the model described in Fig. 6.2 is a simplistic, theoretical model for understanding migration.

One of the most important theoretical conclusions to be drawn here, even at this early point in this chapter, is that *theoretically* migration is a force for good, increasing output and decreasing inequality, supporting poverty, benefiting the world by making the allocation of resources most efficient. Through free[2] migration, workers can freely use their human capital to deploy their knowledge for better pay; firms can hire the best-fit workers for the wage and job type that they need to fill.

Explaining the (Mis)match Between Migration Model Predictions and Reality

Refining migration theory, by adding layers of complexity and changing assumptions, makes migration models more apt for being applied in practice. Significantly, that post-migration wages should necessarily decrease in high-wage areas/countries receiving migrants (as per Fig. 6.2 a) is an effect that is not that simple to observe in real life.

So it *would* be expected that, as migrants increase labour supply in the higher-wage region, and assuming labour demand remained the same, migrants would contribute to an increase in labour demand. Hence, the theoretical expectation *would be* that jobs in the region from which migrants move out, could be filled by firms after lowering the wage. Yet, lowering wages may not be possible for a variety of reasons, such as firms being perceived as discriminating (hiring new workers at lower wages and not being able to renegotiate contracts for their existing workforce), or there being a need for the level of wages to remain higher due to

---

[2] There is actually a strong case and surprising estimates in support of 'open borders'—the worldwide free movement of labour. Here economic modelling shows that free migration could potentially lead to a doubling of world GDP when estimating the gains from this free flow of migrants. If migration could occur freely worldwide, this could lead to the doubling of the world output and could be a significant way to reduce inequality between rich and poor countries (Moses and Letnes 2004; Open Borders). Even if worldwide free borders do not exist, economic estimates of just a 10% increase in international migration suggest it leads to an efficiency gain of US$774 (at 1998 prices) (Moses and Letnes 2004).

investments that firms need to recoup, thus firms also needing higher productivity (and so needing to pay for it).

Therefore, theoretically, it is expected that migration could lead to higher wages in the relatively low-wage countries from where migrants originate, *but findings* suggest that increase in labour supply would *not* lead to lower wages in countries where migrants arrive (unless in very small amounts in case the economy is weak and migrants are low-skilled).

Changes in wages may actually occur in an unexpected way in real life, while theory would also predict them. For example, it may even be that some firms decide specifically to offer a higher wage (known as 'efficiency-wage' theory) than the 'going wage' (the rate at which workers are usually hired), since this decision may 'buy' the company better talent, worker loyalty and productivity. The more profitable the firm, the more able it would be to potentially compete for talent via higher wages. Equally, more productive countries or regions could be able to offer relatively higher wages to attract talent. This practice of offering higher wages could create or exacerbate wage divergence and inequality, triggering migration flows going from less developed, low-wage economic sectors (or countries) towards more developed, higher-wage ones.

Similar developments and departures from the simplistic neo-classical model of the labour market concerned mainly with wages occur by virtue of **government intervention** and **labour market fluctuations or shocks**. Some governmental intervention is generally present in any labour market, for a variety of reasons such as to design a migration system; limit discrimination; introduce health-and-safety regulation; improve information about job vacancies; introduce a minimum wage; collect tax; determine minimum wages and unemployment benefits; and decide on the degree of labour market flexibility allowed (rules related to flexible working and how employers can/should behave e.g. how easy it is to hire and fire workers, unionisation, laws on paid leave or maternity/sick leave pay, working time, etc.).

Moreover, government may wish to intervene to **reduce the impact of supply and demand shocks**, such as economic crises or recessions, for example, the current furloughing of workers applied by the UK government during the COVID-19 pandemic. In relation to labour supply shocks, Europe has been suffering from decreased fertility and an ageing labour market, and thus retirement policies have been altered to encourage workers to stay in their jobs longer, while some governments (in Italy, Hungary and Germany, to name a few) have offered financial incentives for couples to have a baby. Changes in supply of workers are felt most keenly in the short time via migration, since fertility and mortality rates take longer to have an impact. However, changes in demand for labour can be very abrupt (e.g. due to an economic recession or, like in 2020, a pandemic severely affecting economic activity globally within a matter of days); hence there is a continual re-evaluation of the theoretical underpinning of labour markets, that is, the analysis of how supply and demand meet and the related interventions (such as migration systems needed).

Why Migrate? Understanding Migration by Looking at Its Causes

There are many labour market developments in understanding migration, but there is no unifying theory of migration. In their most simpler form, migration models reflect a set of reasons, or motivations for the movement of people which are referred to as **'push and pull factors'**, whereby the attractiveness of the country of destination for a migrant is summed up by its 'pull' factors (higher wages, better jobs, etc.) while the disincentives in the country of origin are its 'push' factors (poverty, unemployment, etc.).

Theoretical models, such as the seminal contribution made by Roy (1951), focus on the **relative skill level** of the migrant flow—this is the number of people migrating. If this flow is relatively higher-skilled compared to the country of origin, for instance, if it is doctors who leave their country to come to the UK, then this is termed positively selected migration. The reverse, whereby it is the relatively less-skilled workers leaving an area (e.g. cleaners from Eastern Europe) to come to the UK, is called negatively selected. Thus, in this theoretical model, there is a sense of the importance attached to the skill level, also known as human capital, accumulated by the migrant, which is brought to a country.

Various models of migration are used by researchers to try to ascertain the impact of migration on wages and employment. It has been found that theoretical implications of a migrant flow arriving in an area do not lead to a longer-term change in the wage level, even if migrant flows can be very large and concentrated within a short time span (see Table 6.1). Similar lack of, or small-size, migration effects on natives' labour market outcomes is found by more recent studies of immigration waves arriving in Germany (Pischke and Velling 1997), Israel (Friedberg 2001), the EU (Angrist and Kugler 2003) or Norway (Erling et al. 2006).

One possible cause of noticing little or no difference is that the outcomes of a migration flow depend on the skill level of the migrant relative

Table 6.1 Historical examples of mass migration with limited evidence for change in wages/employment for natives

Details of mass migration	Impact on labour supply
0.9 m French return in one year to France after Algerian independence in 1962[1]	2% increase in total French labour force
0.6 m Portuguese return to Portugal after it loses its colonies in mid 1970s[2]	7% increase in Portugal's population
The Mariel Boatlift: influx of 8 m Cuban people into Miami (USA) almost 'over-night' in 1980s[3]	7% increase in local population

Notes: Studies of migration effects were carried out by: [1]Hunt (1992); [2]Carrington and de Lima (1996); [3]Card (1990)

Source: The Authors

to native employee and on other factors related to the way the economy utilises and rewards this skill. There are two extreme theoretical cases of migrants, in terms of how different they are relative to native workers, judging by their education, skills, productivity, ability to work, wage and so on. In one extreme case, a migrant could be fully **substituting** a local worker, able to potentially replace them seamlessly in their job. Then, if the migrant were very similar to the local worker, and maybe agreeing to work for a lower wage, which can occur in business sectors such as low-skilled work, natives lose out. In this sense, migration will be job-destroying for natives. In the other extreme case, a migrant and a local worker could be **complementary**—for example, if a dentist migrant opens a new dental practice, this will create a need for a receptionist. Here, migration will be job-creating for natives, maybe leading to more than a 1-2-1 job creation (e.g. if a cleaner were also needed at the new dental practice). In reality, the scenarios encountered will be mixed. Migrants may not be fully substituting, nor fully complementing the local workforce—in general, they may actually be **imperfect substitutes** (e.g. this is the conclusion of a 30-year data analysis for the UK in Manacorda et al. 2010). However, for certain low-wage, low-skill workers, migration of low-skill migrants could lead to downward pressure on wages for natives who can be substituted by firms preferring to higher migrant workers.

An important theoretical conclusion is that the theoretical effect of an inflow of migrants, even if this is large or sudden, will be expected **to depend on a variety of factors (crucially, the particular characteristics of the migrants and natives, and their economies)** and be challenging to estimate in theory and in practice too (see a large and comprehensive review of migration studies carried out by Dustman et al. 2007).

One important factor is the **skill composition** of the influx of migrants—the more skilled the influx, the less likely that these migrants are going to be able to 'replace' the natives in their jobs, and, instead of substituting low-skilled workers, so then migration would generally lead to job creation. The more willing and able to work migrants are, the more the labour market will expand, assuming a flexible, 'healthy' job market, that is, with job information provided easily, investment in jobs, lack of discrimination, government support for natives displaced by migrants via re-training/up-skilling and so on.

Positive effects from migration can arise in various ways, some of which are enumerated here. If additional labour **complements** (rather than substitutes) local labour, thereby enabling increased output (and this benefits the economy as long as remittances remain low), and increase in taxation (from more people being in work). The latter can be invested/spent by the government (to mitigate the housing and other cost pressures that migration brings).

Moreover, **the dynamic effect of migration** (effects taking time, in the longer run, to be observed) can include an increase in business innovation particularly linked to higher-skilled migration and, relatedly, an increase in the average education level and general level of productivity in an economy—ultimately leading to higher average wages. Migrants will also be spending some money in the local economy, therefore contributing to increase in aggregate demand and acting in a protecting way for the economy against adverse shocks such as recessions.

Similarly, a positive and highly desirable consequence of migration is the **access to high-skill migrants gained** by the country of destination of migrants. In most part, this education and skill has been financed by the country of origin of migrants, therefore qualifies as a 'brain drain' to it, yet it is a 'brain gain' to countries receiving migrants.

Migration theoretical models and studies will continue **to need more data,** especially with regard to dynamic effects estimations, such as longer-term analysis of various cohort groups of migrants or inter-generational (second-, third-generation) comparison of migrant outcomes (Dustman et al. 2007: 98).

UK Immigration, Its Poor Image and UK Inequality

Historically, the UK population size *decreased* due to migration up to mid-1980s when immigrants began to outweigh emigrants and the UK started to experience what is termed as positive net migration (see Fig. 6.3 Panel A). After the Second World War, when the UK faced labour shortages, migrants were encouraged to join its labour market. During the next decades, however, EU enlargements, EU treaties and free movement of labour were events triggering larger and larger net migration outcomes. Essentially, around the mid-1980s migrants started to add to the general population and this trend has increased, despite tougher policies such as from Labour Governments (1997–2010), leading to **record high net migration numbers in the recent five years** (see Fig. 6.3 Panel B). Net migration has remained above 50,000 a year since the late 1990s, peaked at over 100,000 people in 1998 for the first time, and has reached a record all-time high in 2015 at 342,000 years (see Fig. 6.3 Panel C)—notably, this is the year just before the 2016 EU Referendum. Post-Referendum, there have been decreases in net migration. These are particularly due to a very dramatic fall in migration from the EU, with **UK net migration from the EU more than halving (dipping below 100,000 for the first time in a decade)**, albeit the **opposite occurred for net UK migration from non-EU countries: it has doubled to over 200,000** (see Fig. 6.3 Panel D). Overall, net migration has decreased in 2018 to 241,000. Moving away from concentrating on net migration, a distinct and useful perspective is offered by migrant employment (see Fig. 6.3, Panel E) showing that EU-immigrants working in the UK labour market outstrip their non-EU counterparts by more than a million (ONS 2020e). EU nationals' presence in the labour market has been on a continual increase in the past two decades, reaching 2.31m (an increase of 36,000), while non-EU nationals reached 1.34m (49,000 more than the previous year) (ibid.).

  The stock of migrants as a share of the UK population has also experienced a continual growth since 1951 standing currently at around 9 million or 14% of the UK's population (See Fig. 6.4 Panel A). This is comparatively high in a global context, with the UK ranking fourth highest in the top ten countries receiving migrants (see Fig. 6.4 Panel B). For an international comparison, there were 21 countries with a migrant population share higher than 10% in 2010, and in 5 countries this share was higher than 20% (Australia, Canada, Luxembourg, New Zealand and

a

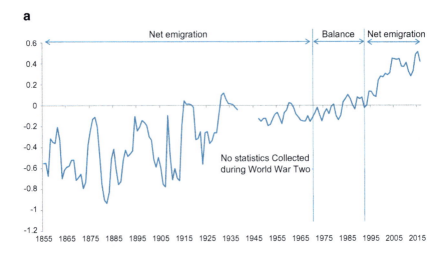

b

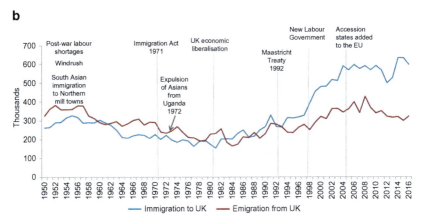

Fig. 6.3 UK net migration and labour employment. Panel A: change in net migration as % of UK population. Panel B: Events that marked changes in UK net migration. Panel C: UK net migration showing immigration and emigration. Panel D: UK net migration based on citizenship. Panel E: EU and non-EU nationals working in the UK. Sources: Panel A and Panel B: Bank of England (2017); Panel C and Panel D: BBC Briefing (2021) using ONS databases. Panel E: ONS (2020e)

c

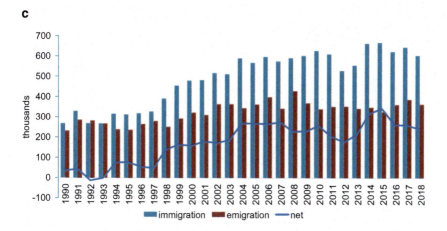

d

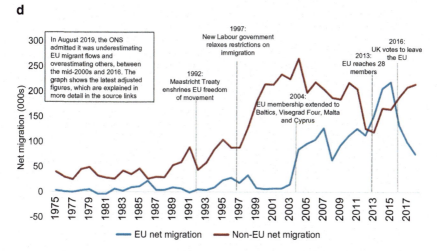

Fig. 6.3 (continued)

Switzerland) (Aubry et al. 2016). Our previous book (Whyman and Petrescu 2017) noted very similar trends in the past five years also shows that the UK's migrant stock figure is comparatively low when considering nations such as Australia, Canada and the USA, which have migrant stock levels of around 28%, 22% and 14% respectively (WDI 2016). Nevertheless,

d

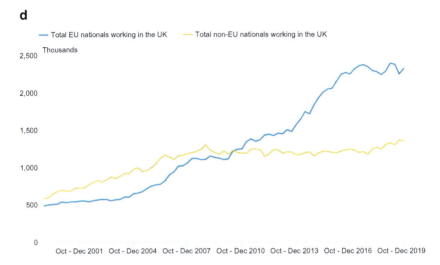

Fig. 6.3   (continued)

the UK has figured among countries with the highest migration stock, relative to its neighbours in west Europe (Whyman and Petrescu 2017).

The most recent migration statistics, available for the year ending June 2019, show that the non-UK-born[3] population was 9.4 million and the non-British (so, here, judging by nationality[4]) population was 6.2 million, remaining similar to the year ending June 2018 (ONS 2019b). India is the most common non-UK country of birth, overtaking Poland for the first time since 2015, followed by Pakistan, Romania and the Republic of Ireland (ONS 2019b). When assessing migration by nationality (as opposed to country of birth, which offers different insights into migration), Polish migrants remain the most common, followed by Romania, India, Republic of Ireland and Italy.

Most EU migrants come to the UK to work, having a definite job, whereas most non-EU migrants come for study or due to family ties (BBC 2017).

---

[3] These include all Polish people but may exclude their children.
[4] These exclude, for instance, Polish people who have obtained British citizenship.

a

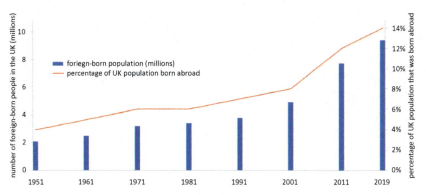

b

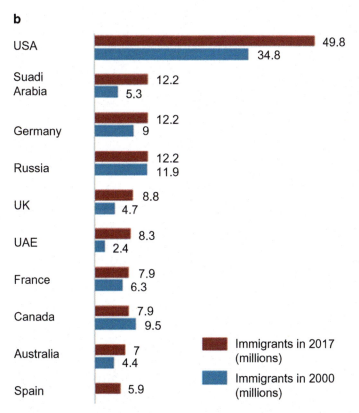

Fig. 6.4 The migrant stock (foreign-born people). Panel A. The continual increase of migrant stock in the UK. Panel B. The UK ranks fourth highest in the world for migrant stock (in million people). Panel C: The migrant stock by nationality, comparison 2001 to 2015. Source: For Panels A and B: BBC Briefing (2021). For Panel C: BBC (2017) based on ONS figures

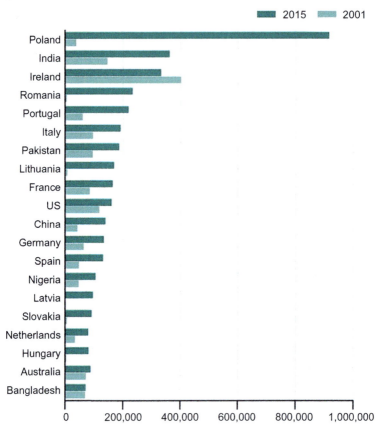

Fig. 6.4   (continued)

MIGRATION'S POOR IMAGE IN THE UK

Public concern in the UK with migration had peaked in September 2015 but after the 2016 EU Referendum they have declined, being rather replaced by general EU and NHS concerns, as of July 2019 (see Fig. 6.5. Panel A). Instead, Brexit had remained the number one issue (for 60% of adults) and the biggest worry (for 47% of adults) (ibid.). This decline in immigration concern may be due to the false assumption that, once Brexit

a

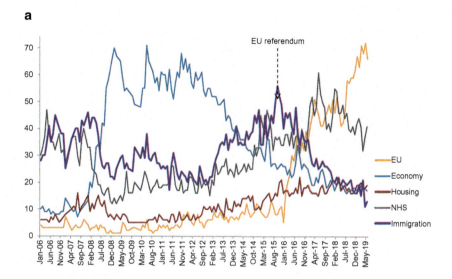

b

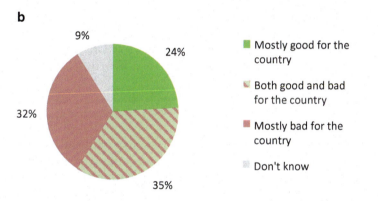

Fig. 6.5 Tracing the British public concern with immigration. Panel A: British adults mentioning important issues to Britain (%), July 2019. Source: Ipsos MORI (2019). Panel B: Public views on whether migration is good for the economy, % (April 2018). Source: Authors' interpretation of YouGov (2018). Panel C. British views on the level of immigration into Britain in the preceding decade, %. Source: Authors' interpretation of YouGov (2018)

c

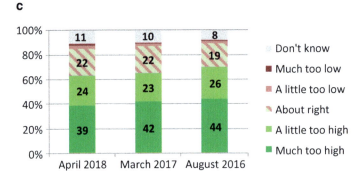

Fig. 6.5   (continued)

had been triggered, immigration would be 'solved', combined with a relatively higher level of integration of more recent (Eastern European) migrants (BBC Briefing 2020: 50). However, public perceptions of migration have continued to be misguided; for example, estimates of migrants leaving in the UK (24%) are more than twice as high as the real figure (14%) (Ipsos Mori 2018), and the general view is that the public is at best split as to whether migration is good for the country (see Fig 6.5. Panel B) with most believing that immigration levels have been too high (see Fig. 6.5. Panel C).

INEQUALITY

At the very basics in terms of theoretical understanding of migration, it is wages that drive workers to move from one job to another and also across countries. **There is a well-known wage variation within the EU,** with higher wages in the older EU member states acting as a pull-factor (while, similarly, lower wages in newer EU member states acting as push-factors) for migration. Moreover, within the UK, there is **marked regional wage variation**, with earnings in England being consistently higher than in Wales, Scotland or Northern Ireland (See Fig. 6.6, Panel A), while London dominates the regional wage distribution (Fig. 6.6, Panel B) having wage levels half as high as the seven regions with lowest average full-time wages (North East, Yorkshire and the Humber, East Midlands, South East, South West, West Midlands, North West). The UK also suffers from a

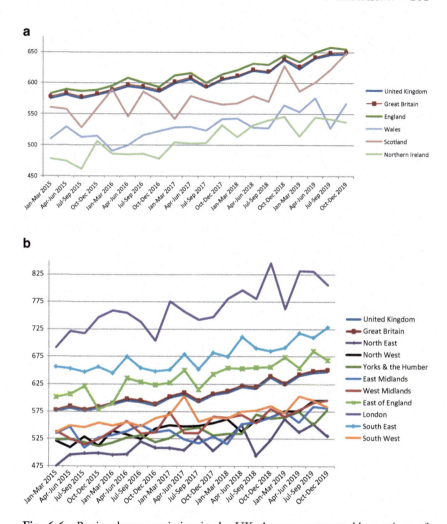

Fig. 6.6 Regional wage variation in the UK: Average gross weekly earnings of full-time employees, by region, 2015–2019. Panel A: Average full-time weekly wage (£), main UK countries. Panel B: Average full-time weekly wage (£), UK regions. Panel C: Average Gini index, selected countries from the EU, outside the EU, and A10 countries, 2000–2014. Source: ONS (2020e) for Panels A and B. For Panel C: WDI (2016). Note: The highest the Gini index, the higher the inequality

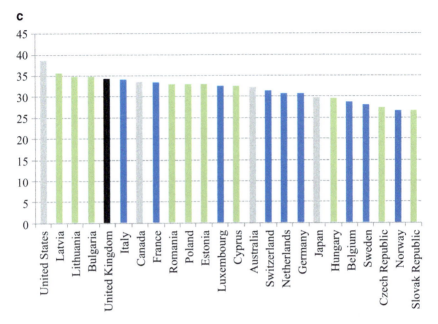

Fig. 6.6   (continued)

relatively high level of inequality (Fig. 6.6, Panel C), alongside a persistent gender pay gap (World Bank, 2016).

Furthermore, even before the EU referendum, there have been intensifying **calls for the government spending policy to address the long-standing North-South divide in the UK,** with the North suffering from low growth, productivity gaps, poor transport connectivity, lack of investment and even with the Treasury spending policy being heavily biased in favour of spending in the South or South East of the UK—for example, the BBC (2019) reported on expected Treasury spending policy changes intended to favour increasing investment in the North. The new government that came to power in December 2019 was elected partly on the promise to deliver growth and a rebalancing of the economy in the North.

Certain areas in the North of UK have already **suffered prolonged periods of lower productivity, lagging behind** other more prosperous South areas. For instance, in Lancashire (a North West English county with about 1.1m people, of which 0.7m workers) there has been lower business growth and marked reduced productivity, with calls for policy makers and business to increase regional investment (Smith et al. 2018). Certain regions in the North West too are marked by **economically disadvantageous elements,** such as in Lancashire, where there is a 4% lower median wage between the county and the wider North West region of England and a nearly 20% productivity gap between Lancashire and the England average gross value added per hour (Whyman and Petrescu 2019). As a consequence, Lancashire is estimated to suffer from **skills drain** worth billions of pounds yearly, due to factors such as one in seven of its workforce commuting to work outside Lancashire (losing thus £4.3b a year), graduates leaving for better-paying jobs (a loss of 0.6b per year to the region) and, most worryingly, via the region suffering for poor investment in high-skill jobs: a mismatch of skills and jobs in Lancashire can lead to £7 b yearly lost by the county's economy (ibid.).

This imbalance in economic growth and other economic aspects is exacerbated by the UK suffering **from a mismatch in skills, with too few high-skill jobs created,** but also a more generally, **unbalanced job creation across regions**. For example, 33% of the population (or 1.8m) live in London and the South East area where a significantly larger share of jobs (47%) in England were created in the past ten years; in contrast 13% of the country's population (or 0.4m) live in the North West where only 11% of the new jobs were created in the past decade (Raikes et al. 2019). Skill imbalances, due to lower availability of highly paid highly skilled jobs in certain regions, lead to internal displacement of workers, and skills drain away from regions that have too few high-skill jobs (see Whyman and Petrescu 2019). This is, in turn, linked to lower productivity and loss of output in regions struck by loss of workforce, via internal migration depleting their pool of talent, or via migrants choosing to also work away from these lower-economic growth areas—a vicious circle and a poverty trap may form, of poor growth and lower productivity.

Indeed, the UK suffers from **inequality in regional growth,** with the southern areas having higher quarterly and annual growth rates (see Fig. 6.7). Most recent figures indicate inequality persists in inter-regional growth rates, with London remaining the fastest growing area at a rate of 3.3%, whereas other regions have a much lower than the UK average growth—Northern Ireland only grew by 1.1% in 2019 and 0.9% in 2018 (ESCoE 2020). The weak growth in Northern Ireland seems to showcase the unease with which the region has experienced the upheaval of

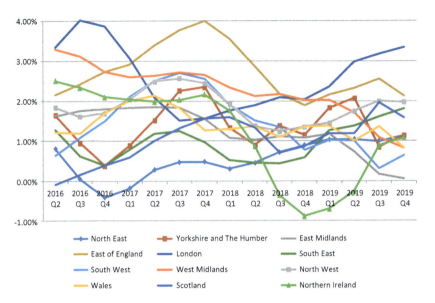

Fig. 6.7 Regional growth inequality in the UK: Growth rates are higher in the southern regions. Source: Authors' interpretation of data available from ESCoE (2020)

regulations and uncertainties post-Referendum 2016, whereas London and the South East have continued to experience the fastest growth in the country.

In the period of five years or more before Brexit, the within-UK (internal) regional migration impact has varied, with **certain UK areas receiving considerably higher numbers of migrants**. Indeed, as predicted by theory, the regions attracting higher numbers of migrants (see Fig. 6.8 Panels A and B), particularly London, are also the ones with relatively higher wages (see Fig. 6.6 on wages).

Migration is a tool that, when managed wisely, may act as an equaliser force. Already it can be noted that most migrants go to live to areas which have previously lower share of migrants in the local population (see earlier in this chapter, subsection on Migration Data). It has been estimated that migration worldwide could significantly reduce inequality and poverty (Moses and Letnes 2004). The literature seems here to suggest the continued opportunity for the UK to utilise migration as a force for good, to the extent that it could help address its unequal regional wage, growth,

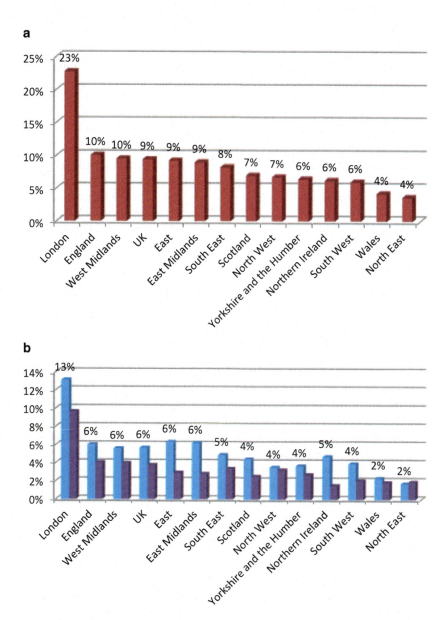

Fig. 6.8 Inequality in UK immigration, by region. Panel A: Non-British migrants, as % of local population. Panel B: EU and non-EU migrants, as % of local population. Source: Authors' calculations based on ONS (2019a) for the period June 2018–July 2019

investment, job creation, skill distribution and other economic imbalance. These are commented upon in the next section.

What Effect Does Migration Have Upon the UK Economy?

Understanding the impact of migration is a more complex, multiple-factor matter as opposed to merely pointing out the gross UK population size increase by 7 million in the past two decades (see Fig. 6.9 Panel A). When assessed in more detail (Fig. 6.9 Panel B), it is apparent that since the late 1990s it was **net migration as the main driving source of this population increase**, adding in the recent year more than twice the people added by natural change (expressed as births minus deaths).

An increase in a country's population, including migrants, is not *per se* a positive or a negative outcome. If it translates into a more efficient allocation of resources, which is the intrinsic goal of economic behaviour analysis, then this increase could lead to more jobs, higher productivity, lower inequality, more output, more government revenue from taxation and so on.

The UK's immigration system did not impose temporary labour market restrictions to immigrants from newer EU member states after the 2004 and 2007 EU enlargements. For these new EU citizens, the British labour market was open, offering the opportunity of earning higher wages and taking advantage of better jobs and livelihoods (Galgoczi et al. 2016). As a result, the UK received a record-high inflow of foreign labour in 2015.

The immigration system is but one facet in a larger picture, one that notably includes **demographic issues needing** to be solved, such as the UK's (and, incidentally European-wide) relatively higher proportions of older people, a lower fertility rate and a problematic 'productivity-puzzle'—the UK's productivity has not increased (see Chap. 7 in this book).

One of the largest impacts of UK migration is most evidently felt in the **increase in the UK labour market**. Migrants have tended to change the UK's demographic for the better, since they tend to be younger (90% are under 45 vs. 60% of the UK population) and have located in areas with previously lower non-UK-born people such as Scotland (experiencing a 138% increase in its migrant population whereas London has experienced only a 51% increase—see ONS, 2019a). The latter leads, thus, to growth

a

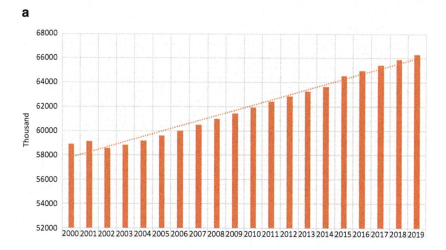

b

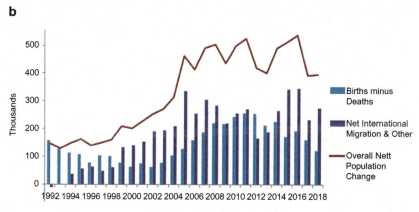

Fig. 6.9 UK population size increase. Panel A. Overall population increase, 2000–2019. Panel B. Overall population change presented alongside net international migration and natural population changes. Source: Panel A: OECD (2020); Panel B: ONS (2019a)

in population numbers in areas where previously there were fewer people, hence boosting growth—**evidence of free migration acting as a balancing force to** distribute access to migrants more equally across the UK.

Business groups have indeed welcomed the addition of migrants to the UK's labour market where about 17% of people employed in 2018 were migrants (Migration Observatory 2019). **Migrants' participation rate in the labour market is the same as the rate of UK nationals** (e.g. Bank of England 2014: 27), which has reached recently historical high levels (above 75% participation rates), hence positive net migration figures translate directly in increases in UK labour market supply. In more detail, based on estimates from a recent survey of 2000 organisation, it appears that migrants (be it from the EU or outside the EU) are working for one in seven employers (CIPD 2019: 6), and are significantly more likely to work in the public sector, relative to the public sector (see Fig. 6.10). It is also apparent that the bulk of migrants employed in the UK are from the EU as opposed to originating from outside the EU.

Certain UK economic sectors rely more significantly on migrant workers than others. A view of the top ten EU-migrant employing sectors, and the top ten non-EU migrant employment sectors, ranked by share of EU migrants that they employ, shows that *Low-skill factory and construction work* is the largest employer of EU migrants when ranked by share of EU migrants in its workforce (at 21%), while the *Low-skill administration and service sector* employs the largest number of EU migrants (nearly 350,000) (see Fig. 6.11). In contrast, for non-EU workers, the sector where they represent the largest share of workforce is *Health professionals* (17%).

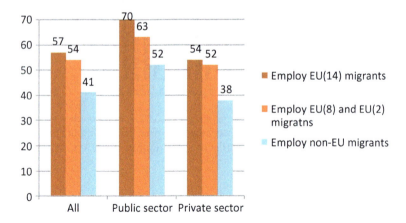

Fig. 6.10 Survey of firms in relation to employment of migrants: percentage of firms employing migrant workers, by sector. Source: The Authors, based on figures from CIPD (2019: 7) from a survey of 2182 firms in the UK

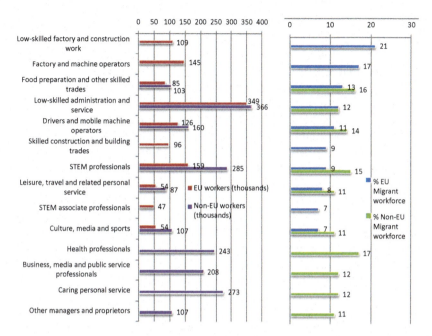

Fig. 6.11 Share of EU and non-EU migrants in the ten highest employing economic sectors. Panel A. Migrant employees (in thousands). Panel B. Share (%) of migrant employees in sector's total workforce. Note: Figures are only provided for the top ten EU-migrant employing sectors and for the top ten non-EU migrant employment sectors, ranked (in Panel B) by their share of EU-migrant workforce and secondarily by share of non-EU migrants. For example, STEM associate professionals ranks as the seventh highest sector by share of EU migrants in its workforce, and it also happens to be among the top ten sectors for employing non-EU migrants, so numbers are provided in the table for non-EU migrants too. However, Caring personal service is a sector which only has figures in the top ten non-EU migrant employers, and hence no figures are provided for EU migrants in this sector. Source: Authors' calculations based on the Migration Observatory (2019)

While some sectors rely heavily on both EU and non-EU migrants, such as *Low-skill administration and service sector*, there are still **important differences in the way EU migrants are represented in the UK labour force**. For instance, migrant workers from EU(14) are **more likely to work in high-skilled jobs than UK-born workers**, while EU workers from newer EU member states are more likely to be in low-skilled work

(Migration Observatory 2019). In detail, prospects of working in a lower job are higher for newer EEA migrants: a larger share, 30% of EEA post-2004 workers are in lower-skilled jobs versus 10% of pre-2004 EEA migrants (ibid.). It is not clear why this discrepancy exists, and it could potentially lead to a reduction in beneficial impact of having migrant workers as part of the UK labour market.

Despite a larger share of migrants from both European Economic Area (EEA) countries and non-EEA countries being high-skilled, when compared to UK-born workers (see Fig. 6.12), **migrants fare less well in their job prospects with regard to utilising their skills**.

More than half of the highly educated EU workers were **mismatched in their jobs**, being employed in low-skill occupation, as opposed to 23% of UK-born workers (ibid.). The latter is evidence of **under-utilisation of labour market resources** and would need to be addressed, such as by measures of increasing employee awareness of job availability and reducing restrictions on migrants' employment requirements imposed by some visa regimes (e.g. whereby a worker must remain employed for a period of time in a particular region/job/company). The reduction of the mismatch would be to the benefit of the UK labour market output, growth and productivity. It could also reduce potential discrimination faced by

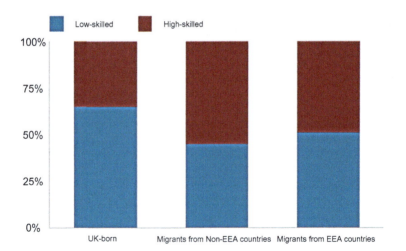

Fig. 6.12   Comparative view of low-skilled and high-skilled share of workers in the UK, by nationality. Source: Migration Observatory (2019)

migrants with regard to job opportunities available, evidenced for instance in findings that migrants suffer from higher involuntary part-time employment, differ in their flexible work patterns, are more likely to work during night shifts and be in non-permanent jobs than the UK born (ibid.; Whyman and Petrescu 2014).

Increases in the stock of migrants in the labour market would have been **helpful to the UK economy** in a variety of ways: **reducing skills bottlenecks**, allowing firms an ample pool of workers for hiring low-skill employees (see Fig. 6.13 Panel A), **keeping labour costs down** (at least in the decade post the 2004 EU enlargement—see Fig. 6.13 Panel B), mitigating the effect of an ageing workforce and **contributing to an increase in output**—which are all welcome by employers (see Fig. 6.9).

Beneficial outcomes include **higher value employment** and increased labour market participation being enabled by the availability of a less skilled migrant workforce. These migrants can, for instance, help support (e.g. via cleaning or childcare services) the higher-paid in their quest for jobs and better labour market participation (MAC 2018).

Similar to the theoretical point of migration (especially open borders) increasing output—point made in the earlier part of this chapter—**empirical studies show that migration flows could be beneficial to a**

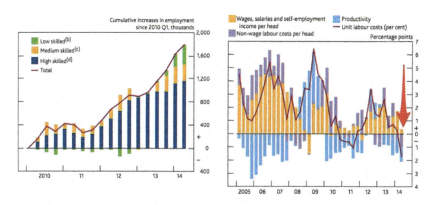

Fig. 6.13 Unit costs have been kept low and job growth was hinged on low-skill jobs. Panel A. Employment growth, by skill level—a large part of the UK's job growth is attributable to low-skilled jobs. Panel B. Unit labour costs decreasing (see red arrow below)—showing decomposition of changes in unit labour costs. Source: Bank of England (2014)

country's GDP/output. The benefit could be felt by more than two-thirds of non-migrant OECD population, benefiting with more than four-fifths of the 22 richest OECD countries' non-migrant population (Aubry et al. 2016). The migration winners are already in countries *receiving* migrants traditionally and countries which benefit from non-OECD migrants' arrival, and the clearest benefit is to consumers who have access to a larger variety of goods (ibid.). Freeing migration into rich countries is also estimated to reduce global poverty by 40–60% (Bradford 2012).

UK's **gross domestic product** (GDP) has increased due to immigration, thus boosting economic prosperity, albeit marginally at individual level (GDP/capita), as found in a number of studies. For example, a 1% in UK GDP per capita increase was estimated for the seven-year period 2010–2016 as being attributable to net migration; or, similarly, a long-run increase of 0.2% in UK GDP per capita was considered to be the result of the A8 countries joining the EU in 2004 (CEP 2018).

The net fiscal contribution (taxes and contributions paid less benefits and public services consumed) has been found to be overall positive for migrants assessed via a static analysis (one year 1999–2000) and valued at £2.5b (Gott and Johnston 2002). It is important to denote the expectation that this estimate could be on over-estimate due to factors such as weaker UK economy than in 1999–2000 (which was a particularly good year), or the analysis being repeated to take into account the life-cycle of migrants (at the time migrants were mostly young, but in time they may have children or retire, thus exist the labour market). Dustmann and Frattini (2014) similarly reported positive fiscal contributions for migrants, while a more recent report for 2016–2017 introduces a welcome disaggregated analysis and finds variation by migrants' nationality: EEA migrants contribute a net of £ 4.7b (£160 per head if originating in the A8 countries, Cyprus or Malta; but a much larger £2870 per head if coming from the rest of the EEA countries); non-EEA migrants receive £9b a year (their labour participation rates are lower, as are their wages since the visa regime has not required them to be highly paid); with UK-born, by comparison, being the highest recipients of government support, receiving the £41.4 (£970 per head) (MAC 2018—Oxford Economics analysis). In a study that does take into account dynamic effects, assuming that patterns of public services use for migrants and UK-born are the same, estimates for the 515,000 migrant wave in 2016 are for a lifetime net contribution of £27b (£78,000 per head for EEA migrants and £28000 per head for non-EEA migrants) (MAC 2018). Children (age 0–19) start with a negative net contribution that turns positive as they enter the labour market; adults close to retirement or retired (age 50 and over) have a negative net contribution, while adults aged 20–49 have a positive contribution until they too retire (ibid.; see Fig. 6.14)

Yet, there are also less desirable macroeconomic effects from the way the UK has seemingly relied on utilising cheap sources of migration, such as resulting **lower wage inflation, that is,** the rate of wage growth (Bank of England 2014). Despite the UK rise in employment rate to 76.5%, and despite the decrease in unemployment rate below 4%, both figures reaching historically high (respectively low) levels (not seen since the early 1970s), real wage growth has been very slow. It has only reached pre-2008 crisis levels in February 2020, more than a painful, austerity decade later (see Fig. 6.15).

Worryingly too, **job vacancies have remained historically high, reaching a record peak of** 861,000 in during November 2018–January 2019; for December 2019–February 2020 the number of vacancies in the UK was 817,000 only lower by 43,000 or 5% compared to its peak (ONS 2020d). These were the periods of time coinciding with a pronounced

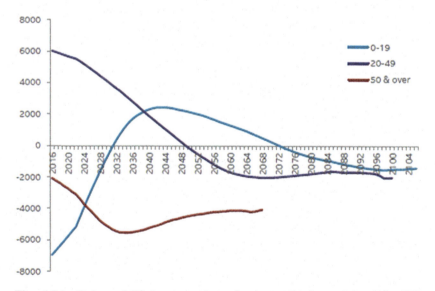

Fig. 6.14 Estimated lifetime annual net fiscal contribution per head for UK migrants arriving in 2016, in £. Source: MAC 2018

Fig. 6.15 Real wages reach pre-2008 crisis levels—showing average weekly wages (inflation adjusted). Source: ONS (2020c)

reduction in EU net migration. In particular, *Human health services and social work services* remained for the ninth consecutive quarter the sector with the largest reported vacancies (136,000 for December 2019 to February 2020) recording one in six (16.6%) of all UK vacancies (ONS 2020a)—echoing fears in the UK that the National Health Service has an increasing gap of doctors, nurses and medical staff, especially in certain regions. Compared to a national average of 2.7 job vacancies in 100 jobs, the highest vacancies rates were recorded for *Accommodation and food service* industries (4 vacancies in 100 jobs). It needs to also be mentioned that the economy experienced an increase (by 67,000) in the number of total jobs available, reaching a record high 35.8m in December 2019 (ibid.). This job growth is apparently on the backbone of a growth in business confidence and recruitment activates post-2019 December election (ONS 2020b) and it has already been severely dented by the current COVID-19 unprecedented economic pressures. Yet, the equally record high job vacancies demonstrate that **employers still clearly demand workers and cannot find them, particularly in certain skill sectors,**

which themselves recorded record high levels of job vacancies (ONS 2020a).

Moreover, this slow economic recovery post-financial crisis appears to be linked particularly to **job growth occurring among lower-paid workers**. Hence, this explains, partly, the weak pressure on wages from this sort of low-pay increase in labour demand (Bank of England 2014). There is worldwide concern that this trend leads to labour market segmentation, also referred to as polarisation, between professional job (with better pay, job security and work conditions) and low-skill jobs (having the opposite characteristics) (see a discussion of economy structural changes in OECD 1989 and a most recent view of job polarisation in OECD 2019).

It is conceivable that, had UK employers faced a **tight** labour market, for example, with harder access to cheap (migrant but also local) work, there would have been investment into automation and a smoother transition into replacing workers with capital, conducive to higher productivity. As things stand, **UK job growth has concentrated on young and low-skilled** (Bank of England 2020), **so this has reduced average pay growth, depressed productivity levels, lead to reduction in tax collected from workers' wages, all the while under-utilising the migrant (and UK-born) skilled workers** (there is a rise in over-qualification). Even if post-Brexit referendum developments (see Fig. 6.16) show increased unit costs, wage growth remains low, and firms are not able to pass this unit cost increase to the consumer as they face competition and pressure on margins, for example, the share of profits in GDP has fallen (Bank of England 2020: 23). Notably, **productivity too remains low and problematic**.

Furthermore, **labour market growth based on low-pay jobs presents challenges** in terms of ensuring decent work, equality of opportunities and exacerbation of the poor outcomes of low-pay trapped workers (be it migrants or UK-born) such as higher risk of in-work poverty, job insecurity or precarious job contracts (zero-hour contracts). In terms of inducing wage inequality, the effects of migration are small, but migration has been found to lower wages at the bottom earnings scale and raise them at the top (Dustman et al. 2007; Nickell and Saleheen 2015; MAC 2018). The magnitude of these changes was estimated to show decreases of 0.6–0.2% in wages for the 5% lowest-paid workers and between 0.3 and 0.7% increase for the highest paid workers (ibid.). Interestingly, it is also found that migrant workers themselves are the ones most likely to feel the effect of lower-wage decreases, in particular for university-educated

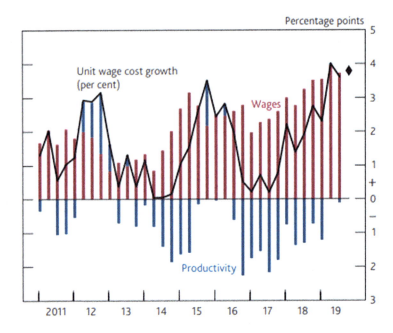

Fig. 6.16 Unit wage cost growth has increased in the late 2010s. Source: Bank of England 2020: 24

immigrants, whereas there is little effect on UK-born workers' wages (Manacorda et al. 2010).

Rises in net migration have added to the strain felt on public resources (education, schooling, housing, health services) in the UK, in particular over the last decade of UK government self-imposed austerity, when growth in public spending per head has been purposely reduced. For instance, migrants tend to have higher fertility rates, to be younger, and, as a result, migrant children and their families have added pressures on schooling, housing and health services particularly in areas of higher migration. Yet, migrants are also over-represented in school workforce with 12% of schools' staff in England being migrant, while, in comparison, 10% of the larger English population are migrant as per MAC (2018); and migrants, overall, make large, positive contributions to the health service (see two paragraphs below).

With regard to house prices, **net migration has contributed to hous-ing inflation**. The UK average house price has increased from £54,000 to £206,000, a 284% increase; or, in real terms, an increase of 137% has occurred which would represent a £70,000 increase in real terms over the 25-year period 1991–2016. This change is estimated to comprise in real terms a 21% (or £11,000) increase directly attributable to net international migration (MHCLG 2018: 7). More than seven times bigger house price changes had been fuelled by incomes rising (150% or £80,000 in real terms). Still, housing supply led to a 40% average house price reduction (£21,000 lower price) in real terms (ibid.). Thus, merely by building houses, that is, increasing housing supply, there has been a reversal of more than twice the magnitude of the price hike effect due to net migration.

Nevertheless, it is important to highlight that net estimates of migrants' health services use have found that on average, due to being younger (and younger people need health services less often and are less costly), **migrants contribute 'much' more to the health service than they con-sume** (MAC 2018). It is worth pointing out that while migrants represent 9% of the UK population and 10% of the UK population, (see Fig. 6.4), fully 23% of NHS doctors in England are non-British and fully 18% of social care workers are also non-British (NHS 2019; Skills for Care 2018).

A critique of cost-benefit analyses of migration is that they tend to remain limited in their coverage and assessment of the larger economic aspects. They undoubtedly offer a useful view of the implications for the UK of having larger net migration figures, on a number of economic out-comes, such as housing or education. Nevertheless, these studies tend to remain quite restrictive, with application limited to a few sectors (such as concentrating on housing or on education), and thus it is usually necessary to widen the analysis and consider more economic factors at play.

Wages and Jobs

The UK **has relied on low-skilled low-wage EU workers** for quite a significant proportion of its workforce, in particular in low-wage indus-tries. For example, in 2017 (the year just after the EU Referendum) an estimated 500,000 EU-born low-skilled migrants were working in the UK (Sumption and Fernandez Reino 2018) in low-wage jobs such as cleaning, processing food or as waiters.

One of the most intensely felt fears for the British public has been that migrants come to the UK and replace jobs, increasing local unemployment, particularly in areas where more migrants settle, and depressing local wages. One of the key reasons for voting Leave in the EU Referendum was the fear of high level of migration, used by anti-EU politicians to obtain support in the Referendum, with more than half of voters surveyed wanting migration levels to fall post-Brexit (Curtice 2017). After 2016, these fears continued to be amplified by politicians and tabloids when referring to immigrants as taking locals' jobs, or to employers' practice of keeping wages low via access to "unlimited pools of labour from other countries" (Boris Johnson's January 2019 JCB headquarters speech, BBC Briefing 2020 :128).

However, **there has been ample and weak evidence on the link between migration and the general wage level**, similarly between **migration and employment (number of jobs).** There is actually an emerging consensus that there is little or no impact on jobs for UK-born workers (see a review by BIS 2014, or MAC 2018), with the UK experiencing historically low levels of unemployment (reaching 4%, lowest since the early 1970s) despite relatively high levels of immigration. This resonates well with the general theoretical view that there is no zero-sum game for the level of jobs available in a country; that is, the arrival of a migrant does not lead necessarily to the direct replacement of a native in the labour market (CEP 2018).

The impact of migration on the labour market is more likely to be felt with respect **to giving rise to market segmentation,** whereby some labour market aspects notice different outcomes (MAC, 2014). Dual or segmented labour markets have been noticed in some low-wage labour markets (e.g. tourism and hospitality, care, food, manufacturing) where migrants represented a high proportion of seasonal or temporary workers. However, this is not true of all EU immigrants, since, for example in London and the South East, there are EU immigrants in higher-paid financial and business sectors, and thus these are highly skilled and earn high wages.

With regard to market segmentation as a consequence of migration, of specific interest is the low-skilled wage market segment. Here, some small negative impact on wage levels has been noticed for the period 1997–2005 (Dustmann and Frattini 2013). This effect was only measurable for the lowest 20% of the wage earners, whose wages were depressed by a small amount, while for the rest of the labour market immigration lead to a higher wage. The relationship found was that for every 1% rise in the foreign-to-native population, the average wage increased by between 0.1 and 0.3% (ibid.).

Similarly, in a more recent study of overall immigration impact since 2004 (the largest EU enlargement) on semi-skilled and unskilled workers' wages, there are estimates that native wages would have reduced by 1% (Nickell and Saleheen 2015), which is relatively small compared to the impact of the National Minimum/Living Wage, taxation or other factors. **In the UK, it seems that there is no displacement of workers by migrants** except for times when the economy **is weak,** such as during economic recessions, when there are job security fears and some employees are prepared to work for lower wage. One size estimate of this replacement concluded that there was a loss of 1 native job for every 13 jobs that were added by total EU and non-EU migrants to the UK economy between 1995 and 2010 (MAC 2012: 2). This was further disaggregated into noting that there was a reduction of 23 jobs for a one-off increase of 100 in the inflow of working-age *non-EU*-born migrants over the period 1995–2010. However, there was no impact on native employment from inflows of working-age EU migrants during 1995–2010—thus no impact of EU enlargement migration into the UK on natives' employment, a statistical finding consistent among other studies too (Gilpin et al. 2006; MAC 2012: 63; Lemos and Portes 2008; Lemos 2010).

FLEXIBILITY AND PRODUCTIVITY

Flexible work has been firmly linked to increases in productivity, in terms of higher business performance, reduced labour turnover and lower absenteeism (Whyman et al. 2015). **A flexible labour market has been linked to general economic benefits** for a nation such as job creation, increased foreign direct investment, business productivity and employee well-being (CBI 2016; Whyman and Baimbridge 2006). Flexible work is ever more popular with the workforce too. Nearly a third (30%) of the UK population, as per a recent UK representative survey (conducted just pre-COVID-19), would prefer flexible work over pay, and a fifth (22%) have already switched to flexible work for a better work/life balance, feeling happier as a result (Theta Financial Reporting 2020).

The UK productivity has stalled since the 2008 crisis (see Chap. 7 in this book) and at its core could be labour market issues related to the poor management of the workforce, such as some employers' rigidity for tradition's sake when considering flexible work requests from their employees; lower investment into skills and training; a counter-productive long-hours culture; and, generally, a less-than-efficient use of human resources—inclusive of the 'gift' presented to the UK economy by **access to the rich pool of skills, high motivation and talent offered by its migrant labour**. There is evidence, for instance, that high-skilled migrants have **boosted UK innovation** (MAC 2018). For instance, highly skilled migrants from the EEA have spurred the UK's research and development activities to levels above G8 and EU averages (ibid.).

Migration is a factor supporting productivity and rises in per-capita income, its contribution ranking even higher than trade openness (Ortega and Peri 2016). A culturally varied workforce, measured via birthplace diversity, is linked to higher levels of productivity, economic output and economic growth, specifically when linked to immigration (Alesina et al. 2016). The richer and more culturally close the immigration flow, the higher its productivity effects at macroeconomic level, increasing performance (Alesina et al. 2016).

In the UK, an increase of 50% in net migration's share of the working-age population would be triggering an increase of 0.32% in GDP per capita in the short term and 2.23% in the long term (Boubtane et al. 2016). This is similar to the estimates obtained for advanced economies, whereby a 1% increase in migrants' share in the adult population is associated with a 2% rise in GDP per capita and productivity (Jaumotte et al. 2016). In line with these estimates too, when focusing on the UK service sector, an increase in immigrants' concentration in local labour markets is found to give rise to an increase by 2–3% in labour productivity (Ottaviano et al. 2015).

High-skill migration in the UK is also found to have a positive impact on productivity in a larger sense, such as having a positive and statistically significant effect on native workers' training when measured in UK-based studies (Campo et al., 2018). Similarly, high-skill migration appears to intensify the local population's desire to increase their own human capital and educational attainment (Campo et al., 2018; Hunt and Gauthier-Loiselle 2010; Kerr and Lincoln 2010).

Migration could be linked to productivity when there is evidence of migrants being **complements** to the local workers, thereby the more migrants there are, the more likely it would be that locals would also be in employment. In this sense, further expectations that migration could raise productivity relate to the mere presence **of low-skill migrants** increasing labour force participation for natives, and this link was found to work for native women's labour market participation (Barone and Moretti 2011), as well as for the wages of low-skilled workers (Foged and Peri 2016).

DESIGNING A POST-BREXIT MIGRATION SYSTEM

A key decision for the UK government has been whether to opt for a form of Brexit which retains a close relationship with the EU or not. If choosing the former, then a close relationship required implicitly a continued acceptance of the four freedoms. If choosing the latter, then a more independent relationship meant the UK could design its own migration system which would not necessarily include unrestricted free movement of people from EU member states. The rest of this chapter examines some of the work that has been done on the migration system already.

A major concern for the UK has been the impact of migration on the UK economy, both for business where firms consistently voiced fears for being unable to fill vacancies, but especially when considering the public's perceived risk of the level of local unemployment rising or wages falling. Thus, intense debate has focused on assessing the impact of migration in terms of the **skill-structure of potential immigrant workforce** and its impact on the local economy.

The preference of the public is clearly in favour of encouraging high-skill migration and discouraging low-skill migration. A majority of the public in the UK (57%) would like to see especially fewer or no low-skilled immigration; in contrast, over 70% would be happy with the same or higher levels of skilled immigration (YouGov 2018).

Mirroring this view on skill preferences for migrants, the government has **published its most recent, newly designed migration policy and has regulated that from 1 January 2021,** with a summary presented in Fig. 6.17.

The new migration system aims to discourage UK firms' reliance on 'cheap labour', incentivising instead a mixture of investing in automation, hiring local workforce (including from the 8m economically inactive population—albeit fewer than 2m of these would like to have a job as per BBC 2020 reporting) and (re)training/up-skilling programmes. Yet, it has been met with scepticism and fear by certain business sectors, in particular the health system and social care where job vacancies remain high and where foreign workers represent a large share of the workforce—for example, one in six of the 840,000 social care workers is foreign, 13% of the NHS workers are foreign (and nearly one in 10 doctors is from the EU).

- **Free movement will end**
- A points-based system for visas will be introduced, with points are assigned to specific skills and qualifications, salaries and shortage occupations)
- Visas will be given only to those who meet or exceed 70 points
- There is lowered £25,600 salary threshold (albeit certain characteristics could be traded for an even lower salary). The UK had previously used a £30,000 (so a higher) salary threshold for non-EU migrants
- The definition of a skilled worker would include not just graduates but also those educated to A-level (Scottish Highers) standard. This definition would exclude skill acquired on the job such as in construction work, putting an emphasis on formal qualifications.
- A PhD in a STEM subject would earn 20 points
- The ability to 'speak English' would be given 10 points
- Having a job offer' before arrival to the UK would be given 20 points
- If the job is at appropriate skill level this would gain 20 points
- **Low-skill migration flows will stop.**
- The list of 'specific shortage occupations' would be revised in time to meet the UK's needs and, at the time of writing, it included: nursing, civil engineering, psychology and ballet dancing, among other occupations.
- Certain parts of the workforce, such as seasonal workers in agriculture, saw their visa scheme quadruple from 2,500 to 10,000 workers per year, while 20,000 young people could come to the UK under the 'youth mobility arrangement' scheme.
- It may be that a specific occupational category could be allowed to deviate, temporarily, from applying this visa system, but these discussions would need to be formalised and the need for work would need to be justified at the time.
- An entrepreneurial route will allow people with start-up ideas, under certain conditions, to have a two-year visa.
- All EU citizens currently in the UK will have to register for an EU Settlement Scheme if they want to stay in the UK after 30 Jun 2021
- The cap on the number of skilled workers arriving in the UK shall be removed, in a change to UK's previous migration system position.
- It is unclear whether students will be allowed to work while studying, a right that currently EU students hold, but they shall be allowed to work in the UK for two years after graduation
- A 'fast-track' route would be available for those deemed to have 'global talent', in an effort to position the UK competitively in the labour market for research and education staff.

Fig. 6.17 A summative list of the main elements in the UK's new points-based immigration system to be enforced from 1 January 2021. Source: The Authors compilation of information available from various governmental notifications inclusive of UK Visas and Immigration 2020

Low-paid sectors, such as retail, nursing, catering and farming,[5] where employers have been facing hard-to-fill vacancies, have also found the new visa system worryingly ill-suited to their labour needs (CIPD 2017b). It is difficult to see how restricting migration numbers will not impact negatively on certain business sectors. Most of the migrants arriving into the UK are coming here for work (70% of EU migrants) and a very large share of EU(8) and EU(2) migrants are actually low-skilled (see Fig. 6.18). With expectations of detrimental worker shortages, in particular for 'key workers' (as determined by the government during the COVID-19 pandemic), there have been renewed voices for the government to revise

---

[5] The farming sector mentions 70,000 seasonal workers are needed, while the government would allow entry to only a seventh of this number.

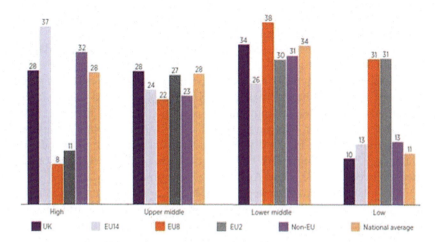

Fig. 6.18 Distribution of workers by nationality and skill level, in per cent, 2016. Source: CIPD 2017b: 19, based on figures from the Annual Population Survey and the Office for National Statistics

is immigration plans by making it more flexible and accommodating business requirements in particular sectors of activity such as health and social care, nursing, agriculture (fruit and vegetable pickers), tourism, hospitality, catering, food processing or transport (CIPD 2017b; People Management 2020).

A New Points-Based Immigration System

A new system of migration has been passed by the UK Parliament in spring 2020 (19 May), in the midst of the COVID-19 pandemic (see Gov.UK 2020). It can be described as being 'off-the-peg': **it has borrowed some elements from other points-based systems across the world** but it is centred on Tier 2 (general work visa) **sponsorship routes** as opposed to having at its core the much-anticipated Australian-style visa system (People Management 2020). The main difference is that the current Tier 2 system of migration will be 'given a makeover' whereby employers need to first be licensed as sponsors, before they can hire European Economic Area workers (ibid.). It is hard to see how the issue of employers needing to apply to be sponsors, and the current pandemic crisis, will be reconciled in the short time until 31 December 2020. Under these rules, only agricultural labourers would be allowed to enter the UK as 'low-skilled' workers, while momentum is gathering for further flexibility.[6]

Nevertheless, lessons need to be learned from Australia, Canada and New Zealand, countries which have a richer past of having adopted points-based migration systems—whereby a specified number of points is given to specific migrant characteristics, and visa are only awarded to individuals accumulating a particular minimum points threshold. In fact, the UK's low-skill immigration ban can be traced as far away as in Japan's immigration system, where unskilled workers only enter the country if they are trainees (BBC Briefing 2020: 179), but the most common comparison has been between the UK's and Australia's visa regimes.

The main difference between the UK and other migration systems is that it **concentrates more narrowly on migrants' skills and less on other migrant characteristics**. For example, unlike the Australian system, the UK does not award points for age, while in Australia being between 25 and 32 years old means obtaining 30 points, or nearly half out of the 65 points required (see Table 6.2).

Similar to Australia's migration policy, a UK immigrant will gain points for having an occupation listed among those with labour shortages in the country or need to be sponsored by employers. So, akin to the Australian, but also Canadian, US and Swiss system of migration, there is a need for UK migrants to show that they are **financially secure** to some degree, such as by having a job offer, a wage above a certain minimum threshold (25,600 a year), or, for students, showing that they have a sponsor, albeit the UK's new visa system seems to be more employer-led when compared to Australia's more government, centrally driven system (Sumption and Fernandez Reino 2018).

Financial security is a widely applied migration system requirement, across various countries, for at least three reasons. Firstly and most evidently, it ensures the UK public finance and government spending/benefit schemes **do not have to worry about providing financial support** to migrants. Secondly, **a higher-pay migration threshold** is an advantageous selection filter for high-skill and most likely high-productivity workers, which again presents an advantage to the migrant-receiving UK areas which can use these migrants to increase their ability to grow their own

---

[6]As of 21 May 2020, the UK government announced, for instance, that bereaved families of migrants who worked in the NHS, during the COVID-19 pandemic, will not need to apply for indefinite leave to remain, being in effect automatically allowed to stay in the UK.

Table 6.2   The Australian points-based system

Elements given points in the Australian visa system for skilled migration visa

Age: 18–24 (25 points); 25–32 (30 points); 33–39 (25 points); 40–44 (15 points); >45 (no points). No migration for >50.
Nominated occupation (in use only up to July 2011)
Nomination or sponsorship by an Australian state or Territory (up to 10 points)
Skilled employment/occupation—chosen from an Australian government list—by length of employment. If within Australia: 1 year (y) at 5 points (pts); 3y at 10pts; 5y at 15pts; 8y at 20pts. If outside Australia: 3y at 5pts; 5y at 10pts; 8y at 15pts. Points can be cumulated up to a maximum of 20 points.
Professional year (completed on in Australia in past 4 years—5 points)
English language ability: superior IELTS (20 points); proficient (10 points); other (no points)
Australian educational qualification
Qualification: PhD (20 points); BA or Master (15 points); Australian Diploma or Trade qualification (10 points); Award or qualification recognised by assessing authority (10 points)
Work experience
Australian work experience
Spoken language
Spouse/partner skills and qualifications (meeting basic requirements: 5 points)

Source: Summative information presented by the Authors

productivity—and cheaply too, as the migrants' education had been done at the expense of a different country. Thirdly, a certain higher ability to earn implies a higher ability to spend. This latter effect then sets in motion a potentially highly advantageous economic mechanism in the UK, economically described via the concept of a **multiplier-effect**: as more affluent (higher-earners) move into an area, they are seen as a start point encouraging a cycle of more consumption, more spending, followed by more output in the area and thus the size of the (local) economy increases, such as via job creation, investment, business start-ups and so on. However, notably Australia's system does not use a wage threshold for its points-based visa system, while in the UK this feature has caused high concern that it is a poor proxy of skill, it neglects the added-value of certain key occupations and it is too narrowly focused since wages depend on much more than skill level. In the long run, if wages do converge across the EU, having a wage threshold would also imply an expectation of reduced migration from the EU newer member states, on which many UK sectors rely.[7]

There are further flexibility differences between the British and Australian systems: Australia enforces a cap on temporary migrants (inclusive of students and workers) and a cap on skilled workers and family-tied immigration, while the UK has not mentioned the introduction of this sort of number cap.

The overall result in Australia's points-based system and other similar systems has been that the number of economic migrants has continued to increase overtime,[8] with a flow being skewed towards skilled migrants in occupations favoured by the respective governments. Under realistic assumptions that workers are different from each other, the latter is expected in most studies to lead to a rise in productivity (measured via GDP/capita for instance).

However, even a points-based system, therefore, cannot be said to be a panacea for controlling, or in particular, reducing migration. In Australia and in other countries, added flexibilities were necessary and this has been most clearly and evidently conveyed by **temporary permits, youth mobility schemes, low-skilled work-permit schemes and/or exceptions for particular sectors**—they are common as supplementary, 'back-door', policy instruments to re-dress otherwise detrimental imbalances created by restrictive visa policies (Sumption and Fernandez Reino 2018). The most recent and key proposals for the UK government include a two-year mobility scheme for all EU citizens, to allow low-skilled EU employment (since a Youth Mobility Scheme or a 12-month temporary visa is feared to be inadequate), and a more flexible salary threshold for some jobs on shortage occupations lists (CIPD 2019).

The UK government has already announced the potential extension to EU countries of its Youth Mobility Scheme already in place for countries

[7] UK employers have expressed high concerns about losing access to EEA migrants, who are a key source of labour based on being described as more likely to take work thought less appealing or working evenings and nights, being better educated than their UK counterparts, more likely to work in high-skilled jobs and generally having a higher motivation to work (MAC 2018). It is estimated that 500,000 EU-born workers are employed in low-wage sectors in the UK (Sumption and Fernandez Reino 2018) and already before January 2020 many UK employers had hard-to-fill vacancies having 'exhausted' the local employment opportunities (CIPD 2019).

[8] As a share of the country's population, more than twice (29%) as many people in Australia are born abroad, versus 14% in the UK (Sumption and Fernandez Reino 2018).

including Australia, New Zealand and Canada (HM Government 2018). This would involve allowing workers of any skill level to take jobs, but numbers could be capped and the scheme may run for a shorter period of time, that is, a temporary scheme. It is estimated that over half of the EU migrants arriving in the UK from the EU in recent years would have been able to come via a youth migration scheme, simply by virtue of their age being 18–30 years old, and some sectors such as hospitality would rely more heavily on this immigrant flow (Sumption and Fernandez Reino 2018). Work-permit schemes, in comparison to youth mobility schemes, can target certain occupations and sectors more specifically, but bring a risk of worker exploitation—wage and working conditions may be abused by employers when workers are dependent on employers, for example, restricted to employment with a particular employer sponsor (e.g. Parliament of Australia 2016).

The skill-filter is clearly put in place in the UK visa system, associated with the desire to assert a better use of control by the UK of the type of migrant who is allowed to come and work here, with low-skill migrants being purposefully denied access to the economy—with the exception of certain occupations or sectors such as in agriculture. The UK government intends to use this opportunity **to wean UK companies from relying on cheap migrant labour**, instead moving towards **automation, using more of the local, native workforce (via training, re-skilling, increasing local supply of jobs**) or using non-EU countries as more main sources of labour[9] (CIPD 2019).

It is hard to predict a priori the level of immigration change post-Brexit. Neo-classical models of migration would also expect a different result in terms of the post-Brexit trade policy impact on the size of the EU immigrant flow. So all migration impact studies, neo-classical or otherwise, could be improved by taking into account whether the UK negotiated an FTA with the EU, or traded according to WTO rules (e.g. see Arregui and Chen, 2018: 16). It is understandable that these factors would introduce a large amount of variety in the post-Brexit migration landscape that the UK would face.

---

[9] Respondents have indicated non-EU countries that would become main sources of labour would be mainly Australia and New Zealand (for 37% of survey respondents), South Asia (35%) and North America (26%), while the occupations for migrant recruitment would be chefs, IT, scientists, teachers, doctors, nurses and engineers (CIPD 2019: 20)

Yet, even estimates for neo-classical assumption-based studies could have large variations, when mentioning, for example, an expected yearly reduction by 50,000 (Hantzsche et al., 2018: F35: 15-17; Hantzsche and Young, 2019: F35), or triple that, so a reduction by 150,000 (BoE 2017). The more realistic, heterogeneous labour models, too, expected a negative impact on UK productivity (Menon et al., 2018: 9-12; Nickell and Saleheen 2015; Portes and Forte 2016: 17).

In fact, the overall outcome of a more restrictive migration policy cannot be judged *a priori* to mean a reduction in GDP. If post-Brexit there shall be a lower number of unskilled migrant workers while there would continue to be increases of skilled immigrants, this should lead in time to a proportional increase (skew in favour) of skilled migrants in the UK's overall migrant workforce. Therefore, the expectation is that UK productivity, *ceteris paribus*, should increase, because skilled workers are more productive, and **the ultimate impact on GDP growth would depend on whether the labour supply (quantity) or productivity (quality) effect predominates.**

A highly skilled migrant flow is, in theory and in practice, crucial to generating much-needed rising productivity. The UK's need for skilled work and the presence of hard-to-fill vacancies contributes to the aggravation of UK's low productivity, also slowing growth due to lower development of the digital sector (EIB 2020: 120). Or, a country's pro-active approach to supporting the development of its digital sector *could* bring faster growth, more productivity and higher wages (EIB 2020). Yet, worryingly, the UK lags behind the USA and most EU countries (fifth from the last) in its digitalisation[10] of the economy (EIB 2020: 9). Moreover, it is mainly due to lack of available staff, and especially so in digital firms, that the UK fares so negatively with regard to investment and development of its digital sector (ibid.; CIPD 2017a). Thus, it is expected that immigration, particularly if skewed in favour of having a higher proportion of migrants being high-skilled, would be helping the UK start to catch-up with other countries, obtain economic growth, supporting an increase in productivity and wages. Organisations know that attracting, developing

---

[10] The Digitalisation Index, on which EU and US inter-country comparisons are made in the EIB (2020) report, measures the following five components: "digital intensity; digital infrastructure; investment in software and data; investments in organisational and business process improvements; and strategic monitoring system" (EIB 2020: 9).

and retaining high-skilled staff is an important strategy, leading to innovation, productivity and competitiveness.

REACTION AND CONSEQUENCES TO THE ANNOUNCED IMMIGRATION SYSTEM

The business reaction to this new immigration system has been mixed. For example, the CBI, collectively representing the UK's business voice, has welcomed the lowering of the salary threshold but echoed concerns about how mid-skilled workers (such as LGV drivers, joiners and technicians) would be allowed entry in particular if they have a lower wage than £25,600 (CBI 2020). For businesses, the two most celebrated aspects were: the removal of the cap on numbers entering the UK, with 26% of employers considering that it shall have a positive impact on UK organisations, alongside the perceived reduction in the bureaucracy of the sponsorship system (welcomed by 25% of organisations) (CIPD 2019).

The design of a well-managed migration system *could* counteract some of the negative effects of inequality within the UK, such as economic growth, skills and regional wage inequality, thereby helping to redress these imbalances. As mentioned in the theory section of this chapter, the theoretical **expectation is that, via migration, a more efficient distribution and use of labour market resources could be achieved, leading to wage convergence,** whereby, in time, with labour mobility being allowed and/or enabled, regional wage variation would decrease.

Taking the example of region wage disparities in the UK, a **regional approach to immigration policy** has already been discussed at the point before deciding the UK's future migration system **salary threshold.** It was found that Scotland would be most interested in this, albeit Scottish employers were also the ones to be most in favour of a national migration policy (CIPD 2019: 17). The point to make is that, depending on extant regional wages, London employers would be, for example, more able to receive migrants, whereas areas with lower regional wages could be negatively affected in two compound ways: firstly, regionally their employment prospects are seen as less desirable by the native population; secondly, they would be less likely to attract migrants since the nation-wide wage threshold would be too high for the respective region. In the event, it remains to be seen how the current policy migration of having a fixed nation-wide wage threshold would affect each region.

The design and application of the final new UK migration policy would need to take into account, at the very least, some of the EU migration policy approaches that it would be wise to mirror, to the extent that the UK would then want to have its citizens treated by the EU in a similar favourable way. Thus, some degree of regulatory compliance of UK migration policy with its EU counterpart may still be desirable, such as with respect to: mutual agreements of visa regulations, student mobility, mobile communication fees, healthcare access or currency transfer for holiday makers, pensions and time limits, alongside, more generally, the treatment of each other's' nationals with regard to living in a foreign country, their access to various services, welfare or benefits, and ultimately to citizenship. The amount of ease (or difficulty) that the new UK system will allow our officials to show to EU citizens whilst in the UK could be mirrored by EU officials when UK citizens travel or intend to live there. Based on this rational expectation, it would be natural to hope that the UK would consider carefully every detail in the design and implementation of its new migration system.

Currently there is a dearth of post-Brexit analyses of GDP and UK growth that take into account of the impact of UK's visa regime, since it is indeed a very recent development. To the extent that trade-based methodology is useful and relevant, a study of the impact of reduced migration from the EU to the UK (carried out pre-Brexit) estimated decreases in GDP, GDP per capita and low-skilled wage levels, albeit modest (see Table 6.3).

In terms of the macroeconomic impact of a skilled-based migration system, if it is assumed that labour is homogenous (workers are similar to each other), a restriction in migration would be expected to cause a direct drop in labour input and inevitably a predicted fall in GDP, but the

Table 6.3 Estimates of the impact of immigration reduction from the EU to the UK by 2030, cumulative, in %

	Scenario	GDP	GDP per capita	Wages
Model 1	Central	2.73	0.92	0.507
	Extreme	4.35	1.53	0.8198
Model 2	Central	5.19	3.38	0.507
	Extreme	8.18	5.36	0.8198

Source: Portes and Forte (2016), Table 9.1

assumptions of homogenous labour are unrealistic (see discussion at the beginning of this chapter, on neo-classical models of migration). Instead, when varying this unrealistic assumption, that is, allowing for the real-world example of heterogeneous labour (by exception, to date, this is done by Gudgin et al. 2017[11]), the analysis of the macroeconomic impact becomes complex and its expected impact less clear. This is because higher-skilled individuals tend to have higher productivity, so fewer but more skilled migrants can have an indeterminate effect upon GDP growth, depending upon which effect predominates (i.e. lower quantity of labour effect vs. higher productivity of labour). Certainly, the expectation is that an increase in the average level of skills amongst the migrant group (and their effect upon the UK population as a whole) would increase GDP-per head. Maybe only time will tell.

Therefore, the UK's new migration system reflects the renewed attempts made by the UK government to strike a better balance between migration and the country's best perceived interest. The expectation is that this new immigration system will allow the government to finally ascertain a degree of control, in line with the Leave Campaign (during the 2016 EU referendum) supporters' mantra of 'taking back control over our borders'. The extent to which this system will also be fit for purpose, satisfying the needs of reducing migration within 'controllable' limits, as well as allowing business to continue to flourish, offering a better way of distributing the benefits and sharing the costs of migration, making best use of limited resources, all these are key question that can only be answered after a period of time of trialling out this system.

CONCLUSION

Migration policy is one of the key areas for the UK government to develop before the end of the transition period, currently lasting until 1 January 2021. The problems with migration are, however, the entrenched negative perception of migrants, such the view that they are stealing natives' jobs, lowering wages and so on.

Migration's poor image problem lies especially in a skewed perception of its benefits versus cost and governments' inability or lack of will to make

---

[11] Estimates here are of lower post-Brexit migration flows (leading to an overall prediction of the UK population reducing by 86,000—OECD), but higher per capita GDP by 2030 (Gudgin et al. 2017).

their voters more conscious of the former, whereas costs usually speak for themselves albeit louder than they should. Migration's benefits tend to be spread to the wide population of a country and hence are almost unseen or barely perceptible, mainly to statisticians, for example, marginally lower prices at the level of a nation, higher variety in goods (for the latter, see Aubry et al. 2016) and easier availability of goods (e.g. if fruit is picked by migrants). Wages and jobs do not tend to be lowered by migrants, except for weaker economic periods, for low-skilled workers and for very small wage changes. In contrast, fears of job loss and wage cuts persist, and some of the negative consequences of migration, such as traffic congestion or increased pressures on health and education systems, are much easily picked up by the media and felt by a local economy.

Migration's image could be redressed by government's design of migration policy that could mitigate better the balance between winners and losers of migration. Otherwise countries are at risk of being too strongly influenced by a negative perception of migration, with too few being the pro-migration advocates. Politicians could be listening too much to parts of their electorate harking back to times when globalisation was slower, harbouring anti-migration biased views, thereby favouring stricter border regulation and the introduction of rather nationalistic-driven migration systems (e.g. Trump's wall to Mexico; the EU's insistence that it helps only Syrian refugees in preference to the 'economic' migrant; resurgence of nationalistic political parties such as in Austria or Hungary). This would risk killing the golden-egg laying goose.

Migrant labour can make positive contributions to our nation in terms of productivity, growth, avoiding skills bottlenecks, reducing inequality and various other labour market and economy-wide aspects. However, costs, such as stresses upon public services (e.g. health, education, transport and housing), need to be recognised.

As a solution, part of the additional income generated for the country as a whole could be invested to alleviate these problems. Indeed, if migration is a net benefit, as many studies suggest, then the issue might be the distribution of this benefit and the associated costs between the likely beneficiaries of migration (largely, firms but the public too) and those who lose out (e.g. people in regions with relatively high migration rates, who need more public services, living in crowded areas, or those workers whose wages might be dampened).

A skills-based migration system could, if designed correctly, enhance productivity, although its net effect on GDP would depend upon whether reduced labour supply predominated over any productivity effect.

Moreover, certain economic sectors will require focused attention to address sector-specific labour supply issues. It may be that short-term or longer-term exemptions from certain migration regulations apply to these sectors, or that seasonal worker schemes or assistance is provided to employers to transform production through introducing more mechanisation where this proves feasible.

The preferred solution based on economic theory, rationale and evidence, one that would offer much needed PR support to migration's image, would be for government, business and the research community to work together to help design a migration policy appropriate to our country's needs, for example, adapted to our country's evolving economic profile of jobs/sectorial occupations and vacancies (be it a service-based economy, a knowledge-based economy, etc.), encouraging higher-skill job creation and investment in training and skilling of its workforce, younger age migration, and with flexibility to adapt its migration policy in time.

REFERENCES

Alesina, A., Harnoss, J., & Rapoport, H. (2016). Birthplace Diversity and Economic Prosperity. *Journal of Economic Growth, 21*(2), 101–138.

Angrist, J. D., & Kugler, A. D. (2003). Protective or Counter-Productive? European Labour Market Institutions and the Effect of Immigrants on EU Natives. *Economic Journal, 113*(June), F302–F331.

Arregui, N., & Chen, J. (2018). *United Kingdom—IMF Country Report No 18/317*. Paris: International Monetary Fund. Available via: https://www.imf.org/en/Publications/CR/Issues/2018/11/14/United-Kingdom-Selected-Issues-46354. Accessed 18 March 2020.

Aubry, A., Burzyńskia, M., & Docquier, F. (2016). 'The Welfare Impact of Global Migration in OECD Countries, *Journal of International Economics*, 101 (July): 1-21. Available online via: https://www.sciencedirect.com/science/article/abs/pii/S002219961630040X.

Bank of England. (2014). Inflation Report. November. Available online via: https://www.bankofengland.co.uk/-/media/boe/files/inflation-report/2014/november-2014.pdf?la=en&hash=B10E1C4E36EBA64D114 2F80E4407798F84F95ADA.

Bank of England. (2017, April 30). A Millennium of Macroeconomic Data for the UK. Version 3.1. Available online via: https://www.bankofengland.co.uk/statistics/research-datasets.

Bank of England. (2020, January). Inflation Report. Available online via: https://www.bankofengland.co.uk/-/media/boe/files/monetary-policy-report/2020/january/monetary-policy-report-january-2020.pdf.

Barone, G., & Moretti, S. (2011). With a Little Help from Abroad: The Effect of Low-skilled Immigration on the Female Labour Supply. *Labour Economics, 18*(5), 664–675.

BBC. (2017). Reality Check: Migration to the UK. Available online via: https://www.bbc.co.uk/news/election-2017-40015269.

BBC. (2019). Treasury to 'Rewrite Rules to Favour the North, News article published online on 27 December. Available online via: https://www.bbc.co.uk/news/business-50925321.

BBC. (2020). Reality Check: Are Economically Inactive People the Answer to Staff Shortages? News article published online on 19 February 2020. Available online via: https://www.bbc.co.uk/news/51560120.

BBC Briefing. (2020, January 20). Immigration. Report. Available online via: http://news.files.bbci.co.uk/include/newsspec/pdfs/bbc-briefing-immigration-newsspec-26148-v1.pdf.

Boubtane, E., Dumont, J. C., & Rault, C. (2016). Immigration and Economic Growth in the OECD countries, 1986-2016. *Oxford Economic Papers, 68*(2), 340–360.

Bradford, S. (2012). The Global Welfare and Poverty Effects of Rich Nation Immigration Barriers. Working paper. January. Available online via https://www.freit.org/WorkingPapers/Papers/Immigration/FREIT432.pdf.

Campo, F., Forte, G., & Portes, J. (2018). *The Impact of Migration on Productivity and Native-Born Workers' Training—paper prepared for the Migration Advisory Committee and reprinted on the UK in a Changing Europe website*. Available via: https://ukandeu.ac.uk/wp-content/uploads/2018/09/Migrationproductivity-and-training.pdf. Accessed on 20 December 2019.

Card, D. (1990). The Impact of the Mariel Boatlift on the Miami Labor Market. *Industrial and Labor Relations Review, 43*(January), 245–257.

Carrington, W. J., & de Lima, P. (1996). The Impact of 1970s Repatriates from Africa on the Portuguese Labour Market. *Industrial and Labor Relations Review, 49*(January), 330–347.

CBI [Confederation of British Industry]. (2016). *Leaving the EU: Implications for the UK Economy*, PwC Report. Available via: http://www.cbi.org.uk/news/leaving-eu-would-cause-a-serious-shock-to-uk-economy-new-pwc-analysis/leaving-the-eu-implications-for-the-uk-economy/.

CBI [Confederation of British Industry]. (2020). *Our Response to Migration Advisory Committee Report*. Released 28 January 2020. Available online via: https://www.cbi.org.uk/media-centre/articles/our-response-to-migration-advisory-committee-report/.

CEP [Centre for Economic performance]. (2018, April 6). The Economic Impacts of Immigration to the UK. Available online via: https://voxeu.org/article/economic-impacts-immigration-uk.

CIPD [Chartered Institute of Personnel and Development]. (2017a). *Resourcing and Talent Planning*. Survey Report. London: UK. Available online via:

https://www.cipd.co.uk/Images/resourcing-talent-planning_2017_
tcm18-23747.pdf.

CIPD [Chartered Institute of Personnel and Development]. (2017b). *Facing the Future: Tackling Post-Brexit Skills and Labour Shortages*. Survey Report. London: UK. Available online via: https://www.cipd.co.uk/Images/facing-the-future_2017-tackling-post-Brexit-labour-and-skills-shortages_tcm18-24417.pdf.

CIPD [Chartered Institute of Personnel and Development]. (2019). *Migration: A Practical Immigration System Post-Brexit Britain*. Report. September. London: UK. Available online via https://www.cipd.co.uk/Images/a-practical-immigration-system-for-post-brexit-britain_tcm18-64059.pdf.

Curtice, J. (2017). Why Leave Won the UK's EU Referendum. *Journal of Common Market Studies, 55*, 19–37.

Dustman, C., Frattini, T., & Glitz, A. (2007). The Impact of Migration: A Review of Economic Evidence. Report. Centre for Research and Analysis of Migration (CReAM), November. Available online via: https://www.ucl.ac.uk/~uctpb21/reports/WA_Final_Final.pdf.

Dustmann, C., & Frattini, T. (2013). *The Fiscal Effects of Immigration to the UK*. CReAM discussionpaper 22/13, UCL. Available via: http://www.cream-migration.org/publ_uploads/CDP_22_13.pdf.

Dustmann, C., & Frattini, T. (2014). The Fiscal Effects of Immigration to the UK. *Economic Journal, 124*, F953–F643.

EIB [European Investment Bank]. (2020). Who Is Prepared for the New Digital Age? Evidence from the EIB Investment Survey. Available online via: https://www.eib.org/attachments/efs/eibis_2019_report_on_digitalisation_en.pdf#IBIS.

Erling, B., Bratsberg, B., & Raaum, O. (2006). Local Employment and the Earnings Assimilation of Immigrants in Norway. *Review of Economics and Statistics, 88*(May), 243–263.

ESCoE [Economic Statistic Centre of Excellence]. (2020, February). Regional Nowcasting Estimates. Available online via: https://www.escoe.ac.uk/regionalnowcasting/.

Foged, M., & Peri, G. (2016). Immigrants' Effect on Native Workers: New Analysis on Longitudinal Data. *American Economic Journal: Applied Economics., 8*(2), 1–34.

Friedberg, R. M. (2001). The Impact of Mass Migration on the Israeli Labor Market. *Quarterly Journal of Economics, 116*(November), 1373–1408.

Galgoczi, B., Leschke, J., & Watt, A. (2016). *EU Labour Migration Since Enlargement*. London: Routledge.

Gilpin, N., Henty, M., Lemos, S., Portes, J., & Bullen, C. (2006). The Impact of Free Movement of Workers from Central and Eastern Europe on the UK Labour Market, Department for Work and Pensions, Working Paper No 29, London: UK.

Gott, C., & Johnston, K. (2002). *The Migrant Population in the UK: Fiscal Effects*. RDS Home Office Report.

Gov.UK. (2020). The UK's Points-based Immigration System: An Introduction for Employers. Published 9 April 2020. Available online via: https://www.gov.uk/government/publications/uk-points-based-immigration-system-employer-information/the-uks-points-based-immigration-system-an-introduction-for-employers.

Gudgin, G., Coutts, K., Gibson, N., & Buchanan, J. (2017). *Defying Gravity: A Critique of Estimates of the Economic Impact of Brexit*, Policy Exchange, London. Retrieved March 10, 2020, from https://policyexchange.org.uk/wp-content/uploads/2017/06/Defying-Gravity-A-critique-of-estimates-of-the-economic-impact-of-Brexit.pdf.

Hantzsche, A., & Young, G. (2019). *The Economic Impact of Prime Minister Johnson's New Brexit Deal*. National Institute Economic Review, 250: F34-7. Available online via: https://www.niesr.ac.uk/publications/economic-impact-prime-minister-johnsons-new-brexit-deal. Accessed 20 March 2020.

Hantzsche, A., Kara, A., & Young, G. (2018). *The Economic Effects of the Government's Proposed Brexit Deal*. London: NIESR. Available via: https://www.niesr.ac.uk/sites/default/files/publications/NIESR%20Report%20Brexit%20-%202018-11-26.pdf. Accessed 17 February 2020.

HM Government. (2018). The Future Relationship Between the United Kingdom and the European Union. Available online via: https://assets.publishing.service.gov.uk/government/uploads/system/uploads/attachment_data/file/786626/The_Future_Relationship_between_the_United_Kingdom_and_the_European_Union_120319.pdf.

HM Treasury [Her Majesty's Treasury]. (2016). *HM Treasury Analysis: The long term economic impact of EU membership and the alternatives, Cm 9250*. London: The Stationery Office. Available via: https://www.gov.uk/government/uploads/system/uploads/attachment_data/file/517415/treasury_analysis_economic_impact_of_eu_membership_web.pdf.

Hunt, J. (1992). The Impact of the 1962 Repatriates from Algeria on the French Labor Market. *Industrial and Labor Relations Review, 45*(April), 556–572.

Hunt, J., & Gauthier-Loiselle, M. (2010). How Much Does Immigration Boost Innovation? *American Economic Journal: Macroeconomics, 2*(2), 31–56.

Ipsos Mori. (2018, December 6). The Perils of Perception. Available online via: https://www.ipsos.com/ipsos-mori/en-uk/perils-perception-2018.

Ipsos Mori. (2019, August 30). Issues Index. Available online via: https://www.ipsos.com/ipsos-mori/en-uk/ipsos-mori-issues-index-july-2019-brexit-nhs-and-crime-are-britons-three-biggest-issues.

Jaumotte, F., Koloskova, K., & Saxena, S. C. (2016). Impact of Migration on Income Levels in Advanced Economies, Spillover Task Force, IMF.

Kerr, W. R., & Lincoln, W. F. (2010). The Supply Side of Innovation: H-1B Visa Reforms and U.S. Ethnic Invention. *Journal of Labour Economics, 28*(3), 473–508.

Kierzenkowski, R., Pain, N., Rusticelli, E., & Zwart, S. (2016). *The Economic Consequences of Brexit: A Taxing Decision,* OECD Economic Policy Paper No. 16, OECD, Paris. Available via: https://www.oecd.org/economy/The-Economic-consequences-of-Brexit-27-april-2016.pdf. Accessed 18 March 2020.

Lemos, S. (2010). *Labour Market Effects of Eastern European Migration in Wales.* Leicester: University of Leicester.

Lemos, S., & Portes, J. (2008). *The Impact of Migration from the New EU Member States on Native Workers.* London: Department for Work and Pensions.

MAC [Migration Advisory Committee]. (2012). Analysis of the Impacts of Migration, Migration Advisory Committee, London. Available via: https://www.gov.uk/government/uploads/system/uploads/attachment_data/file/257235/analysis-of-the-impacts.pdf.

MAC [Migration Advisory Committee]. (2014). *Migrants in Low-Skilled Work.* London: Migration Advisory Committee. Available via: https://www.gov.uk/government/uploads/system/uploads/attachment_data/file/333083/MAC-Migrants_in_low-skilled_work__Full_report_2014.pdf.

MAC [Migration Advisory Committee]. (2018). EEA Migration, September. Available online via: https://www.gov.uk/government/publications/migration-advisory-committee-mac-report-eea-migration.

Manacorda, M., Manning, A., & Wadsworth, J. (2010, August). The Impact of Immigration on the Structure of Wages: Theory and Evidence from Britain. Available online via: https://personal.lse.ac.uk/manacorm/manacorda_manning_wadsworth.pdf.

Menon, A., Portes, J., Levell, P., & Sampson, T. (2018). *The Economic Consequences of the Brexit Deal.* London: UK in a Changing Europe. Available via: http://ukandeu.ac.uk/wp-content/uploads/2018/11/The-economic-consequences-of-Brexit.pdf. Accessed 14 February 2020.

MHCLG [Ministry of Housing, Communities and Local Government]. (2018, April 13). Analysis of the Determinants of House Price Changes. Available online via: https://assets.publishing.service.gov.uk/government/uploads/system/uploads/attachment_data/file/699846/OFF_SEN_Ad_Hoc_SFR_House_prices_v_PDF.pdf.

Migration Observatory. (2019, July 15). Migrants in the UK Labour Market. Available online via: https://migrationobservatory.ox.ac.uk/resources/briefings/migrants-in-the-uk-labour-market-an-overview/.

Moses, J. W., & Letnes, B. (2004). The Economic Costs to International Labour Restrictions: Revisiting the Empirical Discussion'. *World Development, 32*(10), 1609–1626.

NHS [National Health Service]. (2019, March). NHS Workforce Statistics. Available online via: https://digital.nhs.uk/data-and-information/publica-tions/statistical/nhs-workforce-statistics/nhs-workforce-statistics% 2D%2D-march-2019-provisional-statistics.

Nickell, S, & Saleheen, J. (2015). The Impact of Immigration on Occupational Wages: Evidence from Britain, Bank of England, Staff Working Paper No. 574.

OECD [Organisation for Economic Co-operation and Development]. (1989). Employment Outlook. Chapter 5. Characteristics of Employment in Growing and Declining Industries. Available online via: https://www.oecd.org/els/emp/3888296.pdf.

OECD [Organisation for Economic Co-operation and Development]. (2019). Employment Outlook. Chapter 3. The Future of Work: New Evidence on Job Stability, Under-employment and Access to Good Jobs. Available online via: https://www.oecd-ilibrary.org/sites/9ee00155-en/1/2/3/index. html?itemId=/content/publication/9ee00155-en&_csp_=b4640e1ebac05eb-1ce93dde646204a88&itemIGO=oecd&itemContentType=book#sect ion-d1e8141.

OECD [Organisation for Economic Co-operation and Development]. (2020). UK Population Statistics. Available online via: https://stats.oecd.org/.

ONS [Office for National Statistics]. (2019a). Population of the UK by Country of Birth and Nationality. Released on 28 November. Available online via https://www.ons.gov.uk/peoplepopulationandcommunity/populationand-migration/internationalmigration/datas.

ONS [Office for National Statistics]. (2019b). Population of the UK by Country of Birth and Nationality: July 2018 to June 2019. Released 28 November 2019. Available online via: https://www.ons.gov.uk/peoplepopulationand-community/populationandmigration/internationalmigration/bulletins/ukpopulationbycountryofbirthandnationality/july2018tojune2019.

ONS [Office for National Statistics]. (2020a). Vacancies and the Jobs in the UK. Released 17 March 2020. Available online via: https://www.ons.gov.uk/employmentandlabourmarket/peopleinwork/employmentandemploy-eetypes/bulletins/jobsandvacanciesintheuk/march2020.

ONS [Office for National Statistics]. (2020b). Vacancies and Jobs in the UK. Released 17 March 2020. Available online via: https://www.ons.gov.uk/employmentandlabourmarket/peopleinwork/employmentandemploy-eetypes/articles/labourmarketeconomiccommentary/january2020.

ONS [Office for National Statistics]. (2020c). Average Gross Weekly Earnings of Full-time Employees, by Region. Released 5 February 2020. Available online via https://www.ons.gov.uk/employmentandlabourmarket/peopleinwork/earningsandworkinghours/datasets/averageweeklyearnings.

ONS [Office for National Statistics]. (2020d). Labour Market Overview, UK. Released 17 March 2020. Available online via https://www.ons.gov.uk/employmentandlabourmarket/peopleinwork/employmentandemploy-eetypes/bulletins/uklabourmarket/latest#vacancies.

ONS [Office for National Statistics]. (2020e). UK and Non-UK People in the Labour Market. Released 18 February 2020 Available online via: https://www.ons.gov.uk/employmentandlabourmarket/peopleinwork/employmentandemployeetypes/articles/ukandnonukpeopleinthelabourmarket/february2020.

Open Letter to Home Secretary. (2020). UK. 24 January. Available online via https://www.cbi.org.uk/articles/business-unites-on-future-immigration-system/.

Ortega, F., & Peri, G. (2016). Openness and Income: The Roles of Trade and Migration. *Journal of International Economics, 92*(2), 231–251.

Ottaviano, G. I., Peri, G., & Wright, G. C. (2015). Immigration, Trade and Productivity in Services: Evidence from UK Firms, NBER Working Paper No. w21200.

Parliament of Australia. 2016. A National Disgrace: The Exploitation of Temporary Work Visa Holders.

People Management. (2020, May 4). What Does the New Immigration Guidance Mean for Employers? News article available online via https://www.people-management.co.uk/experts/legal/what-does-new-points-based-immigration-guidance-mean-employers?utm_source=mc&utm_medium=email&utm_content=pm_daily_04052020.Employment+law%3a+What+does+the+new+immigration+guidance+mean+for+employers%3f&utm_campaign=7295441&utm_term=5055076.

Pischke, J. S., & Velling, J. (1997). Employment Effects of Immigration to Germany: An Analysis Based on Local Labor Markets. *Review of Economics and Statistics, 79*(November), 594–604.

Portes, J., & Forte, G. (2016, December 7). The Economic Impact of Brexit-induced Reductions in Migration, *National Institute Economic Review*. Available online via: https://www.niesr.ac.uk/sites/default/files/publications/The%20Economic%20Impact%20of%20Brexit-induced%20Reductions%20in%20Migration%20-%20Dec%2016.pdf.

Raikes, L, Giovannini, A., & Getzel, B. (2019). *Divided and Connected: Regional Inequalities in the North, the Uk and the Developed World*. Institute of Public Policy Research North. Report. November. Available online via: https://www.ippr.org/files/2019-11/sotn-2019.pdf.

Roy, A. D. (1951). Some Thoughts on the Distribution of Earnings. *Oxford Economic Papers, 3*(2), 135–146.

Skills for Care. (2018). Adult Social Care Workforce Data. September. Available online via: https://www.skillsforcare.org.uk/adult-social-care-workforce-data/adult-social-care-workforce-data.aspx.

Smith, S., Whyman, P. B., Petrescu, A. I., Wright, A., & Moon, V. (2018). *Productivity in Lancashire—Sparking New Ideas*. Executive Summary. Centre for SME Development. Report, University of Central Lancashire, October.

Sumption, M., & Fernandez Reino, M. (2018, August 30). Exploiting the Opportunity? Low-skilled Work Migration After Brexit. Research Paper. Migration Observatory. London, UK. Available online via: https://ukandeu. ac.uk/research-papers/exploiting-the-opportunity-low-skilled-work-migration-after-brexit/.

Theta Financial Reporting. (2020). The UK Productivity Index 2020. February. Available on request from the authors.

UK Visas and Immigration. (2020). The UK's Points-based Immigration System: An Introduction for Employers. Released 9 April 2020. Available online via: https://www.gov.uk/government/publications/uk-points-based-immigration-system-employer-information/the-uks-points-based-immigration-system-an-introduction-for-employers.

WDI [World Development Indicators]. (2016). World Development Indicators. World Data Bank. Available via: http://databank.worldbank.org/data/reports.aspx?source=world-development-indicators#.

Whyman, P. B., & Baimbridge, M. J. (2006). *Labour Market Flexibility and Foreign Direct Investment, Employment Relations Occasional Paper URN 06 / 1797*. London: Department of Trade and Industry.

Whyman, P. B., Bainbridge, M. J., Buraimo, B. A., & Petrescu, A. I. (2015). Workplace Flexibility Practices and Corporate Performance. *British Journal of Management, 26*(3), 347–364.

Whyman, P. B., & Petrescu, A. I. (2014). Workforce Nationality Composition and Workplace Flexibility in Britain. *International Journal of Manpower, 35*(6), 776–797.

Whyman, P. B., & Petrescu, A. I. (2017). *The Economics of Brexit*. Palgrave. Book Springer Link: https://link.springer.com/book/10.1007%2F978-3-319-58283-2.

Whyman, P. B., & Petrescu, A. I. (2019). *An Evaluation of Skills Drain from Lancashire*. Report. Lancashire Institute for Economic and Business Research, Research Centre for Business Management and Enterprise, University of Central Lancashire.

World Bank. (2016). *Gross Capital Formation Report*. Available via: http://databank.worldbank.org/data/reports.aspx?source=2&series=NE.GDI.TOTL. ZS&country=#.

YouGov. (2018, April 27). Where the Public Stands on Immigration. Politics & Current Affairs. Report. Available online via https://yougov.co.uk/topics/politics/articles-reports/2018/04/27/where-public-stands-immigration.

CHAPTER 7

Economic Growth and Productivity

One of the features of most mainstream economic forecasts relating to Brexit concerns the prediction that it will inhibit productivity and weaken economic growth. Certain theorists take it for granted that Brexit will inevitably result in a less open UK economy and that, in turn, will result in weaker productivity growth (Crafts 2018: 690; Coyle 2019: 62; Wren-Lewis 2019: 44). Some claim that Brexit will cause the unravelling of the central tenants of the "British Model" (Weldon 2019: 12–13).

One of the primary motivations for the UK joining the EU was to reverse UK relative economic decline.[1] Whilst UK growth rates were actually quite reasonable over the early post-war period, certainly when compared to more recent achievements, they were dwarfed by rates of expansion recorded by the six founder members of the EU (Eichengreen 2007). From the UK enjoying a 28% advantage in gross domestic product (GDP) per capita in 1950, compared to the original six members of the EU, by the time the Treaty of Rome was signed in 1957, the gap had narrowed to 15%, and by 1961, when the UK first began openly discussing the option of joining the common market, the gap was 10%. By the time the UK actually joined the EU, in 1973, its GDP per capita was 7% *smaller* than the EU(6) average.[2] Given the EU's superior economic growth over this period, it is easy to understand the attraction for UK political leaders in perceiving EU membership, and the advantages for trade arising from

[1] http://voxeu.org/article/britain-s-eu-membership-new-insight-economic-history
[2] http://voxeu.org/article/britain-s-eu-membership-new-insight-economic-history

© The Author(s) 2020
P. B. Whyman, A. I. Petrescu, *The Economics of Brexit*,
https://doi.org/10.1007/978-3-030-55948-9_7

its associated common market, as a means of arresting the UK's economic disadvantage (Congdon 2013: 44).

Yet, assumptions that European integration was the catalyst behind this relative economic advance of the founder members of the EU, and moreover, that subsequent UK accession to the EU would have a simultaneously positive impact upon its national economy, were always problematic. Economic theory is split over how (or even whether) economic integration may have temporary or permanent stimulus to economic growth rates. Moreover, the various studies undertaken to test this hypothesis have failed to produce the clear and unambiguous set of results that adherents would have anticipated. Nevertheless, predicted productivity and growth effects featured prominently in many of the studies seeking to estimate the potential economic impact of Brexit. Thus, this chapter seeks to draw these threads of theory and evidence together, to try to evaluate the likely growth effect arising from Brexit.

ECONOMIC THEORIES OF GROWTH

The idea that economic integration is capable of improving the efficiency of an economy dates back at least as far as Adam Smith, who famously stated that "the division of labour is limited by the extent of the market" (Smith 1776: 28). According to this viewpoint, a larger market would facilitate a greater division of labour and hence enhanced efficiency.

There are, broadly speaking, three main economic models which have been developed in the attempt to try to understand the determinants of economic growth. These are (i) Keynesian, (ii) neo-classical (Solow) and (iii) endogenous growth models.

Keynesian theory identifies aggregate demand (i.e. consumption plus investment plus net government spending plus the net trade balance) as the key element determining the full employment of resources and realisation of economic growth (Domar 1946; Harrod 1939). A buoyant level of demand both facilitates and encourages business investment, as higher sales provide greater retained earnings available for investment, whilst buoyant trading conditions enhance business expectations and thereby provide the rationale for future investment to take place. A sustainable growth path depends upon their being a sufficient level of aggregate demand in the future to take account of the new capacity created by current investment. Since the Keynesian approach holds that there is no automatic tendency for the economy to tend towards full employment equilibrium, government policy is required to balance demand: if there is insufficient aggregate demand, the economy begins to stagnate; in contrast, an excess in demand leads to over-heating and inflationary pressures. The difficulty in achieving this balance is known as the 'knife edge'. The insight of the Keynesian model of economic growth, therefore, is concerned less with identifying individual determinants of growth and productivity, but rather ensuring the macroeconomic conditions conducive to the realisation of favourable future growth paths.

The Solow (1956) model, by contrast, adopts standard neo-classical assumptions of perfect competition and continuous market clearing. This implies that supply will create its own demand and the economy will tend towards full employment. Within this set of assumptions, economic growth is determined by a combination of the quantity of labour (labour supply) and capital, together with the rate of technological progress. Capital is determined by demand and supply in the neo-classical market for money, via the market interest rate, and hence, domestic savings will determine domestic investment in a closed economy. In an open economy, capital inflow, through the attraction of short-term financial capital or longer-term foreign direct investment (FDI), can have a further effect. Given diminishing returns to investment in physical capital, long-term growth rates will be primarily determined by technological change, which is assumed to be exogenous, or independent of economic behaviour including economic policy intervention. Thus, the neo-classical model maintains that free factor movement promotes a convergence of income levels between nations.

According to this approach, economic integration can have a minor influence upon growth through creating stable economic conditions, encouraging savings and thereby reducing the cost of investment capital, or through the attraction of inward investment capital and/or increasing the labour supply through inward migration. These quantity effects would raise the level of income over the short term. However, unless rates of migration or FDI flows continued to increase exponentially, they would not secure a permanent increase in economic growth rates over the longer term. Thus, arguments that economic integration can have lasting effects upon growth rates are not supported by the neo-classical growth model.

The problem with this theoretical approach, however, is that it does not satisfactorily explain the differences in growth between different nations. The 'residual' for neo-classical growth models is often very high, implying that perhaps up to half of the recorded differences in growth rates between countries is not being successfully accounted for by this approach. Accordingly, a new endogenous growth model was developed, which allowed for heterogeneous capital and labour, whilst firms were assumed to be able to influence technological change through their own investment and strategic planning (Romer 1990). This new theory allows for the possibility of increasing returns to scale and firms having an incentive to invest in new technology and innovate in their production, to reap higher (excess) profits. Furthermore, economic integration can encourage greater competition, across a larger market area, and thereby promote greater efficiency (Baldwin 1989). In this conception, economic integration can have longer lasting affects upon economic growth if increasing the size of the marketplace enables firms to increase production and benefit from greater economies of scale, thereby lowering the costs of production, increasing productivity and hence GDP. Higher profits provide the incentives for further investment and R&D, and this in turn should stimulate further growth. Economic integration may therefore, according to the endogenous growth model, have *permanent* not simply temporary effects upon economic growth rates if it is capable of accelerating technological innovation (Rivera-Batiz and Romer 1991; Cuaresma et al. 2008: 643–4).

Openness and Economic Growth

The insights provided by the neo-classical and endogenous growth theories subsequently led to an association being established between the degree of 'openness' of an economy and economic growth. Openness, in this context, relates to the ease of movement of goods, services, labour and capital across borders (Bank of England 2015: 16). It is thought to assist nations in adopting the latest technologies, which can, in turn, increase the efficiency of their economies, thereby shifting them towards the global productivity frontier (Bank of England 2015: 33). It may change the incentives for firms to innovate and invest in new technology, as openness may increase competition and import penetration (Bloom et al. 2011), whilst simultaneously increasing potential returns that could be achieved through successful exporting into a more accessible overseas market (Rivera-Batiz and Romer 1991; Melitz and Trefler 2012). Furthermore, the inward flow of FDI, as was discussed in Chap. 4, may have positive productivity effects (Aghion et al. 2009).

There is a well-established literature which has sought to establish whether openness results in higher economic growth rates (Edwards 1998; Frankel and Romer 1999). A variety of studies have concluded that openness can increase growth rates due to a rise in investment and technology diffusion (Wacziarg, 1998), and greater R&D (Bloom et al. 2011), whilst there is reasonable evidence that reducing trade barriers raises investment as a share of GDP and thereby *may* stimulate technological change (Barro 1991). However, initial positive findings were criticised on the basis that these studies suffered from missing variable bias—that is, factors, lying outside the model, have a measurable influence upon the results (Rodriguez and Rodrik 2000; Irwin and Terviö 2002). Thus, openness may be acting as a proxy for other more important variables which are not included in the analysis. For example, Rodrik et al. (2004) found that institutional factors were a much larger influence upon economic growth rates than openness. In addition, whilst it can be readily established that wealthier nations tend to engage in a higher proportion of international trade than poorer nations, this is insufficient to establish the degree of causality (Feyrer, 2009a: 2). In other words, does higher trade lead to higher national income, or is the cause the other way around?

One study sought to get around this problem by introducing the idea that distance, in trade terms, is not fixed over time, as reductions in transportation costs (particularly air transport) alters the impact of physical distance between countries over time (Feyrer, 2009a: 3). For example, the cost of air freight declined by more than 92%, from around $3.87 per ton-kilometre in 1955 to under $0.30 in 2004, when expressed in constant currency (Hummels 2007: 137–8). Consequently, whilst spatial distance remains the same, the ability to trade over distance becomes more cost effective, thereby facilitating a large expansion of trade over longer distances and reducing the advantages inherent in trade between close neighbours. The result of this study was to suggest that trade does appear to have a significant effect on income, such that variations in trade patterns can explain around 17% of the differences in growth rates across those nations included in the analysis, between 1960 and 1995 (Feyrer, 2009a: 23).

Other studies have sought to measure the trade impact of political crises or natural disasters. Feyrer (2009b) uses data relating to trade in goods that were negatively impacted by the closure of the Suez Canal between 1967 and 1975, as alternative transport by sea would increase trade costs, followed by a positive shock to trade when the canal reopened. Felbermayr and Gröschl (2013) utilise data from a sample of 162 countries who experienced a large natural disaster (i.e. earthquake, famine, volcanic eruption, storms, floods and droughts), to seek to isolate changes in bilateral trade and the impact upon the GDP of trading partners. These findings were utilised by the Bank of England (2018: 25) in its own forecasts for the potential impact of Brexit upon openness, trade and GDP. This choice is questionable, however, since Felbermayr and Gröschl (2013: 27) themselves acknowledge that their approach only identifies strong and significant associations between trade openness and growth for non-OECD economies, whereas for the more developed (OECD) nations (including the UK), *openness was not found to affect real GDP per capita.*

Competition and Productivity

A second aspect of the proposed openness effect occurs through the impact of greater competition, with subsequent influence upon productivity and growth. Competitive pressures are thought to facilitate productivity through disciplining firms to become more efficient or else they lose market share and through pressuring firms into innovation which can lead to increased efficiency (Pilat 1996: 108–9, 129; CMA 2015: 2). As less efficient firms decline, resources are released and, if certain assumptions hold, are reallocated to the more efficient firms, thereby raising average productivity (Melitz and Redding 2012). Openness amplifies this process as a larger market is likely to enhance competition, certainly in the short run, whilst simultaneously broadening the scope for increased economies of scale (Melitz and Ottoviano 2008: 307–12; CBI 2013: 60). It may also improve the quality of supply chains (CBI 2013: 10). Consequently, were Brexit to result in the UK being excluded from participation in the SIM, concerns have been raised that productivity effects would be weakened (Portes 2013: F6).

There is, however, a critical problem with this rather straightforward view of the positive relationship between competition and productivity growth, namely that it is derived from a neo-classical growth model which is, in turn, founded upon the assumptions inherent within neo-classical economics. The two most prominent of these are (i) perfect competition, where the marketplace is comprised of many small producers and consumers, each too small to influence the market price and with all but essential levels of profitability competed away in the long run; and (ii) Say's Law, which holds that the economy tends towards full employment of all resources, as supply creates its own demand. The operation of these two assumptions enables the neo-classical model to deliver the positive productivity predictions, as perfect competition ensures the continuation of competitive pressures which force firms to become more efficient, whilst Say's Law ensures that any resources released from an inefficient firm leaving the market will be automatically taken up and used by more efficient remaining and new entrant firms. Under these conditions, the Solow growth model holds that competitive pressures drive the expansion of the capital stock which, in turn, is a key determinant of economic growth in the short to medium term.

If these simplifying assumptions do not reflect real-world reality, however, then the link between competition and growth becomes less obvious. For example, given that firms invest in new technology when they see an opportunity to earn profits (Grossman and Helpman 1994: 27), intensive competition can both reduce the incentive to invest by lowering future profit expectations whilst also retarding the ability to do so through retained profits (Romer 1986; Aghion and Howitt 1992). Indeed, the neo-classical assumption of perfect competition makes the reduction in future profitability an inevitable feature of its model of growth. Thus, where domestic firms find it more difficult to compete, greater openness may cause a decline in domestic investment and hence slower rates of growth (Feenstra 1990; Grossman and Helpman 1994).

There have been a number of studies which have examined this issue, but no clear consensus has emerged about whether increased competition will enhance or inhibit innovation and technological advance, or whether this tenuous association depends upon more significant factors (Englander and Gurney 1994). These might include investments in human and physical capital, improvements in infrastructure and the support engendered by a supportive institutional and macroeconomic environment. This is not to dismiss the possibility that openness can have an impact on growth, but rather that it does not necessarily occur through greater competition.

Openness—A Key Determinant of Growth or Proxy for More Important Factors?

Unlike the multifaceted discussion of openness as an economic concept, its measurement is simply the sum of exports and imports divided as a proportion of a nation's GDP. The chain of causation is therefore considered to run from a greater proportion of trade leading to an economy being more 'open' to international competition and less insular, thereby generating productivity and innovation spillovers derived from international production. One problem with this scenario is that it is an observable fact that larger economies tend to have a smaller tradable sector since they are in a position to supply most of their own needs internally, whereas smaller states tend to have a greater propensity for trade as they have less capacity for domestic fulfilment of demand. Consequently, the openness hypothesis would suggest that these larger economies are likely to be less efficient. Yet, the USA and Japan are two examples of larger economies, with comparatively small trade shares, yet it is a gross mischaracterisation to suggest that they are inefficient.

It is plausible that openness and competition have some impact upon productivity and growth. Yet, it is perhaps more likely that their use in economic models is acting as a proxy for more significant determinants of growth, such as the realisation of economies of scale and the rate of capital accumulation. These factors can, of course, be affected by the degree of openness of an economy, but as noted with respect to the USA and Japan, the degree of openness is unlikely to be the *dominant* determinant of this relationship. It is, for example, perfectly possible that the use of a Keynesian economic approach, maintaining a high level of aggregate demand in the domestic economy and providing sufficient investment incentives, could have more effect upon output, economies of scale and capital accumulation.

The endogenous theory of economic growth, by contrast, holds that innovation and technological advance are more significant determinants of economic growth than the level of capital stock *per se* (Grossman and Helpman 1994: 24). It acknowledges that individual sectors are typically characterised by imperfect competition, where it is possible for producers to retain larger (excess) profits beyond the short run, as competition is not sufficiently intense to compete this away. As a result, these firms may respond to the greater market opportunities open to them through greater openness by innovating or investing in new technology because they have the profit incentive and retained earnings to fund such investment (Aghion et al., 2009). In this way, it is possible for openness to impact on growth when competition effects are in fact sufficiently weak to facilitate the investment in technological development, but sufficiently strong to provide a necessary degree of market discipline to prevent inertia.

The problem in seeking to weigh the relative merits of these economic theories is that the evidence is imprecise and difficult to evaluate (Pilat

1996: 122, 130). There is, for example, a certain degree of evidence to support the idea that high rates of product market competition, characterised by high entry and exit rates into a given market, may promote market discipline and productivity growth (Nickell 1996; Disney et al. 2003; Tang and Wang 2005). It may additionally encourage the adoption of new technology (Baily and Gersbach 1995), better management practices (Bloom and van Reenen 2010; Bloom et al. 2012) and innovation (Griffith et al. 2010). However, other theorists found negative associations between product market deregulation and innovation (Griffith and Harrison 2004; Cincera and Galgau 2005), and between import penetration and productivity levels (Pilat 1996: 124).

The discrepancy between the findings of these different studies may indicate that it is not the degree of openness that is important, but rather the ability of domestic producers to be in a position to take advantage of any new market opportunities through investing in new technology, innovating and hence enhancing their productivity and competitive advantage. Interestingly, Aghion et al. (2005, 2009) identified a possible inverted-U shape relationship between competition and innovation in the UK, inferring that, when competition is limited, an increase will result in increased innovation and productivity growth, whereas beyond a certain point, further increases in competition may damage these positive effects. Perhaps, this is why there is only weak evidence that EU membership has had any noticeable impact upon productivity growth in member states (EC 1996: 180).

Openness in the UK and the EU

If economic integration has an economic impact, then there should be overwhelming evidence to be gleaned from the experience of the EU, given that the EU has recorded faster increases in trade openness than other OECD nations (Bank of England 2015: 89). Indeed, it has been described as "the most far reaching and successful integration project in history" (Badinger and Breuss 2011: 285). Perhaps surprisingly, given the importance of this issue, there have been relatively few studies which have sought to test this question (Badinger 2005: 51). Some of these have used the synthetic counterfactuals method, which is where a control group of other countries is chosen to reflect the characteristics of the chosen country(ies) prior to the intervention under investigation, which in this case would be accession to the EU. Estimation of the effect is made by comparing the subsequent behaviour of the target nation with this control group (Campos et al. 2014: 9). The strength and weakness of these studies is therefore quite obviously the closeness of fit of this control group. Other research teams have utilised econometric techniques, whether using cross-sectional or panel data. The issue here concerns the sensitivity of their models to either the sample composition (i.e. the number of countries included and over which time period) and/or the robustness of the model to the inclusion or exclusion of different variables (Sapir 2011: 1213).

There are a number of studies that conclude that European integration has facilitated a temporary period of faster economic growth due to the reduction of trade barriers encouraging investment (Baldwin and Seghezza 1996). Estimates suggest that the GDP of the average EU member state may be between 5% and 20% higher than would otherwise have been the case (Boltho and Eichengreen 2008; Badinger 2005). Henrekson et al. (1997: 1539), in contrast, conclude that European integration led to a *permanent effect* on the growth rate of between 0.6% and 1.3% per annum. This study is particularly interesting because it found similar results for European Free Trade Association (EFTA) nations as for EU member states, which might point towards a general benefit arising from the reduction of trade barriers more generally, but not a specific EU effect *per se*. This conclusion of a permanent increase in economic growth rates is disputed by Eichengreen and Boltho (2008: 24–26), who consider it to be unlikely. Nevertheless, they do accept that integration probably did provide a positive economic impact as trade creation proved to be larger than trade diversion for most of the founder member states (Bayoumi and Eichengreen 1997; Eichengreen 2007). Moreover, whilst economies of scale would no doubt have been secured irrespective of the creation of the common market, this additional trade integration is likely to have provided some additional impetus.

By contrast, there have been a number of studies which have found no evidence that European integration has had any measurable impact upon growth rates, either temporary or permanent (Landau 1995; Vanhoudt 1999). Indeed, much of the observed increase in traded goods may be derived from a catching-up effect, whereby poorer nations benefit far more from accession to the EU than would a more developed economy, such as the UK (Cuaresma et al. 2008: 650–2).

There are, however, a number of weaknesses in utilising the openness concept.

When seeking to measure the impact of EU membership on the degree of trade openness in the UK, for example, a counterfactual has to be constructed—that is, supposing what might have happened had the UK not joined the EU (Bank of England 2015: 10). The robustness of analyses is susceptible to the selection of which countries to include in the analysis, over which time periods and the precise selection (or omission) of particular variables within the model (Cuaresma et al. 2008: 644–5). Missing variable bias is a particular problem, given the difficulties in isolating the effects of European integration from other macroeconomic developments, such as General Agreement on Tariffs and Trade/World Trade Organization (WTO) multilateral liberalisation of international trade (Rodriguez and Rodrik 2000; Rodrik et al. 2004). Analysis should (but often does not) include estimation of trade diversion as well as creation, as EU membership requires the application of the common external tariff. Hence, it is difficult to identify precise causality, and the majority of economic studies concede that their results are fragile and not completely robust (Badinger 2005: 50; Henrekson et al. 1997: 1551; Boltho and Eichengreen 2008: 13; Cuaresma et al., 2008).

There are additional elements which further complicate the interpretation of this evidence. For example, in order to simplify the analysis, studies tend to assume that nations have identical endowments and technologies in order to more easily isolate scale effects that may arise from economic integration. But they clearly do not. Hence, allowing a more realistic assumption of significant differences in endowments and technologies between nations implies that economic integration can result in resources shifting between different sectors and countries, potentially reducing growth rates in some member states even if it rises in others (Rivera-Batiz and Romer 1991: 550).

A further challenge is that the various studies show that any openness effect is not constant over time (Eichengreen 2007). Figure 7.1 indicates that whilst certain economies exhibited a fairly steady increase in openness between 1970 and 2018 (i.e. Germany and EU), others experienced far greater volatility (i.e. Canada), whilst the degree of openness for other nations was little higher at the end of the time period than at the beginning (UK and Japan). Interestingly, the UK was the most open amongst this sample of countries, and around 20 percentage points higher than the global average, before it joined the EU, whereas by 2018, its degree of openness had barely changed and its relative performance was little different from the global average. Thus, whatever other conclusions can be

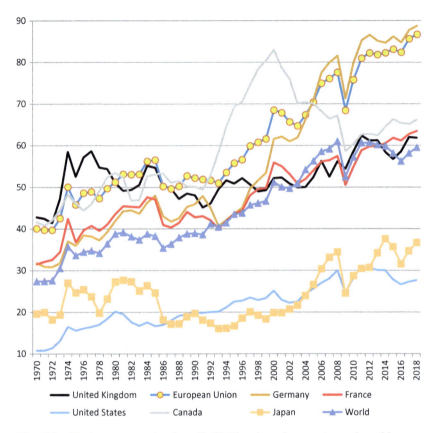

Fig. 7.1   Trade openness (trade as % GDP), selected countries and world areas, 1970–2018. Source: World Bank (2020)

reached concerning the relationship of openness and European integration, the UK does not appear to have become a more open society as a result of membership.

This has two implications for the inclusion of a dynamic (openness) effect in an analysis of Brexit. The first is that the evidence appears to suggest that there is no *a priori* reason why Brexit should automatically and inevitably lead to a reduction in openness. EU membership seems to have had little effect upon the UK's degree of openness, suggesting that the UK is likely to remain an open economy as an independent nation.

Secondly, this evidence casts doubt upon those studies which assume (a) that the past trends in European integration will continue much as they have done previously, despite data indicating that positive trade impetus may being slowly exhausted, (b) that the UK benefits at a similar rate to other EU member states and (c) that this remains constant when predicted into the future. None of these assumptions seem to be warranted by the evidence.

Evidence from the UK—Did Joining the EU Reverse the UK's Relative Decline?

The UK joined the EU, at least in part, to reverse a perceived relative economic decline, in particular, compared to the original founders of the EU. In one sense, this has been successful, given that UK gross national income (GNI) per capita started lower than all but Italy of the EU(6) countries in 1973, but was recorded as being slightly above France in 2015.[3] However, the four decades of membership did not significantly reverse economic weakness identified by those advocating accession. Indeed, the UK actually experienced a reduction in realised growth during the period of EU membership (see Fig. 7.2), where the pre-membership (shown in red) growth trend suggests an average annual growth rate of around 3.1%, with a slightly upward growth trend—so if growth rates continued around this trend growth rates would have been considerably higher (above 5%) at the end of the period under examination. By contrast, the (blue) growth trend during the five decades of EU membership displays a slowing trend, indicating that growth declined during the period of membership, to less than 2% by 2018. Thus, there is a divergence between slowly rising growth trends prior to EU membership and slowly declining growth rates during the membership period.

It is important to note, when interpreting this (and any) economic evidence, that caution is necessary to avoid overstepping what the data is capable of demonstrating. In this case, this evidence does not, indeed *cannot*, prove that EU membership has been detrimental to UK growth performance. It is a simple regression relationship, and there is no attempt to prove causality. Indeed, it is quite possible that the ending of the 'Keynesian era' of macroeconomic policy would have been sufficient to lower UK

---

[3] http://data.worldbank.org/indicator/NY.GNP.PCAP.CD?end=2015&locations=EU-GB-BE-FR-DE-IT-LU-NL&start=1973

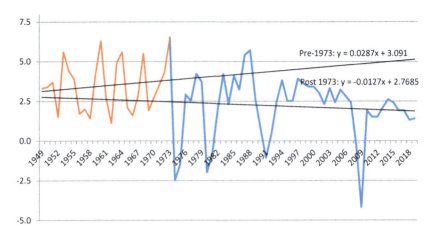

Fig. 7.2   UK annual growth rates (% GDP), with trend lines denoting UK growth performance pre- and post-joining the EU. Source: Authors' presentation of data, based on data available from ONS (2020). Notes: GDP growth rates are measured annually, in %, with GDP being presented as chained volume measure

growth rates irrespective of whether the UK joined the EU. However, it *is* relevant when evaluating whether or not the growth dividends, antici- pated by those who supported EU accession, actually occurred. In the light of this evidence, the conclusion must be that an expected boost to growth simply did not materialise.

A second piece of evidence concerns the relative growth rate of the EU economy compared to the rest of the world. If the EU were growing more rapidly than the global average, then even if the UK failed to reverse its earlier decline relative to other EU member states, the UK could still have benefitted from its accession—as a slower moving boat on a fast-moving tide. Unfortunately, for the UK, this was not the case, as the EU as a whole became a slow growth area during the period of UK membership, with a particularly noticeable deterioration in relative growth performance occurring towards the end of the 1980s.

It has been plausibly suggested that economic tightening, accompany- ing the creation of the EU single currency, together with the subsequent institutional fragility of the Eurozone, has proven to be part of the reason for this poor economic performance (Zarotiadis and Gkagka 2013). However, the slowing of growth rates also coincided with the SIM being established, and thus, it would appear that whatever benefits this may have delivered to the EU economy, it was not sufficient to sufficiently offset any negative effects arising from the single currency's overall macroeconomic framework in order to accelerate EU growth rates. The Confederation of Business Industry (CBI; 2013: 110–1) shares this analysis despite the irony that two decades previously, it had itself advocated UK participation in both the Exchange Rate Mechanism (ERM) and subsequently the single currency (CBI 1989; Eglene 2010: 92).

None of this evidence implies that EU membership has been responsible for this decline in UK economic growth during these four decades. There have been a number of far more potent shocks that the UK economy has experienced over this time period, including the multiple Organization of the Petroleum Exporting Countries (OPEC) oil shocks in the 1970s, the disastrous monetarist experiment in the 1980s, the ERM crisis in 1990 and the financial crisis in 2008. Indeed, it is still possible for advocates of EU membership to argue that UK growth rates would have been *even worse* had the UK not been a member of the EU over this time period. Nevertheless, what this evidence indicates is that EU membership was insufficient to raise UK growth rates by more than whatever factors depressed growth trends. If it did have any positive effects, EU membership must have only a small impact upon economic growth. Hence, Brexit might not prove overtly costly in terms of UK growth rates when measured over the medium term. If, alternatively, EU membership had a negative impact upon UK growth rates, then Brexit should be able to raise UK growth rates over time, by releasing the economy from the constraints imposed by EU membership.

It is, of course, possible that EU membership may be associated with a rise in UK productivity, but that, due to the economy producing at less than capacity, this is not reflected in growth figures. However, evidence from the Bank of England (2015: 48) indicates that UK output per person has remained pretty consistently around 25% lower than that achieved by the USA, and remained below that achieved by the EU(6) countries. A more useful measure of productivity, namely output per hour worked, takes account of the fact that working hours have fallen more rapidly in EU(6) than in the UK or US economies. Using this superior measure, UK output per hour worked increased from around 60% of the US level in 1960, towards 80% of US levels by the start of the 2008 financial crisis, albeit falling back towards 75% in the last few years. EU(6) productivity rose towards parity with US levels, before falling back towards 90% over the past decade.

This evidence leads to three conclusions. The first is that the UK has had a persistent productivity problem when compared to the USA and even the EU(6) nations. This is most likely due to the failure of the UK economy to facilitate comparable rates of productive investment over a long time period. The second conclusion is that membership of the EU was not sufficient to significantly alter this performance. Output per person remained stubbornly unchanged across the whole of this half century period, whilst output per hour worked did increase gradually, but more slowly than comparable EU(6) nations and certainly more slowly than that achieved by Japan. Thus, the third conclusion is that the anticipated productivity effect arising from UK accession to the EU either did not materialise or else any positive effect was overwhelmed by other macroeconomic phenomena. Essentially, if EU membership helped at all, the effect was fairly weak and a superior result could have been achieved by focusing upon other, more proven means of raising productivity. These include increasing the quantity of productive investment in the UK, enhancing education and skills training of the labour force and utilising macroeconomic tools alongside an active industrial policy to reinvigorate UK manufacturing industry, where higher productivity growth is more easily achieved than in the service sector.

THE IMPACT OF BREXIT ON OPENNESS AND PRODUCTIVITY

Despite the relatively fragile evidence contained in the economics literature, that openness is a key determinant of productivity and growth, many of the economic studies examining the impact of Brexit have chosen to include the degree of openness as a key aspect of their models (CBI 2013: 60; Bank of England 2015: 32; BertelsmannStifung 2015: 4; Dhingra et al., 2017; Bank of England, 2018: 3, 13–14, 24–5; CEP 2018: 8; HMG 2018: 26,54; NIESR via Hantzsche et al., 2018: 17). The presumption is that the chain of causality will flow from Brexit increasing barriers to trade with the EU, which will, in turn, reduce openness, which will itself negatively impact upon competition and specialisation effects, thereby resulting in weaker productivity growth. There may, additionally, be a secondary effect as the cost of adapting to technological change may be impacted negatively if Brexit results in a smaller marketplace for UK companies (Coyle 2019: 63).

Certain studies bundle the effects of FDI into this concept of openness and therefore draw from the literature which is generally held to conclude that inward investment and the operation of foreign trans-national corporations within the UK result in innovation spillovers and have positive effects upon productivity (Alfaro and Chen 2018). The review of the evidence in Chap. 4 of this book indicates that the economic literature on this point is not quite so unambiguous in its conclusions since FDI is composed of different forms and it may be that only certain types, in certain industries, have a demonstrably positive effect. As a consequence, many studies struggle to demonstrate a clear link between inward FDI flows and economic growth rates.

For those studies which include an estimation of openness into their modelling, this element tends to have quite dramatic effects upon the outcomes. For example, the CEP (2018: 14) predicted relatively minor static costs associated with different forms of Brexit, including trading according to WTO rules, yet the introduction of dynamic elements into the model, derived from assumptions as to how openness might impact upon productivity, magnified these forecasted costs by a factor of 2.5 (2.9 in the case of the WTO option). This completely changes the conclusions reached by the CEP team, from predicting a modest to a substantial net cost arising from Brexit.

The magnitude of these predicted effects is deeply suspect. Apart from the fragile chain of causality linking openness with productivity, previously discussed in this chapter, there is simply no *a priori* reason why Brexit will *inevitably* lead to a reduction in openness and the UK becoming a more insular, inward-looking country. Close future relationships with the EU, such as the EEA, will include continued regulatory alignment, which would result in little change in trade flows from the status quo. For other options, such as if the UK traded with the EU through a free trade agreement or according to WTO rules, there might be good reason to anticipate a degree of reduction in openness between the UK and the EU. However, since these Brexit options allow the UK to pursue their own independent preferential trade agreements with other nations, it would be the balance between these two effects—any loss of openness between the UK and the EU set against any increase in openness between the UK and the rest of the world—that would determine the net effect. Since approximately 56% of UK exports are purchased outside of the EU, and the fact that the EU's share of the global marketplace is decreasing over time, there is the expectation that non-EU trade will expand significantly over time. It would therefore be expected that economic studies which included this variable in their models should have accounted for global as well as regional openness. Sadly, most did not. This is most unfortunate because, like focusing only on one half of a balance sheet, it biases their predictions.

There are, moreover, two additional aspects that need to be considered when incorporating the concept of openness into economic analysis and yet which are typically assumed away or ignored. The first is that whilst openness may increase the dynamism of the UK economy, it may simultaneously expose the UK economy to real and financial shocks from abroad. Openness may, therefore, help to reduce economic volatility by allowing economic actors to diversify risks (Bank of England 2015: 3), or it might open the economy to international contagion, thereby increasing the risk of the UK importing economic instability (Bank of England 2015: 11). The second consideration relates to the fact that even were European integration proven to have had a significant and lasting positive impact upon economic growth in the past, there is no evidence to suggest that this relationship will necessarily hold in the future (Badinger 2005: 74). It is entirely possible that any economic effects may have been exhausted and that since the degree of openness for most EU member states is already well in excess of 50% of national GDP, there would seem less scope for achieving a similar boost to growth in the future.

These weaknesses in the suggested causal chain, running from a reduction in trade leading to a fall in the UK's openness and a consequent negative impact upon productivity and/or technological progress, must inevitably lead to a questioning of the reliability of those predictions dependent upon this hypothetical effect. Such supporting evidence as does exist tends to be drawn from studies examining the opening up of trade to emerging economies, which is not directly relevant to the position of the UK (Gudgin et al., 2017: 9).

BALANCE OF PAYMENTS CONSTRAINED GROWTH

The standard economic argument for international economic integration is based upon the notion of comparative advantage, first developed by Ricardo (1817). This holds that trade is unambiguous to the advantage of all trade partners because it allows specialisation which, in turn, facilitates economies of scale and lower costs for consumers (Thirlwall 2011: 7). Thus, the balance of trade does not matter, and hence, the argument that leaving the EU might improve the trade position of the UK is unimportant (Portes 2013: F9).

The problem with this idea is that it depends upon two primary assumptions. The first is that the terms of trade (i.e. or the relative prices of exports and imports) are primarily determined by trade flows, and consequently that the market should be self-correcting, through the appreciation of the currencies of nations with a trade surplus and/or depreciation of currencies for countries with a trade deficit. In reality, however, this is no longer the case as financial speculative flows are substantially larger than trade-related flows in international currency markets (Singh 2000: 16). Without this automatic correcting mechanism, national currencies van under- or over-shoot and trade imbalances can persist into the long run.

The second assumption is the standard neo-classical foundation that supply creates its own demand (Say's Law) and therefore the economy remains constantly at or very close to full employment (Perraton 2014: 2). Accordingly, if trade balances automatically correct through market-determined changes in the exchange rate, and full employment is continuously maintained through supply-determined market forces, then economic growth will be determined by the supply of factors of production (capital and labour) and changes in productivity. Nevertheless, to the extent that these assumptions do not accurately describe the real world, outside of economic textbooks, and markets do not automatically self-correct, then large and persistent trade imbalances will have damaging economic consequences (Keynes 1973).

By contrast, Keynesian theory asserts that it is demand that drives the economy, to which supply adapts. Thus, aggregate demand promotes circular and cumulative causation (Myrdal 1957) as output growth induces further investment, technical progress and innovation, thereby facilitating economies of scale and hence generating enhanced productivity growth (McCombie and Thirwall 1994: 19; Thirwall 1997: 379–380; Perraton 2014: 3–4). One variant of this approach has become known as the constrained growth model, and was developed by Thirwall (1979), itself being an extension of the earlier Harrod super trade multiplier (McCombie and Thirwall 1994; Perraton 2003: 2). In essence, it is argued that the growth rate of a country is fundamentally influenced by the growth of its exports and that demand can influence growth through its influence upon output, capacity, technological adaptation and productivity (Thirwall 2011: 4–5).

This virtuous circle can be disrupted, however, by constraints imposed by persistent trade imbalances. For example, should a country suffer a persistent trade deficit as demand expands but before the short-term capacity constraint is reached, then demand will be curtailed unless the nation offsets this trade gap through either overseas borrowing or attracting an inflow of capital. However, these are likely to be relatively short-term options as the former will create obligations for future interest payments and eventual repayment. If the growth rate of the domestic economy exceeds the rate of interest on this foreign borrowing, then the ratio of debt liabilities to domestic income will not rise and the situation is sustainable for a time. Yet, eventually either growth will fall below this level or debt levels will create nervousness and cause investors to increase the risk premium and thereby raise the interest rate. In either case, if corrective measures not taken, the country would be in a debt trap situation (Arestis and Sawyer 1998: 185; Thirwall 2011: 15). Alternatively, inward investment could be attracted to offset any trade deficit on the balance of payments, but this would require the raising of domestic interest rates in order to attract inward flows of capital to finance the deficit, thereby deflating the economy and lowering economic activity. Thus, in either case, persistent trade deficits are likely to have a constraining effect upon national economic development and may well offset any real income gains arising from trade (Thirwall 2011: 8).

If a nation is unable to continue to finance the trade deficit, then demand will be curtailed, causing capacity to remain idle, investment to be postponed or cancelled, technological progress decelerated and product development slowed, thereby leading to less desirable exports for global consumers and further exacerbating trade difficulties. By contrast, a nation with a balance of payments surplus will be able to expand demand up to short-term capacity and, indeed, a virtuous circle might be formed as the pressure of demand causes greater future investment, technological and product development, thereby increasing potential future capacity and the desirability of export products (Thirwall 1979: 429–31).

This theory links aggregate demand and the characteristics of goods produced and through this to the responsiveness of demand (elasticity) for UK exports and imports. 'Thirwall's Law' therefore suggests that long-run national growth rates are determined by the ratio of the responsiveness of the growth of UK exports given an increase in global living standards (income elasticity of demand) relative to the equivalent income elasticity of demand for imports multiplied by world income growth (Arestis and Sawyer 1998). If UK exports are less attractive than the global average and have a low-income elasticity, then the UK will be constrained to grow more slowly than the global average. If, alternatively, income elasticity is higher than the global norm, then growth can exceed the global growth rate (Thirwall 1979: 437–8). Creating favourable conditions for favourable product development through demand management is a necessary but not sufficient part of this process. However, an active industrial policy could make a further contribution (see Chap. 8 for further discussion).

The fact that deficit nations bear the brunt of any economic difficulties caused by trade imbalances does not, however, imply that other nations, whether in balance or running a surplus, will not also experience slower growth. If deficit nations grow more slowly because of their trade imbalances, they will be unable to purchase as many exports from the surplus nations, thereby unnecessarily limiting their growth rates. This global growth constraint is worsened if surplus nations seek to maintain their positive trade balances in the face of deficit nations seeking to restore their own trade balance, since this will cause yet further stagnation, as nations engage in competitive deflation. Keynes noted this unintended economic consequence when considering the design of an appropriate economic architecture for the period following the ending of the Second World War. His proposals for an International Clearing Union were sadly rejected in favour of the Bretton Woods system. Nevertheless, the principle of seeking to secure symmetrical trade adjustment remains an important insight (Thirwall 2011: 36–7; Whyman 2015).

UK Balance of Trade and Brexit

The insight provided by the constrained growth theory indicates how the UK's present very large trade deficit with the EU (see Table 7.1), and conversely trade surplus with North American Free Trade Agreement (NAFTA), Australasia and Commonwealth countries, can have a significant impact upon the growth potential of the economy. As noted in Chap. 3, this trade deficit has been an almost permanent feature for the UK over the 47 years of EU membership and has worsened considerably since the formation of the SIM. As evidenced in Chap. 4, the UK has deferred dramatic economic adjustment to reduce this deficit through its attraction of high levels of inward investment during the last two decades. However, this has meant that large sections of formerly UK-owned industrial and service sectors have been sold to foreign owners, with the result that future production and location decisions taken by these firms might be less

Table 7.1   UK current account balance with trade blocs and selected countries, 2014–2018, in £m

	2014	2015	2016	2017	2018
Total EU28	-107,062	-112,292	-104,875	-96,014	-108,043
Total EFTA	-10,942	-4194	-5493	-8852	-11,997
NAFTA	**32,315**	**26,939**	**24,256**	**34,874**	**41,958**
Commonwealth[a]	**4837**	**4644**	**4889**	**5639**	**6890**
Total Asia	-7049	-8049	-18,194	-11,163	-13,628
China	-16,284	-18,990	-21,503	-20,489	-20,351
Russia	**558**	**881**	**309**	**2**	-2032
Total Americas	**38,537**	**31,623**	**23,404**	**37,368**	**44,430**
Total Africa	-1737	-1866	**505**	**382**	-2894
Total Australasia and Oceania	**7853**	**7746**	**7762**	**10,384**	**11,099**
World total	*-87,925*	*-94,036*	*-103,992*	*-72,306*	*-92,457*

Note: Numbers in bold are showing a current account surplus.

[a]The Commonwealth includes here the following countries: India, Canada, South Africa and Australia. Together these four countries represent the countries producing half of the Commonwealth GDP; they also produce together nearly three quarters of the total GDP of the Commonwealth area when the UK is excluded.

Source: ONS (2019)

influenced by national considerations. Moreover, it is questionable how much longer the UK's trade deficits can be offset in this way, particularly if FDI flows are temporarily reduced as a result of the uncertainty caused by Brexit, whilst future overseas borrowing may prove problematic for a government already struggling to reduce its debt incurred as a result of the 2008 financial crisis. Consequently, it is likely that the post-Brexit economic strategy will need to include a series of measures designed to reduce the current negative trade imbalance, lest it constrain the UK's future growth potential.

Interestingly, whilst Brexit may prove to be the catalyst for government having to address this fundamental economic imbalance, it may also facilitate its solution. For example, a more competitive exchange rate has the potential to have a positive impact upon UK economic growth rates through promoting exports. Simultaneously, an active industrial strategy can facilitate the expansion of those sections of the UK economy with the greatest growth potential, whilst encouraging the development of new product ranges, some of whom may indeed increase the income elasticity of UK exports in the future. The combination of these measures should reduce growth constraints upon the UK economy significantly.

CONCLUSION

The evidence, as it currently stands, is not sufficiently robust to allow a definitive conclusion as to the likely impact of openness upon productivity and economic growth. Nevertheless, there is sufficient information for policy makers to consider when framing policy. For example, whilst competition is often viewed as always and in all cases having beneficial effects, the evidence reviewed in this chapter would suggest that this should be qualified by the ability of domestic (UK) firms to be in a position to respond positively to increased opportunities arising from increased openness. If domestic firms are disproportionately damaged by intensified competition, they may not be in a position to respond in the way the textbooks imagine, by investing in future capacity and new technology. Thus, to ensure that openness produces a positive result for the UK economy, policy makers may need to consider combining openness with an active industrial strategy to ensure that UK firms are in the best position to take advantage of any new opportunities as they arise.

The constrained growth model, furthermore, highlights the importance of the composition of trade between imports and exports, not simply its total volume, in terms of its impact upon aggregate demand and thereby upon investment, R&D, innovation and technological advance. The principle of cumulative causation implies that once a competitive advantage had been established and favourable macroeconomic conditions maintained, this should lead to a dynamic cycle whereby success begets success. However, the opposite is also true. In a situation whereby the UK has run up a massive trade deficit, unless policy intervention can successfully change the parameters sufficiently, cumulative causation will reinforce this economic weakness and this may potentially overwhelm any positive economic benefits arising from favourable trade integration. This, for UK policy makers, is of paramount interest when determining what economic policy framework should be introduced to support the UK economy through the Brexit transition and into the future as an independent nation. That consideration is the focus of the next chapter.

REFERENCES

Aghion, P., Bloom, N., Blundell, R., Griffith, R., & Howitt, P. (2005). Competition and Innovation: An Inverted U Relationship. *Quarterly Journal of Economics, 120*(2), 701–728.

Aghion, P., Blundell, R., Griffith, R., Howitt, P., & Prantl, S. (2009). The Effects of Entry on Incumbent Innovation and Productivity. *Review of Economics and Statistics, 91*(1), 20–32.

Aghion, P., & Howitt, P. (1992). A Model of Growth Through Creative Destruction. *Econometrica, 60*, 323–351.

Alfaro, L., & Chen, M. (2018). Selection and Market Relocation: Productivity Gains from Multinational Production. *Economic Policy, 10*(2), 1–38.

Arestis, P., & Sawyer, M. (1998). Keynesian Economic Policies for the New Millennium. *Economic Journal, 108*(446), 181–195.

Badinger, H. (2005). Growth Effects of Economic Integration: Evidence from the EU Member States. *Review of World Economics/ Weltwirtschaftliches Archiv, 141*(1), 50–78.

Badinger, H., & Breuss, F. (2011). The Quantitative Effects of European Postwar Economic Integration. In M. Jovanovic (Ed.), *International Handbook on the Economics of Integration* (pp. 285–315). Cheltenham: Edward Elgar.

Baily, M., & Gersbach, H. (1995). Efficiency in Manufacturing and the Need for Global Competition. *Brookings Papers on Economic Activity: Microeconomics*, 307–358.

Baldwin, R. E. (1989). *On the Growth Effects of 1992* (NBER Working Paper No. 3119). Cambridge, MA: NBER. Available via: http://www.nber.org/papers/w3119.pdf.

Baldwin, R. E., & Seghezza, E. (1996). *Testing for Trade-induced Investment-led Growth* (NBER Working Paper No. 5416). Available via: http://www.nber.org/papers/w5416.

Bank of England. (2015). *EU Membership and the Bank of England.* London: Bank of England. Available via: http://www.bankofengland.co.uk/publications/Documents/speeches/2015/euboe211015.pdf.

Bank of England. (2018). *EU Withdrawal Scenarios and Monetary and Financial Stability: A Response to the House of Commons Select Committee.* London: Bank of England. Available via: https://www.bankofengland.co.uk/-/media/boe/files/report/2018/eu-withdrawal-scenarios-and-monetary-and-financial-stability.pdf?la=en&hash=B5F6EDCDF90DCC10286FC0BC599D94CAB8735DFB. Accessed on 18 February 2020.

Barro, R. (1991). Economic Growth in a Cross-section of Countries. *Quarterly Journal of Economics, 106*(2), 407–443.

Bayoumi, T., & Eichengreen, B. (1997). Is Regionalism Simply a Diversion? Evidence from the Evolution of the EC and EFTA. In T. Ito & A. O. Krueger (Eds.), *Regionalism vs. Multilateral Arrangements.* Chicago: University of Chicago Press.

BertelsmannStifung. (2015). *Brexit—Potential Economic Consequences If the UK Exits the EU*, Future Social Market Policy Brief 2015/05, Gütersloh. Available via: https://www.bertelsmann-stiftung.de/fileadmin/files/BSt/Publikationen/GrauePublikationen/Policy-Brief-Brexit-en_NW_05_2015.pdf.

Bloom, N., Draca, M., & van Reenen, J. (2011). *Trade Induced Technical Change? The Impact of Chinese Imports on Innovation, IT and Productivity* (NBER Working Paper No. 16717). Available via: http://www.nber.org/papers/w16717.pdf.

Bloom, N., Sadun, R., & Van Reenen, J. (2012). Americans Do I.T. Better: US Multinationals and the Productivity Miracle. *American Economic Review, 102*(1), 167–201.

Bloom, N., & van Reenen, J. (2010). Why Do Management Practices Differ Across Firms and Countries (*Centre for Economic Performance Occasional paper No. 26*). Available via: http://cep.lse.ac.uk/pubs/download/occasional/op026.pdf.

Boltho, A., & Eichengreen, B. (2008). *The Economic Impact of European Integration* (CEPR Discussion Paper No. 6820). Available via: http://eml.berkeley.edu/~eichengr/econ_impact_euro_integ.pdf.

bulletins/ukgrossdomesticexpenditureonresearchanddevelopment/2014.

Campos, N. F., Coricelli, F., & Moretti, L. (2014). *Economic Growth from Political Integration: Estimating the Benefits from Membership in the European Union Using the Synthetic Counterfactuals Method* (IZA Discussion Paper Series 8162). Bonn. Available via: http://anon-ftp.iza.org/dp8162.pdf.

CEP [Centre for Economic Performance]. (2018). *The Economic Consequences of the Brexit Deal*, UK in a Changing Europe, London. Retrieved December 17, 2019, from http://ukandeu.ac.uk/wp-content/uploads/2018/11/The-economic-consequences-of-Brexit.pdf.

Cincera, M., & Galgau, O. (2005). *Impact of Market Entry and Exit on EU Productivity and Growth Performance* (European Economy—Economic Papers No. 222). Brussels: European Commission. Available via: http://ec.europa.eu/economy_finance/publications/publication712_en.pdf.

Competition and Markets Authority (CMA). (2015). *Productivity and Competition: A Summary of the Evidence*. London: CMA. Available via: https://www.gov.uk/government/uploads/system/uploads/attachment_data/file/443448/Productivity_and_competition_report.pdf.

Confederation of British Industry (CBI). (1989). *European Monetary Union: A Business Perspective*. London: CBI.

Confederation of British Industry (CBI). (2013). *Our Global Future: The Business Vision for a Reformed EU*, CBI, London. Available via: http://www.cbi.org.uk/media/2451423/our_global_future.pdf#page=1&zoom=a.

Congdon, T. (2013). How Should Britain Engage with Other Countries? Liberal Internationalism vs Regional Power Blocs. In A. Hug (Ed.), *Renegotiation, Reform and Referendum: Does Britain Have an EU Future?* Foreign Policy Centre, (pp. 42–46). London. Available via: http://fpc.org.uk/fsblob/1616.pdf.

266 P. B. WHYMAN AND A. I. PETRESCU

Coyle, D. (2019). 'Dual Disruptions: Brexit and Technology', in Kelly, G. and Pearce, N. (Eds.), Britain Beyond Brexit. *Political Quarterly*, *90*(S2), 62–71.

Crafts, N. (2018). Industrial Policy in the Context of Brexit. *Fiscal Studies*, *39*(4), 685–706.

Cuaresma, J. C., Silgoner, M. A., & Ritzberger-Gruenwald, D. (2008). Growth, convergence and EU membership. *Applied Economics*, *40*(05), 643–656. Available online via: https://hal.archives-ouvertes.fr/hal-00581990/document. Last Accessed: 28 October 2020.

Dhingra, S., Huang, H., Ottaviano, G., Pessoa, J. P., Sampson, T., & Van Reenan, J. (2017). Trade After Brexit. *Economic Policy*, *32*(92), 651–705.

Disney, R., Haskel, J., & Heden, Y. (2003). Restructuring and Productivity Growth in UK Manufacturing. *Economic Journal*, *113*(489), 666–694.

Domar, E. (1946). Capital Expansion, Rate of Growth, and Employment. *Econometrica*, *14*(2), 137–147.

Edwards, S. (1998). Openness, Productivity and Growth: What Do We Really Know? *Economic Journal*, *108*(447), 383–398.

Eglene, O. (2010). *Banking on Sterling: Britain's Independence from the Euro Zone*. Lanham, Maryland: Lexington Books.

Eichengreen, B. (2007). *The European Economy Since 1945: Coordinated Capitalism and Beyond*. Princeton, NJ: Princeton University Press.

Eichengreen, B., & Boltho, A. (2008). *The Economic Impact of European Integration* (CEPR Discussion Paper No. 6820). London: CEPR. Available via: http://eml.berkeley.edu/~eichengr/econ_impact_euro_integ.pdf.

Englander, S., & Gurney, A. (1994). Medium Term Determinants of OECD Productivity. *OECD Economic Studies*, *22*, 49–109.

European Commission (EC). (1996). Economic Evaluation of the Internal Market (European Economy Reports and Studies, No. 4). Luxembourg: Office for Official Publications of the European Communities. Available via: http://ec.europa.eu/archives/economy_finance/publications/archives/pdf/publication7875_en.pdf.

Feenstra, R. C. (1990). *Trade and Uneven Growth*, (NBER Working Paper No. 3276). Available via: http://www.nber.org/papers/w3276.pdf.

Felbermayr, G., & Gröschl, J. (2013). Natural Disasters and the Effect of Trade on Income: A New Panel IV Approach. *European Economic Review*, *58*(C), 18–30.

Feyrer, J. (2009a). *Trade and Income-exploiting Time Series in Geography, Technical Report* (NBER Working Paper No. 14910). Available via: http://www.nber.org/papers/w14910.

Feyrer, J. (2009b), Distance, Trade and Income: The 1967 to 1975 Closing of the Suez Canal as a Natural Experiment, *NBER Working Papers* 15557, Natural Bureau of Economic Research, Cambridge, Mass. Retrieved December 21, 2019, from https://www.nber.org/papers/w15557.pdf.

Frankel, J. A., & Romer, D. (1999). Does Trade Cause Growth? *American Economic Review*, *89*(3), 379–399.

Griffith, R., & Harrison, R. (2004). *The Link Between Product Market Reform and Macroeconomic Performance* (European Economy—Economic Papers No. 209). Brussels: European Commission. Available via: http://ec.europa.eu/economy_finance/publications/publication652_en.pdf.

Griffith, R., Harrison, R., & Simpson, H. (2010). Product Market Reform and Innovation in the EU. *Scandinavian Journal of Economics, 112*(2), 389–415.

Grossman, G. M., & Helpman, E. (1994). Endogenous Innovation in the Theory of Growth. *Journal of Economic Perspectives, 8*(1), 23–44. Available via: https://www.researchgate.net/profile/Elhanan_Helpman/publication/4722290_Endogenous_Innovation_in_the_Theory_of_Growth/links/56adf60e08ae19a38515eda3.pdf.

Gudgin, G., Coutts, K., Gibson, N., & Buchanan, J. (2017). *Defying Gravity: A Critique of Estimates of the Economic Impact of Brexit*. London: Policy Exchange. Available via: https://policyexchange.org.uk/wp-content/uploads/2017/06/Defying-Gravity-A-critique-of-estimates-of-the-economic-impact-of-Brexit.pdf. Accessed 10 March 2020.

Hantzsche, A., Kara, A., & Young, G. (2018). *The Economic Effects of the Government's Proposed Brexit Deal*. London: NIESR. Available via: https://www.niesr.ac.uk/sites/default/files/publications/NIESR%20Report%20Brexit%20-%202018-11-26.pdf. Accessed 17 February 2020.

Harrod, R. F. (1939). An Essay in Dynamic Theory. *The Economic Journal, 49*(193), 14–33.

Henrekson, M., Torstensson, J., & Torstensson, R. (1997). Growth Effects of European Integration. *European Economic Review, 41*, 1537–1557.

HMG [Her Majesty's Government]. (2018). *EU Exit: Long Term Economic Analysis*, Cm 9742, HMSO, London. Retrieved December 11, 2019, from https://assets.publishing.service.gov.uk/government/uploads/system/uploads/attachment_data/file/760484/28_November_EU_Exit_-_Long-term_economic_analysis__1_.pdf.

Hummels, D. (2007). Transportation Costs and International Trade in the Second Era of Globalization. *Journal of Economic Perspectives, 21*(3), 131–154.

Irwin, D. A., & Terviö, M. (2002). Does Trade Raise Income? Evidence from the Twentieth Century. *Journal of International Economics, 58*(1), 1–18.

Keynes, J. M. (1973). The General Theory and After Part 1—Preparation. In D. Moggridge (Ed.), *The Collected Writings of John Maynard Keynes*. London: Macmillan.

Landau, D. (1995). The Contribution of the European Common Market to the Growth of Its Member Countries: An Empirical Test. *Review of World Economics, 131*, 774–782.

McCombie, J., & Thirwall, A. P. (1994). *Economic Growth and the Balance of Payment Constraint*. London: Macmillan.

Melitz, M. J., & Ottoviano, G. (2008). Market Size, Trade, and Productivity. *Review of Economic Studies, 75*, 295–316.

Melitz, M. J., & Redding, S. J. (2012). 'Heterogeneous Firms and Trade'. *NBER Working Paper 18652*. Available via: http://www.princeton.edu/~reddings/papers/NBERw18652.pdf.

Melitz, M. J., & Trefler, D. (2012). Gains from Trade When Firms Matter. *Journal of Economic Perspectives, 26*(2), 91–118.

Myrdal, G. (1957). *Economic Theory and Underdeveloped Regions*. London: Gerald Duckworth & Co..

Nickell, S. J. (1996). Competition and Corporate Performance. *Journal of Political Economy, 104*(4), 724–746.

ONS [Office for National Statistics]. (2019). *Pink Book—Geographical Breakdown of the Current Account*, The Stationery Office, London, UK. Available via: https://www.ons.gov.uk/economy/nationalaccounts/balanceofpayments/bulletins/unitedkingdombalanceofpaymentsthepinkbook/2019.

ONS [Office for National Statistics]. (2020). *Gross Domestic Product Year on Year Growth*, Chain Volume Measure Release date: 11 February 2020. Available online via: https://www.ons.gov.uk/economy/grossdomesticproductgdp/timeseries/ihyp/pn2.

Perraton, J. (2003). Balance of Payments Constrained Growth and Developing Countries: An Examination of Thirwall's Hypothesis. *International Review of Applied Economics, 17*(1), 1–22.

Perraton, J. (2014). Economic Growth in Open Economies: Balance of Payments Constrained Growth—And Beyond? (*University of Sheffield Department of Economics Working Paper*, No. JP300514). Available via: https://www.post-keynesian.net/downloads/soas14/JP300514.pdf.

Pilat, D. (1996). Competition, Productivity and Efficiency. *OECD Economic Studies, 27*, 106–146. Available via: http://www.oecd.org/eco/reform/17985473.pdf.

Portes, J. (2013). Commentary: The Economic Implications for the UK of Leaving the European Union. *National Institute Economic Review, 266*, F4–9. Available via: http://www.niesr.ac.uk/sites/default/files/commentary.pdf.

Ricardo, D. (1817). *The Principles of Political Economy and Taxation*. New York: Dover Publications.

Rivera-Batiz, L. A., & Romer, P. M. (1991). Economic Integration and Endogenous Growth. *The Quarterly Journal of Economics, 106*(2), 531–556.

Rodriguez, F., & Rodrik, D. (2000). Trade Policy and Economic Growth: A Sceptic's Guide to the Cross-national Evidence. *NBER Macroeconomics Annual, 15*, 261–325.

Rodrik, D., Subramanian, A., & Trebbi, F. (2004). Institutions Rule: The Primacy of Institutions Over Geography and Integration in Economic Development. *Journal of Economic Growth, 9*(2), 131–165.

Romer, P. (1986). Increasing Returns and Long Run Growth. *Journal of Political Economy, 94*(5), 1002–1037.

Romer, P. M. (1990). Endogenous Technological Change. *Journal of Political Economy, 98*, S71–S102.

Sapir, A. (2011). European Integration at the Crossroads: A Review Essay on the 50th Anniversary of Bela Balassa's Theory of Economic Integration. *Journal of Economic Literature, 49*(4), 1200–1229.

Singh, K. (2000). *Taming Global Financial Flows: Challenges and Alternatives in the Era of Financial Globalisation.* London: Zed Books.

Smith, A. (1776). *An Enquiry into the Nature and Causes of the Wealth of Nations.* Oxford: Oxford University Press, 2008 edition.

Solow, R. M. (1956). A Contribution to the Theory of Economic Growth. *Quarterly Journal of Economics, 70*(1), 65–94.

Tang, J., & Wang, W. (2005). Product Market Competition, Skill Shortages and Productivity: Evidence from Canadian Manufacturing Firms. *Journal of Productivity Analysis, 23*(3), 317–339.

Thirwall, A. P. (1979). The Balance of Payments Constraint as an Explanation of International Growth Rate Differences. *Banca Nazionale del Lavoro Quarterly Review, 32*(128), 45–53. Available via: http://ojs.uniroma1.it/index.php/PSLQuarterlyReview/article/viewFile/9407/9302.

Thirwall, A. P. (1997). Reflections on the Concept of Balance of Payments Constrained Growth. *Journal of Post Keynesian Economics, 19*(3), 377–385.

Thirwall, A. P. (2011). *Balance of Payments Constrained Growth Models: History and Overview* (University of Kent School of Economics Discussion Papers, No. KDPE-1111). Available via: https://www.kent.ac.uk/economics/documents/research/papers/2011/1111.pdf.

Vanhoudt, P. (1999). Did the European Unification Induce Economic Growth? In Search of Scale Effects and Persistent Changes. *Weltwirtschaftliches Archiv/Review of World Economics, 135*(2), 193–220.

Wacziarg, R. (1998). Measuring the Dynamic Gains from Trade. *World Bank Economic Review, 15*(3), 393–429.

Weldon, D. (2019). 'The British Model and the Brexit Shock: Plus ça Change?', in Kelly, G. and Pearce, N. (Eds.), Britain Beyond Brexit. *Political Quarterly, 90*(S2), 12–20.

Whyman, P. B. (2015). Keynes and the International Clearing Union: A Possible Model for Eurozone Reform. *Journal of Common Market Studies, 53*(2), 399–415.

World Bank. (2020). *Trade as Percent of GDP. World Development Indicators.* Available via: https://data.worldbank.org/indicator/NE.TRD.GNFS.ZS.

Wren-Lewis, S. (2019). 'Macroeconomic Policy Beyond Brexit', in Kelly, G. and Pearce, N. (Eds.), Britain Beyond Brexit. *Political Quarterly, 90*(S2), 44–52.

Zarotiadis, G., & Gkagka, A. (2013). European Union: A Diverging Union? *Journal of Post Keynesian Economics, 35*(4), 537–565.

CHAPTER 8

Economic Policy After Brexit

One remarkable feature of almost all economic studies which have sought to forecast the impact of Brexit is that they have consistently ignored the role of macroeconomic policy in affecting the outcome. Presumably, this was to simplify the analysis. Yet, this omission is unrealistic for two reasons.

Firstly, one of the main claims for Brexit improving economic performance is that UK policy makers have greater flexibility to implement initiatives designed to meet the particular circumstances and challenges facing the domestic economy. Previous chapters in this book have examined inward investment, trade policy, labour force planning and issues related to productivity. However, greater flexibility in designing macroeconomic strategy, combined with industrial and procurement policy, have arguably an even greater *potential*; the realisation of which depends crucially upon the type of Brexit chosen to replace EU membership, together with whether the government of the day has the insight and determination to design policy to realise potential gains. Consequently, economic studies should have placed greater weight upon the impact of economic policy measures not less.

Secondly, even assuming the predictions made by the mainstream economic studies were correct and that certain aspects of Brexit would inflict net costs upon the UK economy, it is unrealistic to expect policy makers not to react to minimise this effect. Indeed, almost immediately after the referendum result was announced, the Bank of England presented a significant stimulus package, whilst the then Chancellor of the Exchequer,

© The Author(s) 2020
P. B. Whyman, A. I. Petrescu, *The Economics of Brexit*,
https://doi.org/10.1007/978-3-030-55948-9_8

Hammond, announced a partial relaxing of the former tight fiscal stance, thus restoring a measure of confidence and preventing unnecessary economic damage. It is only a pity that this immediate reaction was not carried through into the immediate reversal of austerity measures, combined with a more decisive leadership from parliament to reduce uncertainty during 2017–2019.

The omission of consideration of economic policy variables might be justifiable if study authors made it explicit that they were only concerned with examining the narrow context of what would be likely to occur if policy makers were entirely passive—that is, *what might happen if no other actions were taken*. However, this would have been the limit of these studies. To subsequently present their results as forecasts or predictions as to the likely prospects of the UK economy is deeply problematic. This matters because policy makers and business leaders have relied upon the accuracy of these studies to set their respective future strategies. Failure to properly consider policy actions in these studies sadly undermined their accuracy and hence weakened their utility.

This chapter seeks to rectify this apparent reluctance to include economic policy in consideration of the economic impact of Brexit.

MACROECONOMIC POLICY

Uncertainty

One of the anticipated negative consequences resulting from the Brexit result concerned the uncertainty generated for all economic actors (HMG 2016: 21; Bank of England 2019: 38). To some extent, this was always likely to occur irrespective of the referendum result, as each and every general election results in uncertainty as to the likely result and the subsequent consequences for either continuation or a shift in economic strategy (Credit Suisse, 2016: 6; Punhani and Hill 2016: 5). Yet, the uncertainty relating to Brexit is of a different magnitude since it involves the evolution and partial replacement of a fundamental economic relationship that had formed a key part of the UK economy for more than four decades. Indeed, the Bank of England has argued that Brexit uncertainty has "only exceeded in the financial crisis" (BOE 2019: 48).

The economics literature indicates that there is likely to be a negative impact upon business investment arising from increased uncertainty (Dixit and Pindyck, 1990; Leahy and Whited 1996; Punhani and Hill 2016: 3,

7). Investment may be delayed or deferred (Bloom 2009; Bloom et al. 2014), particularly where firms have large existing fixed investment (sunk costs) (Pindyck 1988; Bank of England 2019: 39). Once uncertainty is resolved, however, there is an expectation that firms will respond to conditions of pent-up demand by unfreezing investment in new capacity and technology (Baker et al. 2016b: 1597). To the extent that investment was merely delayed, rather than cancelled or undertaken in a different jurisdiction, negative effects caused by uncertainty may be limited. Moreover, to the extent that advocates of Brexit are successful in demonstrating potential gains arising from the Brexit process—perhaps through interest expressed by non-EU nations in negotiating future trade agreements with the UK or through utilising the greater policy flexibility post-withdrawal to rejuvenate UK manufacturing industry—this might, to some extent at least, offset other negative expectations (PwC 2016: 6). However, there is no certainty that all deferred investment will, in fact, take place, and moreover, the longer the growth potential in the economy stalls, the more likely that it will have longer-term negative effects (Wren-Lewis 2019: 45). Consequently, there is an incentive for policy makers to resolve uncertainty as swiftly as possible. Keynesian demand management policies could also be helpful in this regard, by creating conditions more conducive for encouraging the realisation of investment decisions in order to take advantage of favourable levels of demand for products and services.

Uncertainty can also affect financial markets, through impacting upon the value of stocks and currencies, or via higher risk premia being charged in credit and equity markets (PwC 2016: 6, 8). In the immediate aftermath of the referendum result, UK stock market valuation fell sharply, although this immediate paper loss was recovered within a few weeks. The value of sterling did, as expected, decline significantly against the Euro (Ebell and Warren 2016; Fairbairn and Newton-Smith 2016: 16; OECD 2016: 12). The extent of this change depends upon the dates selected over which the comparison is made. Thus, if a date of January 2015 is selected as representing a pre-referendum comparator, sterling was trading at €1.28. Since the current value of sterling, in January 2020, is approximately €1.18, this represents a 7.8% fall in the value of the pound over this period. If, however, the value of sterling is taken on the morning of the European referendum itself, when speculation over the result had temporarily increased the value of sterling to €1.31, then the scale of the depreciation has been approximately 10%.[1] Interestingly, the immediate effect of the referendum result was to cause only a 6% depreciation in sterling, whereas the handling of the post-referendum process caused sterling to fall by an additional 12%,[2] before gradually recovering. This would suggest that the decision to withdraw from the EU was only one element of the uncertainty causing depreciation of the exchange rate, with the government's handling of the Brexit process and negotiation with the EU, together with the lack of a parliamentary majority, having a larger effect.

Exchange rate depreciation can have inflationary effects, and indeed, the rate of UK inflation did rise from 0.8% in June 2016 to a peak of 2.8% in October 2018, thereby exceeding the Bank of England's 2% target for most of 2017–2018.[3] However, this is not as significant as it might appear (Baker et al. 2016a: 115). A peak rate of 2.8% is low by historical standards and the starting point of 0.8% inflation had raised concerns that it presaged a period of economic slowdown or recession. In addition, exchange rate volatility can have a detrimental effect upon the cost of trade and trade volumes, yet this only really manifests if volatility persists for a significant period of time, given that companies typically hedge against the effects of currency variability in the short term (Pilbeam 2016). In general, the economics literature is fairly dismissive of the idea that exchange rate volatility has more than a negligible impact upon growth over the medium or longer term (Eichengreen and Boltho 2008: 27). This appears to be confirmed by the evidence relating to the trade effects of the depreciation of sterling following the referendum as the trade gap narrowed. Moreover, the decline in the value of sterling was always expected to have a positive boost to exports and reduce the trade deficit, thereby offsetting (in full or in part) other negative consequences that may arise from Brexit (Armstrong and Portes 2016: 5).

One final Brexit-related effect concerns the ability of the UK government to borrow as cheaply on international markets, as international investors might be less likely to wish to hold gilts, combined with ratings agencies downgrading the value of UK government securities (Baker et al. 2016a: 111). This problem is not as acute for the UK as for many national governments since its gilt market is disproportionately domestic, with international investors only holding around one quarter of the total issue.

---

[1] https://www.finder.com/uk/brexit-pound
[2] 24 June 2016, £1 = €1.23 and 23 August 2017, £1 = €1.08.
[3] https://www.ons.gov.uk/economy/inflationandpriceindices/timeseries/l55o/mm23

Moreover, most government bonds are of longer than average duration, meaning that any short-term problems would take a number of years before their impact became problematic. Hence, little effect has been observed thus far. If, however, Brexit-related uncertainty was to persist into the medium term, the cost of debt financing, for businesses and governments alike, might rise (Baker et al. 2016a: 114).

A number of the economics studies, discussed in Chap. 1, sought to incorporate a variable related to uncertainty in their calculations. The problem is that uncertainty is, by definition, difficult to define and measure. Accordingly, these studies modelled uncertainty as equivalent to risk, which can be calculated based upon probabilities drawn from a well-established dataset. Assumptions were made that Brexit will reduce trade with the EU and lower business export earnings, which would in turn likely raise the cost of capital and temporarily increase the risk premium paid for borrowing to fund investment (Baker et al. 2016a: 109; PwC 2016: 6,22). It is this higher risk premia that is then utilised as a proxy for uncertainty, to produce estimates that UK gross domestic product (GDP) will grow more slowly over the medium term as a result of Brexit, albeit that these negative effects would cease to have an effect thereafter.

The problem with adopting this approach is that there is a key difference between uncertainty and risk. Uncertainty embodies both 'risk', where uncertainty of outcomes can be represented by a known probability distribution, and more general 'uncertainty', when the probability distribution itself is unknown. Former US defence secretary, Rumsfeld, sought to express something of this lack of knowledge in his oft-quoted statement:

> There are known knowns; there are things we know we know. We also know there are known unknowns; that is to say we know there are some things we do not know. But there are also unknown unknowns—the ones we don't know we don't know.[4]

The treatment of uncertainty as being equivalent to risk therefore diminishes its significance. Information remains incomplete in an ever-changing economy, and this is particularly the case with respect to Brexit-related uncertainty because this derives from a unique historical occurrence with no direct precedent. This results in market failure and economic

[4] https://www.thetimes.co.uk/article/despite-the-ridicule-donald-rumsfeld-really-did-know-best-t0022pp5c

actors responding to events through adaptive (not rational) expectations. As a result, policy makers have to resort to judgement about the probable results of actions, costs and benefits associated with various possible outcomes resulting from different policy options (Greenspan 2003). This was the essence of the writings of Keynes, in the 1930s, where the active management of the economy was prescribed as a means of creating conditions conducive for investment and employment, and thereby overcoming caution related to uncertainty about the future.

A second reason why uncertainty cannot be diminished by treating it as equivalent to risk relates to inadequacies with the data upon which risk management and the development of probability distributions are based. These are of three main forms. Transitory statistical uncertainty relates to when provisional data is revised as more information becomes available. Permanent statistical uncertainty occurs when data is incomplete or inadequate. Finally, epistemic uncertainty, arising from a lack of knowledge about current and historical data, which is expected to diminish as data is augmented over time.

There have, nevertheless, been a number of interesting attempts to seek to capture a more accurate appreciation of the comparative level of uncertainty pertaining in a given economy at any one moment in time. One of the most promising is the construction of an index of uncertainty drawn from longitudinal newspaper coverage (Baker et al. 2016a). Whilst this methodology has weaknesses, both in terms of labour intensity of data collection, the narrow range of newspapers utilised in the research and the reliance upon the researcher to identify incidents of uncertainty without unintentionally biasing the data, the approach is nevertheless rather useful in providing a means of comparing general levels of uncertainty over time and between different nations. Using this approach, indications are that uncertainty rose sharply in the period preceding, during and immediately following the 2016 European referendum in the UK, but from 2018 onwards, the level of uncertainty did not appear to be particularly marked (see Fig. 8.1). To the extent that this analysis accurately captures the essence of uncertainty, it would suggest that the most marked and therefore problematic expression of Brexit-related uncertainty was of relatively short duration, lasting perhaps 18 months, whilst what has followed has been difficult to distinguish from more general uncertainty experienced in the period preceding and following the 2008 financial crisis and economic slowdown. This interpretation is quite different from the impression garnered from other sources.

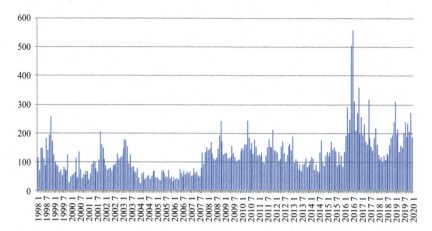

Fig. 8.1 UK economic policy uncertainty, monthly index. Note: Each bar represents a month; however, due to space limitations, horizontal axis labels are only shown every six months. For example, 2019 1 means January 2019, 2019 7 means July 2019. Source: Authors' interpretation of data available to download on the website for UK Economic Policy Uncertainty index, available via: https://www.policyuncertainty.com/uk_monthly.html

A second approach has been to use business surveys to identify an increased frequency of respondents identifying Brexit as a cause of uncertainty (Bank of England 2019: 40). Closer examination of the results suggests that it is difficult to distinguish between a general pessimism over the prospects for the global economy, with those for the UK, and a Brexit-specific element of uncertainty.[5] Moreover, it is not particularly surprising that increasing numbers of respondents mention Brexit as a factor in their investment deliberations as the topic has led most broadcast news bulletins over the past four years. The frequency of mentions, however, does not necessarily equate to action.

Notwithstanding these considerations, the Bank of England (2019: 40–3) appears sufficiently confident that investment and supply capacity have been negatively affected by Brexit-related uncertainty, and has

[5] https://commonslibrary.parliament.uk/economy-business/economy-economy/economic-updates/economic-update-will-less-uncertainty-boost-growth/?utm_source=House+of+Commons+Library+research+alerts&utm_campaign=603e91349f-EMAIL_CAMPAIGN_2020_01_14_08_00&utm_medium=email&utm_term=0_a9da1c9b17-60 3e91349f-102526117&mc_cid=603e91349f&mc_eid=57b30200b0

accordingly internalised these anticipated effects in its own forecast for the future of the UK economy. There is a danger in doing so, in that this creates a self-fulfilling prophesy, as economic actors become more pessimistic precisely because of the Bank's predictions, and their subsequent changes in behaviour are *ex post facto* used by the Bank in the following forecast report as evidence for the accuracy of its previous predictions. This is not simply a matter for the Bank, but also for that range of organisations whose studies were discussed in Chap. 1, where flaws inherent in model design may have inadvertently contributed towards more pessimistic expectations for Brexit than might arguably have been the case.

The difficulties in identifying a Brexit-related element in a more general measurement of uncertainty arise from the latest figures to be published as this book was being finalised. The IHS Markit's Purchasing Managers' Index for services, for example, has risen back to levels previously recorded in early 2018, and which would indicate the economy expanding rather than contracting.[6] Similarly, the Confederation of British Industry (CBI) Industrial Trends Survey recorded business confidence rising in the manufacturing sector.[7] This improvement in business confidence may derive from a reduction in Brexit uncertainty, as the December 2019 General Election result removed the parliamentary deadlock and provided a clearer roadmap for the evolution of the Brexit process during 2020. However, it might equally relate to the preference amongst the business community for the majority won by the Conservative Party in that election. This reduction in uncertainty and improvement in business confidence has not had time to filter through into a noticeable improvement in output and macroeconomic performance. Therefore, these remain only potential early indicators of future developments. Moreover, it is quite possible that any reduction in Brexit uncertainty might be outweighed by future unrelated developments, such as the disruption to production and supply chains caused by the COVID-19 coronavirus or the continuing trade dispute between China and the USA. The complexity of inter-related factors influencing a single forecasting indicator (business confidence) highlights the

---

[6] https://commonslibrary.parliament.uk/economy-business/economy-economy/economic-updates/economic-update-optimism-on-the-up/?utm_source=House+of+Commons+Library+research+alerts&utm_campaign=7079e868bd-EMAIL_CAMPAIGN_2020_02_27_08_00&utm_medium=email&utm_term=0_a9da1c9b17-7079e868bd-102526117&mc_cid=7079e868bd&mc_eid=57b30200b0

[7] https://www.cbi.org.uk/media-centre/articles/early-signs-of-a-turnaround-in-manufacturing-activity-cbi-industrial-trends/

difficulty in isolating the effect of any single contributory factor (i.e. Brexit).

There are two additional points that should be considered in relation to uncertainty. The first is that in acknowledging that change the UK's relationship with the EU will inevitably create risks (CBI 2013: 132) and the time lags involved in implementing these changes will cause uncertainty, this would also have been true when the UK joined the then Common Market in the 1970s and would have been equally true when the CBI and others lobbied for the UK joining the ERM and the Economic and Monetary Union (EMU) in the 1990s. Moreover, risks emanating from Brexit have to be placed against risks that would occur if the UK remained within the EU. For example, it is not certain that the status quo position for the UK would have been tenable in the medium term, even had the UK remained a member of the EU, as Eurozone economies were seeking to strengthen EU economic governance as a means of creating a more supportive infrastructure necessary to sustain the single currency (Armstrong and Portes 2016: 6). In addition, as an EU member state, the UK would have been more affected by further economic contagion arising from the continued fragility of the Eurozone (Business for Britain 2015: 30).

The second point is that Brexit-related uncertainty has not been resolved by the conclusion of the Article 50 process and the UK formally withdrawing from the EU. The transition period is scheduled to end at the end of 2020, at which time, if an agreement has not been reached and enacted, either an extension must be requested and unanimously agreed (not currently the UK government's preference) or trade between the UK and the EU will take place according to World Trade Organization (WTO) rules. Whilst negotiations continue, so will uncertainty (Irwin 2015: 28–9; McFadden and Tarrant 2015: 60).

Has Uncertainty Reduced UK Growth?

This is a difficult question to answer convincingly. What can be noted is that the UK economy generated respectable (but not ebullient) GDP growth rates of 1.8% in 2016 and 2017, in the immediate aftermath of the referendum result, before slowing to 1.4% in 2018 and 1.2% in 2019, and is forecast to remain within the 1.4–1.6% range for the next few years (OBR 2019: 11). The immediate conclusion is that there has not been a substantial deterioration in UK growth performance, following the 2016

referendum result, whilst predictions that the UK would fall into an immediate recession have proven to be inaccurate. Nevertheless, as can be noted
by Fig. 8.2, UK growth performance has been fairly modest by historical
standards.

There are four main factors which might explain this weak
performance.

1. Uncertainty, related to Brexit, has resulted in a proportion of investment being deferred or cancelled, whilst more cautious behaviour
   by consumers might magnify this initial effect.
2. External factors adversely affecting the global economy, such as the
   US–China trade conflict, have been estimated to have reduced
   global GDP in 2020 by around 0.8% (IMF 2019: xiv). This will
   have had a dampening effect upon UK growth performance. In this,
   the UK has not been alone, with Germany being badly affected, due
   to its dependence upon export-driven growth. Indeed, it is worthy
   of note that the UK's slowdown in growth rates, over the past two
   years, has mirrored developments in the Eurozone (IMF 2019: 10).
3. The decade since the 2008 global financial crisis has produced
   amongst the worst growth performance in the last century (Weldon,
   2019: 15–16). Not only did output fail to recover to the pre-crisis

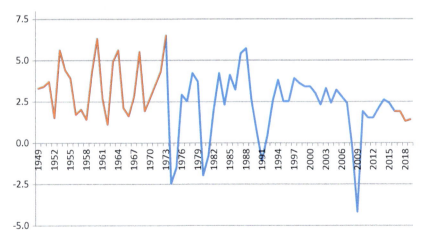

Fig. 8.2 UK gross domestic product, year-on-year growth (%). *Source*:
ONS (2020)

trend, but economic growth rates also declined relative to formerly normal trends (Blanchard et al. 2015: 15; Laeven and Valencia 2018: 23–4). In other words, most advanced economies have not caught up temporarily lost output potential in a post-recession boom, but rather, growth trends have been lowered as a result of the financial crisis. This may be due to credit constraints, frustrating investment recovery or more generally the result of a reluctance to invest, due to adverse economic conditions, resulting in a shortfall of capital stock and thereby slower rates of innovation and adoption of new technology (Chen et al. 2019: 8, 10–11).

4. Domestic austerity policy has constrained UK growth performance over the past decade as depressed aggregate demand caused firms to delay planned investment (Wren-Lewis 2019: 45–6).

Given that the effects of all of these factors produce impacts similar to hypothesised Brexit effects, it is difficult to distinguish between different factors which may all affect economic growth. Moreover, the small number of data points, from which to draw evidence, has led one study, conducted by the Centre for European Reform, to adopt a different methodology to try to answer the question. Their approach has been to establish a 'doppelgänger UK' by means of measuring how the UK performed when compared to a basket of other countries which might arguably be considered to be similar in characteristics to the UK. The countries selected were Germany (32% of the weighting), the USA (28%), Australia (17%), Iceland (9%), Greece (6%), Luxembourg (4%) and New Zealand (4%). Using this approach, Springford (2019: 2) suggests that the "cost of Brexit", due to the uncertainty created, is around 2.9% of GDP.

There are a number of problems with this type of analysis, some of which Springford acknowledges in his report.

Firstly, this is a small data sample, whilst quarterly measures of GDP are volatile and apt to subsequent revision. Thus, small *ex post facto* revisions to the data can have significant effects upon the results.

Secondly, the approach depends heavily upon the validity of the original choice of the pool of countries from which the comparator countries are selected, and this choice is, to some extent, subjective (Bouttellet et al. 2018: 676). Hence, the weightings, calculated by the synthetic control method, are only as accurate as the composition of this original selection of countries. There is a question mark, for example, over the inclusion of smaller OECD in Springford's original pool of countries, from which the sample was selected, since the challenges they face are unlikely to be similar to a larger economy such as the UK. When deconstructing growth performance across the seven country sample, it is noticeable that the three smaller economies—Iceland, Luxembourg and New Zealand—all outperformed the rest of the sample and therefore may have arguably skewed the results.

Thirdly, the time period selected is subjective and may therefore influence the results. In this case, the focus of the analysis is upon divergence following the 2016 referendum. This is barely three years or 12 data points. The small time period is particularly problematic since it is well established that the business cycles between developed nations have different degrees of correlation, with the USA, Japan and Canada tending to have similar business cycle turning points, core EU member states having a slightly different and typically later pattern, whilst the UK is not particularly closely correlated with either group (Artis et al. 1997). As a result, a three-year time period is insufficient to demonstrate whether the observed effect is simply the effect of the UK being out of step with different business cycle timelines.

Fourthly, a study of this type will always suffer from missing variable bias, in that it ascribes the culmination of a multiplicity of different impacts, each result from numerous factors, to one single event, namely the vote for Brexit in the 2016 referendum. Yet, growth is impacted by much more than a Brexit-related uncertainty effect. It will be influenced by global trade patterns, fiscal and monetary policy, and so forth. Yet, in this study, the whole of the variance between UK and the counterfactual scenario is attributed to Brexit. This is, of course, untenable. A simple example makes the point. Using the same weighted group of countries, during the period 2016–2018 inclusive, the 'doppelgänger' counterfactual outperformed not only the UK but also the Eurozone and OECD average. Presumably, the analysis is not suggesting that Brexit had a detrimental effect upon the whole of the OECD or the Eurozone, and therefore, it is difficult to maintain that the variance between UK and 'doppelgänger UK' performance is necessarily solely or even largely due to Brexit-related uncertainty.

Finally, the synthetic control approach only works well if the country of interest (i.e. the UK) is a good fit to the sample as a whole and is not an outlier. It is particularly important that there are no shocks which may contaminate the analysis (Bouttellet et al. 2018: 676). Yet, this is the whole focus for the CEP analysis—that is, testing the impact of the Brexit 'shock' on the UK economy.

Limitations in terms of the short time period following the 2016 referendum and the other factors which are likely to have had significant impact upon growth rates make it difficult to draw firm conclusions regarding the likely impact of Brexit-related uncertainty upon UK economic growth. What seems reasonable to conclude is that following a period of fiscal austerity, when UK growth performance was constrained by low rates of capital formation, and during a period of slowing global growth rates, UK growth rates were underwhelming. It seems probable that uncertainty played a part in this performance; however, the nature of the limited evidence currently available means that ascribing causality to one or more factors is unsafe.

Long-Standing Investment Performance

The 1971 White Paper, which sought to explain or justify the UK's decision to apply for membership of the EU (then the European Economic Community or EEC), raised the possibility that free access for UK exporters to the larger marketplace, comprising all EU member states, would be likely to lead to an increase in investment, production and increased efficiency through the realisation of economies of scale (HMG 1971: 11, 13–14). This is essentially the same point that critics of Brexit have been making in reverse—namely, that leaving the EU would hard investment and productivity through reducing potential scale effects. The effect of uncertainty would, as per the previous discussion, potentially further weaken investment.

Unfortunately, for this narrative, the evidence would seem to indicate that this anticipated acceleration in UK productive investment did not occur. Instead, the UK consistently invests an average of around 2–3% of GDP less than its major competitors (France, Germany and the USA) in fixed capital, and has ranked in the bottom quartile of OECD countries for investment in 48 of the previous 55 years (HMG 2017b: 18). Combined public and private research and development (R&D) expenditure of 1.7% of GDP is similarly insufficient since this is less than the 2.4% OECD average and significantly lower than the economies of Japan, South Korea, Denmark, Finland and Israel, who each allocate in excess of 3% of their GDP to innovation and technological investment (HMG 2017b: 26). Given that the evidence indicates that public investment in R&D tends to encourage ('crowd-in') additional private sector R&D expenditure, there is a clear justification for greater policy intervention to promote greater innovation and technological advances in the UK (see Fig. 8.3). Former Secretary of State for Business, Energy and Industrial Strategy, Greg Clark, made the case for rectifying the poor R&D record, when he noted that without improving this record, the UK "cannot hope to keep, let alone extend, our technological lead in key sectors" (HMG 2017b: 5).

EU membership did not solve this long-standing investment weakness in the UK economy. Indeed, following accession, UK gross capital formation has steadily declined, from around 26% in 1973 to 17.3% in 2015 (see Fig. 8.4).[8] Thus, the UK invests less, as a share of its national income

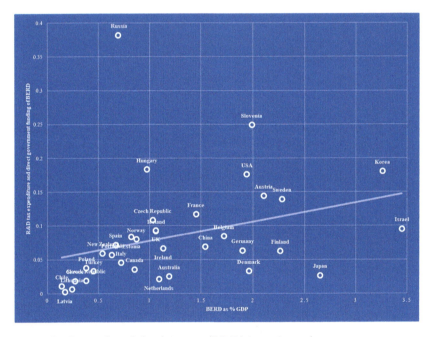

Fig. 8.3 Research and development (R&D) intensity and government support to business R&D (as % GDP), 2013. Source: OECD (2019)

[8] As a technical note, according to the World Bank, this is gross capital formation, not gross fixed capital formation; the difference being that gross capital formation (formerly gross domestic investment) consists of outlays on additions to fixed assets (i.e. land improvements, plant, machinery and other equipment purchases, together with the improvement of physical infrastructure such as roads, railways, buildings, schools and hospitals) and the net change in inventories.

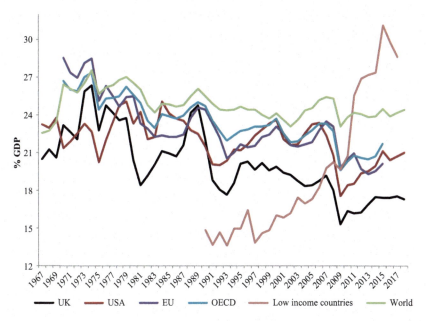

Fig. 8.4 Gross capital formation as % of GDP, selected countries, 1967–2018. Source: World Bank (2020)

today, than it did when it joined the EU four decades previously (Business for Britain 2015: 722–3). Given the evidence presented in the previous chapter, that investment is one of the key determinants of economic growth and productivity, this long-term failure inherent within the UK economy will have significantly limited its growth potential. Moreover, this under-performance is even more manifest when comparing the UK record on investment with other nations. For example, one comparison, based on 2013 figures from the *CIA World Factbook*, ranked the UK only 140 out of 153 countries in terms of its share of GDP devoted to gross fixed investment.[9]

This dismal investment record has occurred despite a sharp increase in inequality levels within the UK. As national income has shifted from wages to capital, orthodox economic theory would have anticipated that productive investment would have risen. Yet, the evidence suggests that lowering

[9] http://www.indexmundi.com/g/r.aspx?v=142

taxes upon entrepreneurs and capital holdings has not worked for the UK, as rising inequality has *depressed*, rather than boosted, economic growth (Chang 2010; OECD 2014).

None of this is to suggest that EU membership *per se* was to blame for this fall in investment, as this had multiple causes. Nevertheless, it does demonstrate that the anticipation of the gains to be made by joining the EU have not materialised in the way that their advocates expected. This conclusion raises questions for those seeking to forecast the likely impact of Brexit and others whose focus is upon aiming to optimise the net benefits from UK withdrawal from the EU. If UK capital formation was inadequate during the period of EU membership, then maximising market access may be one element in encouraging productive investment, but by itself, it is clearly not sufficient. This insight will be discussed in more detail a little later in this chapter.

DESIGNING ECONOMIC POLICY FOR AN INDEPENDENT UK

The long-standing weakness in investment levels and capital formation can be addressed by a more active form of economic policy. This can additionally support the creation of a more favourable economic environment conducive for economic expansion, the rebuilding of parts of the industrial base, support for the creation of new products and new markets, utilisation of procurement and other levers to capture the potential arising from the economics of place, together with management of skills and labour force resources. A balance of macroeconomic and microeconomic policy would produce the best results since thee have the potential to compliment (hence reinforce) one another if designed correctly.

Short Run—Dealing with Uncertainty

The initial challenge, facing an independent UK, is to resolve the uncertainty which has surrounded the Brexit process. The act of withdrawal from the EU will have resolved part of this uncertainty, but negotiations between the UK and the EU will be ongoing throughout the transition period (scheduled to end on 31 December 2020), and uncertainty will remain until a final resolution has been enacted.

There are, however, a number of measures that the UK government could take to mitigate against continuing uncertainty. The first is to explain, in more detail, how their preferred variant of Brexit might work. If the preference is for a simple free trade agreement (FTA) with the EU, economic actors would benefit from understanding how this is likely to affect their businesses and their working lives. Whilst not all features could be outlined until any such agreement has been agreed by all parties, there is still a lot of information that could be disseminated. For example, exporters would benefit from having the maximum amount of time to evolve their systems to address the 'rule of origin' requirements which will form a part of any trade settlement excepting that of a customs union.

A second element is to provide a small stimulus package, of the type introduced by the Bank of England in the immediate aftermath of the 2016 referendum result, to boost aggregate demand and thereby provide more favourable conditions for firms to invest in new plant and technology. The macroeconomic stance of the government is particularly important in creating the parameters within which firms make investment decisions. If the economy can be stimulated to grow at or above trend, firms are more likely to invest as they believe they can sell their products. Indeed, it is the expectations held by business people of future profitability that predominantly determines present investment, whilst realised profits largely finance this new investment (Kalecki 1971; Arestis 1989: 614). Hence, if macroeconomic policy focuses upon promoting growth, it is more likely that investment will be forthcoming as business people will lose out if they fail to invest in new products, processes and technology, in order to take advantage of favourable market conditions. This latter policy stance is particularly important for that proportion of investment which is not financed through borrowing from financial institutions or through equity markets, but rather financed through retained earnings.

This effort could be supplemented by the introduction of a time-limited tax allowance focused upon boosting productive investment. The time limited nature of the scheme would encourage deferred investment plans to be enacted immediately, in order to take advantage of the opportunity, and the resulting boost to the economy would encourage additional output and investment thereafter.

Medium Term—Economic Regeneration

There are three elements to a medium-term redesign of economic policy, namely

i. Macroeconomic management capable of facilitating economic regeneration, promoting economic growth and full employment.
ii. Competitive exchange rate management to offset any increase in trade costs with the EU, whilst facilitating a long-term objective of eliminating the current very large trade deficit and restoring trade balance.
iii. Utilising the UK's independent status to negotiate future trade agreements both with the EU and, perhaps more importantly in the long run, with a range of nations and/or trade blocs in the rest of the world whose rapid growth rates indicate their increasing importance in the marketplaces for UK goods and services in the future.

The rejuvenation and rebalancing of the UK economy will involve an active industrial strategy, but this will, in turn, depend upon government ensuring the maintenance of a sufficiently attractive economy in which economic activity is encouraged to take place. Unfortunately, this is where there is a weakness in much of the analysis that has been undertaken by supporters of Brexit because they tend to base their recommendations upon neo-classical foundations, thereby assuming that the economy will automatically tend towards the full employment of all resources, together with an optimistic reading of the efficient market hypothesis developed at the University of Chicago. On this basis, microeconomic interventions (such as deregulation) or fiscal incentives (such as cutting business taxation) are viewed as providing a sufficient set of incentives to economic actors to reinforce market solutions capable of achieving these goals. This is despite the fact that this approach has been tried repeatedly, over the past few decades, and it has not worked.

The alternative is to acknowledge that businesses produce and invest because they think they can sell their goods or services, rather than because labour or capital have become a little less expensive. Consequently, it is *demand* that drives the economy, not supply. It is the responsibility of government to management the level of aggregate demand in the economy, to ensure that there is a sufficient level to facilitate the full employment of resources, to encourage business investment and to ensure a decent level of economic growth. Aggregate demand impacts directly upon the real economy because it influences, and in turn is influenced by, the rate of investment, which changes the stock of capital and thereby affects productive capacity and employment (Rowthorn 1995, 1999; Alexiou and Pitelis 2003: 628). Moreover, a larger capital stock will permit a higher level of aggregate demand, and hence both higher output and employment, without resulting in an increase in inflation. This approach emphasises the importance of public investment in infrastructure because of the impact this has upon the efficiency and productivity of UK firms, thereby increasing their international competitiveness. It 'crowds in' private investment as firms in the private sector pick up these contracts and expand their operations, thereby increasing their ability and desire to employ more workers and invest greater sums in new machinery and new technology (Aschauer 1990). The importance of infrastructural spending has been recognised by government (HM Treasury 2016). However, there is not yet a clear recognition, by HM Treasury, of the crucial role of aggregate demand as the driver of the economy. Instead, infrastructural spending is viewed rather in isolation, as a stand-alone economic instrument rather than as an integrated overall economic approach. This needs to change if the UK is to create the high growth macroeconomic framework within which firms wish to expand, entrepreneurs wish to invest and consumers wish to continue to spend. In short, macroeconomic policy requires a Keynesian foundation to be truly effective.

Secondly, over the medium term, the depreciation of sterling is likely to boost UK exports whilst reducing the level of imports and/or encouraging import substitution, thereby providing a secondary boost to domestic producers. The economics literature indicates that periods of competitive (or undervalued) exchange rates can have significant positive effects upon those industrial sectors that have significant growth potential (Rodrik 2008). Indeed, there is evidence that exchange rate undervaluation lay behind the rapid increase in the growth rates of European economies up until the 1970s, whereas subsequent revaluation and tighter macroeconomic stance has slowed this pace of development (Perraton 2014: 12). Thus, exchange rate management would appear to be an effective macroeconomic management tool. Data for 2009, drawn from OECD-WTO TiVA datasets, suggest that UK exports are price elastic, which indicates that a change in price will have a proportionately greater impact upon the quantity of that good or service demanded. In this instance, the estimate was made that a 10% change in the price of UK export prices would likely lead to a change in exports volumes of between 15% and 25% (Driver 2014: 7).

The utilisation of this policy tool is, however, circumscribed by two factors. The first is that the weakness of the UK manufacturing sector, in terms of its low international comparative ranking in per capita terms (behind Iceland and Luxembourg), suggests that it might struggle to take full advantage of an increase in international competitiveness (Chang et al. 2013). Moreover, the UK's success in attracting foreign direct investment (FDI) and foreign ownership of a sizeable share of the industrial base may limit the effectiveness of devaluation if these owners preferred to reap increased profits rather than allow currency depreciation from reducing export prices, for fear that this would mean their UK production undercutting their other production facilities elsewhere in the world. Thus, whilst currency management is likely to play a significant role in a post-Brexit macroeconomic strategy, it is likely to be less effective in the absence of complementary measures aimed at regenerating UK manufacturing industry.

Thirdly and finally, Brexit provides the UK with the *opportunity* to explore alternative trade relationships with both EU member states and, more importantly in the long run, faster-growing nations elsewhere in the world. The UK will be free to negotiate its own preferential trade deals with whomever it chooses. This could be with former close trading partners in the Commonwealth and would most likely also embrace the establishment of closer economic ties with the USA. Those few studies which have sought to capture the potential for such FTAs have indicated only limited benefits. However, this analysis inevitably draws upon data relating to current trading patterns, supply chains and existing product ranges. To maximise full advantage of the trade opportunities available to an independent UK, exporters will need to be encouraged to actively seek out new opportunities outside the European regional bloc, whilst new industries, markets and product ranges will need to be developed to augment existing exports in order to reduce the UK's trade deficit. There is no need for this process to be unduly rushed, and nor is there a requirement for the UK to capitulate in negotiations relating to the stated positions of other nations when discussing potential future FTAs. In any case, the net benefit derived from non-EU trade surpluses is likely to rise over time, as faster growth rates outside Europe lead to higher demand for UK products—the precise relationship depending upon the elasticity of the goods and services exported.

MICROECONOMIC POLICY

The macroeconomic policy framework to be set by the UK government following Brexit will be of considerable importance in determining the ultimate success or failure of the decision, taken by the British electorate, for the country to pursue independent economic development. However, microeconomic policy will be no less significant in dealing with challenges that Brexit will entail for specific sectors of the economy. Given that the UK economy has a very large trade deficit, particularly with our EU neighbours, and the economy relies too heavily upon finance and the professional services rather than manufacturing industry to restore trading balance, then industrial policy can play an important role in restoring greater balance to the economy. Rodrik (2006: 986) argues that "more selective, and more carefully targeted policy initiatives ... can have very powerful effects on igniting economic growth in the short run". Thus, microeconomic policy can have a significant effect upon post-Brexit economic development.

Industrial Policy

Industrial policy is intended to resolve market imperfections and thereby enhance the efficiency of the productive sector (Greenwald and Stiglitz 2012). There are two types of industrial policy. 'Vertical' or selective industrial policy seeks to combine planning support for industry, with state investment, infrastructural projects. Policy interventions are targeted at specific firms or sectors, to enhance their efficiency and ultimately secure international competitive advantage, and hence, this has often been characterised by critics as governments attempting to 'pick winners' to create 'national champions' (Cohen, 2007) or in 'choosing races and placing bets' (Hughes 2012). By contrast, 'horizontal' industrial policies are more general and passive in nature, focusing upon reducing constraints to the operation of market forces and the creation of a low tax, low regulation business environment. Horizontal policy could additionally include investment in education and infrastructure, as this benefits the economy in general.

There are, of course, difficulties in maintaining this distinction between vertical and horizontal forms of industrial policy, as any intervention will inevitably disproportionately benefit one firm or industry. Thus, a decision to expand technical education may form part of a horizontal skills policy, yet it will benefit engineering and IT sectors more than agriculture or large parts of the service sector. Similarly, the decision to extend the railway network in the north of England, through the so-called 'Northern Powerhouse' programme, will disproportionately benefit those industrial clusters which are spatially connected to this new infrastructure. Moreover, there is a further weakness with the horizontal approach, in that, because this disproportionate benefit occurs as a by-product of the intervention; rather than through its specific design, it becomes more difficult to monitor the effectiveness of the measure(s) and to prevent 'leakages', thereby potentially reducing the effectiveness of the intervention (Chang 2009: 13–15).

Industrial policy can be viewed narrowly or more comprehensively. For example, corporate governance and financial market structures are not typically incorporated within discussions of industrial policy, yet impatient finance and governance structures—overly concerned with short-term movements in stock market prices, takeover threats and portfolio diversification to minimise risk—tend to result in short-termism in investment decisions (Kay 2012; Crafts and Hughes 2013). Initiatives to deliver more patient forms of finance are, however, firmly within the remit of a more active form of industrial policy (HMG 2017a: 177). Similarly, the enhancement of business networks, often crucial to realise the agglomeration effects arising from clusters of specialised firms operating within a given locality, does not fit easily within the definitions of either vertical or horizontal forms of industrial policy. Nevertheless, the expectation is that networks will generate positive spillovers, whether through the creation of a labour force specialising in the skills and knowledge required by the sector in question or through innovation that emerges through a combination of collaboration and competition (Chinitz 1961; Porter 1998: 78). Consequently, the creation of networks may be categorised as a third type of industrial strategy.

Industrial policy can be justified, in economic theory, on a number of counts. Firstly, can facilitate the efficient development of supply chains by encouraging those industries which are interdependent (hence complimentary) with other sectors of the industrial base (Rosenstein-Rodan 1943; Hidalgo and Hausmann 2009). Secondly, industrial policy may assist the slow and costly process of accumulating productive capacity (Lall 2001). The desire to protect infant industries until they have sufficiently developed these capabilities is one example of this approach. However, so is the 'industrial commons' argument, which notes the interdependent processes of learning and production which spill over across the industrial base, and in this way, encouraging the development of certain key sectors will strengthen the potential of others (Abramovitz 1986; Laranja et al., 2008). A third set of arguments identifies capital market failure in providing sufficient long-term funding for technologically advanced and innovative areas of production, due to their inherent uncertainty and risk profiles (Jäntti and Vartiainen 2009). Finally, industrial policy can facilitate technology transfer by enhancing the "absorptive capacity" of the economy, through skills enhancement, improving management quality and raising levels of R&D expenditure (Crafts 2018: 692).

There are a number of criticisms which are likely to be levied at the introduction of a more active industrial policy. Firstly, there is the suggestion that state investment 'crowds out' private investment. This is based upon the neo-classical theory of the market for money, whereby there is a finite amount of funds available, at the prevailing equilibrium rate of interest, to be borrowed to invest in productive activities as well as less productive forms of assets. If this theoretical construct is accepted, and similarly if the economy is operating at full employment, then any public sector borrowing to invest it in UK businesses will either increase demand relative to the supply of funds, thereby increasing the interest rate paid by all borrowers and thereby making investment less profitable, or else it will substitute public for private borrowing. In either case, the result would be less beneficial than adherents of industrial policy would claim. If the further assumption is added, that private investment is always superior to public investment, then it would be unlikely that state investment will produce beneficial effects that would exceed these predicted costs.

The problem with this critique is that the theory on which it is founded is fundamentally flawed. Whereas money markets might have once resembled the neo-classical characterisation in the early days of capitalism, the reality in the twenty-first century is that most investment occurs through a combination of retained earnings and bank credit (Kalecki 1971). There is not a finite amount of credit, but rather, banks can create money based (sometimes rather loosely) upon their deposits and other assets. Consequently, there is no *a priori* reason for crowding out to necessarily occur. Moreover, to do so, neo-classical theory requires the economy to be operating at full capacity, so there are not underutilised or unused assets that could be seamlessly employed. The theory achieves this through the simplifying assumption of 'Say's Law', which holds that supply creates its own demand, which, in turn, implies that the economy will always be automatically self-correcting towards the full employment of all resources. There can, under this assumption, never be a situation where demand deficiency persists, and both capital and workers remain idle. Yet, any cursory perusal of economic history will demonstrate the fragility of this assumption. The economy is often away from its equilibrium position for long periods of time. Indeed, so much so that many have suggested that the concept of equilibrium itself is a theoretical abstraction from reality. However, the pertinent point for this discussion is that crowding out does not occur if the economy is operating at less than full employment; in circumstances of less than full employment, public investment can often 'crowd *in*' further private sector investment. Moreover, since an essential part of the intention of industrial policy is to actively shape markets, to enhance their future productive potential, then crowding-out arguments are less tenable (Mazzucato and Penna 2014: 27).

A second criticism is that by operating selective measures favouring one firm or industry over another, industrial policy weakens competition policy (Irwin 2015: 17). However, if the free operation of market forces has not been sufficient to deliver the UK sufficient industrial capacity, with future high growth potential, sufficient to eliminate its current large trade deficit, then there would appear to be an *a priori* justification for considering this type of intervention.

A third critique focuses upon the potential for indigenous firms to 'capture' rents from the UK government (Rodrik 2004: 1, 17; HOL 2018: 48). This would represent a Pareto inefficient use of resources. Of course, Pareto efficiency only really exists in a textbook and therefore trade-offs are likely to exist when seeking to achieve economic objectives. It is, for example, quite plausible to anticipate that certain strategically important firms, such as Nissan or Vauxhall, may press for government assistance to mitigate any Brexit-related disruption and ensure the viability of their longer-term operations in the UK. Whilst Crafts (2017: 318) might consider this possibility to be "unedifying", there is a strong argument in favour of using a more active form of industrial policy to secure strategic objectives, if this creates greater benefits for the economy than the cost of any such assistance. It is often necessary, when designing economic policy interventions to deal with real-world problems, not to sacrifice a realisable second-best outcome by chasing after an unrealisable textbook optimum solution. Moreover, the threat of regulatory capture would be reduced if industrial policy measures were time-limited, to prevent the entrenchment of vested interests, together with a rigorous monitoring and policing of the various initiatives. Democratic accountability and transparency could help to prevent the abuse of policy intervention measures.

A fourth criticism is that industrial policy does not work because the state is incapable of 'picking winners'. Presumably, those who advocate this position also hold that venture capital funds, and the financial markets more generally, are presupposed to have a monopoly of insight into future market conditions and the growth potential of each and every individual firm and productive sector (Baldwin 1969). This viewpoint is largely based upon a vague understanding of the 'efficient market hypothesis' (Farma 1970). Contrary to popular belief, this theory does not state that markets are always and everywhere efficient and do not exhibit excessive volatility, but rather that even if they should do so, predictions of future movements in securities prices are a random walk and hence, on average, no investor can make consistently greater returns than another. Yet, the rather limited scope of the original theory has been taken by policy makers and some economists (who perhaps should read the original texts) to imply market superiority.

The fact that industrial policy may occasionally fail in its choice of investments does not undermine the need for the state to undertake this role if the private sector is unable or unwilling to nurture these developments. Venture capitalists often fail in their investment selections, but they are judged not on individual interventions, but rather upon the balance of their entire portfolio. State investments should be similarly assessed on the same basis, so the inevitable losses sustained in certain businesses are likely to be more than offset by the successes in other ventures (Mazzucato and Penna 2014: 23–4). If governments make no mistakes when operating an active industrial policy, it implies that they are not trying sufficiently hard (Rodrik 2004: 25).

There are plenty of examples that can be given where vertical industrial policy has assisted in the development of international competitive industries—whether car production in Japan or steel in South Korea—because the state had the long-term vision often lacking in financial markets more focused upon short-term gains (Chang 2002).[10] Nations which have utilised active forms of industrial policy have included Japan, South Korea, Taiwan, Singapore, France, Finland, Norway, Austria, Germany, Italy and, more recently, China. Moreover, the UK was only the first amongst multiple nations (including Germany) which pursued what would now be

---

[10] http://www.ibtimes.com/yes-government-can-pick-winners-ha-joon-chang-268043

described as an infant industry programme, where the development of selected industries was protected by high tariffs; the UK's later championing of free trade allowed these same (now mature) industries to realise their competitive advantage (Chang 2009: 10).

This list could additionally include the USA since the state financed between half and two-thirds of national R&D expenditure between the 1950s and 1980s, principally in the fields of defence-aerospace and healthcare, and it is in many of these areas where the USA subsequently established a technological lead (Chang 2009: 2–8). Indeed, the USA is a good example of how government has the ability to create a direction for technological change, and by investing according to this vision, new firms and new markets will be created (McFadden and Tarrant 2015: 5). Many of the most prominent recent examples of product innovation, including pharmaceuticals, renewable energy and personal electronics such as the iPod, iPad and battery technology, depended upon foundations created by publically funded research (Mazzucato 2013). The fact that the USA funds and organises this level of innovation and technological support through a multitude of channels, rather than through a single, and hence more visible, industrial strategy, has resulted in the USA being described as a "hidden development state" (Block 2008: 2).

The economics literature has not, unfortunately, produced a clear consensus upon the effectiveness of different modes of industrial policy. There have, for example, been a number of studies which have concluded that vertical policy fails to deliver its intended increase in productivity (Krueger and Tuncer 1982; Lee 1996). Yet, these studies typically suffer from problems of omitted variable bias and difficulties in interpretation of causality. For example, if a study records a negative association between intervention and industrial performance, does this indicate that industrial strategy has had negative effects upon the industry or alternatively that the problems of the industry were so intractable that a more sizeable state intervention was necessitated to try and solve deep-set problems? Moreover, other econometric studies indicate that total factor productivity is higher in those nations which adopt an import-substitution form of industrial policy rather than a market-orientated alternative although, again, it is difficult to assign causality (Bosworth and Collins 2003). Hence, there is no persuasive body of evidence which can point conclusively to whether one form or another of industrial policy produces superior or inferior economic outcomes (Rodrik 2006: 9–10).

The historical record is a little clearer when considering the effectiveness of industrial strategies in aggregate as those economies which have utilised active industrial policy outperformed other large OECD economies between 1950 and 1987 (Chang 2009: 7–8). This might help to explain why there has been a significant increase of interest in a more active industrial policy proving indispensable to national economic development (Lin and Monga 2010).

Industrial Policy Within the EU
The EU initially pursued a vertical form of industrial policy, seeking to develop a set of European businesses capable of competing with US transnational corporations (TNCs). However, during the past two decades, policy has shifted towards a horizontal approach. Indeed, to illustrate the extensiveness of this shift in approach, the former European Commissioner in charge of competition policy, Kroes, argued that concerns over retaining national control over what are regarded to be 'strategic assets' is "outdated—the language and the mindset are those of yesterday's people, not of these who have the guts to look forward with ambitious realism"—a viewpoint dismissed as "contrary to the spirit and the letter of the laws underpinning the European Union" (Kroes 2006: 3). Vertical industrial policy was, furthermore, rejected by Kroes (2006: 4,6) on the grounds that it would result in decreasing competitiveness, whilst state aid was decried as crowding out private sector investment.

The advent of the single internal market (SIM) further reinforced this shift in approach as the Commission held that national promotion of domestic industry was discriminatory and therefore not consistent with competition rules. Vertical industrial policy would, by definition, give preference to, or advantage for, domestic products vis-à-vis those produced elsewhere in the EU (Kennedy 2011: 47–8; Barnard 2016: 82–4). Whilst these restrictions upon industrial policy initially focused upon goods, a combination of the approach taken by the Commission and decisions of the European Court of Justice gradually extended these constraints to include services and issues related to tax (Reynolds and Webber 2019). This additionally includes the use of 'buy British', 'buy Irish' and even 'buy local' campaigns, due to concerns over unfair competition within the SIM. Yet, by doing so, this frustrates using 'buy local' campaigns to reduce food miles and thereby benefit the environment. Similarly, European Court rulings prevent national or regional rules requiring electricity suppliers to purchase specific quantities of renewable energy from their local region (Barnard 2016: 83), despite this frustrating the establishment of local energy generation, which many experts suggest can be produced at lower levels of energy lost through transmission grids, with resultant cost and emissions advantages (Armstrong 2015).[11]

Public authorities are required to make public procurement tender details widely available across the EU and may not discriminate against any firm because it is registered or located in a different EU country.[12] The intention is to create a 'level playing field' for firms across the EU to bid for tenders that, in aggregate, approximate to 14% of EU GDP per annum.[13] However, this constrains the ability for public procurement to be used to establish a core market for local producers, to meet developmental or environmental objectives. It could, for example, introduce a preference for local produce to reduce food miles and raise nutritional food provision for public services (i.e. hospitals, schools, retirement homes and prisons) or to help to establish a market for local renewable energy. Similarly, it could facilitate the expansion of the UK engineering industry by ensuring that local producers receive part of the increased demand arising from the Northern Powerhouse public investment intended to renew transportation links in the north of England. In the absence of the greater industrial policy flexibility which will arise post-Brexit, comments from Sir Andrew Cook, Chairperson of William Cook Rail (a large engineering employer in South and West Yorkshire), would suggest that this opportunity is currently being squandered.[14]

A third area where the EU restricts industrial policy relates to its rules relating to state aid. This may be defined as where public assistance is provided on a selective basis to a firm or group of firms either directly by public authorities or via an instrument over which the state has significant control (BIS, 2015: 4–5). This would include not only subsidies and tax credits funded through the national budget but also assistance from regional or local government, public guarantees, state holdings or all or part of a company, the provision of goods and/or services on preferential terms, and funding provided via quasi-public bodies such as the National

---

[11] See also UK government select committee conclusions, contained within http://www.publications.parliament.uk/pa/cm201314/cmselect/cmenergy/180/18006.htm

[12] http://europa.eu/youreurope/business/public-tenders/rules-procedures/index_en.htm

[13] https://ec.europa.eu/growth/single-market/public-procurement_en

[14] http://www.bbc.co.uk/iplayer/episode/b083gkjs/look-north-yorkshire-late-news-01122016

Lottery.[15] If this assistance has any effect, it will strengthen the firm or firms targeted by the measure, and will therefore be deemed as distorting competition and fall foul of EU SIM competition laws.

There are exceptions to this rule. The first relates to the provision of very small amounts of assistance (de minimis rule), where each business receives less than €200,000 over three years; lesser sums apply in the agricultural (€15,000) and road transport (€100,000) sectors (Jozepa 2018: 4). A second set of exemptions fall under the category of 'General Block Exemption Regulation'. These include development assistance for disadvantaged regions of the EU, infrastructure funding, environmental protection, cultural and heritage conservation, aid to facilitate recovery from natural disasters, employment and training for disabled or disadvantaged workers, provision of assistance for small and medium-sized enterprises (SMEs) and innovation funding to facilitate R&D through, for example, helping with patent costs (Jozepa 2018: 9–10).[16] Each of these categories has its own rules and ceilings placed upon the maximum amount of permitted state aid (BIS, 2015: 9). Moreover, these exemptions only apply when assistance is provided to any and all eligible firms from across the EU, irrespective of their nationality of ownership, where their headquarters are located and even, perhaps surprisingly, whether they have any current operations within the country offering the aid. It is, however, permissible to restrict assistance to those firms that have some form of operations within the national boundary of the government offering the assistance at the time that the assistance is provided (EC 2016: point 7).

It is a fair point to note that the UK has chosen not to utilise its flexibility within these exemptions to operate a more active form of industrial policy (HOL 2018: 44). For example, in 2016, the UK allocated only 0.36% of its GDP to state aid (excluding railways), compared to 0.65% in France and 1.31% in Germany (Jozepa 2018: 4). Hence, the limited forms of industrial policy that are permitted by the EU could have been pursued more vigorously (Crafts 2017: 317). Nevertheless, EU rules necessarily limit the potential for the full range of options available to a more active form of industrial policy. Instead, the EU has placed greater emphasis upon regional (EU-wide) competitiveness, utilising measures to encourage the development of SMEs and the knowledge economy (Bartlett 2014: 4–5). This was latterly extended, through provisions established in

[15] http://ec.europa.eu/competition/state_aid/overview/index_en.html
[16] http://ec.europa.eu/competition/publications/cpb/2014/009_en.pdf

the Lisbon Treaty, to provide elements of sector-specific support (EC 2010; Uvalik 2014: 2–3). The stated goal was to support the growth of the EU's industrial sector to approximately one-fifth of EU GDP by 2020 (Pellegrin et al. 2015: 10).

The Potential for Industrial Policy Following Brexit

Brexit offers the potential to operate a more active industrial policy unhindered by SIM competition and state aid rules. For those critical of the Brexit project, industrial strategy will be "a necessity" to prevent unnecessary harm to the UK industrial base (Jones 2016: 827). To those less antagonistic towards Brexit, industrial policy offers the opportunity to transform the fortunes of UK manufacturing and achieve a rebalancing of the economy otherwise difficult to achieve within the strictures of EU rules and regulations (Whyman 2018: 5,8,16). Whereas the current UK industrial strategy has been developed within the existing constraints imposed by EU membership, and as a result is rather limited in a number of key respects (Crafts 2017: 317, 319), the potential for industrial strategy to form a central pillar of economic strategy post-Brexit has been recognised by government and opposition parties (Conservative Party 2017: 12–13; HMG 2017a: 11, 15–16, 20, 212–3; HMG 2017b: 13, 62–4; Industrial Strategy Commission 2017: 10, 12; Labour Party 2019: 12–3, 16–18).

WTO Rules and Industrial Policy

Withdrawal from the EU does not mean that there are *no* constraints remaining upon the use of industrial policy measures. The UK remains a member of the WTO and hence must follow its rules which are contained in the Agreement on Subsidies and Countervailing Measures (ASCM).[17] Crucially, however, these restrictions are not as comprehensive and "intrusive" as the EU regime (HOL 2018: 47–8, 53).

The WTO approach, for example, allows the use of public subsidies unless these are focused upon export activity or import substitution (Article 3 of the ASCM), or unless another country can prove that these measures are damaging their domestic industries and/or their trade in general (Articles 5 and 6) (Jozepa 2018: 16–17). Whereas the default EU position is to prohibit such subsidies in advance of their introduction, and businesses have to repay any aid which is found to breach EU rules, the

---

[17] This was incorporated into GATT 1994 as part of Annex 1A to the WTO Agreement 1994

WTO merely requires the withdrawal of any measure found to breach the ASCM, without any similar requirement for recipients to repay any assistance received prior to any judgement (HOL 2018: 47). Moreover, the WTO can accept retention of subsidies, even if found to have convened its own rules, but allow the aggrieved party to introduce a countervailing tax to offset and competitive advantage secured via the subsidy (Jozepa 2018: 17).

There are other significant differences between the EU and WTO approaches. Whereas WTO rules apply only to goods, EU rules apply to all economic activities including services (HOL 2018: 47; Jozepa 2018: 5, 17). WTO rules only apply to trade-related activities, whereas EU rules apply indiscriminately to all economic activity occurring within the UK economy, whether or not this was intended for purely domestic use and consumption or for export (HOL 2018: 48). WTO rules are reactive, depending upon a complaint being made by a signatory nation before investigation takes place, whilst EU rules are applied prospectively and do not require a formal complaint before action is taken (Jozepa 2018: 17). In addition, under the EU system, individuals and companies can lodge complaints to the Commission or through domestic courts, whereas the WTO approach is based upon dispute settlement between state actors (UKCE 2018: 8).

WTO rules *generally* prohibit local content requirements (Article III:4 of the GATT [General Agreement on Tariffs and Trade] 1994; Article 2.1 of the Technical Barriers to Trade Agreement; 3.1(b) of the ASCM). However, local preference is permitted in public procurement and when adopting policies aimed at avoiding environmental problems (EC 2017; Rubini 2004: 152). Similarly, subsidies can be used where they seek the protection of public health and/or public morals, the environment and the conservation of natural resources (Bohanes, 2015: 3). Non-discriminatory measures, such as labelling standards or strict hygiene requirements, would not breach WTO rules, despite their potentially having a disproportionate benefit to certain domestic industries. Industrial policy measures could be used, under WTO rules, to promote regional regeneration, the restructuring of certain industrial sectors particularly responding to changes in trade and economic policies such as presumably the impact of Brexit, encouraging R&D especially in high-tech industries, assisting the development of infant industries, introducing local preference in public procurement and when avoiding environmental problems (Rubini 2004: 152).

The degree of policy flexibility for the UK, if operating under WTO rather than EU rules, is therefore quite significant. It broadens the scope of what is a permissible use of industrial policy rather considerably which is potentially very valuable for an independent UK, seeking to rebalance its economy through rejuvenating its manufacturing industry, seeking to encourage higher rates of investment and innovation, and ensuring that any resultant economic growth is spread more evenly across the whole nation.

What Might an Active Post-Brexit Industrial Policy Look Like?
There is no reason why an industrial strategy, designed to meet the persistent weaknesses in the UK's economic model and the particular challenges and opportunities presented by Brexit, needs to follow approaches adopted by other nations. However, there are a number of features that can be highlighted in other successful examples of industrial strategy which might inform a UK scheme.

The first element concerns the necessity for a "national vision" around which to frame the development of an industrial policy (Chang et al. 2013: 46–7). If the UK, following withdrawal from the EU, commits itself to the goal of transforming the UK economy, to deliver higher productivity and more inclusive growth, then it is much easier to achieve broad support for the principles of the industrial strategy and its policy initiatives.

A second aspect concerns the ability to coordinate activity through "thick" networks (Chang et al. 2013: 48). Certain nations utilised indicative planning to perform this function (France, Japan and Korea), whilst others adopted corporatist approaches (Finland), utilised workers councils (Germany) or specially established deliberation councils (Japan and Korea). These networks facilitate communication and coordination, which in turn both informs and facilitates the enactment of industrial policy initiatives. Coordination additionally requires the ability to coordinate across government departments, and this leadership role has been undertaken successfully by the Ministry of International Trade and Industry in Japan, the Planning Commission in France and the Economic Planning Board in Korea. The Department for Business, Energy and Industrial Strategy could perform this leadership function in the UK, but it may find the task of coordination more difficult in the absence of a well-established range of intermediate institutions or "industrial commons" (Abramovitz 1986) who are able to fully engage with the development and implementation of the industrial strategy.

The third element that typically forms a foundation of industrial policy programmes concerns the provision of affordable, patient investment finance. Japan ensured this through the Long-Term Credit Bank of Japan and the Industrial Bank of Japan, Korea through state-owned banks, whilst Finland utilised public savings, which at their peak comprised almost one-third of total domestic savings, to support productive investment (Chang et al. 2013). Given their provision of lower cost credit and financial services to businesses not adequately served by the private sector financial institutions, state investment banks have the ability to support capital development more generally and potentially enhance countercyclical macroeconomic policy in the process (Mazzucato and Penna 2014: 4–5). The current state-owned British Business Bank could develop into fulfilling this more strategic role, possibly along the lines of the German Kreditanstalt für Wiederaufbau, which both fulfils the role of a national state investment bank whilst simultaneously provides funding to regional state investment banks in Germany.[18] Previous proposals have been made along these lines in the UK (Dolphin and Nash 2012).[19] However, they have not, as yet, been implemented.

The provision of patient finance for productive investment is a necessary but not sufficient feature of industrial strategies. It is typically complemented by financial regulation aimed at rationing credit consumer credit and thereby steering resources towards the productive sector (Korea). Forced savings schemes have also been utilised as a means to generate and then steer funding towards productive investment (Singapore), whilst similar approaches have also been utilised through the development of public sector savings surpluses (Finland and Sweden).

The provision of patient capital to fund productive investment has implications for corporate governance. If this is subject to overt short-termism, the industrial policy objectives of rebuilding the UK's industrial base will falter. In other countries, firms have been partially insulated from short-term pressures through cross-shareholding (Japan) or codetermination (Germany) (Chang et al. 2013: 50). Whatever the approach, in order to ensure that this active industrial policy is sustainable, it is important to ensure that public and private stakeholders have a "symbiotic" rather than

---

[18] https://www.dbresearch.com/PROD/DBR_INTERNET_EN-PROD/PROD0000000000380779.pdf
[19] https://www.theguardian.com/politics/2016/jul/18/labour-vows-to-set-up-national-investment-bank-to-mobilise-500bn

304 P. B. WHYMAN AND A. I. PETRESCU

"parasitic" relationship (Mazzucato 2013: 30). Too often state support for innovation in the private sector combines the socialisation of risk with the privatisation of gains, which is precisely the flawed balance of costs and benefits that underpinned the irrational exuberance and excessive risk taking by the financial institutions, thus precipitating the 2008 global financial crisis (Mazzucato 2013: 34, 203).

A true partnership requires a means of sharing both the costs and the benefits derived from the initial public investment. This could involve the state taking a stake in the enterprise, thereby receiving a share of the rewards arising from the development of products drawing upon this publically funded invention or innovation. In addition, active industrial policy could additionally include the re-institution of a public interest test for takeovers, thereby preventing the foreign takeover of strategic industries. A variant of this approach could involve the state acquiring a 'golden share' in certain sectors to prevent outcomes that might prove undesirable to the economy as a whole, such as the relocation of the headquarters, or R&D functions, offshore.

Having drawn upon the common elements present in successful examples of industrial policy, the next step is to determine the form that industrial policy intervention will take. Rodrik (2008) suggests that this should be one that combines vertical and horizontal elements, namely where the government identifies specific sectors with high growth potential and provides targeted support to aid their development, whilst simultaneously creating a broader framework conducive to industrial development more generally. The former could include tax credits, subsidies or directed credit.

A good starting point would be to identify emergent sectors with good productive growth potential, such as alternative energy and those developing applications from new materials, on the basis that there are fewer established firms dominating these markets.[20] Government action cannot be judged as distorting a newly created market since there is no historical precedent against which to assess any alleged distortion arising from public policy actions (Bohanes, 2015: 8). In terms of renewable energy, one obvious field in which successful innovation could generate large returns, would concern battery technology, both for personal electrical devices and perhaps more significantly for electric cars and to be able to successfully store renewable energy power generation. Research is currently examining the potential for lithium-air batteries, which are hypothetically far more

[20] http://www.ibtimes.com/yes-government-can-pick-winners-ha-joon-chang-268043

efficient than the current ion batteries in contemporary usage, together with sodium-ion and redox flow batteries, which, should technical issues be satisfactorily resolved, be scaled up to facilitate renewable energy from providing a greater share of UK energy needs, even when the wind is not blowing or the sun shining.[21] The current UK industrial strategy concurs with this emphasis upon battery technology, energy storage and smart grid technology (HMG 2017b: 16). However, the scale and scope of policy interventions to date remains far too limited to deliver the type of transformational effect proposed by advocates of active industrial policy.

A second example might be to focus upon applications of new materials such as graphene, which was discovered at the University of Manchester and for which two academics won the 2010 Nobel Prize in Physics. Graphene is a crystalline form of carbon, in which a single layer of carbon atoms are arranged in a regular hexagonal pattern. It is the thinnest known material yet discovered, yet is also the strongest; indeed, it is estimated to be 100 times stronger than steel. Despite being crystalline in structure, it is quite elastic and has the best thermal conductivity of any material. As a consequence, the range of potential applications to which this substance can be put signifies the potential gains for those organisations that are able to establish themselves as first-movers in these markets. Yet, despite graphene being discovered in Manchester, the UK has filed less than 1% of graphene-related patents (IPO 2015: 7). China, by contrast, has 29% of patents, whilst fully 47% have been filed in China; the difference presumably relating to non-Chinese companies deciding to file patents in China as this is where they propose developing the related product range(s) (IPO 2015: 7–9). This is not simply a reflection of the relative sizes of individual nations, since South Korea has registered almost as many graphene-related patents as their larger neighbour, with 25% of the global total. The response by the UK government, to establish a £235 million advanced manufacturing research centre at the University of Manchester, is a welcome but rather belated recognition of the significance of this sector (HM Treasury 2014: 50).

A second strategic approach that a more active industrial strategy could pursue is to identify those types of technologies which have scale or agglomeration economies, and which are unlikely to receive sufficient

---

[21] https://www.theguardian.com/business/2016/aug/20/do-we-even-need-hinkley-point-smart-usage-windpower-hi-tech-batteries?CMP=Share_iOSApp_Other

long-term investment in the absence of public intervention. There are a number of reasons why this may be the case. It may be that certain industries are capital intensive and thereby requiring a substantial initial fixed-cost outlay before economies of scale can be realised (e.g. the national grid, telecommunications networks or the railways). Or alternatively, it might be that the financial markets perceive that investments are too risky or too long term to realise reasonable shorter-term profits (e.g. aerospace in the 1970s). A third category concerns technologically advanced or innovative industries. The problem for investors is that innovation is fundamentally uncertain, and hence it is problematic to accurately predict returns. Hence, innovation requires the type of patient, long-term finance that state investment banks or other forms of public investment are perhaps more capable of providing, alongside a supportive policy environment designed to support high-tech and high growth business development (Industrial Strategy Commission 2017: 10). Industrial policy could provide assistance for these activities, but it would do so less by identifying specific industries to receive public support, but rather the specific types of technological innovation to promote (Rodrik 2004: 14). This is the framework that some have characterised as an "entrepreneurial state" (Mazzucato and Penna 2014: 23).

Alongside the provision of funding for dynamic industries or areas of technological innovation, industrial policy has the potential to create a supportive business environment within which these firms can operate. Given that innovation can be constrained by the lack of demand for the resulting products or activities, particularly where large initial investments are required to realise the innovative gains, businesses are likely to remain cautious or slow to innovate unless they are confident about future market conditions (Rodrik 2004: 4, 12–13). Expectations about future profitability are the motivation behind future investment, whilst realised past profits largely finance such investment (Keynes 1936: 135–141; Kalecki 1971). Moreover, historical evidence would suggest that investment tends to be concentrated where capital productivity is growing the fastest (Baumol et al., 1989). Thus, if industrial policy can contribute towards stimulating industrial expansion and enhancing total factor productivity, it should enhance broader economic policy objectives. There are clear synergies between macroeconomic and industrial policy; the former can create a supportive structure within which the latter can better operate, whilst the latter can stimulate industrial expansion and thereby support macroeconomic goals.

One area where Rodrik (2004: 30) does not suggest focusing industrial policy is, perhaps surprisingly, the attempt to influence the locational decisions of TNCs and thereby attract FDI. His reasoning is quite clear: that there is insufficient evidence to justify the belief that FDI results in significant productive externalities and that associations between higher productivity and exporting firms are the result of selection effects (i.e. that successful and efficient firms tend to export rather than exporting causing their productivity advantage). Hence, directing public funds to subsidise the activities of TNCs would be an inefficient use of resources and do little to enhance productive capacity. Where factors of production are mobile (as is the case with TNCs, by definition), there is an argument for industrial policy focusing upon specific stages of the supply chain, low mobility factors and/or increasing the 'stickiness' of economic activity, through skills development and institutional architecture, to increase the embeddedness of activity within the UK economy (Crafts and Hughes 2013).

Industrial policy would be particularly important for the UK to deal with the consequences of Brexit. Irrespective of the final form of trade agreement negotiated with the EU, there will be a degree of industrial restructuring which will inevitably follow. This could involve some repositioning of European supply chains, and whilst certain industries are likely to expand due to a more competitive exchange rate and global sales opportunities, other industries may contract as a result of their reliance upon European trade in protected sectors. Industrial policy can help to ease this transition, through provision of information, the financing of infrastructure improvement and compensation for externalities (Lin and Monga 2010). Indeed, Rodrik (2004: 15) notes that industrial restructuring rarely occurs in the absence of government involvement and assistance.

Industrial policy could provide a means of assisting sectors such as vehicle manufacture, which could be affected by an increase in non-tariff barriers amidst most Brexit scenarios, and might additionally face a tariff rate of around 8.5% if trade with the EU reverted to WTO rules. In Chap. 3, it was noted that this may raise costs for the industry by around £1.4 billion. This could be offset indirectly through industrial policy support for R&D, which WTO rules to be provided up to three quarters of the total cost. Indeed, this would appear to be an obvious means of achieving a 'double dividend' in terms of negating additional costs for a strategically important industry whilst simultaneously most likely increasing investment and productivity in the process. Other permitted (indirect) options for support would be through the development of disadvantaged areas of the country, where a car plant may happen to be situated, or through horizontal measures to support export activities, which would benefit an export-intensive industry (Chang 2009).

It is important to note that the permitted forms of industrial policy are dependent upon the form of post-Brexit agreement that is agreed between the UK and the EU. The closer the relationship between the UK and the EU, the less scope will exist for the type of active industrial policy described in this chapter. Thus, European Economic Area, customs union[22] or FTA options, complete with 'common rule book' provisions, permit little if any variance from the current position. A simple FTA or WTO option, by contrast, would enable the UK far greater flexibility in the use of an active industrial and procurement policy (Crafts 2017: 317). Indeed, it might be argued that the adoption of such an approach, were the UK to adopt a more independent stance in relation to the EU, would be 'essential' to enhance economic resilience and transform the industrial base into a form more capable of taking advantage of those opportunities that may arise (Whyman 2018: 34,42).

The UK's stated preference for the negotiation of a simple form of FTA is consistent with this position (Jozepa 2018: 4)[23] as state aid control is not typically included in more basic forms of FTA (Reynolds and Webber 2019: 5). The Comprehensive Economic and Trade Agreement, ratified between the EU and Canada, contains no extension of state aid provisions over and above those contained within WTO agreements (Jozepa 2018: 28). Nor, indeed, do the vast majority of Switzerland's multiple bilateral accords with the EU (HOL 2018: 46). Similarly, the FTA between the EU and South Korea also rests upon the WTO (not EU) rulebook in terms of governing the use of industrial policy, with the minor exception that the list of WTO prohibited subsidies was slightly extended in the agreement (HOL 2018: 47). Thus, there is ample precedent established for the UK

---

[22] Labour Party policy was to attempt to negotiate exemptions from EU rules constraining the use of state aid and procurement within its preferred Brexit option of a customs union (https://brexitcentral.com/full-text-jeremy-corbyns-speech-labours-brexit-policy/#menu). It is questionable as to whether this would have proved possible to negotiate with the EU; however, the election result made this a moot point.

[23] https://www.reuters.com/article/us-britain-election-johnson-buy/johnson-pitches-buy-british-and-new-state-aid-rules-after-brexit-idUSKBN1Y317M; https://www.indepen-dent.co.uk/news/uk/politics/boris-johnson-brexit-eu-state-aid-deal-labour-voters-general-election-a9226151.html

to negotiate a form of FTA with the EU which depends upon the WTO and not the EU framework.

PUBLIC PROCUREMENT

Public procurement, if used strategically, can build supply chains and has been used in countries such as the USA to further innovation and develop high technology industries (Chang et al. 2013: 28–9; HMG 2017b: 18). Procurement can contribute towards reducing the economic imbalances pertaining across the UK and thereby facilitate more sustainable economic development (HMG 2017b: 21). It can facilitate environmental goals, by encouraging small-scale farmers to link more directly with sections of the public sector (i.e. schools, hospitals, elderly care facilities and/or prisons), where the sourcing of local foods could enhance the quality of meals but also reduce food miles. Moreover, local procurement can be used to reduce leakages from a local economy, whilst strengthening supply chains, attracting skilled workers to an area and boosting growth potential (HMG 2017b: 120).

EU membership has constrained the UK's ability to utilise procurement policy to further strategic aims for much the same reason as it limits the ability for a nation state to realise the full potential of industrial strategy, namely that the dictates of protecting the integrity of the single market prevent preference being given to a particular firm or industry in the awarding of a contract. To do so would be viewed as anti-competitive. Thus, all procurement contracts, above a certain size,[24] have to be publicised across the EU (using the standardised Tenders Economic Daily process), to ensure transparency and enhance competition (HMG 2017b: 71). Any firm, operating within the EU, therefore has the right to bid for procurement contracts on an equal basis.

As with other aspects of industrial policy, there are exemptions to the EU procurement framework. For example, the 2014 Procurement Directive allowed member states to take into consideration the needs of SMEs when designing procurement procedures and, most significantly, to

---

[24] These limits are typically €139,000 for most inputs of materials and services purchased by central government, and €5.35m for construction contracts. For more detailed discussion, see https://europa.eu/youreurope/business/selling-in-eu/public-contracts/public-tendering-rules/index_en.htm and https://ec.europa.eu/growth/single-market/public-procurement/rules-implementation/thresholds_en.

take into account a wider range of social and environmental goals. In the UK, the Public Services (Social Value) Act 2012 has reinforced this approach. It enabled the UK government to splitting large procurement contracts into smaller segments and through the "balanced scorecard" approach which sought to take into account factors other than cost, such as skills development and the inclusion of apprenticeship schemes, when considering value for money criteria (HMG 2017b: 18, 71–2). Furthermore, it enabled the well-documented 'Preston Model' to encourage local anchor institutions to adopt 'social value' criteria in their procurement policies, and thereby significantly enhance the development prospects of the local economy (Manley and Whyman 2020). These exemptions are limited in scope, however, as procurement preference given to local food producers, as an attempt to reduce food miles and secure environmental benefits, attempted in the UK, Ireland and Sweden, was found to breach competition and public procurement rules (Barclay, 2012).

Following the completion of the transition period, however, the UK would shift to WTO rules, unless precluded by specific agreement reached with the EU (Irwin 2015: 16).[25] Procurement is not included in the GATT 1994 treaty focusing on traded goods, nor the General Agreement on Trade in Services treaty focusing upon services, and therefore, for most WTO members, there is no restriction upon using public procurement as an adjunct to industrial policy, to favour local or domestic over imported goods (Bohanes, 2015: 14). This is the default position that the UK could choose to adopt as an independent nation. This would preclude the UK from having an *automatic* right to be able to tender for public procurement contracts across the remaining 27 EU member states—a market valued at around €1.59 trillion or 14% of EU GDP (EU Commission 2016: 1). It is estimated that UK firms secure between £1 billion and £1.4 billion of this market and therefore withdrawal from the EU may place some of this at risk (Clifford Chance 2019: 10). Set against this, however, the UK would have the ability to use its own £286bn worth of public procurement to achieve strategic goals (HMG 2017b: 18). Given that EU figures suggest that between 2009 and 2015, on average around 44.8% of UK public procurement contracts, worth a total of £72.4bn, was awarded to foreign bidders (£7.3bn) or UK-based subsidiaries of foreign companies (£65.1bn), this would suggest that a nationally focused procurement

---

[25] https://www.wto.org/english/tratop_e/gproc_e/gproc_e.htm

policy has the potential to generate significant net gains (Clifford Chance 2019: 10).

A second alternative would be for the UK to sign the Government Procurement Agreement (GPA) which requires nations to operate open and transparent conditions for competition to be included in all public procurement procedures.[26] The intention is to enable greater reciprocal access to the procurement markets (above certain minimum thresholds) of all 32 signatory nations. The EU is a signatory to the GPA, and therefore, whilst it remains a member state, the UK is bound by this agreement. However, following the end of the transition period, the UK could opt out of the GPA or take advantage of an exception from the GPA rules, in that local preference in public procurement is allowed when the policy intervention is intended to avoid environmental problems (Rubini 2004: 152). Given that one primary focus of industrial policy would be to trans-form the UK economy, through enhancement of the renewable industry sector, whilst other 'buy local' policies could reduce transport-related car-bon emissions and/or food miles, this could offer some scope for a more strategic procurement policy. Finally, since it is only those procurement activities that form part of the nation's coverage schedules that are bound by the GPA, and not the full range of public procurement contracts (as under EU rules), the UK could remain a GPA signatory but limit the range of its schedules to create a greater scope for the use of strategic pro-curement policy initiatives in specific areas of its economy.[27]

UK intentions remain confused at present. The UK government announced its intention to become an independent signatory of the GPA in June 2018, and this was provisionally agreed by the WTO in February 2019 (HMG, 2019b: 10–11).[28] Ratification could therefore take place around one month after the UK formally withdraws from the EU, once the UK has deposited the instrument of accession with the WTO (Clifford Chance 2019: 4). However, these negotiations took place under the previ-ous Prime Minister (May), whilst the current Prime Minister (Johnson) has advocated adopting a 'buy British' preference in public procurement

---

[26] In addition to the EU member states, the current GPA signatories are Armenia, Canada, China, Hong Kong, Iceland, Israel, Japan, Korea, Liechtenstein, the Netherlands with respect to Aruba, Norway, Singapore, Switzerland, Chinese Taipei and the USA.

[27] https://www.wto.org/english/tratop_e/gproc_e/gp_gpa_e.htm

[28] https://www.instituteforgovernment.org.uk/explainers/public-procurement

to "turbo-charge" the UK economy (Clifford Chance 2019).[29] Moreover, the Industrial Strategy Commission (2017: 5) has highlighted the importance of using procurement policy to develop new technologies.

ACTIVE LABOUR MARKET POLICY

An active industrial policy would be enhanced if it were operated within a supportive macroeconomic framework, and alongside measures adopted to enhance human capital development. Active labour market policies can embody both demand and supply side measures (see Table 8.1). The former reinforce countercyclical stabilisation by eliminating skills shortages and structural rigidities, whilst the latter ease market adjustment by achieving a higher employment level at a given rate of inflation and promote structural change by reducing structural rigidities, search and transaction costs (Layard et al. 1991). Examples of demand measures include public works schemes, employment subsidies to individual firms, control over the release of tax-exempt private investment funds and state purchases placed with firms and in localities where unemployment would otherwise increase. Supply side measures, in contrast, focus upon skill enhancement and enabling individuals to adapt to changing needs of the labour market (DfEE 1997). These measures seek to ease the market adjustment process by achieving a higher employment level at a given rate of inflation whilst simultaneously accommodating structural change (Whyman 2006).

Policy interventions to promote education and skills formation, in order to close skills shortages and improve the functioning of the labour market, are useful policy instruments for government to utilise in any circumstances. The UK compares poorly with other OECD countries in

Table 8.1 Different types of labour market policies

Matching	Supply	Demand
Public employment services • Information • Job placement • Counselling	Subsidised geographical mobility Free labour market training Subsidised in-house labour training	Public relief work Recruitment wage subsidies Youth teams Sheltered employment

---

[29] https://www.theguardian.com/business/2019/dec/01/johnson-spots-an-opportunity-over-state-aid-and-it-may-work

terms of the skills distribution across the whole of its population, due to the persistence of a significant proportion of individuals with low skills. Moreover, even when considering the proportion of the labour force with high (degree level) skills, the prevalence of skills mismatching, with 28.9% of the labour force working in jobs not suited to their abilities, means that many of these skills are being currently under-utilised (Industrial Strategy Commission 2017: 11). An expansion in intermediate and vocational training might help to address part of this problem, as might the adoption of Korean-style sector-specific skills formation (Chang et al. 2013).

In addition to these long-standing concerns relating to the UK skills base, the particular circumstances following Brexit are likely to create necessitate additional labour market measures, given the fact that many businesses have become perhaps overly dependent upon the importation of migrant labour to meet various labour force requirements. Should Brexit result in a reduction in the quantity of net migration, labour market policy could provide one means of reducing the production constraints imposed by persistent skill shortages in specific sectors. Given that any system of immigration control is difficult to apply with flexibility, it is probable that active labour market policy would be a useful means of moderating any unintended effects of a new work permit system, whilst providing assistance to UK companies as they might seek to expand their internal training and/or apprenticeship schemes.

Conclusion

In contrast to the many economic studies which seek to marginalise or simply ignore the significance of economic policy measures, this chapter has sought to outline the key features of a more active economic policy stance in order to demonstrate how it has the potential to maximise the benefits, and minimise the costs, arising from Brexit. The maintenance of a high level of aggregate demand provides the platform for the economy to continue to expand, as businesses overcome the inevitable degree of uncertainty that will arise during the withdrawal process and continue to invest in new capacity and innovative technology, whilst a competitive exchange rate will offset some or all of the additional export costs that may arise from trading with the EU, depending upon which model of relationship is ultimately negotiated. Industrial and labour market policy will become more essential post-Brexit, as the UK economy has the potential to rebuild its industrial base, if freed from some of the constraints imposed by SIM rules, and thereby start to address some of the fundamental weaknesses with the UK economy—that is, low productivity and high trade deficit. The successful design and implementation of this more active role for economic policy will determine its success, and very possibly also the success or failure.

References

Abramovitz, M. (1986). Catching Up, Forging Ahead, and Falling Behind. *Journal of Economic History, 46*(2), 385–406.
Alexiou, C., & Pitelis, C. (2003). On Capital Shortages and European Unemployment: A Panel Data Investigation. *Journal of Post Keynesian Economics, 25*(4), 613–631.
Arestis, P. (1989). On the Post-Keynesian Challenge to Neo-classical Economics: A Complete Quantitative Macro-model for the UK Economy. *Journal of Post-Keynesian Economics, 11*(4), 611–629.
Armstrong, A., & Portes, J. (2016). Commentary: The Economic Consequences of Leaving the EU. *National Institute Economic Review, 236*, 2–6.
Armstrong, H. (2015). *Local Energy in an Age of Austerity: Preserving the Value of Local and Community Energy.* London: NESTA. Available via: http://www.nesta.org.uk/sites/default/files/local_energy_in_an_age_of_austerity.pdf.
Artis, M. J., Kontolemis, Z. G., & Osborn, D. R. (1997). Business Cycles for G& and European Countries. *The Journal of Business, 70*(2), 249–279.
Aschauer, D. (1990). *Public Investment and Private Sector Growth.* Washington DC: Economic Policy Institute.
Baker, J., Carreras, O., Ebell, M., Hurst, I., Kirby, S., Meaning, J., et al. (2016a). The Short-Term Economic Impact of Leaving the EU. *National Institute Economic Review, 236*, 108–120.
Baker, S. R., Bloom, N., & Davis, S. J. (2016b). Measuring Economic Policy Uncertainty. *The Quarterly Journal of Economics, 131*(4), 1593–1636.
Baldwin, R. E. (1969). The Case Against Infant-Industry Protection. *Journal of Political Economy, 77*(3), 295–305.
Bank of England. (2019). Monetary Policy Report—November, Monetary Policy Committee, Bank of England, London. Retrieved January 7, 2020, from https://www.bankofengland.co.uk/-/media/boe/files/monetary-policy-report/2019/november/monetary-policy-report-november-2019.pdf.
Barclay, C. (2012). Food miles. House of Commons Library, No. SN/SC/4984. http://researchbriefings.parliament.uk/ResearchBriefing/Summary/SN04984.
Barnard, C. (2016). *The Substantive Law of the EU: The Four Freedoms* (5th ed.). Oxford: Oxford University Press.

Bartlett, W. (2014). *Shut out? South east Europe and the EU's new industrial policy* (LSE Europe in Question (LEQS) Discussion Paper No. 84/2014). Available via: http://www.lse.ac.uk/europeanInstitute/LEQS%20Discussion%20 Paper%20Series/LEQSPaper84.pdf.

Baumol, W. J., Blackman, S. A. B., & Wolff, E. N. (1989). *Productivity and American Leadership*, MIT Press, Cambridge, MA.

BIS [Department for Business Innovation and Skills] (2015). *State Aid: The Basics Guide*. London: BIS. Available via: https://www.gov.uk/government/ uploads/system/uploads/attachment_data/file/443686/BIS-15-417-stateaid- the-basics-guide.pdf.

Blanchard, O., Cerutti, E., & Summers, L. (2015). Inflation and Activity—Two Explorations and Their Monetary Policy Implications, *IMF Working Paper* 230, IMF, New York. Retrieved January 13, 2020, from https://www.imf. org/external/pubs/ft/wp/2015/wp15230.pdf.

Block, F. (2008). Swimming Against the Current: The Rise of a Hidden Developmental State in the United States. *Politics and Society, 36*(2), 169–206.

Bloom, N. (2009). The Impact of Uncertainty Shocks. *Econometrica, 77*(3), 623–685.

Bloom, N., Floetotto, M., Jaimovich, N., Saporta Eksten, I., & Terry, S. (2014). Really Uncertain Business Cycles, *US Census Bureau Center for Economic Studies*, No. CES-WP-14-18. Available via: https://www2.census.gov/ces/ wp/2014/CES-WP-14-18.pdf.

Bohanes, J. (2015). WTO Dispute Settlement and Industrial Policy, International Centre for Trade and Sustainable Development (ICTSD) and World Economic Forum, Geneva, Switzerland. Retrieved January 9, 2020, from http://e15ini-tiative.org/wp-content/uploads/2015/09/E15-Industrial-Policy-Bohanes-FINAL.pdf

Bosworth, B. P., & Collins, S. M. (2003). The Empirics of Growth: An Update. *Brookings Papers on Economic Activity, 34*(2), 113–179.

Bouttellet, J., Craig, P., Lewsey, J., Robinson, M., & Popham, F. (2018). Synthetic Control Methodology as a Tool for Evaluating Population-Level Health Interventions. *Journal of Epidemiol Community Health, 72*, 673–678.

Business for Britain. (2015). *Change or Go: How Britain Would Gain Influence and Prosper Outside an Unreformed EU*. London: Business for Britain. Available via.: https://forbritain.org/cogwholebook.pdf.

Chang, H.-J. (2002). *Kicking Away the Ladder: Development Strategy in Historical Perspective*. London: Anthem Press.

Chang, H.-J. (2009). Industrial Policy: Can We Go Beyond an Unproductive Confrontation? Plenary Paper for Annual World Bank Conference on Development Economics, Seoul, South Korea, 22–24 June. Available via: http://siteresources.worldbank.org/INTABCDESK2009/Resources/Ha-Joon-Chang.pdf.

Chang, H.-J. (2010). *23 Things They Don't Tell You About Capitalism*. London: Allen Lane.

Chang, H-J., Andreoni, A., & Kuan, M. L. (2013). *International Industrial Policy Experiences and the Lessons for the UK*, Future of Manufacturing Project: Evidence Paper 4, Government Office for Science, HMSO, London. Retrieved January 17, 2020, from https://www.bl.uk/britishlibrary/~/media/bl/global/business-and-management/pdfs/non-secure/i/n/t/international-industrial-policy-experiences-and-the-lessons-for-the-uk.pdf.

Chen, W., Mrkaic, M., & Nabar, M. (2019). The Global Economic Recovery—10 Years After the 2008 Financial Crisis, *IMF Working Paper* 83, IMF, New York. Retrieved January 13, 2020, from https://www.imf.org/en/Publications/WP/Issues/2019/04/26/The-Global-Economic-Recovery-10-Years-After-the-2008-Financial-Crisis-46711.

Chinitz, B. (1961). Contrasts in Agglomeration: New York and Pittsburg. *American Economic Review: Papers and Proceedings, 51,* 279–289.

Clifford Chance. (2019). *Public Procurement, Brexit and Boris Johnson's 'Buy British' Pledge*, Clifford Chance, London. Retrieved January 20, 2020, from https://www.cliffordchance.com/content/dam/cliffordchance/briefings/2019/10/public-procurement-brexit-and-boris-johnsons-buy-british-pledge.pdf.

Cohen, E. (2007). Industrial Policies in France: The Old and the New. *Journal of Industry, Competition and Trade, 7*(3–4), 213–227.

Confederation of British Industry (CBI). (2013). *Our Global Future: The Business Vision for a Reformed EU*. CBI, London. Available via: http://www.cbi.org.uk/media/2451423/our_global_future.pdf#page=1&zoom=auto,-119,842.

Conservative Party. (2017), *Forward Together: Our Plan for a Stronger Britain and a Prosperous Future—The Conservative and Unionist Party Manifesto 2017,* Conservative party, London. Retrieved January 10, 2020, from https://s3.eu-west-2.amazonaws.com/conservative-party-manifestos/Forward+Together+-+Our+Plan+for+a+Stronger+Britain+and+a+More+Prosperous....pdf.

Crafts, N. (2017). A New Industrial Strategy: Making Britain Great Again? *Political Quarterly, 88*(2), 315–319.

Crafts, N. (2018). Industrial Policy in the Context of Brexit. *Fiscal Studies, 39*(4), 685–706.

Crafts, N., & Hughes, A. (2013). Industrial Policy for the Medium to Long-Term, in Hughes, A. (Ed.), *The Future of UK Manufacturing: Scenario Analysis, Financial Markets and Industrial Policy*, UK-RIC, Cambridge and London. Retrieved January 8, 2020, from http://www.uk-irc.org/wp-content/uploads/2015/02/Future_of_Manufacturing_ebook.pdf.

Credit Suisse. (2016). *Brexit: Breaking Up is Never Easy, Or Cheap, Global Markets Research*, 25 January. Available via: https://research-doc.creditsuisse.com/

docView?language=ENG&format=PDF&document_ id=1060751681&source_id=emrna&serialid=EVlEmyReyn5h4J%2fdAJdjfrma xSOfiIkDYuLRaL%2bvH3U%3d. Accessed 2 November 2020.

Department for Education and Employment (DfEE). (1997). *Learning and Working Together for the Future*. London: Department for Education and Employment.

Dixit, A. K., & Pindyck, R. S. (1990). *Investment under Uncertainty*. Princeton: Princeton University Press.

Dolphin, T., & Nash, D. (2012). *Why We Need a British Investment Bank*, London: Institute for Public Policy Research (IPPR). Available via: http://www.ippr. org/files/images/media/files/publication/2012/09/investmentfuture-BIB_ Sep2012_9635.pdf?noredirect=1.

Driver, R. (2014). *Analysing the Case for EU Membership: How Does the Economic Evidence Stack Up?* London: The City UK. Available via: https://www.thec-ityuk.com/research/analysing-the-case-for-eu-membership-does-theeconomic-evidence-stack-up/.

Ebell, M., & Warren, J. (2016). The Long-term Economic Impact of Leaving the EU. *National Institute Economic Review, 236*, 121–138.

Eichengreen, B., & Boltho, A. (2008). *The Economic Impact of European Integration* (CEPR Discussion Paper No. 6820). London: CEPR. Available via: http://eml.berkeley.edu/~eichengr/econ_impact_euro_integ.pdf.

EC [European Commission]. (2010). *An Integrated Industrial Policy for the Globalisation Era: Putting Competitiveness and Sustainability at Centre Stage*. COM(2010) 614, Commission of the European Communities, Brussels. Available via: http://eur-lex.europa.eu/legal-content/EN/TXT/?uri=cele x:52010DC0614.

EC [European Commission]. (2016). *General Block Exemption Regulation (GBER): Frequently Asked Questions*. Brussels: Commission of the European Communities. Available via: http://ec.europa.eu/competition/state_aid/leg-islation/practical_guide_gber_en.pdf.

EC [European Commission]. (2017). *Public Procurement – European Semester Thematic Factsheet*, European Commission, Brussels. Retrieved January 20, 2020, from https://ec.europa.eu/info/sites/info/files/file_import/ european-semester_thematic-factsheet_public-procurement_en_0.pdf.

Fairbairn, C., & Newton-Smith, R. (2016). *Brexit—The Business View*. Lecture at London Business School, Monday 21st March. Available via: http://news.cbi. org.uk/business-issues/uk-and-the-european-union/eu-business-facts/ brexit-the-business-view-pdf/.

Farma, E. F. (1970). Efficient Capital Markets: A Review of Theory and Empirical Work. *Journal of Finance, 25*, 383–417.

Greenspan, A. (2003). Monetary Policy Under Uncertainty. Presented as a *Symposium Sponsored by the Federal Reserve Bank of Kansas City*. Jackson Hole,

Wyoming, 29 August. Available via: http://www.federalreserve.gov/board-docs/speeches/2003/20030829/default.htm.

Greenwald, B. C., & Stiglitz, J. E. (2012). Industrial Policies, the Creation of a Learning Society and Economic Development. In J. E. Stiglitz, J. Esteban, & J. L. Yifu (Eds.), *The Industrial Policy Revolution I: The Role of Government Beyond Ideology* (pp. 43–71). London: Palgrave.

Hidalgo, C. A., & Hausmann, R. (2009). The Building Blocks of Economic Complexity. *Proceedings of the National Academy of Sciences of the United States of America, 106*(26), 10570–10575.

HM Treasury. (2014). *Autumn Statement 2014*. Cm 8961. London: The Stationery Office. Available via: https://www.gov.uk/government/uploads/system/uploads/attachment_data/file/382327/44695_Accessible.pdf.

HM Treasury. (2016). *Autumn Statement 2016*, Cm 9362. London: The Stationery Office. Available via: https://www.gov.uk/government/uploads/system/uploads/attachment_data/file/571559/autumn_statement_2016_web.pdf.

HMG [Her Majesty's Government]. (1971). *The United Kingdom and the European Communities—White Paper, Cmnd 4715*. London: HMSO.

HMG [Her Majesty's Government]. (2016). The process for withdrawing from the European Union, Cm 9216, The Stationery Office, London. https://www.gov.uk/government/uploads/system/uploads/attachment_data/file/504216/The_process_for_withdrawing_from_the_EU_print_ready.pdf

HMG [Her Majesty's Government]. (2017a). *Industrial Strategy: Building a Britain Fit for the Future*, Cm 9528, HMSO, London. Retrieved January 9, 2020, from https://assets.publishing.service.gov.uk/government/uploads/system/uploads/attachment_data/file/730043/industrial-strategy-white-paper-print-ready-a4-version.pdf.

HMG [Her Majesty's Government]. (2017b), *Building Our Industrial Strategy—Green Paper*, HMSO, London. Retrieved January 9, 2020, from https://www.gov.uk/government/uploads/system/uploads/attachment_data/file/585273/building-our-industrial-strategy-green-paper.pdf.

HMG [Her Majesty's Government] (2019b), Political Declaration Setting Out the Future Framework for the Future relationship Between the European Union and the United Kingdom, Presented to Parliament pursuant to Section 1 of the European Union (Withdrawal) Act (No. 2) 2019 and Section 13 of the European Union (Withdrawal) Act 2018, HMSO, London. Available via: https://assets.publishing.service.gov.uk/government/uploads/system/uploads/attachment_data/file/840656/Political_Declaration_setting_out_the_framework_for_the_future_relationship_between_the_European_Union_and_the_United_Kingdom.pdf

HOL [House of Lords]. (2018), *Brexit: Competition and State Aid*, House of Lords European Union Committee 12th Report of Session 2017-19, HL 67,

HMSO, London. Retrieved January 9, 2020, from https://publications.parliament.uk/pa/ld201719/ldselect/ldeucom/67/67.pdf.

Hughes, A. (2012), 'Choosing Races and Placing Bets: UK National Innovation Policy and the Globalisation of Innovation Systems', in Greenaway, D. (Ed.), *The UK in a Global World: How Can the UK Focus on Steps in Global Value Chains That Really Add Value?*, CEPR, London, 37-70. Retrieved January 10, 2020, from https://voxeu.org/sites/default/files/file/UK_in_a_global_world.pdf.

IMF [International Monetary Fund]. (2019). *World Economic Outlook: Global Manufacturing Downturn, Rising Trade Barriers*, IMF, Washington DC. Retrieved January 13, 2020, from https://www.imf.org/en/Publications/WEO/Issues/2019/10/01/world-economic-outlook-october-2019.

Industrial Strategy Commission. (2017). *Laying the Foundations*, Industrial Strategy Commission, London. Retrieved January 9, 2020, from http://industrialstrategycommission.org.uk/wp-content/uploads/2017/07/Laying-the-Foundations-the-Industrial-Strategy-Commission.pdf?mc_cid=d198df0f93&mc_eid=65e35d7be8.

Intellectual Property Office (IPO). (2015). *Graphene: The Worldwide Patent Landscape in 2015*. Newport: Intellectual property Office. Available via: https://www.gov.uk/government/uploads/system/uploads/attachment_data/file/470918/Graphene_-_the_worldwide_patent_landscape_in_2015.pdf.

Irwin, G. (2015). *Brexit: The impact on the UK and the EU*. London: Global Counsel. Available via: http://www.global-counsel.co.uk/system/files/publications/Global_Counsel_Impact_of_Brexit_June_2015.pdf.

Jäntti, M., & Vartiainen, J. (2009). 'The Finnish Developmental State and its Growth Regime', *World Institute for Development Economics Research Paper* No. 2009/35, UNU World Institute for Development Economics Research (UNU-WIDER), Helsinki. Retrieved January 16, 2020, from https://www.wider.unu.edu/sites/default/files/RP2009-35.pdf.

Jones, A. (2016). The Return of Industrial Policy. *Local Economy, 31*(8), 827–829.

Jozepa, I. (2018). House of Commons Library Briefing Paper 06775, Retrieved January 9, 2020, from https://researchbriefings.parliament.uk/ResearchBriefing/Summary/SN06775.

Kalecki, M. (1971). *Selected Essays on the Dynamics of the Capitalist Economy 1933–1970*. Cambridge: Cambridge University Press.

Kay, J. A. (2012). *The Kay Review of UK Equity Markets and Long-term Decision-Making*, HMSO, London. Retrieved January 10, 2020, from https://assets.publishing.service.gov.uk/government/uploads/system/uploads/attachment_data/file/253454/bis-12-917-kay-review-of-equity-markets-final-report.pdf.

Kennedy, T. P. (Ed.). (2011). *European Law* (Vol. 5). Oxford: Oxford University Press.

Keynes, J. M. (1936). *The General Theory of Employment, Interest and Money.* London: Macmillan. 1973 edition.

Kroes, N. (2006). Industrial Policy and Competition Law and Policy. *Speech given at Fordham University School of Law, New York City,* 14th September 2006. Available via: http://europa.eu/rapid/press-release_SPEECH-06-499_en.htm?locale=en.

Krueger, A. O., & Tuncer, B. (1982). An Empirical Test of the Infant Industry Argument. *American Economic Review, 72*(5), 1142–1152.

Labour Party. (2019), Its Time for Real Change—The Labour Party Manifesto 2019, Labour Party, London. Retrieved January 10, 2020, from https://labour.org.uk/wp-content/uploads/2019/11/Real-Change-Labour-Manifesto-2019.pdf.

Laeven, L., & Valencia, F. (2018). *Systematic Banking Crises Revisited, IMF Working Paper 206.* New York: IMF. Retrieved January 13, 2020, from https://www.imf.org/en/Publications/WP/Issues/2018/09/14/Systemic-Banking-Crises-Revisited-46232.

Lall, S. (2001). *Competitiveness, Technology and Skills.* Cheltenham: Edward Elgar.

Laranja, M., Uyarra, E., & Flanagan, K. (2008). Policies for Science, Technology and Innovation: Translating rationales into regional policies in a multi-level setting. *Research Policy, 37*(5), 823–835.

Layard, R., Nickell, S., & Jackman, R. (Eds.). (1991). *Unemployment: Macroeconomic Performance and the Labour Market.* Oxford: Oxford University Press.

Leahy, J., & Whited, T. M. (1996). The Effects of Uncertainty on Investment: Some Stylized Facts. *Journal of Money, Credit, and Banking, 28*(1), 64–83.

Lee, J.-W. (1996). Government Interventions and Economic Growth. *Journal of Economic Growth, 1*(3), 391–414.

Lin, J. Y., & Monga, C. (2010). *Growth Identification and Facilitation: The Role of the State in the Dynamics of Structural Change* (The World Bank Policy Research Working Paper No. 5313). Available via: http://documents.worldbank.org/curated/en/438321468164948980/pdf/WPS5313.pdf.

Manley, J., & Whyman, P. B. (2020). *The Preston Model and Community Wealth Building.* London: Routledge.

Mazzucato, M. (2013). *The Entrepreneurial State: Debunking Public v's Private Sector Myths.* London: Anthem Press. 2015 edition.

Mazzucato, M., & Penna, C. C. R. (2014). Beyond Market Failures: The Market Creating and Shaping Roles of State Investment Banks. *Science Policy Research Unit* (Working Paper No. SWPS 2014–21), University of Sussex. Available via: https://www.sussex.ac.uk/webteam/gateway/file.php?name=2014-21-swps-mazzucato-and-penna.pdf&site=25.

McFadden, P., & Tarrant, A. (2015). *What Would 'Out' Look Like? Testing Eurosceptic Alternatives to EU Membership.* London: Policy Network. Available via: http://www.policy-network.net/publications/4995/What-would-outlook-like.

OBR [Office for Budgetary Responsibility]. (2019). *Economic and Fiscal Outlook— March 2019,* CP 50, HMSO, London. Retrieved January 13, 2020, from https://obr.uk/forecasts-in-depth/the-economy-forecast/real-gdp-growth/.

OECD. (2014). *Focus on Inequality and Growth.* Paris: OECD. Available via: https://www.oecd.org/social/Focus-Inequality-and-Growth-2014.pdf.

OECD. (2016). *The Economic Consequences of Brexit: A Taxing Decision* (OECD Economic Policy Paper, No. 16). Available via: http://www.oecd.org/eco/The-Economic-consequences-of-Brexit-27-april-2016.pdf.

OECD [Organisation for Economic Co-operation and Development]. (2019). Science, Technology and Patents Dataset. Available online via https://stats.oecd.org/Index.aspx?DatasetCode=SNA_TABLE1.

ONS [Office for National Statistics]. (2020) Gross Domestic Product Year on Year Growth, Chain Volume Measure Release date: 11 February 2020. Available online via: https://www.ons.gov.uk/economy/grossdomesticproductgdp/timeseries/ihyp/pn2.

Pellegrin, J., Giorgetti, M. L., Jensen, C., & Bolognini, A. (2015). *EU Industrial Policy: Assessment of Recent Developments and Recommendations for Future Policies.* Director General for Internal Policies—European Parliament, Brussels, PE 536.320. Available via: http://www.europarl.europa.eu/RegData/etudes/STUD/2015/536320/IPOL_STU%282015%29536320_EN.pdf.

Perraton, J. (2014). Economic Growth in Open Economies: Balance of Payments Constrained Growth—and Beyond? *University of Sheffield Department of Economics* (Working Paper, No. JP300514). Available via: https://www.post-keynesian.net/downloads/soas14/JP300514.pdf.

Pilbeam, K. (2016). *How Brexit Fears Are Shaking the Currency Markets.* The Conversation, London. Available via: http://theconversation.com/howbrexit-fears-are-shaking-the-currency-markets-61057.

Pindyck, R. S. (1988). Irreversible Investment, Capacity Choice, and the Value of the Firm. *The American Economic Review, 78*(5), 969–985.

Porter, M. (1998). Clusters and the New Economics of Competition. *Harvard Business Review, November–December, 76*(6), 77–90.

PricewaterhouseCoopers LLP (PwC). (2016). *Leaving the EU: Implications for the UK economy.* London: PricewaterhouseCoopers LLP. Available via: http://news.cbi.org.uk/news/leaving-eu-would-cause-a-serious-shock-to-ukeconomy-new-pwc-analysis/leaving-the-eu-implications-for-the-uk-economy/.

Punhani, S., & Hill, N. [Credit Suisse Report]. (2016). *Brexit: Breaking Up Is Never Easy, or Cheap.* Zurich: Credit Suisse. Available via: https://doc.research-and-analytics.csfb.com/docView?language=ENG&format=PDF&do

cument_id=806936650&source_id=emrna&serialid=lPu6YfMSDd9toXKa9E
Pxf5HiNBEoWX2fYou5bZ6jJhA%3D.

Reynolds, B., & Webber, J. (2019). The Withdrawal Agreement, State Aid and UK Industry: How to Protect UK Competitiveness, Politeia, London. Retrieved January 9, 2020, from http://www.politeia.co.uk/wp-content/ Politeia%20Documents/2019/05.02.19%20Reynolds%20&%20Webber/ The%20Withdrawal%20Agreement,%20State%20Aid%20&%20UK%20 Industry%20by%20Barnabas%20Reynolds%20&%20James%20Webber.pdf.

Rodrik, D. (2004). *Industrial Policy for the Twenty-First Century.* Available via: https://myweb.rollins.edu/tlairson/pek/rodrikindpolicy.pdf.

Rodrik, D. (2006). Goodbye Washington consensus, hello Washington confusion? *Journal of Economic Literature, 44*(4), 973–987.

Rodrik, D. (2008). Industrial policy: Don't ask why, ask how. *Middle East Development Journal,* (Demo Issue), 1–29. Available via: https://www.sss.ias. edu/files/pdfs/Rodrik/Research/Industrial-Policy-Dont-Ask-Why- Ask-How.pdf.

Rosenstein-Rodan, P. N. (1943). Problems of Industrialisation of Eastern and South-Eastern Europe. *Economic Journal, 53*(210/211), 202–211.

Rowthorn, R. E. (1995). Capital Formation and Unemployment. *Oxford Review of Economic Policy, 11*(1), 26–39.

Rowthorn, R. E. (1999). Unemployment, Wage Bargaining and Capital-labour Substitution. *Cambridge Journal of Economics, 23*(3), 413–425.

Rubini, L. (2004). The International Context of EC State Aid Law and Policy: The Regulation of Subsidies in the WTO. In A. Biondi, P. Eeckhout, & J. Flynn (Eds.), *The Law of State Aid in the European Union* (pp. 149–188). Oxford: Oxford University Press.

Springford, J. (2019). The Cost of Brexit to June 2019, Centre for European Reform, London. Retrieved January 14, 2020, from https://www.cer.eu/ insights/cost-brexit-june-2019.

UKCE [UK in a Changing Europe]. (2018). *What Would 'Trading on WTO Terms' Mean for the UK?,* UK in a Changing Europe, London. Retrieved January 22, 2020, from https://ukandeu.ac.uk/wp-content/ uploads/2018/12/What-would-trading-on-WTO-terms-mean- Long-Guide.pdf.

Uvalik, M. (2014). *The Role of the State in Economic Growth: Industrial Policy in Europe.* Columbia: Centre on Global Economic Governance. Available via: http://cgeg.sipa.columbia.edu/sites/default/files/cgeg/Paris%20Brief%20 -%20Milica%20Uvalic%20-%20Industrial%20Policy%20in%20 Europe_1.pdf.

Weldon, D. (2019). The British Model and the Brexit Shock: Plus ça change?. *Political Quarterly, 90*(S2), 12–20.

Whyman, P. B. (2006). *'Third Way' Economics.* London: Palgrave.

Whyman, P. B. (2018). *The Left Case for Brexit: Active Government for an Independent UK.* London: CIVITAS.

World Bank. (2020). *Gross Capital Formation Report.* Available via: http://databank.worldbank.org/data/reports.aspx?source=2&series=NE.GDI.TOTL.

Wren-Lewis, S. (2019). Macroeconomic Policy Beyond Brexit, in Kelly, G. and Pearce, N. (Eds.), Britain Beyond Brexit, *Political Quarterly*, 90(S2): 44–52.

CHAPTER 9

Alternative Trading Models After Brexit

The economic impact arising from Brexit will depend, in large part, upon the successful formation of new trading relationships with both the EU and the rest of the world. Whilst the Article 50 process has been completed, and the UK formally withdrawn from the EU, the future relationship has yet to be determined. The political declaration, contained in the withdrawal agreement, indicates the preferred direction of travel. However, until an agreement has been agreed and ratified by all parties, a wide range of potential Brexit options remain viable alternatives. Each of these has its own relative merits and drawbacks. Furthermore, each option will have a significant effect upon the ability of the UK to negotiate trade agreements with other nations and trading blocks and, moreover, will either facilitate or constrain policy solutions to many domestic economic challenges. This chapter, therefore, will seek to outline the range of alternative trading models that could be utilised, together with their likely consequences for the UK economy.

Alternative Trade Arrangements

There have been various alternative trading models which have been advanced in the literature as the basis for UK-EU future economic relations. These include:

© The Author(s) 2020   325
P. B. Whyman, A. I. Petrescu, *The Economics of Brexit*,
https://doi.org/10.1007/978-3-030-55948-9_9

1. Membership of the European Economic Area (the Norway model) or, alternatively, a variant of the EEA designated by advocates as 'SIM-lite'
2. Customs union with the EU (the Turkey model)
3. Norway-plus or customs union II
4. Bilateral agreements with the EU (the Swiss model)
5. Concluding an FTA with the EU (the Canadian or South Korean model)
6. Reliance upon World Trade Organization (WTO) rules for trade with the EU (the WTO or Greenland model)
7. Unilateral free trade (the Hong Kong model)

In addition, a number of alternative trade arrangements have been suggested for an independent UK to pursue, including:

1. European Free Trade Association (EFTA)
2. The Commonwealth
3. The Anglosphere
4. Joining the North American Free Trade Agreement (NAFTA)
5. Reviving the proposed Trans-Pacific Partnership (TPP) or joining the Comprehensive and Progressive Agreement for Trans-Pacific Partnership (CPTPP)

When examining the various options for the UK's future trade relationships, it is important to be clear about the terminology. The 'single market', or more accurately the single internal market (SIM), is more than an internal free trade agreement, where tariff-free trade has been agreed for goods and a limited range of services. It is also more than a customs union, which is what the UK joined in 1973 and involves an FTA being extended by the imposition of a common external tariff, levied on non-members; it may, as in the case of the EU, additionally involve a common external trade policy. Instead, the EU SIM extends trade integration, by adopting harmonisation of trade regulations and guaranteeing the freedom of movement of goods, services, capital and people. These 'four freedoms' form an integral part of the SIM and it would be difficult to negotiate a withdrawal agreement which sought to retain full access to the SIM without acceptance of this core element of the arrangement. Thus, when commentators discuss the option of the UK remaining within the SIM without the need for free movement of labour and possibly also free of EU trade regulation, it is difficult to conceive how this would work. It is certainly possible to negotiate a new trade arrangement with the EU which delivers various degrees of free trade in some if not all sectors, and which does not involve the free movement of labour and/or capital, but this does not constitute full access to the SIM.

When considering options for future trading arrangements between the UK and the EU, it is important to recognise the trade-offs involved. None of the various alternatives is cost free. None provides a 'free lunch'. All possess potential advantages and disadvantages. Therefore, it is the choice that the negotiating parties make that will determine the type of Brexit impact that will be experienced by the UK and EU member states, and consequently, it will go some way to determine the degree to which Brexit will deliver modest or substantial future economic development opportunities.

The myriad possible options for future trading arrangements with the EU can be a little confusing as they all contain slightly different variants of a standard set of features which, when combined, create a distinctive economic relationship. However, there is an economic theorem which can be used to conceptualise the Brexit options available to voters during the referendum, and moreover the choices facing policy makers in determining which set of economic arrangements the newly independent UK should follow.

Rodrik's "inescapable trilemma of the world economy" asserts that it is impossible to achieve deep economic integration (hyper-globalisation), national sovereignty and democracy (mass politics) simultaneously (Rodrik 2012; 2000: 180-3) (see Fig. 9.1). Thus, voters and policy makers have to prioritise either: (i) pooling sovereignty and pursuing a form of global federation through continued membership of the EU, even though this limits national sovereignty or self-determination; or (ii) accepting the constraints of the 'golden straightjacket' on democracy (Friedman, 1999: 87) by using sovereignty to pursue global integration to the exclusion of other domestic goals, such as occurred during the Gold Standard or perhaps New Labour's "determined passivity"[1] with respect to globalisation; or alternatively (iii) sacrificing a measure of economic integration in the interests of sovereignty and democracy, such as occurred during the period of the Bretton Woods international monetary system, where limited trade liberalisation was combined with financial regulation and capital controls.

---

[1] https://www.ft.com/content/63246e18-72b4-11e7-aca6-c6bd07df1a3c

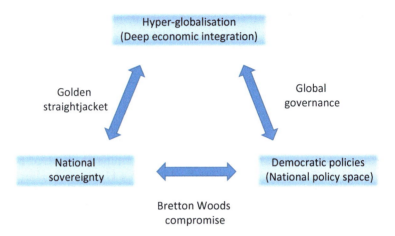

Fig. 9.1 Rodrik international political economy trilemma. Source: Authors' development of ideas, based on Rodrik (2000: 18) and Palley (2017)

Note to editors: if needing to have the figure above as a stand-alone image, then please use the version below:

For Rodrik (2000:182-3), "the essential point is this: once the rules of the game are set by the requirements of the global economy, the ability of mobilized popular groups to access and influence national economic policy-making has to be restricted". Other theorists prefer to discuss this trade-off in terms of the degree of national policy space which is compatible with different degrees of globalisation or economic integration (Palley 2017: 8). Policy options can be constrained through formal international trade agreements or membership of a supra-national body such as the EU, or through concerns that pursuing certain policies might render the country less competitive (Palley 2017: 16). Indeed, Keynes (1933) himself made a similar argument, when he debated the merits of greater national self-sufficiency and the control of capital to create a sufficient economic policy space to promote national self-determination and full employment.

Viewed in this light, the referendum decision to 'take back control' can be understood as one solution to the trilemma trade-off, whilst the vociferous debate that has occurred both within and between political parties, during the past three years, can be perceived as the struggle between alternative competing trilemma outcomes.

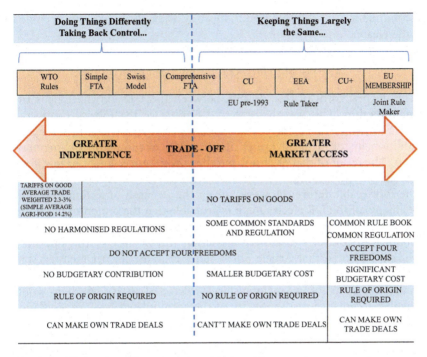

Fig. 9.2   The trade-off between greater independence and greater market access. Source: The Authors

Consideration of the trade-offs involved in the choice of the UK's favoured form of post-Brexit trade relationship with the EU, and as a result the global economy, can be further illustrated in Fig. 9.2. Given the fact that the UK's withdrawal from the EU, completed on 31 January 2020, precludes (at least in the short run) the option of pursuing regional (European) governance, the choice remaining to UK policy makers concerns acceptance of rule-taking as a result of EU demands for regulatory harmonisation (the 'golden straightjacket') or putting aside certain aspects of deeper economic integration in order to create greater policy space at national level. In essence, this choice is between 'keeping things largely the same' between the EU and the UK, by prioritising the maintenance of greater market access, or 'doing things differently' by establishing a different model of economic development through creatively utilising the greater flexibility and policy space that derives from a more independent economic relationship. Viewed in this way, the policy trade-offs become a little clearer.

Access Prioritised over Independence

The deepest form of relationship, between the UK and the EU, is **full membership**. This was the preferred option for the Liberal Democrats and Scottish National Party, in the December 2019 General Election, and additionally for many advocates of a second referendum on EU membership. The result of that election, and the current government having completed the UK's formal withdrawal from the EU, curtails this option for the foreseeable future. However, given the strength of feeling in certain segments of the UK electorate, it is probable that the option of re-joining the EU, at some future point in time, will remain a feature of the UK's political discourse. For those considering the viability of this option, it should be noted that Article 50(5) states that any former member state would have to re-apply as if it were a new applicant, with no concessions made due to its former membership (Miller et al. 2016: 26). This would involve acceptance of the totality of the accumulated body of legislation and court decisions (*acquis communautaire*) which would apply at the time of re-joining. There would neither be an opt-out from the UK having to join the single currency nor a rebate on the UK budget contributions. Moreover, it is likely that, after a difficult Brexit process, the UK would benefit from less goodwill than previously existed, which would have probable repercussions upon stipulations contained in any accession agreement. This could make re-joining the EU a less attractive proposition than if the UK had remained a member on its original terms.

Outside of full membership, the **European Economic Area (EEA)** would secure greater access to the EU's SIM but would require compliance with EU standards and regulations and the acceptance of the free movement of trade, capital and people (the 'four freedoms'). The EFTA countries (Iceland, Liechtenstein and Norway) which formed the EEA with the EU in 1992, are additionally automatically part of the Schengen border-free travel area, which the UK, as full EU member, has refrained from joining and this would therefore represent an *extension* to the free movement of people than the UK has to date accepted. Acceptance of the 'four freedoms' might additionally prove problematic for certain sections of the electorate. This has not been the case for Norway, for example, who have welcomed the reduction in skill shortages (NOU 2012a, 2012c).

However, it is worth noting that, as an EEA member, Norway has actually accepted more than twice the number of EU migrants per head of population than the UK as a full member of the EU (Booth et al. 2015:53-4). The EEA agreement does not involve participation in the Common Agricultural Policy (CAP) or the Common Fisheries Policy (CFP),[2] and nor does it include common foreign and security policy. Since it does not involve participating in the EU's customs union, EEA nations can operate their own external trade policy, subject to rules of origin regulations for exports into the EU (HoC 2013: 74).

The disadvantages of this option relate primarily to the loss of self-determination that the EEA agreement represents, which would be difficult to reconcile with the referendum result indicating a preference for the UK to take back control over wider aspects of its policy making. It would require the adoption of around two-thirds of the EU's *acquis communautaire*, thus narrowing the freedom of movement that the UK would gain from withdrawal from the EU (Miller et al. 2016: 40). It would involve the acceptance of EU rules and regulations pertaining to competition, goods standards, consumer and environmental protection (NOU 2012c), which may minimise whatever loss of trade opportunities might arise with EU member states due to the UK's withdrawal (CEPR 2013: 43), but at the cost of adversely affecting the probability of negotiating independent trade deals with other nations. Whilst EEA members can participate in preparatory work relating to those laws and regulations pertaining to the SIM, and have a theoretical right of veto over unfavourable new regulations, in practice this has never been exercised because it would prevent all EFTA nations from continuing to trade freely in the SIM (Singham et al. 2017: 27-8). EEA members are, therefore, 'rule takers' and this option has been criticised as offering "integration without representation" (Sejersted and Sverdrup 2012). Furthermore, EEA membership would necessitate the continuation of UK financial contributions as a *quid pro quo* for access to the SIM and/or in contribution towards the less developed EU member states. Norway currently contributes a gross figure of around 0.76% of its GDP to the EU,[3] or around 0.38% (net) (NOU

---

[2] Supplemental to the EEA agreement, Iceland has negotiated tariff-free access to EU markets for its fishery exports by allowing limited access for EU fishing vessels in Icelandic territorial waters.

[3] http://www.ssb.no/en/nasjonalregnskap-og-konjunkturer/statistikker/knr/kvarta l/2016-05-12?fane=tabell&sort=nummer&tabell=265699

2012a:784; CBI 2013: 142). Since Norway has a higher GDP per capita, an equivalent figure for the UK might be in the region of 0.22% or £4.4bn per annum. Nevertheless, this still represents a significant reduction in anticipated fiscal savings following Brexit (see Chap. 2).

Trading with the EU through the EEA requires the use of 'rule of origin' regulations to prevent tariff-jumping. This is where exporters in a third country seek to evade higher tariffs by exporting first to whichever member of the FTA has the lowest tariffs and, once their products are circulating within that country, re-exporting them (tariff free) to other parties to the agreement, thereby evading the higher part of prevailing national tariffs. Rule of origin regulations place lower limits on the proportion of a good which is to be deemed as originating in the country party to the EEA, and therefore solves the problem, albeit at an additional regulatory (administrative) cost for the exporting firms (Dinnie 2004; Fawcett 2015). Overall, therefore, it is perhaps worth noting that, for Norway, the EEA represents a political compromise and is, as such, a second best solution, given that it limits the policy independence of the state (NOU, 2012b).

There is one final consideration for those advocating the EEA option. EFTA membership is a prerequisite for EEA participation and, as such, has to be ratified by all EU member states in addition to these three EFTA members (Miller et al. 2016:39-40; Piris 2016: 7). Consequently, it is entirely plausible that any attempt made by the UK to join the EEA may be frustrated by a veto, of either an EU member state or, indeed, an EFTA nation which prefers to preserve the current composition of the organisation and does not want the UK to re-join EFTA.

The formation of a **customs union** between the EU and the UK, such as that adopted in 1996 between the EU and Turkey, would represent another Brexit option. This would include free trade in goods but not agriculture, services or procurement. This was the approach favoured by the Labour Party at various points during the last parliament. In many respects, it would revert the trade relationship between the UK and the EU to how it was between 1973 and the advent of the SIM in 1992. The customs union would involve the adoption of the EU's common external tariff and commercial policy which would, in turn, enable tariff-free trade in goods (services are not typically included) (HoC 2013: 74; Miller et al. 2016: 37). Rule of origin designation would not be required as the common tariff would prevent tariff-jumping (CEPR 2013: 40-1). It is the adoption of the common external tariff being imposed on all imports from countries not party to the customs union, and the adoption of a common trade policy whereby the EU continues to have sole control over the negotiation of trade agreements with third parties, which distinguishes a customs union from an FTA.

The customs union approach would not require the free movement of labour. However, Turkey was required to accept all aspects of the EU's *acquis communautaire* as part of the arrangement. Thus, whilst some aspects of social, employment, energy and environment policy might be less harmonised than required by full EU membership, there is likely to be a requirement to adopt trade-related regulations determined in Brussels. Customs unions do not typically include agricultural and fisheries support, nor is it likely to impose constraints imposed upon public procurement, although EU negotiators may seek to depart from precedence on this point. Furthermore, Turkey has set a precedent since it participates in EU schemes such as Erasmus and is a net recipient of EU regional and transport funding.[4] Thus, should the UK wish to continue participation in such programmes, there should be no impediment to its so doing.

There are a number of disadvantages with the customs union option. The first relates to its sole focus upon goods and not services, while it is in the latter that the UK has a particular comparative advantage (Ottaviano et al. 2014). This weakness is somewhat alleviated since the SIM has never properly operated where services are concerned and hence the UK will probably not be too badly affected by losing a theoretical advantage which has never been fully realised in any case (Capital Economics 2016:14). Nevertheless, customs unions may be less effective in reducing non-tariff barriers (NTBs) such as health and technical standards, together with those administrative regulations which impose a delay or other costs upon trade, thereby reducing the volume traded (CBI 2013: 16). It is difficult to quantify the magnitude of NTBs (as noted in Chap. 3), although it is generally accepted that they impose a trade cost perhaps twice that of formal tariff barriers, albeit that the combination of multilateral and preferential trade agreements mean that their significance is being steadily reduced over time (De Sousa et al. 2012; UNCTAD 2013: 1, 14-15).

Membership of a customs union would, moreover, require the maintenance of the EU's common external tariff and the UK could not operate its own independent trade policy and it could not strike its own trade deals with other countries (CEPR 2013: 41). One issue which has arisen for

[4] http://ec.europa.eu/enlargement/pdf/turkey/20160122-turkey-factograph.pdf

Turkey, in relation to EU negotiated trade agreements with third party countries, is that they are asymmetric since Turkey has to allow their goods to enter its market but there is no automatic reciprocal arrangement for Turkish goods. In the case of South Africa and Algeria, subsequent attempts made by Turkey to negotiate reciprocal arrangements were refused.[5] Thus, Turkey has been left in an invidious position of having to grant free access to its own markets but not receiving the same in return. This would hardly represent a sustainable position for the UK.

The UK would be expected to make a financial contribution to EU programmes, although the expectation is that this would be more modest than the EEA option. It is probable that the UK would be expected to accept EU rules pertaining to competition and company takeovers and preclude certain forms of industrial policy, which would, in turn, limit its policy flexibility as an independent nation (Reynolds and Webber, 2019:5).

It is interesting to note that the CBI (2013:12, 148) has expressed its concern that the 'Turkey model' would be "the worst of the 'half-way' alternatives, leaving the UK with very limited EU market access and zero influence over trade deals". This strong expression of dissatisfaction is a little odd given the CBI's strong support for the UK's accession to the 'Common Market' in the 1970s, since this was, of course, a customs union. Yet, it is perhaps instructive that, when considering the best alternative model for the UK to pursue in its future trade relationship with the EU after Brexit, the CBI considers customs unions to be inferior to all other options.

The **common market 2.0** or **Norwegian-plus** option provides a hybrid of EEA and customs union approaches. It would combine acceptance of regulatory harmonisation and the 'four freedoms', as per the EEA, but it would also involve acceptance of customs union features, such as the EU common external tariff and its continued monopoly on negotiating future trade deals. In doing so, it would provide a resolution to the Northern Ireland 'backstop' problem[6] through locking the UK close to the EU, thereby securing more frictionless trade. As such, this is a defensive option, focused upon minimising anticipated economic costs arising from Brexit. Like the EEA, it would lead to the UK being a 'rule taker'

[5] http://data.parliament.uk/writtenevidence/committeeevidence.svc/evidencedocument/eu-external-affairs-subcommittee/brexit-customs-arrangements/written/85217.pdf
[6] https://ukandeu.ac.uk/norway-or-common-market-2-0-the-problems-are-not-where-they-seem-to-be/. The backstop is discussed, in more detail, later in this chapter.

and having little influence over the development of the regulations under which its industries operate, whilst, like the customs union approach, it would prevent the UK from negotiating its own future trade deals. Accordingly, this option has been described as a "Hotel California Brexit", where the UK technically withdraws from the EU but continues to follow its rules as if it were still a member.[7] This does not appear to be an optimum choice. Nevertheless, it does represent a potential solution for the political elite who would prefer to remain an EU member or at least remain as close to this position as possible and yet keep faith with an electorate who do not share this opinion.

TRADE-OFF ACCESS FOR INDEPENDENCE AND FLEXIBILITY

The prioritisation of greater policy flexibility and a greater degree of self-determination requires the selection of a looser form of future economic relationship between the UK and the EU. One option would be to seek to negotiate a series of **bilateral agreements** with the EU, covering as many aspects of trade and economic cooperation as is practicable. Switzerland adopted this approach and has successfully negotiated 20 major, and more than 100 lesser, bilateral agreements. The bilateral treaties provide tariff-free trade in goods but are rather more limited in terms of services. Thus, for example, cross-border services are restricted to a maximum of 90 days in a calendar year (Booth et al. 2015:58), whilst financial services (except insurance) are not covered by 'EU passport' arrangements, necessitating Swiss banks to establish subsidiaries within EU member states if they wish to operate freely within that market (Keep 2015:12; Miller et al. 2016:40-1).

The advantages of this approach are that only those areas where mutual agreement can be forged are included in the series of treaty's (CBI 2013: 16). Hence, participation in EU agricultural, energy, foreign, social and employment policies is excluded (Booth et al. 2015: 57). Moreover, Switzerland does not have to accept the importation of legislation and regulations designed in the EU (the *acquis communautaire*), but only has to commit to *equivalent* legislation. Given criticisms of the regulatory burden imposed on UK companies who do not trade with the EU, this might be viewed as a distinct advantage. Furthermore, the 'Swiss model' does

---

[7] https://www.theguardian.com/commentisfree/2019/apr/01/customs-union-brexit-conundrum-no-deal-eu-peter-mandelson

not involve any transfer of decision-making to a supra-national authority set up for the purpose of facilitating the trade agreement(s), and it is entitled to negotiate other trade deals with third parties and does not have to impose the EU's common external tariff (CEPR 2013: 45). The bilateral agreements enable cooperation in research and access to public procurement opportunities, although the latter is secured through acceptance of EU rules constraining the use of strategic procurement measures, as were discussed in Chap. 8.

Disadvantages of the bilateral treaty approach include the lack of flexibility that Switzerland has encountered when seeking to extend basic trade in goods into areas where it has a comparative advantage (Booth et al. 2015: 46). Switzerland is also committed to make a financial contribution to EU social and regional programmes in addition to those areas in which the bilateral agreements permit Swiss participation (Miller et al. 2016: 43). If the UK adopted the Swiss model under the same conditions, given the fact that Swiss GDP per capita is approximately 1.5 times the UK rate, UK contributions to the EU might be expected to fall to around £2.1 billion (Thompson and Harari 2013: 26-7).

A more problematic aspect, for Switzerland, concerns the fact that the bilateral agreements stipulate its acceptance of the free movement of labour from the EU (CBI 2013: 145). Given its high GDP per capita and its geographical location towards the centre of the EU landmass, Switzerland has accepted a greater proportion of EU migrants per head of population than the UK. Thus, in 2013, fully 15.6% of the Swiss population had been born in an EU country, whereas the equivalent figure for the UK was 4.2% (Booth et al. 2015: 59-60). A referendum decision for Switzerland to introduce quotas on EU migrants would have breached the free movement of labour clause and the EU threatened to suspend the relevant trade deals until Switzerland set aside the referendum decision and introduced only minor local job preferences.[8] The dissatisfaction with this solution, alongside concerns raised by the EU relating to the Swiss not having to automatically adopt new regulations pertaining to areas covered by the bilateral agreements, raises questions as to the long-term sustainability of this Brexit option (HoC 2013: 76-7). As a result, it may be difficult to persuade the EU to concede a similar approach to the UK (Booth et al. 2015: 73; Miller et al. 2016: 41).

---

[8] https://www.theguardian.com/world/2016/sep/22/switzerland-votes-for-compromise-to-preserve-relations-with-eu

A more straightforward option would be for the UK to negotiate a **free trade agreement (FTA)** with the EU. FTAs are the most common form of preferential trade agreements (PTAs) in operation across the globe (CEPR 2013: 16). Prominent examples of countries which have an FTA with the EU include South Africa, Mexico, South Korea and Canada (CETA). Given the enthusiasm with which the EU has begun embarking upon negotiating FTAs with individual countries and groups of nations, it would be slightly surprising if the EU were not interested in doing the same with the UK—a former member state and a large market for EU goods and services (Springford and Tilford 2014: 9).

If successfully negotiated, an FTA would have a number of advantages over the EEA since it is more narrowly focused upon the facilitation of international trade without having to accept additional elements of political and social integration (Milne 2004: 1). Similarly, an FTA has the advantage over a customs union that the UK would be free to determine the level of any tariffs it decided to levy and negotiate preferential trade agreements with other nations. However, FTAs do necessitate the introduction of 'rules of origin' regulations to prevent tariff-jumping, which would impose additional administrative costs upon exporters alongside verification procedural costs on importers, which might prove disruptive for those exporters who are part of time sensitive supply chains (CEPR 2013: 36; Miller 2016: 21). Economic studies have identified costs associated with 'rules of origin' regulation of between 1% and 8% of the value of traded goods, albeit with most results lying within the lower part of this range (Herin, 1986; USITC 1996; Cadot et al. 2006; Manchin 2006; Brenton 2010; Abreu 2013: 19). Set against this cost, country of origin marking can deliver some economic benefits to exporters, if consumers use it as a proxy for the quality of goods and services (Hui and Zhou 2002). Moreover, it could facilitate a 'buy British' campaign, of the type currently forbidden by EU rules but which would be available to policymakers post-Brexit. The evidence is that these campaigns, if designed correctly, can have a positive economic impact, both for UK exporters but also for domestic producers reducing import penetration (Chisik 2003; Dinnie 2008).

An FTA is also unlikely to involve any budgetary contribution to the EU, of the type required from other types of preferential trade deal (Emmerson et al. 2016: 15-16). Certainly, CETA involves no budgetary contributions in return for market access.[9] It is also possible for FTAs to be expanded to include provisions on areas which usually lie outside of a standard trade agreement, such as the mobility of staff, FDI and other capital movements, intellectual property and so forth (CEPR 2013: 36-39). Whether the UK, having just decided to withdraw from a more comprehensive set of arrangements bundled together within EU membership, desires to move beyond a standard FTA is, however, another question.

The average time for negotiating an FTA is 28 months. The average for the USA is only 18 months, albeit that implementation tends to take a similar additional period.[10] These figures disguise the fact that certain trade deals can be achieved considerably quicker. For example, the FTA negotiated between Jordan and the USA was signed in only 4 months and implemented in 18, whilst an FTA with Australia was signed in 14 months and implemented in less than 2 years. Since the transition arrangement with the EU terminates at the end of 2020, and current UK government policy is not to request an extension beyond that point, this gives negotiators nine months to conclude an FTA with the EU, otherwise trading will revert to WTO rules. This is a short time period and made more difficult by the impact of the COVID-19 virus distracting from future trade negotiations, nevertheless, given the starting position of common standards and regulatory harmonisation, it would be likely that an agreement between the UK and the EU could be concluded more rapidly, *if all parties wished this to be the case* (Singham et al. 2017: 16).

It is not, however, necessarily the ability to negotiate an FTA with the EU that might concern the negotiators, but rather whether the terms that can be negotiated would prove sufficiently favourable to EU and UK economies. Accordingly, there are a number of issues which negotiators should consider.

The first issue that will determine the sustainability of the FTA relates to the breadth of its coverage. It would most likely secure tariff-free trade in goods but not necessarily services. Given the UK's particular competitive advantage in financial, educational and business services, it would be in the UK's interests to secure the maximum inclusion of services in any FTA, whereas the EU might be content to limit any agreement to goods,

---

[9] https://www.theguardian.com/politics/2016/dec/01/brexit-secretary-suggests-uk-would-consider-paying-for-single-market-access

[10] Peterson Institute for International Economics, 2016. https://piie.com/blogs/trade-investment-policy-watch/how-long-does-it-take-conclude-trade-agreement-us

since this is where it has a large trade surplus. There should be scope for a mutually beneficial agreement, given the juxtaposition of the relative trade strengths, but it may require UK negotiators to display resolution and be willing to accept potential trade according to WTO rules, to secure a favourable deal for the UK. It is worth noting, in this regard, that the FTA negotiated with Canada includes some agricultural goods and a significant proportion of services, although financial services are excluded (Emmerson et al. 2016: 15-16).

A second issue may concern the potential inclusion of "third party MFN provisions" in the FTA. This would ensure that any subsequent preferential trade agreement negotiated with one of the FTA partners would also apply to the other automatically (CEPR 2013: 37). This is a two-edged sword, because it could be used by the UK to ensure that it benefits from any more favourable trade agreements that the EU is able to negotiate with other nations, as a result of its greater bargaining position, or else it could be used by the EU to ensure that the UK could not secure for itself a more favourable trade deal with a third party without the EU having access to the same favourable trade conditions. It might, therefore, be more difficult for the UK to gain a competitive advantage for its exporters over European rivals through negotiating FTAs with fast-growing developing economies, if the EU insisted upon this type of clause in its FTA with the UK (CEPR 2013: 47).

A third negotiating issue might relate the EU's desire to include harmonisation of regulations in any FTA. This may include competition policy, oversight of mergers and acquisitions, health and safety rules, labour market regulation, product standards and technical specifications for goods and services entering its market. These features are not typically included in FTAs, and this includes the trade deals that the EU has negotiated with Canada and South Korea (Reynolds and Webber, 2019: 5). Nevertheless, the EU has made clear its preference to establish a 'common rule book' to underpin any such future trade agreement with the UK. This would fatally weaken any attempt to utilise strategic procurement policy or an active industrial policy to regenerate the UK's industrial capacity.

This raises two rather interesting questions. The first relates to the concern being shown by EU member states that any potential divergence away from EU norms and regulations would prove to be economically successful, otherwise it would not be perceived as an effective competitive threat. This contradicts those economic studies which tend to ignore or marginalise the effectiveness of economic policy autonomy to drive future

UK growth performance. The second question relates to the degree to which it is reasonable for a supra-national organisation to seek to control the ability of a nation state, which has ceased to be part of this bloc, to determine its own economic policy priorities. What for one nation may represent unfair competition and social dumping, may for another be no more than the natural consequence of choosing a different approach to economic development

Public procurement is likely to form a fourth area for discussion. There is a trade-off involved in determining the UK negotiating stance on this issue. UK producers may benefit from having the ability to bid for public contracts across the EU. Yet, as noted in Chap. 8, the size of the UK's market for public procurement dwarfs the amount of EU procurement work won by UK firms, and therefore utilisation of UK procurement expenditure as part of a broader industrial strategy may prove more beneficial.

A final issue concerns whether or not to include investment protection and the associated Investor-State Dispute Settlement (ISDS) into any FTA (Singham et al. 2017: 12). The inclusion of investor protection and ISDS clauses in FTAs is a fairly recent phenomenon, and the stated intention is to prevent unjustified expropriation and unequal treatment by providing foreign investors with the same rights and benefits as local (indigenous) firms (Hufbauer 2016: 197). This sounds to be perfectly reasonable. However, the ISDS provides foreign-owned trans-national corporations (TNCs) a privileged position, able to by-pass local courts and litigate against national governments. It is asymmetric in that it allows foreign firms to litigate against national governments, but it does not provide for governments suing foreign firms for breaches of national law. Critics, such as the US Senator, Warren, describe the ISDS as a threat to national sovereignty[11] whilst Reich (2015) described it as a "Trojan horse in a global race to the bottom, giving big corporations and Wall Street banks a way to eliminate any and all laws and regulations that get in the way of their profit".[12] The ETUC suggests that this "privileges big multinational

---

[11] https://www.washingtonpost.com/opinions/kill-the-dispute-settlement-language-in-the-trans-pacific-partnership/2015/02/25/ec7705a2-bd1e-11e4-b274-e5209a3bc9a9_story.html
[12] https://www.salon.com/2015/01/07/robert_reich_the_trans_pacific_partnership_is_a_disaster_in_the_making_partner/

corporations and can be used to intimidate democratic institutions from acting in the public interest" (ICTU 2016; SETUC 2016). UNCTAD figures suggest that TNCs win around 60% of the cases taken through ISDS procedures, with the primary beneficiaries being very large corporations and very wealthy individuals (De Zayas 2015: 25). However, even where claims are not successful, the existence of the ISDS can cause "regulatory chill" leading to governments abandoning or modifying measures intended to promote social benefits. In addition, the UN Independent Expert has documented a number of cases where the ISDS process has been used as a means of TNCs evading their breaching of national laws and regulations, most particularly in the case of national health and environmental damage (De Zayas 2015: 10, 13-16). As a result, they recommended the abolition of ISDS approaches in international trade treaties, and its replacement by either the creation of an impartial international investment court, which has to take into account the social impact of its decisions, or a state-to-state dispute settlement along the lines of that operated by the WTO, or alternatively reliance upon domestic dispute settlement (De Zayas 2015: 20-22).

In view of the criticism of the ISDS and investor protection aspects included in some of the more comprehensive FTAs, there is a strong argument for the UK to seek to limit the scope of its preferred FTA with the EU to focus upon trade-related matters. By doing so, the UK would avoid the problems that arise from investor clauses which unduly privilege TNCs and weaken the ability of democratic governments to make laws and set regulations in the best interests of their citizens.

If it were not possible to negotiate a mutually satisfactory FTA, within the timescale allotted, the alternative would be for the UK to revert to trading with the EU according to the rules set down by the WTO, whose membership of 164 nations represents approximately 98% of global trade and GDP.[13] This is typically discussed as the '**WTO option**' or the no-deal scenario in the literature, although earlier pioneering studies often described it as the 'Greenland model' (Burkitt et al. 1996).

The WTO upholds multilateral international trade rules, originating from the General Agreement on Tariffs and Trade (GATT) and General

---

[13] https://www.wto.org/english/thewto_e/history_e/history_e.htm;   https://www.wto.org/english/thewto_e/acc_e/cbt_course_e/c1s1p1_e.htm

Agreement on Trade in Services (GATS). The most prominent of these rules concerns 'Most Favoured Nation' (MFN) requirements, whereby WTO members are required to offer all other members equal same access to their markets unless a PTA, such as a customs union or FTA, has been separately agreed. This means that, in the case of the UK withdrawing from the EU, the latter cannot impose higher tariffs on imports from the UK than it does on the same goods imported from another WTO member nation with whom the EU does not have a form of PTA. Moreover, whilst PTAs have expanded rapidly over the past three decades, it is unlikely that they account for more than around one-third of total trade, once the share of trade between PTA signatories that attracts little or no MFN duties is taken into consideration (Medvedev 2006: 47-8; WTO 2011: 7). Hence, the majority of international trade occurs within the remit of WTO MFN rules.

The imposition of tariffs would be the largest disadvantage inherent within the 'WTO model'. When weighted according to the value of UK exports to the EU, these MFN tariffs may only impose an average cost upon UK exports of around 2-3% (WTO 2016: 75; World Bank, 2020), which is a sum easily absorbed by UK exporters as it lies within the monthly fluctuations of a floating currency. However, since the tariff cost would fall disproportionately upon certain industries, such as car production, chemicals, tobacco, clothing, together with food and beverages, it might be advisable for the UK government to seek to use a proportion of budgetary savings arising from Brexit to compensate producers in these sectors. This might occur through a combination of research grants and training subsidies, aiming at enhancing the productivity of these industries whilst simultaneously compensating them for the rise in costs caused by tariffs. This was discussed in more detail in Chap. 3 (see Figs 3.8, 3.9, 3.10 and 3.11 in particular).

A second disadvantage stemming from reliance upon WTO rules relates to the imposition of non-tariff barriers (NTBs), such as administrative, licensing and other regulatory procedures which may delay shipments and add to export costs. As noted in Chap. 3, it is estimated that NTBs may be around twice as significant as tariff costs. Moreover, they could be of particular concern for service exporters, which is where the UK currently has a comparative advantage (and trade surplus), where continued export activity depends upon mutual recognition of professional qualifications and/or permitted access to service professionals to undertake this activity. GATS provisions provide some assistance in this regard, but progress in multilateral agreements in services was never as advanced as that for trade in goods.

In terms of advantages, the 'WTO model' offers the greatest degree of independence from the EU (Booth et al. 2015: 61-2; Minford 2016: 8). The UK would no longer have to implement EU-determined regulations and technical specifications for goods and services across the whole of the UK economy, but only that part which desired to export into the EU SIM. There would be no budgetary cost for trading along WTO lines, unless the UK sought access to specific EU programmes, such as Horizon 2020, for research collaboration, or Erasmus, to facilitate student mobility. The UK would have maximum freedom to negotiate its separate trade agreements with other countries and/or trade blocks, although the CBI (2013: 16) disputes the probable realisation of superior deals than membership of the EU or the EEA could secure. The UK could also resume its seat and vote at the WTO, rather than have to defer to the EU position, given its reserving trade policy to itself (Milne 2004: 42-5). In addition, one further advantage arising from the WTO model is the gain to the public purse arising from tariff revenues (CEPR 2013: 16).

One variant of the WTO option would be for the UK to follow the **'Hong Kong model'** and unilaterally eliminate all tariffs with all nations. Neo-classical international trade theory would predict that the result would be lower prices for imported goods for UK consumers and manufacturers who use inputs from abroad, leading to lower inflation, increased consumer welfare, whilst the lower cost of inputs together with competitive effects arising from the removal of trade protection would increase efficiency and improve the international competitiveness of UK exporters (Minford et al. 2005; Booth et al. 2015: 63, 73; Minford et al. 2015: 116; Economists for Brexit 2016). One estimate suggests that this approach could provide a net benefit for the UK economy of perhaps 0.75% UK GDP by 2030 (Ciuriak et al. 2015: 25-6).

These conclusions are, however, dependent upon the theoretical underpinning of neo-classical theory. For example, it is assumed that factors of production are relatively homogenous and therefore easily interchangeable, whilst wages and prices are sufficiently flexible as to facilitate a relatively rapid movement from one equilibrium situation to another. Thus, the economy will remain at full employment for all of those who are willing to work at the prevailing market wage rate. Say's Law will prevail, in that supply will create its own demand, and therefore factors will move rapidly to new employment opportunities created by this new demand, particularly in the services sector (Minford et al. 2015: 17, 73). There may be temporary (frictional) unemployment, but this will not persist into the medium term (Booth et al. 2015: 73-5). None of this is very likely in the real world.

The experience of the recent financial crisis should have demonstrated to all but the most enthusiastic adherents to economic orthodoxy, that disequilibrium can persist for more than a short transitional period and that the economy can find itself in a demand deficient position, where individuals who want to work find it difficult to do so, and that firms that cease to trade often leads to capital scrapping rather than reallocation. Should structural reorganisation not occur rapidly, through price flexibility, it will likely do so through quantity effects, such as impacting upon output and/or employment. Unemployed workers would need to retrain before being able to find alternative employment, whilst any resulting economic downturn would likely result in depressed demand, investment and employment. The creation of depressed areas in certain regions of the country may take a long time to reverse. Moreover, to the extent that the net negative effects were concentrated upon manufacturing industry, this would have a disproportionate effect upon productivity growth and negatively impact the trade balance. This would contradict the conclusion reached in Chap. 8 of this book that the greater freedoms offered by Brexit should be utilised in order to strengthen not weaken the UK manufacturing sector.

The 'Hong Kong' option would, moreover, reduce the probability of the UK being able to negotiate advantageous trade access to other nations. If a country has already secured tariff-free access to the UK market as a result of the unilateral liberalisation approach, there would be little advantage for it to provide a similar benefit to UK exporters. As noted earlier in this chapter, Turkey has discovered this weakness in the asymmetric nature of its customs union with the EU, and it would be likely that the UK would find itself in a similar position. Thus, unilateral liberalisation is unlikely to produce benefits for UK exporters.

OTHER BESPOKE SOLUTIONS

The option to re-join **EFTA** is typically discussed alongside a supplementary application for membership of the EEA. However, there is nothing to prevent the UK from eschewing the latter and instead participating in EFTA as one element in a post-EU strategy. EFTA is a much smaller entity than the EU, having only four member nations—Iceland, Liechtenstein, Norway and Switzerland—and representing a total GDP of €0.9bn.[14] UK membership could be attractive to other EFTA members, who would otherwise lose tariff-free trade with the UK market. Set against this, the UK would become far the largest single member of EFTA and this would change the dynamic of the organisation, which some current members may find unsettling.

Whilst potentially attractive as part of any post-Brexit global trading realignment, EFTA membership in isolation is simply too small to replace any significant amount of lost trade with the EU should negotiations fail to agree some form of free trade agreement. Hence, whilst not necessarily agreeing with Piris (2016: 7-8) that, due to the advent of the EEA, the EFTA has become "an empty shell", it is certainly true that, as currently constituted, it is too small to represent more than part of any future trade strategy developed by the UK.

A more promising source of future trade opportunities, neglected during the UK's focus upon regional European trade, concerns the 54 nation **Commonwealth**.[15] These markets formed a significant proportion of UK trade before EU accession; the application of the EU's Common External Tariff (CET) and the ending of the 'imperial preference' system which formerly prioritised trade between the UK and Commonwealth countries, caused trade displacement in favour of the EU internal market. Whilst Commonwealth nations have often been viewed as part of the UK's trading past, it is noteworthy that the growth rates of core Commonwealth nations have exceeded that of the EU for the whole of the period since 1971 (Fig. 9.3). Moreover, the entire Commonwealth represents around 15% of global GDP, which is larger than the Eurozone and, mainly due to the high growth rates recorded by India, is predicted to overtake the EU by the end of the decade.[16] Consequently, there is a good argument to be made for an independent UK to have a greater focus upon exploring potential trade opportunities within this group of nations, with which it has historic ties and pre-existing layers of cooperation.

[14] http://www.efta.int/statistics/efta-in-figures
[15] Perhaps this should be more accurately 53 member nations, since Fiji is currently suspended.
[16] http://www.telegraph.co.uk/news/newstopics/eureferendum/12193101/Brexit-will-allow-Britain-to-embrace-the-Commonwealth.html;   http://www.worldeconomics.com/papers/Commonwealth_Growth_Monitor_0e53b963-bce5-1ba1-9cab-333cedaab048.paper

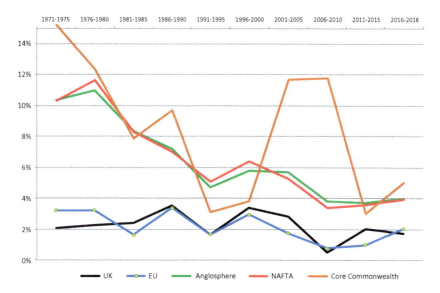

Fig. 9.3 Annual average growth rates (GDP), selected areas and countries. Notes: The EU here consists of the EU(15) member countries. The core Commonwealth area includes here the top six countries by GDP in the Commonwealth (excluding the UK) amounting to about two-thirds of the total Commonwealth GDP. The Anglosphere includes the USA, Canada, Australia and New Zealand. Source: Authors' calculations based on UNCTAD (2020) and OECD (2019)

Given that there are already FTAs in place between the EU and 18 Commonwealth nations, with a further 14 awaiting ratification,[17] it is possible that gains from closer trading ties between an independent UK and many Commonwealth nations might be limited.[18] Nevertheless, it would be churlish to fail to recognise the fact that membership of a regional trade bloc tends to cause exporters to focus upon regional trade opportunities, particularly when encouraged to do so by a common external tariff that makes the forging of complex supply chains a little more complex and

---

[17] http://eulawanalysis.blogspot.co.uk/2015/11/the-eu-or-commonwealth-dilemma-for-uk.html
[18] http://blogs.lse.ac.uk/brexitvote/2015/12/10/the-commonwealth-and-the-eu-lets-do-trade-with-both/; http://www.economist.com/blogs/bagehot/2011/10/britain-and-eu-3

expensive than would otherwise be the case. Withdrawal from the EU will therefore focus attention upon trade opportunities outside Europe, and the Commonwealth nations with shared history, language and cultural ties would seem like a good starting point (Algan and Cahus 2010; Guiso et al. 2009).

Similar arguments have been used to promote the potential of what has been termed an **'Anglosphere'** might provide the basis for economic and political partnership for an independent UK (Nesbit 2001; Bennett 2004). When considered as a bloc, the Anglosphere (USA, Britain, Ireland, Canada, Australia and New Zealand) has more than one quarter of the world's GDP, and this advantage is amplified if considering GDP per capita measured according to purchasing power parity (Kotkin and Parulekar 2011: 29-30). These nations share a common language, operate according to common law, together with shared cultural and historical ties, all of which has been found to be conducive to trade (Algan and Cahus 2010; Guiso et al. 2009). Moreover, the growth performance of Anglosphere countries has been considerably superior to that of the EU for the past half century (see Fig. 9.3).

Taking into account these potential advantages, it has been reported that a number of leading political figures, in the UK, Australia and Canada, have stated an interest in this concept (Miller et al. 2016: 46). Whilst both the new President of the USA and the New Zealand Prime Minister have expressed their interest in negotiating a free trade agreement with the UK shortly after the Brexit withdrawal process has been completed.[19] This has led a former Conservative MEP, Daniel Hannan, to argue that, when comparing EU membership to the perceived advantages of the Anglosphere argued that "far from hitching our wagon to a powerful locomotive, we shackled ourselves to a corpse". However, it should be noted that, whilst countries may share elements of culture, they do not necessarily have shared interests. Nor is the Anglosphere concept a new proposal, having been first proposed in imperial terms in 1911, when it received only scant support (Harries 2001). Nevertheless, like the Commonwealth option, the cultural and other ties between Anglosphere nations may facilitate closer trade arrangements and other forms of economic cooperation between sovereign nations.

[19] http://www.bbc.co.uk/news/uk-politics-38608716;   http://www.telegraph.co.uk/news/2017/01/27/congress-pushes-donald-trump-form-bilateral-trade-deal-uk/

A perhaps more immediately practical option, considered by the US Senate Finance Committee, is whether an independent UK could join **NAFTA**, which currently operates between the USA, Canada and Mexico. Like the Anglosphere, the NAFTA countries have recorded far better growth rates than the EU for the time period included in Fig. 9.3. This option has been discussed by sections of the US Congress and the US International Trade Commission (USITC) completed a report on the likely impact that UK participation in NAFTA may have upon the economies of all four nations. Conducted in 2000, but based upon trade data drawn from 1995, the report suggested that there would be significant trade effects, with UK exports to Canada rising by approximately 24% and the USA by 12.5%, with similar although smaller rises in imports from NAFTA nations, leading to an improvement in the UK's trade balance. This would not, by itself, be sufficient to compensate for a probable reduction of UK exports to the EU, albeit that due to imports into the UK would fall faster than exports, resulting in the UK's trade deficit with the EU being reduced and its overall trade balance improved (USITC 2000: 4-13-14). The impact on FDI would likely reduce the output of US-owned manufacturing affiliates in the UK by 0.56%, which is a significantly smaller effect than many more recent predictions (USITC 2000: 4-19). Overall, in terms of macroeconomic effects, the report suggests that prices may decline slightly in the UK, whilst the modelling predicted insubstantial changes in national GDP, ranging from -0.02% for the UK to a zero change for the USA (USITC 2000: 4-16-17).

The USITC study is interesting partly because it was one of the first studies to seek to model the economic effect of UK withdrawal from the EU, and its prediction of an insubstantial impact on the UK economy of only -0.02% GDP is in sharp contrast to more recent studies outlined in Chap. 1. Moreover, it is probable that the results of its analysis would be more favourable to the UK, if the exercise was repeated in 2020, because the share of UK exports taken by the EU is significantly lower now than it was in the mid-1990s, whilst the average trade-weighted MFN tariff levied by the EU has fallen from a little over 6% in 1995 to around 2–3% today (Thompson and Harari 2013:7; WTO 2016: 75; World Bank, 2020). Hence, whilst it would be unwise to base current economic policy upon one study, conducted using data from two decades previously, the USITC predictions do provide a tantalising piece of evidence that UK withdrawal from the EU, and subsequent membership of NAFTA or alternatively a broader Anglosphere, might provide an interesting option for an independent UK. At the very least, it would be worth UK policy makers examining this option in more detail.

Another option for the UK to consider would be to follow the advice of US Trade Representative Michael Froman[20] to join the **CPTPP**. This is an FTA negotiated between the following countries in the Asia-Pacific region, namely: Australia, Brunei, Canada, Chile, Japan, Malaysia, Mexico, New Zealand, Peru, Singapore and Vietnam. The CPTPP emerged from the previous Obama administrations attempt to create a TPP, but which was vetoed when President Trump took office.[21] With USA involvement, the TPP would have created a trade bloc of 800 million people and representing around 40% of global GDP and around one-third of world trade.[22] In the absence of the USA, once fully implemented, the CPTPP will include 495 million people and represent around 13.5% of global GDP. This is slightly larger in population terms than the EU (447 million people), represents a similar share of global GDP to that of the EU and is larger than the Eurozone. If the UK joined, the trade bloc would have a larger GDP than the EU.

The TPP, from which the CPTPP evolved once the USA withdrew from the arrangement, was criticised for its anticipated effect upon employment and wages in the USA,[23] whilst concerns were raised that market access rules might enable the penetration of national public services by TNCs and Investor-State Dispute Settlement (ISDS) clauses might undermine national policy sovereignty (Backer 2014: 54-5).[24] The CPTPP agreement suspended 22 provisions relating to 'investor agreement' and 'investor authorisation' from the former TPP approach, which has narrowed the scope of the ISDS, providing additional protection for national health services in their efforts to secure the best price for drugs and safeguards for national governments being able to regulate in the national

---

[20] http://www.express.co.uk/news/uk/687484/Obama-admin-Brexit-Britain-not-back-queue-trade-deal

[21] https://www.cfr.org/backgrounder/what-trans-pacific-partnership-tpp; https://www.politico.com/story/2019/01/23/trans-pacific-trade-pact-2017-1116638

[22] https://www.bbc.co.uk/news/business-32498715

[23] http://www.independent.co.uk/voices/ttip-american-ttp-trade-deal-bernie-sanders-hillary-clinton-donald-trump-barack-obama-looks-set-for-a7194336.html

[24] http://inthesetimes.com/article/18695/TPP_Free-Trade_Globalization_Obama; https://www.washingtonpost.com/opinions/kill-the-dispute-settlement-language-in-the-trans-pacific-partnership/2015/02/25/ec7705a2-bd1e-11e4-b274-e5209a3bc9a9_story.html

interest.[25] Clauses concerning public procurement were also delayed for a period of time. However, the rest of the investment chapter remains unaltered in the CPTPP (Yu 2018: 2). Therefore, UK trade experts would need to assure themselves that the additional safeguards built into the agreement are sufficient to safeguard UK interests, otherwise participation would remain problematical.

A different type of settlement, which would depend upon a significant shift in the adherence to 'the project' by leading members of the EU, would be to accept the existence of a '**variable geometry Europe**', whereby different nation states participate to a varying degree in the various aspects of economic integration pursued by the EU (see Fig. 9.4). To a certain extent, this would be to formally recognise differences which currently exist, with certain long-standing EU member states reluctant to participate in the single currency or the Schengen agreement, whilst others would be content to have a looser association rather than implement the full *acquis communautaire* (HoC 2013: 78-9; Booth et al. 2015: 64). It might provide the basis of a new settlement, between the EU and the UK, but would additionally solve certain tensions persisting within the EU, between participants in the Eurozone and other members (Chopin 2013: 9). It might additionally facilitate a more general realignment between core membership and those seeking looser alignment, such as EFTA members, Switzerland and possibly the UK (van Hulten 2011; Chopin 2016). Nevertheless, it is unlikely to occur. Previous suggestions to introduce a two-speed EU, including those made by former UK Prime Minister Major, did not attract sufficient support across other EU member states. If the opportunity for such realignment existed, during the recent Euro crisis, this now seems to have passed, and one supporter of this variable geometry framework considers that it is unlikely to receive serious consideration unless the UK makes a success out of its independence from the EU (Owen 2016: 2).

CHEQUERS AND THE JOHNSON WITHDRAWAL AGREEMENT

Having outlined the main generic Brexit options available to UK policy makers, it is perhaps easier to understand the motivations and choices made by successive UK governments in their development of the two

---

[25] https://www.mfat.govt.nz/en/trade/free-trade-agreements/free-trade-agreements-in-force/cptpp/understanding-cptpp/tpp-and-cptpp-the-differences-explained

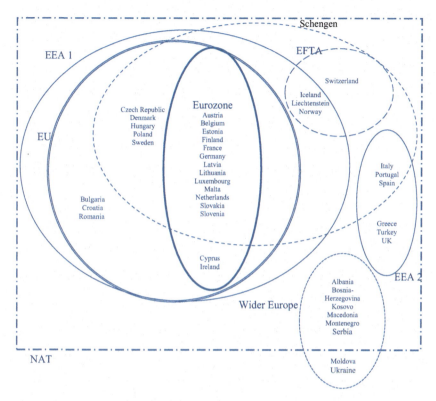

Fig. 9.4 An illustration of the highly complex variable geometry Europe and the potential for a new realignment between Eurozone-Core and SIM-lite-Periphery groupings. Source: Authors' drawing, based on Owen (2016:2-3)

versions of the withdrawal agreement set before Parliament. To distinguish between the two, former Prime Minister May's proposals are discussed as the Chequers Plan, following the dramatic events which occurred during the cabinet discussions that took place at the Prime Minister's countryside retreat and the subsequent resignations. It is the Chequers Plan that suffered three of the largest parliamentary defeats in UK history. The replace of May with Prime Minister Johnson, led to the renegotiation of the withdrawal agreement with the EU, the December 2019 General Election victory and the implementation of the revised withdrawal

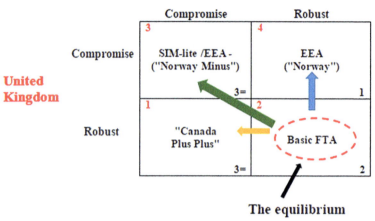

Fig. 9.5 Game theory potential bargaining solution. Source: Authors' revised version of material drawn from the academic blog, available via: https://blogs.lse.ac.uk/brexit/2018/07/16/two-years-after-the-vote-there-is-little-certainty-where-the-uk-eu-relationship-is-heading/

agreement, cumulating in the UK withdrawing from the EU on 31 January 2020. This is described as the Johnson Plan.

Chequers

The Chequers proposals sought to reconcile a challenging if not contradictory set of negotiating criteria, or 'red lines', imposed upon the process by UK and EU authorities. The UK government sought to end freedom of movement of labour, whilst the EU sought to protect the integrity of the SIM, which for them included the four freedoms as a key foundation. The UK sought to regain the ability to negotiate trade deals with third parties, which was incompatible with remaining within the customs union. These 'red lines' are relatively easy to resolve, through the negotiation of an FTA. Indeed, prior to the Chequers meeting, the Department for Exiting the EU had been in the process of developing a 'Canada-Plus-Plus-Plus' FTA proposal.

The final EU 'red line' proved to be more difficult to reconcile. This is related to the EU's desire to avoid the (re-)imposition of a hard border, between its member state the Republic of Ireland and Northern Ireland. Whilst the Belfast (Good Friday) Agreement[26] does not actually commit the UK to maintaining an open border—the only related clause concerning the removal of security installations—it is probably accurate to conclude that the reintroduction of border infrastructure could become a security target and thereby destabilise the peace process (Phinnemore and Hayward 2017: 26, 34, 47).

Borders manage the flow of goods and people. Since a common travel area has existed since 1922 between the Republic of Ireland and the UK, the flow of people was a lesser concern for UK negotiators, as passport control could always be exercised upon arrival onto the British mainland. Customs duties could always be collected by the relevant parties to the agreement, as part of a customs partnership arrangement. However, the EU's concern over the integrity of the SIM focused attention upon how the passage of goods across the Irish-Northern Irish border could be facilitated. If the UK were to diverge from EU rules and regulations, checks would need to be imposed to ensure that goods entering the SIM through this route complied with EU standards. The EU's conclusion, therefore, was that the only solutions would involve the UK or Northern Ireland remaining in a customs union (or EEA or customs union-plus) arrangement with the EU, or via the UK's voluntary acceptance of regulatory harmonisation with EU rules, standards and regulations. This meant that, either the whole of the UK was required to follow EU rules (i.e. become a rule-taker) or Northern Ireland would have to do so alone, which would necessitate different parts of the UK being subject to different laws and regulations. Complaints lodged by the UK that this created a democratic deficit were dismissed and in December 2017, the UK negotiating team reluctantly agreed to the proposal.[27]

The resulting Chequers Plan and subsequent White Paper (HMG 2018b), therefore, was composed of elements of the EEA, FTA and customs union options. It sought to maintain frictionless trade in goods with the EU (section 1.2.1.15), whilst ending freedom of movement of labour (section 1.1.7c), thereby moving outside the SIM, and regaining an

[26] https://assets.publishing.service.gov.uk/government/uploads/system/uploads/attachment_data/file/136652/agreement.pdf

[27] https://www.politico.eu/article/how-uk-lost-brexit-eu-negotiation/

independent trade policy (sections 1.1.7h, 1.8.155), which necessitated leaving the customs union. The Chequers Plan also sought to maintain the UK's regulatory autonomy *in services*, whilst accepting regulatory harmonisation with the EU ('a common rule book') for goods and agricultural products (sections 1.1.7a, 1.2.11, 1.2.3.25-28, 1.2.4.35, 1.3.48-9).[28] It further accepted non-regression of labour standards (section 1.6.1.123), both to neuter internal criticism from the UK trade unions and Labour opposition, but additionally to mollify EU negotiators concerned over the UK gaining a competitive advantage through a 'race to the bottom' in social policy and labour standards.

The Protocol on the Republic of Ireland and Northern Ireland comprised around one-third of the content of the Withdrawal Agreement, thereby indicating its importance and complexity. The 'backstop' solution it contained committed the UK as a whole to acceptance of a customs union with the EU, covering all goods (except for fish), which would come into force unless the two negotiating parties could reach a mutually satisfactory alternative arrangement (Article 2). It would require the whole of the UK to accept 'level playing field' restrictions, including continued acceptance of EU competition, procurement and state aid rules (sections 1.1.7f, 1.6.106-108, 1.6.1.109-111), alongside commitments to maintain high standards in the areas of labour and social policy. Northern Ireland would additionally be subject to EU regulations in agriculture, VAT, the environment and customs (Articles 10:4, 11-12, Annex 4:4 and Annex 8) (Reynolds and Webber, 2019: 1-3).

The Chequers Plan sought to evade the necessity of invoking the backstop through the introduction of what it described as a "facilitated customs arrangement", whereby the UK would apply EU tariffs for goods whose ultimate destination would be the SIM and UK tariffs for those destined for the UK market (sections 1.2.12, 1.2.1.14, 18). The intention was that this would remove need for customs checks as if a combined customs territory was in operation (HMG 2018a). This type of revenue sharing is complex, but the experience of the MERCOSUR trade bloc indicates how it can be operated.[29]

---

[28] https://www.gov.uk/government/speeches/sos-dominic-raab-statement-on-the-future-relationship-between-the-united-kingdom-and-the-european-union-12-july-2018; https://assets.publishing.service.gov.uk/government/uploads/system/uploads/attachment_data/file/723460/CHEQUERS_STATEMENT_-_FINAL.PDF

[29] https://www.instituteforgovernment.org.uk/sites/default/files/publications/IfG_Brexit_customs_WEB_0.pdf

Technological solutions (often described as 'max-fac' or 'smart borders') were proposed in the Chequers Plan as a means of avoiding customs checks taking place at the point of border crossing, through the use of Authorised Economic Operator ('trusted trader') arrangements (sections 1.2.1.16-17) (HMG, 2017: 7). Trusted traders can make use of advance electronic cargo information and pre-declaration, customs duties paid on account (subsequently audited), whilst risk targeting can identify items for inspection to be carried out by X-ray and other non-invasive equipment or by mobile customs teams up to a designated distance from the border (Karlsson 2017: 41; HMG 2018c: 8-9; WCO 2018: 2, 4).[30] RFID tags and GPS can be used to track registered commercial vehicles, whilst automatic number plate recognition can facilitate passenger vehicles (Karlsson 2017: 25-6). These approaches have been trialled along the US-Canada border and in its most advanced form along the Swedish-Norwegian border (Karlsson 2017: 22, 24, 29). In the latter case, most goods are cleared through the border within 3–9 minutes (Karlsson 2017: 30).

The smart borders proposals were dismissed by the EU negotiators as "magical thinking",[31] which is a little disappointing given the support for the approach as a potential solution to the Irish border issue in a report produced by the European Parliament's Policy Department for Citizens' Rights and Constitutional Affairs (Karlsson 2017). It is certainly the case that the introduction of smart borders would require considerable investment in technological solutions, whilst the trusted trader scheme would have to be considerably extended.[32] One complication to any extension of trade-related infrastructure stems from the UK having privatised its ports, and consequently the government has no direct control over capacity and equipment (Owen et al. 2017: 16). Moreover, the current Customs Handling of Import and Export Freight (CHIEF)[33] system is scheduled to be replaced by a new Customs Declaration Service (CDS), in part to extend capacity, towards the end of 2020 which coincides with the end of

[30] http://www.wcoomd.org/-/media/wco/public/global/pdf/topics/facilitation/instruments-and-tools/tools/safe-package/safe-framework-of-standards.PDF?la=en
[31] https://www.theguardian.com/uk-news/2017/aug/25/uk-accused-of-magical-thinking-over-brexit-plan-for-irish-border
[32] http://data.parliament.uk/writtenevidence/committeeevidence.svc/evidencedocument/eu-external-affairs-subcommittee/brexit-customs-arrangements/written/83040.pdf
[33] https://assets.publishing.service.gov.uk/government/uploads/system/uploads/attachment_data/file/209612/Customs_Handling_of_Import_and_Export_Freight__CHIEF_.pdf

the transition period and is, in any case, a "demanding" timetable according to the National Audit Office.[34]

There has, moreover, been a degree of controversy over the potential cost that may be involved in the extension of customs declarations that may accompany any new trading system. One suggestion is that an additional 180,000 traders will need to make customs declarations, which could cost in the region of £4bn per annum (Owen et al. 2017: 4). More troubling, the head of the HMRC, Thompson, suggested that the cost of additional customs declarations could be as high as £17–20bn per annum,[35] although this claim was later criticised by Gudgin and Mills whose own estimate for customs costs was a significantly smaller £2bn per annum.[36]

Johnson Revision

The failure of former Prime Minister May to secure parliamentary approval for her version of the Withdrawal Agreement led to a change in Prime Minister and a renegotiation of certain elements of the Chequers proposals.[37] These changes were agreed in October 2019 and constituted a revised Withdrawal agreement (HMG 2019c). Most of the content of the withdrawal agreement remains identical to that of the previous iteration. However, the primary strategic choice made by the Johnson government was to accept Northern Ireland remaining subject to EU harmonised rules and regulations, for goods and agricultural produce (Articles 5–10), in order to remove backstop provisions and enable the rest of the UK to diverge. Notwithstanding this regulatory alignment with the EU, the revised withdrawal agreement made it clear that Northern Ireland remains part of the UK's single customs territory (Article 4), and can benefit from the UK's independent trade policy (Article 5).[38] One important caveat concerns the EU's acceptance that this arrangement is subject to the ongoing consent, expressed through a majority vote of the Northern Ireland Legislative Assembly, reaffirmed every four years (Article 18) (HMG 2019a).

---

[34] https://www.nao.org.uk/report/the-customs-declaration-service-a-progress-update/
[35] https://www.ft.com/content/fbdc5d58-5e97-11e8-9334-2218e7146b04
[36] https://briefingsforbrexit.com/customs-costs-post-brexit-long-version/
[37] https://www.politico.eu/article/how-uk-lost-brexit-eu-negotiation/
[38] https://assets.publishing.service.gov.uk/government/uploads/system/uploads/attachment_data/file/840230/Revised_Protocol_to_the_Withdrawal_Agreement.pdf

The political declaration expressed the intention of the UK and EU negotiating a comprehensive and balanced FTA, which would be based upon regulatory autonomy (HMG 2019b). At the same time, however, Clause XIV.77 introduces the notion that, because of the UK's "geographic proximity and economic independence", any future relationship should be based upon "open and fair competition, encompassing robust commitments to ensure a level playing field", particularly in the areas of state aid, competition, social and employment standards, environmental measures and taxation (HMG 2019b: 14-15). Given other statements made by EU negotiators and the leaders of both France and Germany, over their concerns that the grater policy freedoms secured by Brexit will enable the UK to become a competitive rival to the EU, it would seem that this single paragraph may foreshadow the forthcoming negotiations between the UK and the EU over their future relationship, with the UK seeking to widen its policy space following independence and the EU seeking to continue to constrain the ability of the UK to use this greater flexibility to improve its competitive position.

Future Trade Relationships

Looking forward to the negotiations to be held regarding the form of future economic relationship between the UK and the EU, the experience gleaned from the past few years would suggest that this may be a difficult and not straightforward process. The EU has been particularly effective in setting the agenda and controlling the negotiations process through sequencing and channelling negotiations through a single conduit (Ries et al. 2017: 38).[39] This approach is unlikely to change given the success achieved to date. In addition, the former Greek finance minister, Varoufakis, has suggested that the EU bureaucracy will wish to frustrate the negotiation of a mutually beneficial agreement in order to protect the stability of the European project.[40] Thus, the forthcoming negotiations between the UK and the EU over the framework of the future trade relationship may be difficult.

[39] https://www.politico.eu/article/how-uk-lost-brexit-eu-negotiation/;   https://www.theguardian.com/politics/2017/jun/19/uk-caves-in-to-eu-demand-to-agree-divorce-bill-before-trade-talks
[40] https://www.newstatesman.com/politics/brexit/2018/11/yanis-varoufakis-eu-declared-war-and-theresa-may-played-along

Consideration of the economic 'game theory' approach suggests that there may be a bargaining solution which would meet the preferences of both sides. Whilst the EU would prefer an EEA-style agreement, to ensure a 'common rule book' and secure the integrity of the SIM, and the UK would prefer a comprehensive FTA to include financial and business services, unless one or more parties to the negotiations are prepared to make major concessions, the likely equilibrium position that both parties would accept would be a simple form of FTA,[41] a solution certain commentators have dubbed 'Canada minus' (UK&EU 2019: 4-5). This option would deliver an FTA without the UK having to become a rule-taker and being subject to EU-imposed constraints (Menon et al. 2018: 8). It has the advantage of being straightforward to negotiate, given that it would not include clauses concerning investor protection, social, labour and environmental policies, which is important given the fact that the transition period terminates at the end of 2020. It would provide the basis for continued free trade in goods, following the end of the transition period, and could be extended by mutual agreement to include elements of services in the future. Mutual agreements relating to professional qualifications are already in place and this should be straightforward to roll over into the new arrangement.

Note to editors: if needing to have the figure above as a stand-alone image, then please use the version below:

The one potential roadblock in reaching this mutually acceptable solution concerns the stated intention of EU negotiators to force the UK to agree to 'level playing field' provisions, intended to prevent what the EU considers to be the "undercutting of EU standards to gain competitive advantage" (UK&EU 2019: 5). This could simply be the EU's 'robust' negotiating stance. Yet, even if it is not, it is unlikely that the current UK administration would accede to this position, as it would negate the policy flexibility that Brexit delivers. In effect, they would be accepting the 'golden straightjacket' option described in the Rodrik trilemma. Or, in Varoufakis' prose, it would mean accepting a 'Hotel California Brexit' where the UK "could check out but never leave".[42] Thus, it is probable that this will be the end result of the negotiations between the UK and the

---

[41] https://blogs.lse.ac.uk/brexit/2018/07/16/two-years-after-the-vote-there-is-little-certainty-where-the-uk-eu-relationship-is-heading/

[42] https://www.newstatesman.com/politics/brexit/2018/11/yanis-varoufakis-eu-declared-war-and-theresa-may-played-along

EU, with the option of trade according to WTO rules if negotiators miscalculate.

Of course, the completion of the UK's withdrawal from the EU signifies its ability to seek new trading relationships with other nations and trade blocs. The Change Britain organisation has reported that 14 nations, including China, Brazil, India, Argentina and Australia, have publically stated their interest in negotiating an FTA with the UK once the Brexit process has been completed. Were these agreements successfully completed, this would represent a potential marketplace for UK exports of around £16.8 trillion,[43] which is considerably larger than the GDP of the EU(27). Moreover, the Trump administration has emphasised its willingness to negotiate an FTA with the UK and has even set out its own preferred set of negotiating priorities (USTR 2019). Certain of the more unpalatable aspects of the US negotiating position—that is, food safety rules, investor protection, access to public health systems and control over exchange rates—would be negated if the UK were to advocate a simpler, more basic form of FTA. This would still deliver some benefits in terms of expanded trade opportunities, but would avoid the more troublesome aspects that might be contained within a more comprehensive agreement.

Interestingly, those studies which have sought to estimate the economic impact of FTA agreements, between the UK and other nations, have indicated how effective this independent trade policy might be in offsetting the impact arising from potential trade losses with the EU. For example, one study predicts that the negotiation of FTAs with Anglosphere countries could increase trade between themselves and the UK by around 12%, whilst similar arrangements with BRIICS countries (Brazil, Russia, India, Indonesia, China and South Africa) could increase bilateral trade by 19%. This would result in a boost to total UK trade of around 4.8% (Ebell, 2017). This would imply only a 0.2% gain to UK GDP (Hantzsche et al., 2018: 23). By contrast, another study suggested that an FTA between the UK and the USA would offset half of any predicted economic cost arising from the worst-case Brexit scenario (Ries et al. 2017: 57-9). Adding in other NAFTA countries would further reduce any Brexit cost to negligible levels (USITC 2000: 4-16-17). Extending trade opportunities to include leading Commonwealth countries, or other members of the Anglosphere, or alternatively considering participation in the CPTPP, would provide a

---

[43] http://www.telegraph.co.uk/news/2016/10/29/hard-brexit-could-help-secure-trade-deals-worth-double%2D%2Deu-agree/

further economic boost to the UK economy. This is irrespective of whether the UK and the EU can negotiate an FTA. If this was added into the calculations, the predicted effect would be a net *gain* for the UK economy over and above former EU membership (Ries et al. 2017: 57-9, 67).

It is difficult, as highlighted in Chap. 1, to make precise predictions concerning the potential economic impact arising from Brexit. Partly that is because such calculations do not take place in a vacuum. The world is constantly changing. The advent of the COVID-19 virus, as this book was in the finishing stages of completion, demonstrates this only too clearly. Thus, whilst the EU SIM is likely to remain the largest single consumer of UK exports for the foreseeable future, its importance seems likely to decline over time due to a combination of faster growing areas of the global economy and the income elasticity of trade (Milne 2004; CBI 2013: 27; Business for Britain 2015: 30-2, 697; ONS 2016). Thus, a reorientation of trade relationships with more focus upon global (rather than regional) opportunities, could deliver greater long-term benefits. Similarly, Brexit offers the opportunity for the UK to recalibrate its economic stance away from attempts to secure regional governance through the EU and policy makers must determine whether to opt for a 'golden straightjacket' for of Brexit, trading rule-taking and policy constraints against greater SIM market access, or preferring to pursue greater national self-determination and using the greater policy space to transform its productive sector. The choice will determine not only the success or failure of the Brexit project, but additionally the life chances for UK citizens for decades to come.

CONCLUSION

This book has evaluated the existing evidence relating to the economic impact that is likely to arise from Brexit. It has noted the methodological flaws of many of the more prominent studies on which policy makers and other economic actors reply, reaching the conclusion that the magnitude of their predicted negative consequences are most likely exaggerated. These studies do, however, highlight the areas that are disproportionately prone to negative consequences, such as in trade with the EU and in relation to investment being deferred due to the uncertainty caused by the Brexit process. However, other factors are too often either ignored or marginalised, such as the potential to expand trade and investment with the rest of the (non-EU) world and the potential for government policy to ameliorate negative, and magnify positive, effects. What is needed is for policy makers and other economic actors to base their decision making on a broader range of economic evidence. It is hoped that this book plays a small part in this endeavour.

The choice of future economic relationship, between the UK and the EU, will play a critical role in determining whether Brexit will ultimately be viewed as a success or failed experiment. There is a trade-off between greater trade access into the EU SIM, which may deliver short-term benefits, and securing a greater degree of policy flexibility, which may deliver longer-term gains. Judgements concerning the merits of either option will be, at least in part, determined by perceptions concerning the significance of economic problems facing the UK and the potential for economic policy intervention to provide a solution. If the UK economy is viewed as essentially sound, and/or policy interventions are viewed as having only weak effects, then there would appear to be little to gain by more independent action and therefore continued market access is the overwhelming priority. EEA or customs union membership would therefore appear to be the most preferable Brexit options.

If, however, the UK economy is viewed as suffering from a number of longstanding problems, not least the very large trade deficit and productivity weaknesses, then a more independent stance would appear more advantageous. If, in addition, the evidence is accepted that active forms of economic policy can have significant impact upon the economy—and the reader needs to look no further than the stabilisation achieved amidst the recent financial crisis or indeed the action of the Bank of England to reduce uncertainty immediately after the European referendum—then the most obvious Brexit option would be to seek to negotiate an FTA, including as greater portion of services as possible. Should this not prove to be possible, then it would be preferable for trade to revert to WTO rules rather than accept a form of trade agreement which unduly restricted the policy flexibility for the now independent UK. This would provide sufficient policy flexibility to reduce uncertainty through the stimulation of aggregate demand, utilise an active industrial and procurement policy to strengthen the UK's productive base, whilst targeting national regulation upon the needs of the domestic economy and maintaining a competitive exchange rate to facilitate international competitiveness. Given the evidence presented in this book, this independent option would appear to offer the greater potential.

REFERENCES

Abreu, M. D. (2013). Preferential Rules of Origin in Regional Trade Agreements, *World Trade Organisation Staff Working Paper* No ERSD-2013-05. https://www.wto.org/english/res_e/reser_e/ersd201305_e.pdf.

Algan, Y., & Cahus, P. (2010). Inherited Trust and Growth. *Amerssican Economic Review, 100*(5), 2060–2092.

Backer, L. C. (2014). The Trans-Pacific Partnership: Japan, China, the U.S., and the Emerging Shape of a New World Trade Regulatory Order. *Washington University Global Studies Law Review, 13*(49), 49–81.

Bennett, J. C. (2004). *The Anglosphere Challenge: Why the English-speaking Nations Will Lead the Way in the 21st Century*. Lanham: Rowman and Littlefield.

Booth, S., Howarth, C., Persson, M., Ruparel, R., & Swidlicki, P. (2015). *What If...?: The Consequences, Challenges and Opportunities Facing Britain Outside EU*. Open Europe Report 03/2015, London. http://openeurope.org.uk/intelligence/britain-and-the-eu/what-if-there-were-a-brexit/.

Brenton, P. (2010). Preferential Rules of Origin. In J. P. Chauffour & J. C. Maur (Eds.), *Preferential Trade Agreement Policies for Development: A Handbook* (pp. 161–178). Washington DC: World Bank.

Burkitt, B., Baimbridge, M., & Whyman, P. B. (1996). *There is an Alternative: Britain and Its Relationship with the EU*. Oxford: CIB/Nelson and Pollard.

Business for Britain. (2015). *Change or Go: How Britain Would Gain Influence and Prosper Outside an Unreformed EU*. London: Business for Britain. https://forbritain.org/cogwholebook.pdf.

Cadot, O., Carrère, C., de Melo, J., & Tumurchudur, B. (2006). Product- Specific Rules of Origin in EU and US Preferential Trading Arrangements: An Assessment. *World Trade Review, 5*(2), 199–224.

Capital Economics. (2016). *The Economics Impact of 'Brexit': A Paper Discussing the United Kingdom' Relationship with Europe and the Impact of 'Brexit' on the British Economy*. Oxford: Woodford Investment Management LLP. https://woodfordfunds.com/economic-impact-brexit-report/.

CBI [Confederation of British Industry]. (2013). *Our Global Future: The Business Vision for a Reformed EU*. London: CBI. http://www.cbi.org.uk/media/2451423/our_global_future.pdf#page=1&zoom=auto,-119,842.

CEPR. (2013). *Trade and Investment Balance of Competence Review*. London: Department for Business Innovation and Skills. https://www.gov.uk/government/uploads/system/uploads/attachment_data/file/271784/bis-14-512-trade-and-investment-balance-of-competence-review-project-report.pdf.

Chisik, R. (2003). Export Industry Policy and Reputational Comparative Advantage. *Journal of International Economics, 59*(2), 423–451.

Chopin, T. (2013). Two Europe's. In S. Nevin & R. Thillaye (Eds.), *Europe in Search of a New Settlement: EU-UK Relations and the Politics of Integration* (pp. 9–10). London: Policy Network. http://www.policy-network.net/publications_download.aspx?ID=8274.

Chopin, T. (2016). After the UK's EU Referendum: Redefining Relations Between the "Two Europe's". *European Issues*, No. 399, Robert Schuman Foundation. http://www.robert-schuman.eu/en/doc/questions-d-europe/qe-399-en.pdf.

Ciuriak, D., Xiao, J., Ciuriak, N., Dadkhah, A., Lysenko, D., & Narayanan, G. B. (2015). *The Trade-related Impact of a UK Exit from the EU Single Market.* April, Ciuriak Consulting, Ottawa: Research Report. https://papers.ssrn.com/sol3/papers.cfm?abstract_id=2620718.

De Sousa, J., Mayer, T., & Zignago, S. (2012). Market Access in Global and Regional Trade. *Regional Science and Urban Economics, 42*(6), 1037–1052. http://econ.sciences-po.fr/sites/default/files/file/tmayer/MA_revisionRSUE_jul2012.pdf.

De Zayas, A-M. (2015). Promotion of a Democratic and Equitable International Order, United Nations General Assembly Seventeenth Session, Item 73(b), A/70/285. Retrieved February 2, 2020, from https://www.un.org/en/ga/search/view_doc.asp?symbol=A/70/285.

Dinnie, K. (2004). Country of Origin 1965–2004: A Literature Review. *Journal of Customer Behaviour, 3*(2), 165–213.

Dinnie, K. (2008). *Nation Branding: Concepts, Issues, Practice.* Abingdon: Routledge.

Ebell, M. (2017). *Will New Trade Deals Soften the Blow of Hard Brexit?.* NIESR Blog, 27 January 2017. Available via: https://www.niesr.ac.uk/blog/will-newtrade-deals-soften-blow-hard-brexit.

Economists for Brexit. (2016). *A Vote for Brexit: What Are the Policies to Follow and What Are the Economic Prospects?* London: Economists for Brexit. Available via. http://www.economistsforbrexit.co.uk/a-vote-for-brexit.

Emmerson, C., Johnson, P., Mitchell, I., & Phillips, D. (2016). *Brexit and the UK's Public Finances* (IFS Report 116). Institute for Fiscal Studies, London. Available via: http://www.ifs.org.uk/uploads/publications/comms/r116.pdf.

Fawcett, J. (2015). Origin Marking Research—full report phases 1 and 2, Department for Business Innovation and Skills, London. https://www.gov.uk/government/uploads/system/uploads/attachment_data/file/408476/bis-15-94-compulsory-origin-marking-research-phase-1-and-2.pdf.

Friedman, T. L. (1999). *The Lexus and the Olive Tree: Understanding Globalization.* New York: Farrar, Straus and Giro.

Guiso, L., Sapienza, P., & Zingales, L. (2009). Cultural Biases in Economic Exchange? *The Quarterly Journal of Economics, 124*(3), 1095–1131.

Hantzsche, A., Kara, A., & Young, G. (2018). *The Economic Effects of the Government's Proposed Brexit Deal.* London: NIESR. Available via: https://

www.niesr.ac.uk/sites/default/files/publications/NIESR%20Report%20 Brexit%20-%202018-11-26.pdf

Harries, O. (2001). *The Anglosphere Illusion*. Spring: *The National Interest*. http://www.prospectmagazine.co.uk/features/anglosphereillusions.

Herin, J. (1986). *Rules of Origin and Differences between Tariff Levels in EFTA and in the EC*, EFTA Occasional Paper No. 13, EFTA Secretariat, Geneva.

HMG. (2018a). *Statement from HM Government*. Retrieved February 3, 2020, from https://assets.publishing.service.gov.uk/government/uploads/system/ uploads/attachment_data/file/723460/CHEQUERS_STATEMENT_-_ FINAL.PDF.

HMG. (2018b). *The Future Relationship Between the United Kingdom and the European Union (White Paper), CM 9593*. London: HMSO. Retrieved February 3, 2020, from https://assets.publishing.service.gov.uk/govern- ment/uploads/system/uploads/attachment_data/file/725288/The_future_ relationship_between_the_United_Kingdom_and_the_European_Union.pdf.

HMG. (2018c). *Future Customs Arrangements: A Future Partnership Paper*. London: HMSO. Retrieved February 6, 2020, from https://assets.publishing. service.gov.uk/government/uploads/system/uploads/attachment_data/ file/637748/Future_customs_arrangements_-_a_future_partnership_ paper.pdf.

HMG. (2019a). *Declaration by Her Declaration by Her Majesty's Government of the United Kingdom of Great Britain and Northern Ireland concerning the oper- ation of the 'Democratic consent in Northern Ireland' provision of the Protocol on Ireland/Northern Ireland—Presented to Parliament pursuant to Section 1 of the European Union (Withdrawal) Act (No. 2) 2019 and Section 13 of the European Union (Withdrawal) Act 2018*, HMSO, London. Retrieved February 7, 2020, from https://assets.publishing.service.gov.uk/government/uploads/system/ uploads/attachment_data/file/840658/Statement_that_political_agreement_ has_been_reached_and_that_the_United_Kingdom_has_concluded_an_agree- ment_with_the_European_Union_under_Article_50_2__of_the_Treaty_on_ European_Union.pdf.

HMG. (2019b). *Political Declaration Setting Out the Framework for the Future Relationship Between the European Union and the United Kingdom*. London: HMSO. Retrieved February 7, 2020, from https://assets.publishing.service. gov.uk/government/uploads/system/uploads/attachment_data/ file/840656/Political_Declaration_setting_out_the_framework_for_the_ future_relationship_between_the_European_Union_and_the_United_ Kingdom.pdf.

HMG. (2019c). *Agreement on the Withdrawal of the United Kingdom of Great Britain and Northern Ireland from the European Union and the European Atomic Energy Community—Presented to Parliament pursuant to Section 1 of the European Union (Withdrawal) Act (No. 2) 2019 and Section 13 of the*

European Union (Withdrawal) Act 2018 [revised October 2019], HMSO, London. Retrieved February 7, 2020, from https://assets.publishing.service. gov.uk/government/uploads/system/uploads/attachment_data/ file/840655/Agreement_on_the_withdrawal_of_the_United_Kingdom_of_ Great_Britain_and_Northern_Ireland_from_the_European_Union_and_the_ European_Atomic_Energy_Community.pdf.

HMG [Her Majesty's Government]. (2017). *Future Customs Arrangements: A Future Partnership Paper.* London: HMSO. Retrieved January 21, 2020, from https://assets.publishing.service.gov.uk/government/uploads/system/ uploads/attachment_data/file/637748/Future_customs_arrangements_-_a_ future_partnership_paper.pdf.

HoC [House of Commons Foreign Affairs Committee]. (2013). *The Future of the European Union: UK Government Policy—First Report of Session 2013–2014, Volume 1, HC-87-1.* London: The Stationery Office. http://www.publications. parliament.uk/pa/cm201314/cmselect/cmfaff/87/87.pdf.

Hufbauer, G. C. (2016). Investor-State Dispute Settlement. In C. Cimino-Isaacs & J. J. Schott (Eds.), *Trans-Pacific Partnership: An Assessment* (pp. 197–212). New York: Columbia University Press.

Hui, M. K., & Zhou, L. (2002). Linking Product Evaluations and Purchase Intention for Country-of-origin Effects. *Journal of Global Marketing, 15*(3/4), 95–116.

ICTU [Irish Congress of Trade Unions]. (2016). No Deal: Why Unions Oppose TTIP and CETA, Irish Congress of Trade Unions, Dublin. Retrieved February 2, 2020, from https://www.ictu.ie/download/pdf/no_deal.pdf.

Karlsson, L. (2017). *Smart Border 2.0: Avoiding a Hard Border on the Island of Island for Customs Control and the Free Movement of Persons,* PE 596.828, Director General for Internal Policies of the Union, European Parliament, Brussels. Available via: http://www.europarl.europa.eu/RegData/etudes/ STUD/2017/596828/IPOL_STU(2017)596828_EN.pdf.

Keep, M. (2015). EU Budget 2014–2020. *House of Commons Library Briefing Paper (HC 06455),* The Stationery Office, London. http://researchbriefings. files.parliament.uk/documents/SN06455/SN06455.pdf.

Keynes, J. M. (1933). National Self-Sufficiency. *The Yale Review, 22*(4), 755–769.

Kotkin, J., & Parulekar, S. (2011). The Anglosphere: We Are Not Dead Yet. In J. Kotkin (Ed.), *The New World Order* (pp. 28–38). London: Legatum Institute. http://www.li.com/docs/default-source/surveys-of-entrepreneurs/new- worldorder-2011_final.pdf.

Manchin, M. (2006). Preference Utilisation and Tariff Reduction in EU Imports from ACP Countries. *The World Economy, 29*(9), 1243–1266.

Medvedev, D. (2006). 'Preferential Trade Agreements and their Role in World Trade', *World Bank Policy Research Working Paper 4038.* Washington DC:

World Bank. Retrieved February 10, 2020, from http://documents.world-bank.org/curated/en/672601468332692068/pdf/wps4038.pdf.

Mendes, A. J. M. (1986). An Alternative Approach to Customs Union Theory: A Balance of Payments Framework to Measure Integration Effects. *Journal of International Economic Integration, 1*(1), 43–58.

Menon, A., Bevington, M., & Wager, M. (2018). The Context. In UKCE [UK in a Changing Europe] (Eds.), *The Brexit White Paper—What It Must Address*, UK in a Changing Europe, London, 7-10. Retrieved February 3, 2020, from http://ukandeu.ac.uk/wp-content/uploads/2018/07/The-Brexit-white-paper-what-it-must-address.pdf.

Miller, V., Lang, A., Smith, B., Webb, D., Harari, D., Keep, M., & Bowers, P. (2016). Exiting the EU: UK Reform Proposals, Legal Impact and Alternatives to Membership. *House of Commons Library Briefing Paper* No. HC 07214. http://researchbriefings.parliament.uk/ResearchBriefing/Summary/CBP-7214#fullreport.

Milne, I. (2004). *A Cost Too Far? An Analysis of the Net Economic Costs and Benefits for the UK of EU Membership*. London: Civitas. http://www.civitas.org.uk/pdf/cs37.pdf.

Minford, P. (2016). *The Treasury Report on Brexit: A Critique*. London: Economists for Brexit. http://static1.squarespace.com/static/570a10a460b5e93378a26ac5/t/5731a5a486db439545bf2eda/1462871465520/Economists+for+Brexit+-+The+Treasury+Report+on+Brexit+A+Critique.pdf.

Minford, P., Gupta, S., Le, V. P. M., Mahambare, V., & Xu, Y. (2015). *Should Britain Leave the EU? An Economic Analysis of a Troubled Relationship—Second Edition*. Cheltenham: IEA and Edward Elgar.

Minford, P., Mahambare, V., & Nowell, E. (2005). *Should Britain Leave the EU? An Economic Analysis of a Troubled Relationship*. Cheltenham: IEA and Edward Elgar.

Nesbit, J. C. (2001). *An Anglosphere Primer*. http://explorersfoundation.org/archive/anglosphere_primer.pdf.

NOU [Official Norwegian Report]. (2012a). *Utenfor og Innenfor: Norges avtaler med EU*. [Outside and Inside: Norway's agreement's with the EU].

NOU [Official Norwegian Report]. (2012b). *Outside and Inside: Norway's Agreements with the European Union—Other Parties' Views on Norway's Agreements with the EU—Chapter 13, NOU 2012:2*. Oslo: Norwegian Ministry of Foreign Affairs. http://www.eu-norway.org/Global/SiteFolders/webeu/NOU2012_2_Chapter%2013.pdf.

NOU [Official Norwegian Report]. (2012c). *Outside and Inside: Norway's Agreements with the European Union—The Way Forward—Chapter, 28.*

OECD [Organisation for Economic Co-operation and Development]. (2019). *GDP, Volume—Annual growth rates in percentage.* Available via: https://stats. oecd.org/Index.aspx?DataSetCode=SNA_TABLE1

ONS [Office of National Statistics]. (2016). *UK's Top 10 Trading Partners.* http://visual.ons.gov.uk/uk-perspectives-2016-trade-with-the-eu-andbeyond/.

Ottaviano, G., Pessoa, J. P., & Sampson, T. (2014). The Costs and Benefits of Leaving the EU. CEP mimeo. http://cep.lse.ac.uk/pubs/download/pa016_tech.pdf.

Owen, D. (2016). *Europe Restructured: Vote to Leave.* London: Methuen. http://www.lorddavidowen.co.uk/wp-content/uploads/2016/03/Europe-Restructured-160301.pdf.

Owen, J., Shepheard, M., & Stojanovic, A. (2017). *Implementing Brexit: Customs.* London: Institute for Government. Retrieved February 6, 2020, from https://www.instituteforgovernment.org.uk/sites/default/files/publications/IfG_Brexit_customs_WEB_0.pdf.

Palley, T. (2017). *The Fallacy of the Globalisation Trilemma: Reframing the Political Economy of Globalisation and Implications for Democracy, Forum for Macroeconomics and Macroeconomic Policies (FMM) Working Paper 8.* Hans-Bockler-Stiftung: Macroeconomic Policy Institute. Retrieved February 3, 2020, from https://www.boeckler.de/pdf/p_fmm_imk_wp_08_2017.pdf.

Phinnemore, D., & Hayward, K. (2017). *UK Withdrawal ('Brexit') and the Good Friday Agreement,* PE 596.826, Policy Department for Citizens' Rights and Constitutional Affairs, European Parliament, Brussels.. Retrieved January 22, 2020, from http://www.europarl.europa.eu/RegData/etudes/STUD/2017/596826/IPOL_STU(2017)596826_EN.pdf.

Piris, J.-C. (2016). *If the UK Votes to Leave: The seven alternatives to EU membership.* London: Centre for European Reform. https://www.cer.org.uk/ sites/default/files/pb_piris_brexit_12jan16.pdf.

Reich, R. (2015). Robert Reich: The Trans-Pacific Partnership is a disaster in the making. *Salon.* Available online via: https://www.salon.com/2015/01/07/robert_reich_the_trans_pacific_partnership_is_a_disaster_in_the_making_partner/. Last accessed: 20 November 2020.

Reynolds, B., & Webber, J. (2019). *The Withdrawal Agreement, State Aid and UK Industry: How To Protect UK Competitiveness.* London: Politeia. Available via: http://www.politeia.co.uk/wpcontent/Politeia%20Documents/2019/05.02.19%20Reynolds%20&%20Webber/The%20Withdrawal%20Agreement,%20State%20Aid%20&%20UK%20Industry%20by%20Barnabas%20Reynolds%20&%20James%

Ries, C. P., Hafner, M., Smith, T. D., Burwell, F. G., Egel, D., Han, E., Stepanek, M., & Shatz, H. J. (2017). *After Brexit: Alternative Forms of Brexit and Their Implications for the United Kingdom, the European Union and the United*

States, The Rand Corporation, Cambridge. Retrieved January 22, 2020, from https://www.rand.org/pubs/research_reports/RR2200.html.

Rodrik, D. (2000). How Far Will International Economic Integration Go? *Journal of Economic Perspectives, 14*(1), 177–186.

Rodrik, D. (2012). *The Globalization Paradox*. Oxford: Oxford University Press.

Sejersted, F., & Sverdrup, U. (2012, October 5). Eurosceptics Be Warned—The 'Half In, Half Out' EU Integration Model Option Is Best Left to Norway. *The Independent*. http://www.independent.co.uk/voices/comment/eurosceptics-be-warned-the-half-in-half-out-eu-integration-modeloption-is-best-left-to-norway-8199849.html.

SETUC [Syndicat European Trade Union Confederation]. (2016). ETUC Assessment on the EU-Canada Comprehensive Economic and Trade Agreement (CETA)—Statement Approved at the Executive Committee, 14-15 December 2016.. Retrieved February 2, 2020, from https://www.etuc.org/sites/default/files/document/files/07-en-statement_-_etuc_assessment_on_ceta_-_final.pdf.

Singham, S., Tylecote, R., & Hewson, V. (2017). *The Brexit Inflection Point: The Pathway to Prosperity*. London: Legatum Institute. Retrieved January 22, 2020, from https://britainsfuture.co.uk/documentation/the_brexit_inflection_point_the_pathway_to_prosperity.pdf.

Springford, J., & Tilford, S. (2014). *The Great British Trade-Off: The Impact of Leaving the EU on the UK's Trade and Investment,*. Centre for European. tableView.aspx.

Thompson, G., & Harari, D. (2013). The Economic Impact of EU Membership on the UK. *House of Commons Library Briefing Paper* SN/ EP/6730. http://researchbriefings.parliament.uk/ResearchBriefing/Summary/SN06730#fullreport.

UK&EU [The UK in a Changing Europe]. (2019). *The Economic Impact of Boris Johnson's Brexit Proposals*. London: UK in a Changing Europe. Retrieved February 7, 2020, from https://ukandeu.ac.uk/wp-content/uploads/2019/10/The-economic-impact-of-Boris-Johnsons-Brexit-proposals.pdf.

UNCTAD [United Nations Conference on Trade and Development]. (2013). *Non-Tariff Measures to Trade*. Geneva: United Nations. http://unctad.org/en/PublicationsLibrary/ditctab20121_en.pdf.

UNCTAD [United Nations Conference on Trade and Development]. (2020). *Annual average growth rate*, GDP. Available via: http://unctadstat.unctad.org/wds/TableViewer/tableView.aspx

USITC [United States International Trade Commission]. (1996). *Country-of- origin Marking: Review of Laws, Regulations and Practices*. Washington DC: USITC. https://www.usitc.gov/publications/332/pub2975.pdf.

USITC [United States International Trade Commission]. (2000). *The Impact on the US Economy of Including the United Kingdom in a Free Trade Agreement with the United States, Canada and Mexico.* Investigation No. 332–409, USITC, Washington DC.

USTR [US Trade Representative]. (2019). *United States-United Kingdom Negotiations: Summary of Specific negotiating Objectives, Office of the United States Trade.* Washington DC: Representative. Retrieved January 22, 2020, from https://ustr.gov/sites/default/files/Summary_of_U.S.-UK_Negotiating_Objectives.pdf.

van Hulten, M. (2011). *To Get Out of This Crisis We Need to Rebuild Europe from Scratch.*. European Council on Foreign Relations. http://www.ecfr.eu/article/commentary_to_get_out_of_this_crisis_we_need_to_rebuild_europe_from_scratch.

WCO [World Customs Organisation]. (2018). *SAFE Framework of Standards—2018 edition.* Brussels: World Customs Organisation. Retrieved February 6, 2020, from http://www.wcoomd.org/-/media/wco/public/global/pdf/topics/facilitation/instruments-and-tools/tools/safe-package/safe-framework-of-standards.PDF?la=en.

World Bank. (2020). *MFN (Most Favourite Nation) tariff rate 1988–2014.* http://data.worldbank.org/indicator/TM.TAX.MRCH.WM.AR.ZS?locations=EU.

WTO [World Trade Organization]. (2011). *World Trade Report 2011: The WTO and Preferential Trade Agreements—From Coexistence to Coherence.* Geneva: World Trade Organisation. https://www.wto.org/english/res_e/booksp_e/anrep_e/world_trade_report11_e.pdf.

WTO [World Trade Organization]. (2016). *Tariffs and Imports—Part, A2.* http://stat.wto.org/TariffProfile/WSDBTariffPFView.aspx?Language=E&Country=E28.

Yu, P. K. (2018). Investor-State Dispute Settlement and the Trans-Pacific Partnership, *Texas A&M University Legal Studies Research Paper Series* 18-32. Retrieved February 2, 2020, from https://papers.ssrn.com/sol3/papers.cfm?abstract_id=3237541.

CONCLUSION

This book has evaluated the existing evidence relating to the economic impact that is likely to arise from Brexit. It has noted the methodological flaws of many of the more prominent studies on which policy makers and other economic actors reply, reaching the conclusion that the magnitude of their predicted negative consequences are most likely exaggerated. These studies do, however, highlight the areas that are disproportionately prone to negative consequences, such as in trade with the EU and in relation to investment being deferred due to the uncertainty caused by the Brexit process. However, other factors are too often either ignored or marginalised, such as the potential to expand trade and investment with the rest of the (non-EU) world and the potential for government policy to ameliorate negative, and magnify positive, effects. What is needed is for policy makers and other economic actors to base their decision making on a broader range of economic evidence. It is hoped that this book plays a small part in this endeavour.

The choice of future economic relationship, between the UK and the EU, will play a critical role in determining whether Brexit will ultimately be viewed as a success or failed experiment. There is a trade-off between greater trade access into the EU SIM, which may deliver short-term benefits, and securing a greater degree of policy flexibility, which may deliver longer-term gains. Judgements concerning the merits of either option will be, at least in part, determined by perceptions concerning the significance

© The Author(s) 2020
P. B. Whyman, A. I. Petrescu, *The Economics of Brexit*,
https://doi.org/10.1007/978-3-030-55948-9

of economic problems facing the UK and the potential for economic policy intervention to provide a solution. If the UK economy is viewed as essentially sound and/or policy interventions are viewed as having only weak effects, then there would appear to be little to gain by more independent action and therefore continued market access is the overwhelming priority. European Economic Area (EEA) or customs union membership would therefore appear to be the most preferable Brexit options.

If, however, the UK economy is viewed as suffering from a number of long-standing problems, not least the very large trade deficit and productivity weaknesses, then a more independent stance would appear more advantageous. If, in addition, the evidence is accepted that active forms of economic policy can have significant impact upon the economy—and the reader needs to look no further than the stabilisation achieved amidst the recent financial crisis or indeed the action of the Bank of England to reduce uncertainty immediately after the European referendum—then the most obvious Brexit option would be to seek to negotiate a free trade agreement, including as greater portion of services as possible. Should this not prove to be possible, then it would be preferable for trade to revert to WTO rules rather than accept a form of trade agreement which unduly restricted the policy flexibility for the now independent UK. This would provide sufficient policy flexibility to reduce uncertainty through the stimulation of aggregate demand, and utilise an active industrial and procurement policy to strengthen the UK's productive base, whilst targeting national regulation upon the needs of the domestic economy and maintaining a competitive exchange rate to facilitate international competitiveness. Given the evidence presented in this book, this independent option would appear to offer the greater potential.

Appendix: Brexit After the COVID-19 Pandemic

One difficulty in writing any book examining topical issues concerns the ability of events to impact upon the narrative. This has been particularly true in this case as the COVID-19 pandemic was emerging at the time that this book was in the final stages of completion. Yet, even in the early stages of this crisis, the experience of other nations and the most recent announcement of a package of support for the economy, by the Chancellor of the Exchequer, both suggest the emergence of a substantial shock to the UK economy with the potential to exceed anything experienced in living memory.

Whilst this book is scheduled to enter its printing and publication phase before the full extent of the pandemic has been revealed, two points have already emerged which are of importance to the content of this book.

The first is to note that in an economic crisis, there is a tendency for Keynesian solutions to be more prevalent, in the sense that governments seek to do whatever is necessary, using what for many may be viewed as unorthodox measures, to prevent unnecessary and long-lasting damage to the economy. This was the case during the 2008 global financial crisis, although not (sadly) in its immediate aftermath as austerity measures unnecessarily prolonged the recovery phase, and it will be the case in the current pandemic. The extent of the support package, intended to 'bridge' the UK economy over the inevitable downturn in economic activity caused by measures taken to avoid the loss of life caused by the pandemic, is already unprecedented in scale in modern peacetime, and it is likely to be

© The Author(s) 2020
P. B. Whyman, A. I. Petrescu, *The Economics of Brexit*,
https://doi.org/10.1007/978-3-030-55948-9

only the first step that government will take to support the economy. These measures are wholly necessary to prevent severe economic damage and credit should be given to policy makers who may be going against the grain of their inherent economic orthodoxy to grasp the importance of adopting such measures. Yet, their adoption could have one of two effects upon the scope of future economic policy initiatives, once the pandemic is past its worst and attention returns to the Brexit process.

The first effect could be that the degree of government intervention in the economy, necessitated by the scale of the pandemic shock, generates a greater degree of acceptance for a more active economic policy framework in the future. The discussion contained in Chap. 8 outlined how a more active economic policy, utilising industrial and procurement policy, combined with macroeconomic Keynesian demand management, could create conditions conducive to the rebalancing of the UK economy and creating growth potential. Consequently, to the extent that the policy response to the pandemic crisis creates greater acceptance of a more active economic policy approach amongst the population as a whole, but additionally amongst the financial and business communities more generally, this may encourage policy makers to utilise the full range of economic levers newly available to them, and in the process, if done correctly, this could prove beneficial to post-Brexit performance.

Alternatively, however, the measures undertaken during the pandemic could equally cause a backlash against future forms of active policy measures. Even during the early stages of the pandemic, commentators wedded to economic orthodoxy have sought to limit the extent to the business support package by questioning the cost of public support being provided and the accompanying rising levels of public debt. Supporters of a smaller state have raised their concerns about future tax implications even before the peak of the pandemic has been reached. It is probable that these opinions will become more prominent over time, and it is possible that they will succeed in prematurely constraining the economic support measures before growth potential has been restored or that a new period of austerity is implemented which will impair recovery. In this case, a backlash arising from the pandemic may have negative consequences for the post-Brexit UK economy.

The second issue which is likely to arise in the aftermath of the pandemic relates to the reinvention of the argument that the UK is too weak to develop successfully outside the economic orbit of the EU, and therefore, the UK should pursue a form of economic relationship with the EU as close as possible to full membership. This could potentially involve application to join the EEA and/or a customs union. If this should occur, it is worth noting that this argument is, in essence, simply a restatement of the same argument that was voiced against the economic viability of the Brexit vote back in 2016.

As noted on a number of occasions in this book, there is an essential choice to be made between adopting a close trading relationship with the EU to avoid short-term losses in trade, but at the expense of tying the UK into EU rules and regulations, and the alternative strategy of having a looser relationship with the EU to facilitate greater economic policy flexibility designed to rejuvenate our productive base, whilst developing preferential trade relationships elsewhere across the globe. The economics of the pandemic will have little effect upon this calculation. Whilst advocates of a closer relationship may point towards greater security in existing trade relationships, advocates of economic independence may focus upon the even greater necessity to use all economic levers to rebuild the economy in the aftermath of the pandemic shock. The economic environment may have changed significantly due to the pandemic, but the fundamental choice associated with Brexit will not. This book has sought to outline as many of the economic studies and evidence that is currently available in order to allow you, the reader, to form your own opinions on the correct set of actions that the UK should take in the future, to maximise the benefits arising from Brexit and minimise the costs.

Place Index[1]

---

[1] Note: Page numbers followed by 'n' refer to notes.

© The Author(s) 2020   377
P. B. Whyman, A. I. Petrescu, *The Economics of Brexit*,
https://doi.org/10.1007/978-3-030-55948-9

SUBJECT INDEX[1]

---

[1] Note: Page numbers followed by 'n' refer to notes.

© The Author(s) 2020
P. B. Whyman, A. I. Petrescu, *The Economics of Brexit*,
https://doi.org/10.1007/978-3-030-55948-9

Printed by Printforce, United Kingdom